A Question of Commitme

Studies in
Childhood and Family
in Canada

A broad-ranging series that publishes scholarship from various disciplines, approaches and perspectives relevant to the concepts and relations of childhood and family in Canada. Our interests also include, but are not limited to, interdisciplinary approaches and theoretical investigations of gender, race, sexuality, geography, language, and culture within these categories of experience, historical and contemporary.

We welcome proposals and manuscripts from Canadian authors. For further information, please contact the Series Editor:

Professor Cynthia Comacchio
History Department
Wilfrid Laurier University
75 University Avenue West
Waterloo, ON N2L 3C5, Canada
Phone: (519) 884-0710 ext. 3422
Email: ccomacchio@wlu.ca

A Question of Commitment
THE STATUS OF CHILDREN IN CANADA
second edition

Thomas Waldock, editor
Foreword by R. Brian Howe
and Katherine Covell

WILFRID LAURIER
UNIVERSITY PRESS

Wilfrid Laurier University Press acknowledges the support of the Canada Council for the Arts for our publishing program. We acknowledge the financial support of the Government of Canada. This work was supported by the Research Support Fund.

Library and Archives Canada Cataloguing in Publication

Title: A question of commitment : the status of children in Canada / Thomas Waldock, editor ; foreword by R. Brian Howe and Katherine Covell.
Other titles: Status of children in Canada
Names: Waldock, Thomas, 1962– editor. | Howe, Robert Brian, writer of foreword. | Covell, Katherine, writer of foreword.
Series: Studies in childhood and family in Canada.
Description: Second edition. | Series statement: Studies in childhood and family in Canada | Originally published: Waterloo, Ont.: Wilfrid Laurier University Press, 2007. | Includes bibliographical references and index.
Identifiers: Canadiana (print) 20190148659 | Canadiana (ebook) 2019015067X | ISBN 9781771124058 (softcover) | ISBN 9781771124072 (PDF) | ISBN 9781771124065 (EPUB)
Subjects: LCSH: Convention on the Rights of the Child (1989 November 20) | LCSH: Children's rights Canada. | LCSH: Children—Government policy—Canada. | LCSH: Child welfare—Canada.
Classification: LCC HQ789 .Q48 2020 | DDC 323.3/520971—dc23

Front-cover photo © Zaikina | Dreamstime.com. Cover design and interior design by Angela Booth Malleau, designbooth.ca.

© 2020 Wilfrid Laurier University Press
Waterloo, Ontario, Canada
www.wlupress.wlu.ca

This book is printed on FSC® certified paper. It contains recycled materials and other controlled sources, is processed chlorine free, and is manufactured using biogas energy.

Printed in Canada

Every reasonable effort has been made to acquire permission for copyright material used in this text, and to acknowledge all such indebtedness accurately. Any errors and omissions called to the publisher's attention will be corrected in future printings.

No part of this publication may be reproduced, stored in a retrieval system, or transmitted, in any form or by any means, without the prior written consent of the publisher or a licence from the Canadian Copyright Licensing Agency (Access Copyright). For an Access Copyright licence, visit http://www.accesscopyright.ca or call toll free to 1-800-893-5777.

This book is dedicated to the memory of my father, Frank Waldock, and to my mother, Beverly Waldock

Contents

Foreword   ix
R. Brian Howe and Katherine Covell

Acknowledgements   xiii

Chapter 1   Introduction: Children's Rights: A Question of Status and Recognition   1
Thomas Waldock

POLICY AND PRACTICE AREAS

Chapter 2   Do Canadian Education Practices Respect the Rights of the Child?   17
Katherine Covell

Chapter 3   Parenting Education and Support: A Children's Rights Perspective   35
R. Brian Howe

Chapter 4   Promising Policies, Ambiguous Practices: An Exploration of the Status of Children in Canadian Health Care Settings   55
Cheryl van Daalen-Smith, Brenda LeFrançois, and Devon MacPherson-Mayor

Chapter 5   Young People, Justice, and Children's Rights in Canada: Critical Reflections at the Edge of Abeyant Action   87
Shannon A. Moore

Chapter 6   Child Welfare and the Status of Children Requiring Support and Care   107
Thomas Waldock

Chapter 7   Assessing the Rights and Realities of War-Affected Refugee Children in Canada   131
Myriam Denov and Maya Fennig

CHILDREN AND THE LAW

Chapter 8   The Supreme Court of Canada and the Convention   161
J. C. Blokhuis

Chapter 9	More Than a Symbol: Canada's Legal Justification of Corporal Punishment of Children Joan Durrant	179
Chapter 10	A Children's Rights Perspective on "Wrongful Life" Disability Medical Negligence Cases Sonja C. Grover	205
Chapter 11	The Extraordinary Cases of J. J. and Makayla Sault J. C. Blokhuis and Amy Smoke	223

PARTICIPATION RIGHTS, STATUS, AND RECOGNITION

Chapter 12	Participation Rights of the Child: At the Crossroads of Citizenship Jan Hancock	241
Chapter 13	Canadian Child and Youth Advocates' Roles in Supporting Children's Rights M. Theresa Hunter	267
Chapter 14	Shaking the Movers: A Decade Later – Does Our Voice Stick? Judy Finlay and Landon Pearson	293
Chapter 15	Conclusion: A Children's Rights Pathway to Status and Recognition Thomas Waldock	315
	About the Contributors	337
	Index	343

Foreword

R. Brian Howe and Katherine Covell

In 2007, we edited a collection of writings on the status of children's rights in Canada—*A Question of Commitment: Children's Rights in Canada*. Several years had passed since Canada ratified the United Nations Convention on the Rights of the Child in 1991, committing federal, provincial, and territorial governments to the progressive implementation of children's rights. The overarching question of our book was whether Canada had demonstrated genuine commitment, as reflected in its actions, or whether the commitment was merely symbolic. We concluded that although Canada did show some signs of commitment, the commitment was wavering and inadequate. Efforts to move forward in implementing children's rights were underwhelming.

But we were not pessimistic. We believed that it was possible the status of children in Canada would improve over time. There was reason to believe that with the continuing evolution of rights consciousness, and of a political culture increasingly supportive of the value of human rights, more attention would be paid to the rights of children. We hoped that Canada would come to realize the importance of honouring its commitment to children and take action to implement their rights. After all, with ratification of the Convention, Canada had officially agreed to respect the rights of the child and to honour children by putting their rights into effect. It was reasonable to believe that over time, Canada would recognize its obligations and act on what it had agreed to.

A significant amount of time has passed since the first edition of *A Question of Commitment*. What measures have been taken since then to secure the rights of children in Canada? How have things improved? An updated edition is needed to assess Canada's performance and answer such questions. We are very grateful to Tom Waldock for bringing together this second collection to determine whether our hope—and the hope of so many child advocates across the country—has been realized. The essential questions of this book are these. In line with the Convention, have Canadian children finally been given the status of individual bearers of rights? Are their protection, provision, and participation rights now respected? Or are they still assumed to be not-yets and objects of paternalistic concern, deserving of charity but not yet deserving of enjoying the rights of personhood and citizenship? Is it even possible that children continue to be seen—after all this time—as essentially the property and responsibility of their parents?

In assessing Canada's commitment to children, we need to be mindful of the difference between what Canadian governments say that they are doing for children and what they are actually doing. Canada is required to report to the United Nations Committee on the Rights of the Child—the committee responsible for monitoring compliance with the Convention—on the measures it has taken to implement the rights of children in policies, laws, and practices. In its reports, the government says many positive things. But what we really need to watch are the government's responses to the committee's criticisms and recommendations for improvement, as stated in their reports called Concluding Observations. In their comments, the committee has repeatedly criticized Canada for its lack of serious implementation of children's rights, and expressed its concern and disappointment that Canada has continued to disregard its recommendations. The committee has pointed to many failures and problem areas. It is a long list. Included are the lack of mechanisms for meaningful participation, insufficient supports and services for parents, inadequate rights-consistent responses to refugee and asylum-seeking children, high rates of child poverty, the continuing practice of corporal punishment, the lack of public education about the Convention, and of children's rights education in schools, the lack of incorporation of the Convention into Canadian law, inadequate early childhood education, punitive elements in the youth justice system, and overrepresentation of Indigenous youth in the justice system.

To what extent and in what areas has Canada addressed the committee's concerns? Or has the government continued to disregard the committee's calls for improvements? Has real progress been made in implementing the rights of the child? In the chapters that follow, the contributors examine the current status of children in Canada in the various contexts of their development. This is important reading. It will tell us much about Canada, about Canadians, and about where children fit into the priorities of governments in Canada. It will tell us if there continues to be a gap between Canada's official commitment to children and the reality of their experiences. If the gap has been closed or significantly narrowed, then our country deserves praise for taking seriously the rights of the child. But if there is a continuing gap, we need to know this. It will tell us that the task of building a culture of respect for the rights of the child remains unfinished.

Acknowledgements

The editor wishes to express his appreciation to the contributing authors for their dedication not only to this book, but also to research and advocacy efforts in their respective areas of focus.

He also would like to thank Wilfrid Laurier University Press for their contributions throughout the process, and more generally express his appreciation for their commitment to the Studies in Childhood and Family in Canada series.

Chapter 1
Introduction: Children's Rights
A Question of Status and Recognition
Thomas Waldock

This book is preoccupied with the following question: To what extent has Canada fulfilled its obligations under the United Nations Convention on the Rights of the Child (UNCRC) to treat children as rights-bearing citizens, respecting their dignity as fully human persons in their own right? Underlying the important principles and rights articulated in the UNCRC, the Convention represents a significant evolution in conceptualizations of children and childhood, both in Canada and around the world. From views of children as "property" to full recognition as subjects and citizens with specific rights, the road travelled is a familiar one for human rights advocates, and at its foundation has to do with questions of status and recognition. While obligations under the UNCRC are apparent, and the trajectory of this evolution is relatively clear, countries can be at different stages of the journey; and within countries, development can be uneven, with different areas of public policy and law reflecting varying levels of progress. In the chapters to follow, the book's contributing authors attempt to answer the aforementioned question as it relates to the Canadian context and their respective areas of expertise.

CHILDREN'S RIGHTS: A BRIEF HISTORY

In 1989, the UN General Assembly unanimously approved the UNCRC. Subsequently, it was signed and ratified by almost every country in the world. Indeed, the UNCRC has the distinction of being the most widely ratified human rights Convention in history (UNICEF, 2005)—196 countries and all but one UN member nation (United Nations Treaty Collection, 1989). It is important to put this relatively recent culmination of efforts to formalize children's rights in international law—as well as the widespread support for the UNCRC itself—into context. While the Western origins of the modern idea of rights figure prominently in most historical accounts, the "more fully global history of children's rights nevertheless has a rich if somewhat briefer history …" (Stearns, 2017, p. 3). Since children's rights are a particular category of human rights, the evolution toward conceptualizing children as independent bearers of rights also calls forth a rich history because it involves the human rights story generally. The idea that human beings have inalienable, universal rights by virtue of being human, and that their humanity is characterized by an essential equality, dignity, and autonomy, is centuries old and traceable to the second half of the seventeenth century, even if the formal regime of universal human rights—of which the UNCRC is part—is largely a twentieth-century creation (Donnelly, 2013, p. 75).

Prior to the emergence of the "human rights idea" (Stearns, 2017)—and later children's rights specifically—parental authority over children largely was unquestioned. Over time, pre-modern, agricultural societies did begin to offer some minimal protections for children; for example, the practice of infanticide was banned, and this occurred across regional and religious lines. So the situation for children was somewhat improved over, for example, Roman times, when fathers—under the principle of *patria potestas*—literally had the power of life and death over their children. There were some signs, then, of a very preliminary foundation of sorts for later developments associated with the protection of children, if only in the most minimal sense that the need for intervention against arbitrary parental authority was acknowledged, at least in some instances. In addition, parents came to be required by common law to provide children with the necessities of life (Covell & Howe, 2001, p. 17)—similarly, a preliminary foundation for later developments associated with provision for children. But irrespective of these minimally discernible improvements in the condition of children, children in agricultural societies largely were subject to the authority of parents. With a status akin to property, and state involvement in their welfare virtually non-existent, children were extremely vulnerable, both within the context of the family, and in society generally.

From the late seventeenth century onward in western Europe, against the backdrop of a developing belief in universal human rights, new ideas about children began to emerge. As Stearns notes, this was evident in the intellectual realm. John Locke (1690/1937) argued that children at birth were "blank slates," neither good nor evil but capable of improvement through education. To be sure, children were viewed as "citizens in the making" or incomplete adults (Archard, 2004; Albanese, 2009), but Locke's position contrasted with the dominant sensibilities of the time—at times associated with the Christian doctrine of original sin—whereby children required harsh discipline in order to control their inherently evil nature. In contrast, children were to be treated with kindness and care, and given opportunities through education to develop good character (Stearns, 2017). Later, in the eighteenth century, Jean-Jacques Rousseau (1762/1973) went further in suggesting that children were naturally good, with childhood being a time of innocence and honesty; again, the onus was on education broadly conceived not to spoil these admirable qualities (Stearns, 2017; Albanese, 2009). Such new ideas called into question the conceptualization of children as property and shifted the focus somewhat to parental obligations regarding children's care and education.

These new sensibilities concerning children were developing in conjunction with the general evolution of the human rights story. While a full accounting of this history is beyond our scope here, suffice to say that Rousseau and other Enlightenment thinkers emphasized human equality and shared rights. The state came to be viewed as having a more positive role in enhancing human freedoms, including safeguarding and promoting human rights. Moreover, states that violated such freedoms and human rights had their legitimacy questioned. In the late eighteenth century, revolutions in France and the United States were premised on the inalienable "rights of man." Of course, these human rights were not yet applied to children, but it was only a matter of time before the tides converged. As Stearns observes: "Both the revision of ideas about childhood, and the effective emergence of a concept of human rights, had obvious potential bearing on the treatment of children. If human beings had a firm claim on rights, and if children were in fact worthy beings, might children have rights directly? Hints of this connection did begin to emerge" (Stearns, 2017, p. 7). From early signs and examples in the late eighteenth century, ideas about children's rights advanced in the nineteenth century—spurred on by practical concerns about child labour and education, policy areas now associated with protection and provision rights respectively—and real agendas and campaigns for children's rights became discernible in the early twentieth century (Stearns, 2017).

Demands concerning the welfare of children began to be phrased in terms of rights, with children starting to be seen as autonomous beings in their own right. The early British pioneer for children's rights, Eglantyne Jebb, campaigned for better protection of the world's children, and was arrested for obscenity for simply displaying pictures of starving children in the aftermath of World War One (Hammarberg, 1990). Jebb was instrumental in the founding of the Save the Children movement, and also herself sponsored a Declaration of the Rights of the Child in 1923, the five principles of which ultimately were adopted in 1924 as the Declaration of Geneva by the newly formed (1920) League of Nations. The Declaration enshrined the principle of "children first," which became somewhat of a rallying cry for children's advocates moving forward. Lest we underestimate the breadth of the movement during even the earliest formalized campaigns, it should be acknowledged that the title of early pioneer for children's rights also applies to Janusz Korczak, the Polish advocate whose writings in the 1920s and 1930s became very influential. While the need to protect and provide for children was becoming more widely acknowledged and increasingly framed as rights claims, it has been suggested that Korczak's writings were progressive in calling for positive freedom of expression for children themselves (Stearns, 2017, p. 13), an early statement of the significance of children's participation for full status and recognition as subjects and citizens.

After World War Two and with the establishment of the United Nations in 1948, momentum built toward more formalized human rights obligations generally, which included the call for a more precise and elaborate statement of the rights of children. In 1959, the UN General Assembly adopted the UN Declaration on the Rights of the Child, expanding upon the Declaration of Geneva by now enshrining ten principles; this represented another step forward in the children's rights journey. But at bottom, Declarations—including the 1924 Declaration of Geneva (League of Nations) and the 1959 Declaration on the Rights of the Child (United Nations)—are really statements of principle, largely moral appeals without the clout of international law. In order to achieve the status of international law, a Convention on children's rights would be required. That was the logical next step in the historical evolution of children's rights.

By the 1970s, the effort to make children's rights a part of international law was in full swing. Of assistance was the fact that there was a growing awareness of children's psychological needs, and that aside from the consensus around rights in the areas of protection and participation, there was growing recognition of a child's right to participate in decisions affecting his or her situation (Hammarberg, 1990, p. 98). By 1979, during the International Year of the Child, the Polish government proposed a Convention for children's rights, and this set in motion a painstaking ten-year process of negotiation and compromise that culminated in 1989 with the United Nation's adoption of the UN Convention on the Rights of the Child (Jupp, 1990). Negotiations were complex, given the many potential areas of contention, not the least of which concerned the relationship between children's rights and the role of parents and families. Also at issue was the framing of participation rights for children, given the contentious question of the relationship between age and associated capacity. But in the end, with the ratification of the UNCRC, the rights of children were enshrined in international law. While it may have taken somewhat longer, children's rights are certainly enmeshed within the general history of human rights, and are now an integral part of the human rights story.

THE UNCRC: A LEGAL AND NORMATIVE FRAMEWORK

With the ratification of the UNCRC in 1991, Canada made an official (legal and moral) commitment to the Convention's guiding principles: non-discrimination (Article 2)—the child is to be protected from all forms of discrimination; the best interests of the child (Article 3)—in all actions concerning children, the best interests of the child shall be a primary consideration; survival and development (Article 6)—ensuring the survival and development of the child to the maximum extent possible; and participation (Article 12)—the child has the right to be heard and his or her views given due consideration in accordance with the age and maturity of the child. Canada also committed to the implementation of the rights of the child in the three categories under which the UNCRC's rights can be organized: protection rights (for example, protection from abuse and neglect that relates to an area like child welfare); provision rights (for example, in areas like education and health care); and participation rights (facilitating the participation of the child in all decisions related to the child) (Hammarberg, 1990). Taken together, the principles and articles of the UNCRC provide legal and normative standards by which to assess a country's level of progress in areas of public policy, practice, and law that relate to children.

It is important to note that the UNCRC's provisions bind Canada and other UN member states as a matter of international law. On the international stage, the UNCRC shifted the conversation from the largely moral ideals and guidelines of the Declaration on the Rights of the Child (1959) to the arena of international law and legal obligation. Despite debates over the efficacy of international law, this was a significant development. As Howe and Covell note in the first edition of this book, *A Question of Commitment* (Howe & Covell, 2007, p. 3), the UNCRC is a systematic and comprehensive statement on children's rights that did not exist before; as such, they suggest—in agreement with Verhellen (2000)—that the UNCRC provides a new global standard on the treatment of children. Moreover, the UNCRC alters the nature of our obligations to children. Rights claims rooted in the inherent rights of children as specified in international law have a forcefulness that extends beyond enjoinders based on pity or duty.

Countries are legally and morally committed to children's rights as articulated in the UNCRC, and over time are supposed to bring their laws and public policies in line with its dictates. As Article 4 states, "States Parties shall undertake all appropriate legislative, administrative, and other measures for the implementation of the rights recognized in the present Convention," and they are to do so "to the maximum extent of their available resources...." Belgium has been at the forefront in terms of making the UNCRC "self-executing," directly incorporating the Convention into domestic law; this is the most effective way of making the UNCRC enforceable in a country's domestic courts, granting it the status and legal clout of "hard law." Belgium subscribes to the doctrine of monism, whereby ratified international treaties have automatic legal application in domestic courts. Other countries, including Canada, subscribe to dualism; they remain legally bound by ratified international treaties, but must incorporate treaties through legislation into domestic law for them to have the force of hard law in their domestic courts. On the leading edge here is Norway, a country that has incorporated the UNCRC into key pieces of legislation, for example, their human rights act. Canada, on the other hand, has for the most part not directly incorporated the UNCRC into domestic legislation and policies. Aside from some progress in this regard in a limited number of public policy areas—and authors in this book provide more detail in their respective areas of focus—Canada largely has resisted the call to directly incorporate the UNCRC into domestic law, with authorities tending to assume that laws and policies already are sufficiently in conformity with the Convention's dictates (Howe & Covell, 2007).

In such a situation, the UNCRC attains only the status and legal clout of "soft law." It is not enforceable in domestic courts. That is not to say that the UNCRC would not be appealed to in domestic courts. Indeed, the principles and values of the Convention have helped to provide context for statutory interpretation and judicial review (Birdsell & Chan, 2017). But in the absence of direct incorporation into domestic law, the UNCRC is not legally enforceable in domestic courts. As soft law, accountability largely comes through a reporting system. Every five years, a country makes a report to the committee overseeing the UNCRC—the UN Committee on the Rights of the Child—chronicling its efforts to bring laws and policies into conformity with the principles and articles of the Convention. The UN Committee also receives reports from other organizations and agencies concerned with the welfare of children and families, and these reports help to offset any biases likely to appear in the country's report. The committee takes all of the information provided into account and ultimately provides a report on the country in question, referred to as the "Concluding Observations" (on the number of the respective report—in the cycle—and the country). The committee highlights both areas of progress and required areas of improvement, and also makes recommendations. Countries are supposed to take these recommendations into account, and improve the situation for children, certainly prior to the next reporting cycle. Accountability, then, can come through domestic and international pressure, both from public opinion and peer (other countries) pressure. Countries generally don't want to be called out by the committee or other groups for not abiding by international law.

While direct incorporation into domestic law is clearly preferable and is itself a sign of a country's level of commitment, regardless the UNCRC has become an important basis for advocacy on many levels, two of which will be highlighted here. First, it provides a legal and normative framework by which to judge a country's progress or lack thereof when it comes to children's rights. With regard to areas of public policy and practice, the Convention provides an overarching governing philosophy or theoretical framework based on children's rights—on the principles and articles contained therein.

Principles and articles that are particularly relevant to an area can be identified, and by bringing these together, a framework of assessment can be constructed that enables a focused assessment of whether or not the UNCRC's principles and articles have been sufficiently incorporated into the field of policy and practice. The authors in this book each undertake this exercise, and academic assessments of this type can provide support to advocacy efforts.

But at an even more basic level, an awareness and consciousness of rights as entitlements enhances the power of advocacy generally and, even more significantly, empowers children themselves. As noted by well-known children's rights scholar Michael Freeman, to accord rights is to respect dignity; to deny rights is to cast doubt on humanity and on integrity. Historically, the deprivation of rights has been a precursor to extreme vulnerability and at times has even led to assaults on the right to live. The UNCRC is an important advocacy tool because it articulates the rights of children, and can be employed in the battle to secure recognition. Rights are entitlements, and in this battle for status and recognition, they allow for demands to be made. Without rights, children and those advocating on their behalf can make requests and implore, relying on others being charitable or having a sense of duty and obligation, but they can't make demands because there is no entitlement (Freeman, 2007).

When assessing the evolving status of children in history—manifested in ideas and attitudes about children, as well as in law and public policy— there is a general recognition that the ratification of the UNCRC marked a turning point in our conceptualizations of children and childhood, both in Canada and globally. One historian has referred to this evolution and historical transformation in ideas about children as "one of the most consequential developments in world history" (Strong-Boag, 2002, p. 32). This is not to say that countries aren't at varying stages of progress in terms of actually abiding by the dictates of the Convention. But it is to recognize that to a large degree the UNCRC laid the foundations for progress by outlining the legal and normative standards by which nations could be judged. There is no doubt that these legal and normative standards have made their way into national conversations about children and childhood within nation-states. While the evolution of ideas and attitudes about children continues, there is little doubt that the UNCRC has been instrumental in terms of bringing children into the human rights conversation in a more pronounced way. In highlighting the status of children as rights bearers with entitlements, obligations followed to have this status reflected in public policy, practice, and the law.

THE CANADIAN CONTEXT: THE STATUS OF CHILDREN IN POLICY, PRACTICE, AND THE LAW

After the United Nation's adoption of the UNCRC in 1989, commentators began to situate the evolution of the status of children within the context of the familiar trajectory from "property to persons" (Hart, 1991) that had characterized other human rights stories. A general awareness ensued that the evolution of the status of children was following a similar path. Canadian children's rights scholars, Katherine Covell and Brian Howe, provided a more specific template of analysis for understanding this evolution. They identified three overlapping, evolutionary stages of development as children gradually transitioned from being regarded as objects to subjects in their own right: social laissez-faire, paternalistic protection, and children's rights (Covell and Howe, 2001). In the social laissez-faire stage, children are regarded as objects, and largely as the property of parents. In the paternalistic protection stage, children are seen as vulnerable and in need of protection; the focus is children's protection and provision needs, and the state recognizes its role in this regard. Finally, the children's rights stage is defined by an emphasis on children as rights bearers, as individuals in their own right with entitlements in all three typically referenced categories of rights: protection, provision, and participation rights. The children's rights stage is unique in emphasizing participation rights, with children being regarded as actors and agents, entitled to participate in decision making. In terms of international human rights law, the UNCRC exemplifies and reflects the children's rights stage in terms of the evolving status of children.

Of course, ideas and attitudes about the status of children are reflected in developments over time in the areas of public policy, practice, and the law. Covell and Howe provided a general overview of such developments in establishing their three-stage framework of assessment, while also identifying an evolutionary timeline for the three stages in the Canadian context. In the social laissez-faire policy stage—dated from colonial times to the nineteenth century—children were viewed as objects of parental authority. They were regarded as parental property or possessions, and as "appendages of the father in patriarchal and authoritarian families" (Covell & Howe, 2001, p. 17).

This view of the status of children was reflected in public policy, and parents largely were given a free hand in child rearing. Protective laws for children in the family and society were virtually non-existent; for example, there were no laws against abuse and neglect. There were also no protective systems for children; for example, there was no system of juvenile justice. In short, children had no basic rights and were vulnerable to abuse and exploitation. In the paternalistic protection stage—roughly from Confederation (1867) to the mid-twentieth century—children began to be regarded as "a separate and special class of immature persons, vulnerable and in need of state paternalism and state protection" (Covell & Howe, 2001, p. 17). While children continued to be viewed largely as objects and the possessions of their parents, society had an obligation to protect children from maltreatment, and provide a protective and nurturing environment. During this time frame, legislation and systems emerged in areas such as child welfare and juvenile justice. While state paternalism offered children more protection, it stopped short of recognizing their voice and status as independent persons. Only with the advent of the children's rights stage (stage three)—dated from World War Two onward—did children begin to be regarded as independent bearers of rights. Particularly characteristic of this stage is the recognition of children's right to participation—the right to have their voice as independent persons acknowledged and incorporated into areas of public policy, practice, and the law.

Covell and Howe's instructive framework outlines the general stages of evolution as children's status develops from property to persons. In terms of the status of children, and its relationship to areas of public policy and the law, it is clear that the drawing of definitive lines between stages within the three-stage framework is not possible or necessary. The development of views of children has occurred incrementally and gradually over time. Older ideas may be superseded by newer and more dominant understandings, but often they do not recede completely into the past. In other words, the stages clearly overlap. At the same time, development can be uneven, not only between countries but within them as well. For example, in terms of incorporating the view of children as independent bearers of rights (stage three), different areas of public policy may exemplify varying rates of progress. Covell and Howe clarify the general trajectory through their articulation of evolutionary stages, and in so doing invite in-depth analysis and evaluation of different areas of public policy, practice, and the law.

Individual authors are invited to assess their respective areas of public policy and law in arriving at their own conclusions about the status of children and the extent to which children have been afforded the type of recognition associated with the children's rights evolutionary stage (stage three). Authors critically assess the extent to which the UNCRC principles and articles most relevant to their area of focus—those that, taken together, form a framework of assessment—have been recognized and incorporated into their respective areas, drawing conclusions about what the situation reveals in terms of the status of children. Authors address the fundamental question of whether or not Canada has fulfilled its obligations under the UNCRC to treat children as rights-bearing citizens in their respective areas of focus. Depending on the answer to this question, other related questions may arise:

- If Canada is falling short of fulfilling its obligations in a particular area, where would you place the country on the evolutionary three-stage spectrum from children being regarded as property through to children being viewed as rights bearers?
- Has Canada made much progress in the respective area of focus?
- What do historic and more recent developments in the area signify?
- Are you optimistic or pessimistic about the children's rights evolutionary stage being achieved in the near future?

Authors take a critical perspective and provide in-depth analysis, keenly aware of the caution that one must get beyond the "rhetoric of rights" (Freeman, 2007, p. 8) and put rights into effect. The bar in this regard is high; regardless of the area of focus, there has to be a substantial commitment to animating the principles and standards of the UNCRC within the lived experiences of children. It certainly isn't enough to pay lip service to the principles and standards of the UNCRC. But beyond that, even the incorporation of UNCRC into domestic law in a particular policy and practice area, which would demonstrate a more substantial commitment to children's rights, is not in itself enough. As Howe and Covell have argued, governments "still must put laws into effect, and courts must interpret the law in such a way that governments have a positive obligation to implement rights. Governments have been known, of course, to stall on their obligations, and the courts have been known to interpret rights in a restrictive manner" (2007, p. 9).

In addition, other factors are significant in determining the nature of commitments and whether or not children are being fully respected as rights-bearing citizens. For example, actually realizing the provision, protection, and participation rights of children in particular areas may require the injection of resources. It may also require advocacy support for children and various forms of representation. As Freeman notes, "rights without remedies" are of symbolic importance only (2007, p. 8). And of particular importance is the extent to which children's voices are being respected and heard in the area in question.

As noted previously, the granting of participation rights in international law sets the UNCRC apart and largely defines the achievement of the "children's rights stage" (stage three) in the Howe and Covell framework. Of course, it remains necessary for countries to demonstrate a high level of commitment to protection and provision rights in order to fully respect children as rights-bearing citizens, and therefore gauging levels of commitment to these rights remains important. But in both a theoretical and practical sense, the acknowledgement of participation rights marks the evolution to stage three in terms of recognizing rights related to children's agency—no longer restricting the focus to rights related to children's interests (protection and provision rights)—and calling for their incorporation into law and policy. It has been suggested that on a global scale there has been a "noticeable shift in orientation from a focus on children's rights to protection and provision to an emphasis on children's participation and self-determination" (Ruck, Peterson-Badali, & Freeman, 2017, p. xiii). Whether there are signs of this shift in the Canadian context remains an open question, but the chapters to follow will be helpful in terms of drawing some conclusions in this regard.

Readers have the opportunity to reflect—along with children's rights commentators—on the status of children in Canadian society as revealed in different areas of policy, practice, and the law. The book is divided into three sections: "Policy and Practice Areas"; "Children and the Law"; and "Participation Rights, Status, and Recognition." The first section—"Policy and Practice Areas"—includes the significant areas of education, health care, juvenile justice, child welfare, and refugee policy and practice. The examination of policy and practice areas begins with two chapters on education, highlighting the potential significance of this area in fostering a child's rights consciousness among children and adults alike. In chapter 2, Katherine Covell examines whether Canadian educational practices respect the rights of the child. In chapter 3, R. Brian Howe employs a children's rights perspective to focus on parental education and support. In chapter 4, Cheryl van Daalen-Smith, Brenda LeFrançois, and Devon MacPherson-Mayor analyze the status of children in Canadian health care settings. In chapter 5, Shannon Moore critically reflects on the youth justice system and children's rights. In chapter 6, Thomas Waldock discusses the extent to which the field of child welfare treats children as rights-bearing citizens. The final chapter in this section focuses on an area of significant scrutiny at the present time, and also allows for coverage of a particularly marginalized group of children, war-affected refugees. In chapter 7, Myriam Denov and Maya Fennig assess Canada's record when it comes to the rights and realities of war-affected refugee children.

The second section—"Children and the Law"—includes chapters dealing with the status of children as reflected in Canadian law and significant court decisions. The chapters range from general overviews to more specific interrogations of particular court decisions related to the question of status. In chapter 8, a general and appropriate lead-in chapter to this section, J. C. Blokhuis discusses the Supreme Court of Canada and the Convention. In chapter 9, Joan Durrant examines Canada's legal justification of corporal punishment and relates this to the status of children. Chapter 10 provides a very specific interrogation of "wrongful life" disability medical negligence cases; the question of status is again at the forefront as Sonja Grover analyzes the implications of particular court decisions for the status of children with disabilities. The final chapter in this section focuses on Indigenous children and the law; in chapter 11, J. C. Blokhuis and Amy Smoke discuss the revealing and extraordinary cases of J. J. and Makayla Sault. Given that the particular marginalization of Indigenous children relates to numerous areas of policy and practice, this chapter supplements—in its examination of legal cases—the ongoing focus on Indigenous children in many chapters throughout the book, notably those addressing health care, youth justice, and child welfare, but also in chapters in the last section of the book dealing with participation rights and advocacy. The work of the Truth and Reconciliation Commission confirms the reality that concerns about the marginalization of Indigenous children cross policy and practice boundaries (Truth and Reconciliation Commission of Canada, 2015).

The last section—"Participation Rights, Status, and Recognition"—emphasizes the connection between the participation rights of children and the children's rights stage (stage three). In chapter 12, Jan Hancock provides a lead-in analysis of the significance of participation rights for children's empowerment as rights-bearing citizens. In chapter 13, M. Theresa Hunter examines the roles of Canadian child and youth advocates in supporting children's rights. And finally, in chapter 14, Judy Finlay and Landon Pearson take an informal approach in conveying lessons from their own journeys as child advocates attempting to support children's voices and provide opportunities for participation and engagement in the public policy process. They provide a history and overview of "Shaking the Movers" (STM), annual participatory workshops for children and youth that have taken place since 2008. The chapter highlights in microcosm the potential effects of participation and engagement, not the least of which is child and youth empowerment associated with the children's rights stage (stage three).

The book's subject matter relates to a variety of academic disciplines concerned with the well-being of children and families. Contributing authors reflect this disciplinary diversity; fields represented include the following: child and youth studies, child and youth care, child and family studies, community health sciences, psychology, political science, nursing, education, social development studies, social work, and law. In addition, authors are drawn from universities across the country, including the following: Memorial University (Newfoundland), Cape Breton University (Nova Scotia), McGill University (Quebec), Nipissing University (Ontario), York University (Ontario), Ryerson University (Ontario), Brock University (Ontario), Lakehead University (Ontario), the University of Waterloo (Ontario), the University of Manitoba (Manitoba), and the University of Victoria (British Columbia).

REFERENCES

Albanese, P. (2009). *Children in Canada today* (2nd ed.). Don Mills, ON: Oxford University Press.

Archard, D. (2004). *Children: Rights and childhood*. London: Routledge.

Birdsell, M., & Chan, E. (2017). *Application of the UNCRC in Canadian law—children's participation in justice processes: Finding the best way forward*. Retrieved from http://findingthebestwaysforward.com/Materials/4B%20PPt%20CRC%20and%20Charter%20-%20Birdsell%20Chan.pdf

Covell, K., & Howe, R. B. (2001). *The challenge of children's rights for Canada*. Waterloo, ON: Wilfrid Laurier University Press.

Donnelly, J. (2013). *Universal human rights in theory and practice* (3rd ed.). Ithaca, NY: Cornell University Press.

Freeman, M. (2007). Why it remains important to take children's rights seriously. *International Journal of Children's Rights, 15*, 5–23.

Hammarberg, T. (1990). The UN Convention on the Rights of the Child—and how to make it work. *Human Rights Quarterly, 12*(1), 97–105.

Hart, S. N. (1991, January). From property to person status: Historical perspective on children's rights. *American Psychologist, 46*(1), 53–59.

Howe, R. B., & Covell, K. (Eds.). (2007). *Children's rights in Canada: A question of commitment*. Waterloo, ON: Wilfrid Laurier University Press.

Jupp, M. (1990). The UN Convention on the Rights of the Child: An opportunity for advocates. *Human Rights Quarterly, 12*, 130–136.

Locke, J. (1690/1937). *Treatise of civil government and a letter concerning toleration*. New York: D. Appleton-Century Company.

Rousseau, J.-J. (1762/1973). The social contract. In *The social contract and discourses* (pp. 163–278). London: Dent & Sons/Everyman's Library.

Ruck, M. D., Peterson-Badali, M., & Freeman, M. (2017). Preface. In M. D. Ruck, M. Peterson-Badali, & M. Freeman (Eds.), *Handbook of children's rights: Global and multidisciplinary perspectives* (pp. xiii–xxi). New York: Routledge.

Stearns, P. N. (2017). History of children's rights. In M. D. Ruck, M. Peterson-Badali, & M. Freeman (Eds.), *Handbook of children's rights: Global and multidisciplinary perspectives* (pp. 3–20). New York: Taylor and Francis.

Strong-Boag, V. (2002). Getting to now: Children in distress in Canada's past. In B. Wharf (Ed.), *Community work approaches to child welfare* (pp. 29–46). Peterborough, ON: Broadview Press.

Truth and Reconciliation Commission of Canada. (2015). *Honouring the truth, reconciling for the future: Summary of the final report of the Truth and Reconciliation Commission of Canada.* Retrieved from http://www.trc.ca/websites/trcinstitution/File/2015/Findings/Exec_Summary_2015_05_31_web_o.pdf

UNICEF. (2005). *Convention on the Rights of the Child—frequently asked questions.* Retrieved from http://www.unicef.org/crc/index_30229.html

United Nations Treaty Collection. (1989). *Convention on the Rights of the Child.* Retrieved from https://treaties.un.org/Pages/ViewDetails.aspx?src=TREATY&mtdsg_no=IV-11&chapter=4&lang=en

Verhellen, E. (2000). *Convention on the Rights of the Child* (2nd ed.). Antwerpen, Belgium: Garant Uitgevers.

POLICY AND PRACTICE AREAS

Chapter 2
Do Canadian Education Practices Respect the Rights of the Child?
Katherine Covell

Writing on the aims of education, the United Nations Committee on the Rights of the Child emphasized that "children do not lose their human rights by virtue of passing through the school gates" (*General Comment No. 1*, 2001). This means that Canadian education practices—the curricula, the pedagogy, and the school environment—should be guided by and consistent with the United Nations Convention on the Rights of the Child (hereafter the Convention). The question addressed in this chapter is the extent to which such consistency is characteristic of Canadian public schools. Although the articles of the Convention are interdependent, those that are of specific relevance to education (12–15, 28, 29, and 42) are considered here, with a focus on Article 29 as the most comprehensive of the education-specific articles.

The chapter is organized in three sections. The first section summarizes the education system in Canada. The second describes the relevant rights of the Convention. The third provides a summary of failures, shortcomings, and successes in the provinces and territories in meeting their education obligations. The chapter concludes with a discussion of whether public school education in Canada generally is consistent with the rights of the child, and the prospects for change. If educators continue to perceive children as property of their parents or those acting *in loco parentis*, then practices will overall be inconsistent with the Convention, instead reflecting an authoritarian or adult-centred approach to education. If children are perceived as not-yets and objects of paternalistic concern, there may be some indication of rights consistency. However, overall, practices will reflect an assumption that children are incapable of meaningful participation or agency in their education and are future rather than contemporaneous citizens. But if children are understood to have status as independent bearers of human rights, then practices largely will be consistent with the Convention or transitioning to that end.

CANADA'S EDUCATION SYSTEM

Canada has no national system of education and no federal department of education. There is one national body—the Council of Ministers of Education, Canada (CMEC). The CMEC comprises provincial and territorial ministers who are responsible for education, and who are, in essence, a national voice for education in Canada. However, the reach of the CMEC is limited. It may discuss policy issues, undertake initiatives, consult with governments, and represent the interests of individual jurisdictions, but it cannot exert any control over action. Action is not within the federal jurisdiction. It may be worth noting that the ministers of this council are elected politicians, not bureaucrats, and that limits their cohesiveness (since they may represent different political parties) and long-term planning (since they face elections and cabinet shuffles).

Within the federal system of shared powers, the 10 provinces and three territories have responsibility for the organization, delivery, and assessment of education within their jurisdiction. As a result, there are some basic differences across the country. One is in the age of available or compulsory schooling. Kindergarten may be compulsory or not, and may be available at age four or age five. Although in most jurisdictions the age for compulsory school attendance is six to 16 years, some start at five and end at 18 years. There are differences also across the country in curricula, assessments, and accountability policies and further variations are possible within each jurisdiction. Local school boards or district education councils, whose members are democratically elected, have some control in the operation and administration of schools in their area, curriculum implementation, personnel, enrolments, and capital expenditures. The extent of their power is determined by the province or territory in which they function. There are also school councils in several jurisdictions, which add a layer between the board and the school. In some jurisdictions, there are separate English and French school boards. In fact, in a single geographic area there may be four different school boards.

One exception to this system of schooling is seen in education on First Nations reserves. Details on such education are beyond the scope of this chapter; however, it should be noted that the federal government is fully responsible for funding (or, as it seems, underfunding) schools on reserves, and that some First Nations (for example, 11 bands in Nova Scotia) have entered into self-governing agreements with respect to the education of First Nations children. With this exception, most children are in schools governed by the provinces and territories.

It is not only public schools that come under the jurisdiction of provincial or territorial departments of education; it is also private schools and home-schooling. It is noteworthy that across Canada, there has also been a sizable increase in private school enrolment and in home-schooling both in terms of absolute enrolment and as a share of total enrolment (Covell, Howe, & McGillivray, 2017; MacLeod & Hassan, 2017). Funded or otherwise, private and home schools generally are exempt from regulations. In British Columbia, for example, parents who wish to home school are neither supervised by certified educators, nor required to meet any provincial standards, nor are they are inspected (Covell, Howe, & McGillivray, 2018). In fact, parents actually have a statutory right to educate their children any way they choose (BC Ministry of Education, 2015). As with home schools, faith-based private schools that are not funded also are fully exempt from regulations (see, for example, Manitoba Education, 2015). Across the country, while private schools that receive some public funding may be required to teach at least some part of the public school curriculum, the means to assure quality education for children are absent (Jones, 2012). As a result, it is not possible to draw any general conclusions about the rights consistency of private or home schools. In this chapter, then, the discussion of rights and the analyses of rights consistency are limited to public schools. Public education remains of primary importance as it is within public schools that most Canadian children receive their education. The most recent figures show over five million children enrolled in public schools in Canada (Statistics Canada, 2013).

THE CONVENTION'S EDUCATION RIGHTS

In the Convention, education is recognized not only as a right itself, but also as a means to the realization and promotion of other rights. The architects of the Convention assume children's rights education to be a means of empowering children to participate as active citizens in the decisions that affect them, to advance their own rights, and to promote and protect the rights of all others (Howe & Covell, 2007). Taken together, the Convention rights of relevance to education describe child-centred and child-friendly schools that model and respect the rights of the child in both the official curricula (the content of subjects taught) and the hidden curriculum (the norms, values, and beliefs conveyed by the teaching methods and the school's social environment).

Articles 12 to 15 describe children's rights to participation and expression. Article 12 describes children's rights to express views freely in all matters affecting them and requires that children's views are given due weight in accordance with their age and maturity. It is not a right of self-determination but of meaningful participation. Within schools, Article 12 means that children have a right to participate in both school and classroom functioning.

This includes the following: organizing and contributing to school websites; democratic involvement in student councils, disciplinary, other judicial or administrative proceedings, including budgetary and hiring decisions; and in the development and evaluation of school curricula. Students can also participate in their own education through self-directed and co-operative group learning, critical thinking, social issues discussion, role play, and project-based learning. Systematic opportunities for each form of participation should occur at all grade levels, but children's views should be given *increased* weight as they mature. As part of participation, under Article 13, children also have the right to access and impart information from a wide range of print and digital information subject to reasonable limits. Article 14 allows for freedom of thought, conscience, and religion; and Article 15 provides the right to freedom of association and peaceful assembly. Again, these rights are subject to limitations in order to ensure the rights and reputations of others are respected.

Article 28 focuses upon the obligations of state parties to establish and ensure access to education. Education is to be provided for all children with measures taken to encourage regular attendance and reduce dropout rates. Within education, children should have access to educational and vocational guidance counselling, and importantly, school discipline is to be non-violent with respect for the child's dignity. One aspect of Article 28 that has been given inadequate attention is that education is to be provided "on the basis of equal opportunity." This is not just a challenge for the developing world. It is of concern for all children whose families are living in poverty. Children who are socio-economically disadvantaged are less likely to be prepared for school, more likely to have behavioural challenges at school, less likely to perform well in school as measured through national and international tests, more likely to repeat grades (which is detrimental socially and academically), and more likely to drop out of school (Howe & Covell, 2013).

Article 42 is not one of the substantive rights of the Convention, but one of general measures of implementation. Nonetheless, it is of critical relevance since rights are of little importance if the holders and those who work with and for them are unaware of their existence. Article 42 requires Canada to ensure that adults and children are aware of the Convention through "appropriate and active means," which generally is interpreted to mean through children's rights education. The Committee on the Rights of the Child (hereinafter the committee) repeatedly has called for the Convention to be incorporated both into school curricula and teacher training (Covell, Howe, & Blokhuis, 2018).

Article 29, which describes the aims of education, is perhaps the most challenging. Going well beyond teaching for numeracy and literacy, Article

29 calls for schools to pay attention to the development of the whole child. Schools are charged with developing each child's skills, talents, and personality, and with imbuing in children the values of understanding, peace, and tolerance, and respect for human rights and the natural environment. Article 29 requires education that is child-friendly and empowering, education that provides life skills, human dignity, self-esteem, and self-confidence (UN Committee on the Rights of the Child, 2001). In essence, schools are to work toward maximizing the child's capacity and opportunities for meaningful participation in democratic society. In its emphasis on the need for a holistic and balanced approach to the development of the child, the committee has criticized the traditional styles of teaching that focus on the accumulation of knowledge, encourage competition, and compromise the child's development of potential.

The wide-ranging scope of the aims of education reflects the interconnected nature of children's Convention rights. The full implementation of Article 29 requires attention also to the four principles of the Convention: non-discrimination (Article 2), best interests of the child (Article 3), survival and development (Article 6), and participation (Articles 12–15). In addition, Article 29's aims of education subsume the rights of children with disabilities (Article 23), the right to health education (Article 24), the right to education (Article 28), and the linguistic and cultural rights of children belonging to minority groups (Article 30) (UN Committee on the Rights of the Child, 2001). In its comprehensiveness, then, Article 29 addresses the three fundamental aspects of schooling: the content of curricula, the pedagogical methods, and the school environment.

Curricula Content

The committee affirms that the effective implementation of Article 29 requires the fundamental reworking of curricula and the systematic revision of textbooks and other teaching materials (UN Committee on the Rights of the Child, 2001). Article 29 requires that curricula content be relevant to the child, prepare the child for a responsible life in a free society, and be infused with rights across subjects, including traditional subjects such as science, math, and language skills.[1] Beyond the basics, children should be taught budgeting, social relationships, environmental education (including sustainable development), sexual and reproductive health, critical thinking (e.g., philosophy for children), and national and international human rights treaties with, as noted above, an emphasis on children's own rights. It is not enough, however, to simply talk about children's or other human rights. It is not enough to memorize what is in human rights treaties, or what articles provide which rights. Children should also learn about human rights by experiencing human rights standards implemented in practice. At its core, this requires rights-consistent pedagogy.

Pedagogical Methods

The teaching methods used in schools should be those that are in the best interests of the child: democratic, evidence-based, and reflective of the spirit and educational philosophy of the Convention's aims of education. Teaching occurs not only through explicit lessons in the classroom, but also through how rights are implemented in practice. First, for consistency with the Convention, students should systematically be provided with opportunities for participation in school and classroom functioning. At the level of the school, there should be democratically elected student representation on all committees, including disciplinary, budgetary, resource acquisitions, and personnel/hiring committees. In the classroom, students should participate in the articulation of behaviour codes and sanctions for misbehaviours, and opportunities should be provided for self-directed learning, small-group and peer learning, student-teacher interviews, reflective writing, and self-assessments (for example, addressing "What I did, What I learned, Questions I still have"). Experiential learning is important also. For example, the committee emphasizes that environmental education must not be solely theoretical. Rather, children should be actively involved in local, regional, or global environmental projects. Second, teacher assessment strategies should incorporate a variety of techniques that allows for students' diverse backgrounds, needs, and learning styles. In addition to self-assessment strategies, the use of group projects, journals, art, photography, websites, blogs, and so forth allow for every child to develop skills and talents.

Third, school management strategies must respect the privacy, dignity, and rights of every child. There has been significant attention over the past few years to the unconstitutional locker and sniffer-dog searches in a number of high schools. And as recently as 2015, a 15-year-old girl at Neuchatel High School in Quebec City was actually strip-searched by the principal and one other member of staff. On the assumption that she was trafficking drugs, she was told to remove all her clothing, including her underwear. No drugs were found (La Chance, 2015). This situation represents an egregious violation of the child's privacy, dignity, and rights. A complete ban on such physical assault (which is what a strip search is) and physical punishment is necessary as is a ban on verbal abuse, humiliation, and emotional violence.

School Environment

The school environment not only affects children's engagement and success in school; it also teaches values (e.g., Fullan, 2007; Peterson & Deal, 2009). According to the committee, the school environment must reflect the values of the Convention: respect for rights, peace, tolerance, and equality. School environments comprise two aspects: school cultures and school climates (Van Houtte, 2005). The school culture refers to the shared values, beliefs, norms, assumptions, and expectations that inform and guide practices. Critical to consistency with the Convention are school cultures that fully embrace children's rights, cultures in which the rights of the child are the values shared by all levels of staff and students. In turn, respect for children's rights is the criteria against which all school functioning is assessed with practices altered to achieve rights consistency where necessary. The school climate is the subjective aspect of the school culture. School climate is the experience of the school culture by students, teachers, administrators, parents, and members of the local community. It is a key means of imparting values. A rights-consistent school culture will be experienced by students as a welcoming, supportive, respectful, and safe school climate. Children will feel engaged and empowered, unwanted behaviours—absenteeism, early school leaving, and bullying—will decrease, and the value of human rights for all will become integrated into the child's sense of self (Covell, 2010, Covell, McNeil, & Howe, 2009; Howe & Covell, 2007, 2013).

These demanding three aspects of education are not easily achieved. Recognizing the need for, in some cases, extensive change, the committee has urged pre-service and in-service training to promote the principles reflected in Article 29(1) for teachers, educational administrators, and others involved in children's education. In addition, it has called on state parties, including Canada, to develop a comprehensive national plan of action, from a child's rights perspective, to realize the objectives listed in Article 29(1). The committee further states that resource constraints cannot be used as a justification for any state party to fail to take measures to implement Article 29, and emphasizes that the necessary human and financial resources should be available to the maximum extent possible. Canada is a wealthy country. Is it in compliance? Has the Canadian Council of Ministers heeded the committee? Are any provincial or territorial departments of education rights consistent? These questions will now be addressed.

IS CANADIAN EDUCATION RIGHTS CONSISTENT?

The short answer, according to the Committee on the Rights of the Child, is no. In its report to Canada (UN Committee on the Rights of the Child, 2012), the committee expressed a number of concerns about Canada's lack of compliance with the rights of the child in schools as elsewhere. The committee expressed its particular concern with the lack of children's rights education in schools, and with the continuing high rates of bullying in schools and with the rate of early school leaving. Despite previous urgings, they noted, knowledge of the Convention remains very limited among children and those working with them. The committee urged the development and use of curriculum resources on children's rights, the integration of knowledge and exercise of children's rights in curricula, policies, and practices in schools, and the necessary teacher training to allow these changes. Appropriate teacher training is, of course, fundamental to the realization of rights-consistent curricula, policies, and practices.

Like the education system, teacher training varies widely across the country in structure and duration (Van Nuland, 2011). Nowhere, however, is it rights consistent, or is there evidence of changes resulting from Canada's ratification of the Convention in 1991. In fact, reflecting on changes in teacher education over the past 40 years, Edward Howe concludes that the core of teacher education programs has remained relatively unchanged, and that "Generally, the classrooms of today look remarkably similar to the classrooms of the 1970s" (2014, p. 592). One of the few but most profound changes, he notes, is the increasing incorporation of technology into teaching and learning. Others also have noted the increasing use of social media and changing technologies in the classroom (e.g., Crocker & Dibbon, 2008; Van Nuland, 2011), much in the absence of benefits (Oppenheimer, 1997). As Todd Oppenheimer points out, each new technological development from the 1920s motion picture onward has been embraced as the means of improving student outcomes. None has done so.

Unfortunately, the attention to the use of technology in teacher training far outweighs that given to education about classroom management strategies, motivation, and teaching methods, which remain superficial with little time or attention given to pedagogy and virtually none to classroom management (Crocker & Dibbon, 2008; Howe, 2014). This despite the increasing rates of bullying at school and the numbers of children living in poverty, with special needs, or with English as a second language (Van Nuland, 2011). Ultimately it is the behaviour of the teacher in the classroom that is most predictive of student engagement and achievement (Howe & Covell, 2013).

In general, the federal government has responded to the criticisms and concerns of the committee with the excuse of provincial or territorial responsibility for education and teacher training. It is a weak excuse. The federal government could take action. First, it could play a key role in disseminating information about the Convention to education department officials, teacher training programs, and the Canadian Teachers' Federation (a national organization that acts in the interests of teachers).

Second, with national programs of early childhood education and the elimination of child poverty, the federal government could ensure that education is provided on the basis of equal opportunity by removing the basic barriers that compromise many children's capacity to achieve potential (Howe & Covell, 2013). This also would reduce the outcomes of behaviour difficulties, bullying, and early school leaving, which are correlated with lack of preparedness for school.

Third, the federal government could partner with the CMEC to encourage and support implementation of rights-consistent education in all jurisdictions. A possible foundation for this was established after a request from the United Nations Educational, Scientific and Cultural Organization (UNESCO) and the UN High Commissioner for Human Rights for a report on human rights education in Canada (Council of Ministers of Education, Canada/ Canadian Commission for UNESCO, 2010). The report, prepared by CMEC with the Canadian Commission for UNESCO, clearly illustrates the disregard for the Convention on the Rights of the Child that exists. Primary attention is given to the Canadian Charter of Rights and Freedoms, and to issues of diversity and equity. Shockingly, of the long list of human rights legislation, codes, and commissions said to guide education in Canada, the Convention is absent. And it is not that there is a complete absence of international conventions (which are legally binding documents). For example, the UN Convention on the Rights of Persons with Disabilities is included. Neither is it the case that the CMEC is ignorant of the existence of the Convention on the Rights of the Child. It does note that some provinces have initiatives for student participation that are consistent with the Convention, and that the Canadian Coalition for the Rights of Children has provided booklets about the Convention's education rights. The Convention on the Rights of the Child simply does not seem to be salient to the CMEC. Rather, it sees human rights in education in terms of inclusive education, safe school initiatives, initiatives to assist Indigenous, at-risk, and immigrant students, and programs to protect minority language rights. It is a view that discounts or ignores the importance of the Convention. It is a view that disregards the legitimacy of the Convention as an overarching framework for the concerns and initiatives.

The CMEC could commit to pan-Canadian strategies of implementation of children's rights in education if it so chose. And it could co-operate to make rights-consistent schooling a reality in all 13 jurisdictions. Instead, the CMEC apparently has chosen to ignore the Convention and the committee recommendations, and continue to aim for the type of education that the committee finds inadequate and inappropriate. *Learn Canada 2020* describes the CMEC's vision of the appropriate direction for Canadian schools, and outlines a framework intended to enhance education. It is a framework that emphasizes the development of skills in literacy, numeracy, and science. There is only one activity area identified that is consistent with Article 29's curricula content requirement: education for sustainable development. Human rights treaties and children's rights education are remarkably absent from the CMEC vision of an ideal future in education, as are the teaching of life skills and the development of the whole child to potential.

Clearly, neither the federal government (current and past) nor the national education body (the CMEC) have taken their Convention obligations or the committee's urgings seriously. What about the departments of education in the provinces and territories? It is important to emphasize here that although it is the federal government that ratified the Convention, the provinces have approved the Convention and so are required to act in ways that are consistent with its principles and provisions. Those relating to education are no exception. Even if the federal government is silent and missing in action, the provincial governments should fulfill their obligations. To what extent have they done so?

Not surprisingly, given the CMEC vision of ideal education, an examination of the 13 provincial and territorial education legislation and documents (with the exception of those with access restricted to teachers only) showed little evidence of consistency with the education provisions of the Convention. Prior to addressing specifics, it may be worth noting that an examination of education acts, regulations, and policies in all jurisdictions, and a sample of school boards and individual schools provided no evidence that the Convention has had any influence on policies. Nonetheless, there is some consistency with the Convention.

Consistency with the Convention

Despite jurisdictional variation in policies and practices, patterns emerge in those that are somewhat consistent with the education provisions of the Convention. Most jurisdictions allow students to have access to a range of print and digital information subject to various limitations (Article 13), freedom to practise religion (Article 14), and provide some opportunities for students to participate in extracurricular activities. Consistent with Article 28(1d), guidance counselling is available across the country. However, for the most part, access to a counsellor is limited to high school students, and the availability of counselling varies among districts and individual schools. All school districts and schools have some measures for monitoring attendance (Article 28[1e]), and many have sanctions for non-attendance. The Yukon, for example, has provisions to fine parents if their children are not attending school. Nonetheless, none has any proactive measures to encourage attendance or reduce dropout. Finally, consistent with Article 28, corporal punishment is explicitly prohibited in education acts in all jurisdictions except Ontario. Ontario does, however, refer to a variety of non-violent disciplinary measures. Student participation in codes of conduct or discipline is very limited. British Columbia and the Yukon have some provisions for students to appeal certain decisions; and there has been some student involvement in codes of conduct in New Brunswick, Prince Edward Island, and Nova Scotia. Consistency with the other education provisions of the Convention is woefully lacking.

Inconsistency with the Convention

First, although there is some evidence of consistency with articles 13–15, there is little meaningful participation in schools as required by Article 12. Some jurisdictions have mechanisms for student representation on school councils or district boards, but this is minimal and seen only in higher grades. A few provinces do seem to be making an effort to allow for or facilitate student participation. In 2009, New Brunswick became the first jurisdiction to appoint a student member with voting rights (with some exceptions) to each of its 14 district councils. Ontario's Student Voice project, online at the government website, encourages students to express their thoughts and ideas about their education and promises to listen to their suggestions. Ontario is to be commended as the only provincial government education site to acknowledge that children may be there and have something to say. It does not, however, promote participation in either the school or classroom. Nova Scotia's *Education Act* specifies that "Students may participate in decisions that affect their schools through representation on school advisory councils or committees in accordance with school board policy" (Nova Scotia, 2016). Unfortunately, few boards, other than Cape Breton district, do include representation. No jurisdiction has provisions for the participation of children in their schools and classrooms. Far from providing opportunities for meaningful participation in their education to all children, Canadian schools limit participation to a few older students and to a few narrowly defined areas. Of course, participation in schools is more likely if children know that they have the right to express their thoughts and be listened to. Most remain unaware of this because they remain uninformed about their rights.

There is no evidence that the Convention has been incorporated into school curricula or teacher training as called for by the committee. On the contrary, the Convention is notably absent across the country with few exceptions. In some jurisdictions (British Columbia, Saskatchewan, Ontario, New Brunswick, Prince Edward Island, Nova Scotia, and Newfoundland and Labrador), the Convention makes a fleeting appearance, usually at the elementary level. For example, in the Atlantic shared curriculum, the kindergarten unit on identity and personal characteristics has the following suggestion: "Teachers can discuss a child's right to a name. The right to a name is one of the articles of the United Nations Convention on the Rights of the Child. It is important that all people honour the name given to a child. It is something to be respected. On chart paper, teachers can write the name of each child after each child gives his/her own name orally. When finished, the class can celebrate the diversity of special names they have. The teacher can prominently display the chart of names in the classroom" (Newfoundland and Labrador, 2004). While this arguably may be better than nothing, it is far from consistent with Article 42.

There is also evidence of mention of the Convention in a global context in some curricula. In Quebec, for example, students in grades 5 and 6 learn to compare what the Convention says and what is actually happening *in the world*—but not in their schools. And in Ontario, the elementary curriculum says that "By the end of Grade 6, students will explain why Canada participates in specific international accords and organizations (e.g., the North American Free Trade Agreement [NAFTA]; Asia-Pacific Economic Cooperation [APEC]; the World Health Organization [WHO]; the North Atlantic Treaty Organization [NATO]; the United Nations [UN], including the Declaration on the Rights of Indigenous People and/or the Convention on the Rights of the Child" (Ontario, 2013).

Here also the Convention is not presented as relevant to the student. Moreover, teaching it is an option: teachers may choose between it and the Declaration on the Rights of Indigenous Peoples. It is, of course, also noteworthy that the Convention is presented as the last option. In fact, all too often the inclusion of human rights in classroom teachings is at the discretion of the individual teachers.

The German gestalt psychologist Kurt Koffka made the now famous statement: "The **whole** is other than the **sum** of its parts" (Heider, 1977). This is certainly true when applied to the implementation of the Convention's aims of education as described in Article 29. Across the country, there is evidence of some of the *parts*: citizenship education, environmental education, anti-discrimination policies, and so forth. But in the absence of children's rights, there is no *whole*. The whole requires the overarching and integrative framework that the Convention can provide. At this time, curricula are not infused with rights, pedagogy is non-democratic with little (if any) allowance for participation, and school cultures do not embrace and reflect the rights of the child. Current practices across jurisdictions do not recognize the child as a contemporaneous citizen. Rather, they teach adult citizenship rights or rights of particular minorities. While they teach about rights violations, the environment, and climate change, students are not empowered to effect change (Howe & Covell, 2007). There are anti-bullying weeks and diversity days, but these are isolated, unconnected to the basic curriculum or school functioning, and there is little attention to underlying principles.

Without the overarching framework of the Convention to guide school functioning, teaching—both formal and informal—is fragmented. Disconnected teachings are an ineffective means of fulfilling the aims of education. During the course of a month or a semester, children may learn about the need for environmental protections, that they must behave in non-discriminatory ways, about historic rights violations of adults, and about democratic structures that will affect them when they are adults. But the relevance to the children and the common concerns or values implications across the issues remain unlearned because they remain unsaid (Howe & Covell, 2007). Children do not spontaneously apply what they learn to their daily lives. They do not extrapolate commonalities or generalize among issues in the absence of a specified coherent or cogent framework. Children, at all ages, need to be provided with a relevant context—that of respect for the rights of every child—which engages them, and allows them to coordinate and reconcile the values, behaviours, and the information they are being taught.

Similarly, policies that guide school environments lack a coherent rights-based framework. Much of the emphasis is on how to respond to unwanted behaviours such as bullying, and on student responsibilities rather than their rights. In addition, they often are aspirational and vague. The Safe and Caring Schools policy, for example, a model for a number of jurisdictions, describes the ideal school as one in which "the whole school community develops awareness, skills, and knowledge for well-being, positive relationships, and solution-focused problem solving" (Manitoba Education and Training, 2017, p. 3). How this is to occur and how it is to fit with existing policies and practices is not explained.

In summary, there is very little evidence of consistency with the education obligations of the Convention in Canadian public schools. There is anecdotal evidence of some teachers and some classrooms adopting a rights-based approach. But in the absence of political commitment and a national or jurisdictional strategy, children remain unaware that they have rights. And with the lack of rights-consistent schooling, children generally remain unprepared for respecting or promoting rights, or for democratic participation. Clearly we have not yet reached a stage in the evolution of human rights where children are understood to be and treated as independent bearers of rights. Rather, much of the evidence suggests that current education is best described as transitioning from understanding children as parental property to not-yets.

There are some efforts at allowing children to participate in education decisions that affect them, and there is some inclusion of rights in curricula. However, overwhelmingly, consistency with the Convention is lacking: Canadian education practices do not fully respect the rights of the child. In many areas, parents and teachers continue to make all decisions for the children. Participation in particular classes (for example, sexual health or religion) can be disallowed by a parent, and policies generally are decided in the absence of student input. Schools continue to act as authoritarian parents. One example of the latter is seen in the Saskatchewan *Education Act*, which states that "every pupil shall ... submit to any discipline that would be exercised by a kind, firm and judicious parent" (Saskatchewan, 2017). And in Ontario, the only persons allowed to appeal decisions of suspension or expulsions are parents or guardians (Justice for Children and Youth, 2013). Such policies exemplify lingering concepts of children as parental property. The disregard for student participation, together with the orientation toward preparing children for future (adult) citizenship, may also be seen as indicators of beliefs in children as not-yets.

Is Consistency Possible?

Consistency with the Convention is attainable. One approach is through incremental change. Already, topics such as the environment, diversity, and bullying are addressed in both policy and curricula, and many social studies curricula pay attention to raising the child to be a responsible citizen who understands rights and cultural issues. Incorporating, and teaching, the Convention as an overarching principle would be a good first step. As new curriculum documents are developed, and as new policies are adopted, the rights of the child can be infused into them. Simultaneously these can be supported and reinforced by the inclusion of the Convention into teacher pre- and in-service training and by the provision of Convention resources.

Ultimately, consistency requires changing the culture of schools (Howe & Covell, 2013). As has been detailed extensively elsewhere (Covell, 2010,

2013, 2014, 2016; Covell & Howe, 2018; Covell, Howe, & McNeil, 2008, 2010; Covell, Howe, & Polegato, 2011; Covell, McNeil, & Howe, 2009), the *Rights, Respect and Responsibility Initiative* (RRR) in Hampshire, England, illustrates that such change is possible and desirable. In brief, in the RRR schools the rights of the Convention provide the overarching framework for all school policy and practice. Democratic participation is encouraged in classroom learning, in class and school behavioural codes, budgetary allocations, spending, and hiring. Rights are incorporated into all curricula and used as a standard and framework for problem solving, discussion, critical thinking, and the evaluation of ideas. With this initiative as a model, Canadian schools could, if the will was there, become the rights-respecting and rights-promoting institutions that governments agreed to when they approved the Convention. Maybe then our children would not lose their rights "by virtue of passing through the school gates."

QUESTIONS FOR DISCUSSION

1. How might your school experience have been different if it was consistent with the Convention?
2. How could you convince education officials and teachers to take children's education rights seriously?
3. What would be the advantages of systematically providing for the participation of all students in their education?

NOTE

1 For examples, see Howe & Covell, *Education in the best interests of the child*, pp. 159–175.

REFERENCES

BC Ministry of Education. (2015). *Home schooling*. Retrieved from www.bced.gov.bc.ca/home_school

Council of Ministers of Education, Canada/Canadian Commission for UNESCO. (2010, December). *Report to UNESCO and the UN High Commissioner for human rights on human rights education: Report for Canada 2005–2009*. Retrieved from http://www.cmec.ca/Publications/Lists/Publications/Attachments/267/hr-canada-report-2005-2

Covell, K. (2010). School engagement and rights-respecting schools. *Cambridge Journal of Education, 40*(1), 39–51.

———. (2013). Children's human rights education as a means to social justice: A case study from England. *International Journal of Education for Social Justice*, 2(1), 35–48.

———. (2014). Awareness, learning and education in human rights. In A. Mihr & M. Gibney (Eds.), *SAGE handbook of human rights* (pp. 821–839). London: Sage.

———. (2016). The value of children's rights education in school. *Education Review*, Special Issue, 5(1), 14–18.

Covell, K., and Howe, R. B. (2017). Rights-based schooling: The Hampshire experience. In M. Zembylas & A. Keet (Eds.), *Critical human rights, citizenship, and democratic education* (pp. 191–207). London: Bloomsbury.

Covell, K., Howe, R. B., & Blokhuis, J. C. (2018). *The challenge of children's rights for Canada* (2nd ed.). Waterloo, ON: Wilfrid Laurier University Press.

Covell, K., Howe, R. B., & McGillivray, A. (2018). Implementing children's education-rights in schools. In M. Ruck, M. Peterson-Badali, & M. Freeman (Eds.), *Handbook of children's rights: Global and multidisciplinary perspectives* (pp. 296–311). New York: Taylor and Francis.

Covell, K., Howe, R. B., & McNeil, J. K. (2008). If there's a dead rat, don't leave it. Young children's understanding of their citizenship rights and responsibilities. *Cambridge Journal of Education*, 38(30), 321–339.

———. (2010). Implementing children's human rights education in schools. *Improving Schools*, 13(2), 1–16.

Covell, K., Howe, R. B., & Polegato, J. L. (2011). Children's human rights education as a counter to social disadvantage: A case study from England. *Educational Research: Special Issue Intercultural, Citizenship and Human Rights Education*, 53(2), 193–206.

Covell, K., McNeil, J. K., & Howe, R. B. (2009). Reducing teacher burnout by increasing student engagement. *School Psychology International* 30(3), 282–290.

Crocker, R., & Dibbon, D. (2008). *Teacher education in Canada*. Kelowna, BC: Society for the Advancement of Excellence in Education.

Fullan, M. (2007). *The new meaning of educational change*. New York: Teachers College.

Heider, G. M. (1977). More about Hull and Koffka. *American Psychologist*, 32(5), 383, quoted in R. A. Dewey, *Psychology: An introduction*. Retrieved from http://www.psywww.com/intropsych/ch04-senses/gestalt-psychology.html

Howe, E. R. (2014). A narrative of teacher education in Canada: Multiculturalism, technology, bridging theory and practice. *Journal of Education for Teaching*, 40(5), 588–599. doi: 10.1080/02607476.2014.956540

Howe, R. B., & Covell, K. (2007). *Empowering children: Children's rights education as a pathway to citizenship*. Toronto: University of Toronto Press.

———. (2013). *Education in the best interests of the child: A children's rights perspective on closing the achievement gap*. Toronto: University of Toronto Press.

Jones, C. (2012). *A cruel arithmetic: Inside the case against polygamy*. Toronto: Irwin Law.

Justice for Children and Youth. (2013). *Children's right to be heard in Canadian administrative and judicial proceedings*. Retrieved from http://jfcy.org/wpcontent/uploads/2013/10/UNDiscussionPaper.pdf

La Chance, N. (2015). *Je me sentais violée*. Retrieved from http://www.journaldemontreal.com/2015/02/16/je-me-sentais-violee

Learn Canada 2020. (2020). Retrieved from https://www.cmec.ca/Publications/Lists/Publications/Attachments/187/CMEC-2020-DECLARATION.en.pdf

MacLeod, A., & Hassan, S. (2017). *Measuring student enrolment in Canada 2017*. Barbara Mitchell Centre Fraser Institute. Retrieved from https://www.fraserinstitute.org/sites/default/files/where-our-students-are-educated-measuring-student-enrolment-in-canada-2017-execsum.pdf

Manitoba Education. (2015). *Schools in Manitoba: Non-funded independent schools*. Retrieved from www.edu.gov.mb.ca/k12/schools/ind/non

Manitoba Education and Training. (2017). Safe and caring schools: A whole-school approach to planning for safety and belonging. Retrieved from www.edu.gov.mb.ca/k12/docs/support/whole_school/document.pdf, p. 3

Newfoundland and Labrador. (2004). *Kindergarten–grade 2 social studies curriculum guide*. Retrieved from http://www.ed.gov.nl.ca/edu/k12/curriculum/guides/socialstudies/k2/Kindergarten%20to%20Grade%202%20Social%20Studies%20Curriculum%20Guide.pdf

Nova Scotia. (2016). *Education Act, 1995–96*. s. 24 (3). Retrieved from http://nslegislature.ca/sites/default/files/legc/statutes/education.pdf

Ontario. (2013). *The Ontario curriculum: Social studies, grades 1 to 6; history and geography, grades 7 and 8*. Retrieved from http://edu.gov.on.ca/eng/curriculum/elementary/sshg18curr2013.pdf

Oppenheimer, T. (1997). The computer delusion. *Atlantic Monthly*. Retrieved from https://www.theatlantic.com/magazine/archive/1997/07the-computer-delusion/376899/

Peterson, K., & Deal, T. (2009). *The shaping school culture fieldbook*. San Francisco: Jossey-Bass.

Saskatchewan. (2017). *Education act, 1995*. s.150, 3(f). Retrieved from http://www.publications.gov.sk.ca/freelaw/documents/English/Statutes/Statutes/E0-2.pdf

Statistics Canada. (2013). *Elementary-secondary education survey for Canada, the provinces and territories*. Retrieved from http://www.statcan.gc.ca/daily-quotidien/131204/dq131204c-eng.htm

UN Committee on the Rights of the Child. (2001). *General comment no. 1*. CRC/GC/2001/1(para. 13) 009-en.pdf

———. (2012). *Concluding observations: Canada*. Retrieved from http://rightsofchildren.ca/wp-content/uploads/2016/03/Canada_CRC-Concluding-Observations_61.2012.pdf

Van Houtte, M. (2005). Climate or culture? A plea for conceptual clarity in school effectiveness research. *School Effectiveness and School Improvement, 16*(1), 71–89.

Van Nuland, S. (2011). Teacher education in Canada. *Journal of Education for Teaching, 37*(4), 409–421. Retrieved from http://dx.doi.org/10.1080/02607476.2011.611222

Chapter 3
Parenting Education and Support
A Children's Rights Perspective
R. Brian Howe

Parenting matters. Children who are well parented are more likely to experience healthy development and have their basic rights provided for as described in the UN Convention on the Rights of the Child. Conversely, children who are not well parented are more at risk of having their rights and well-being compromised. Parenting education also matters. Parents who may face challenges in their parenting are given valuable help and support through evidence-based programs of parenting education. These programs serve as a protective factor for children, reducing the risk of unhealthy development. Because of this, the programs also serve as a valuable means of promoting the rights and best interests of the child under the Convention.

The purpose of this chapter is to show that although programs of parenting education have grown in Canada, they fail to live up to their potential as a valuable means of advancing the rights and best interests of children. Their failure is due not only to their inadequate implementation but also their disregard of the Convention. Such disregard reflects the fact that the status of children has yet to move forward from objects of charity to persons with inherent rights. The chapter proceeds as follows. The first part shows how parenting education is a responsibility for Canadian governments under the Convention; the second explains the importance of parenting education; the third reviews evidence of its effectiveness; and the fourth shows how programs in Canada have failed to live up to their potential. The final part explains why there has been failure.

The term "parenting education" is used here to refer to organized educational programs that attempt to equip parents (and guardians) with knowledge, skills, and confidence, in order to improve parenting and advance the rights and best interests of children. It is important to note that although parenting education is a form of support for parents, it is one support among many. Alone, it cannot meet the needs of all parents. Support also is required in areas such as health care, child care, parental leave, addiction services, and income support. Nevertheless, parenting education is a significant component of the comprehensive range of supports that are in the best interests of children and families. The intention here is not to provide a full analysis of the design, content, and delivery of parenting education programs. Rather, it is to examine these programs from the point of view of the rights and best interests of the child.

THE UN CONVENTION

In ratifying the Convention on the Rights of the Child in 1991, Canada officially approved the principle that not only do children have fundamental rights but also that governments have the obligation to ensure the progressive realization of those rights. As part of this obligation, in matters of parenting, Canada also approved the principle that governments have the responsibility to assist parents (and guardians) in providing for the rights and best interests of their children.

That families and parents play a vital role in the lives of children is clearly recognized in the Convention (Detrick, 1999; Hodgkin & Newell, 2007). In the preamble of the Convention, it is stated that the family is the fundamental group of society and, in Article 18, that parents have the primary responsibility for raising their children. Parents do not have inherent or unconditional rights in relation to their children. Under the Convention it is children who have inherent rights. But parents do have important responsibilities to fulfill in order for children to enjoy their rights and experience healthy development. Thus, Article 5 says that parents have the obligation to provide appropriate direction and guidance to their children as their children exercise their rights. And Article 18 says that parents have as their basic concern the best interests of the child. But the Convention also recognizes that many or most parents need assistance and support in order to successfully fulfill their obligations. Thus, in appreciation of the principle that it takes a village to raise a child, the Convention requires the state to partner with parents and provide them with assistance where needed.

The Convention directs governments to provide support to parents in specific areas. Under Article 18(3), governments are to assist working parents in making child-care arrangements. Under Article 23, governments are to provide help to parents of children with physical or mental challenges. Under Article 24, governments are to provide prenatal and postnatal health care for mothers and to ensure health care education and supports for parents.

And under Article 27, governments are to take measures to assist parents in providing a standard of living adequate for their children's development.

Apart from specific areas, the Convention directs governments to provide support to parents in general. In the words of Article 18(2), governments "shall render appropriate assistance to parents and legal guardians in the performance of their child-rearing responsibilities ..." And in determining appropriate assistance, government decisions are to be governed by the principle of the best interests of the child. In the words of Article 3, "In all actions concerning children ... the best interests of the child shall be a primary consideration." So parents have the responsibility of providing for the best interests of their child and governments have the responsibility of providing assistance to parents in order to advance the best interests of the child.

The question arises: What is meant by the best interests of the child? As pointed out by Michael Freeman (2007), although the Convention provides a normative statement on the need to consider best interests, it does not provide a full substantive definition of what best interests actually are. However, from the wording of the Convention in combination with the comments of the UN Committee on the Rights of the Child—the highest international authority in interpreting the Convention—there are a number of signposts for decision makers to follow in determining best interests (Alston, 1994; Freeman, 2007; Howe & Covell, 2013). One obvious and basic signpost is for decisions to optimize the well-being and healthy development of children. This includes not only basic physical health but also positive social, emotional, and cognitive development. Another signpost is for decisions to incorporate the rights of the child. It is in children's best interests that their basic rights are respected and implemented. It is also in children's best interests that conditions are identified for the realization of their rights. In the area of parenting, for example, these conditions include providing parents with supports to make for more effective parenting. Finally, another signpost is that decisions be informed by evidence. It is in children's best interests that decision makers consider the impact of alternative courses of action on children and, where possible, gather evidence through research and child-impact assessments. Selecting courses of action that are evidence-based is very much acting in the best interests of the child.

THE IMPORTANCE OF PARENTING EDUCATION

Recognizing their importance, there has been growth of parenting education programs in recent decades in Canada and across the developed world (Ponzetti, 2016). The programs come in a variety of forms in terms of modes of delivery, timing of sessions, content, and approach. There are programs with particular purposes, such as helping parents with their parenting during times of separation or divorce. There are also general programs of prevention and support, which may be universal or targeted to families at risk. Parents may voluntarily enrol in these programs, or be referred, or be required to participate as part of a court ruling. But despite the variations, the overall aims of programs are to assist parents in acquiring the knowledge, skills, and abilities that contribute to their children's healthy development (NREPP, 2015; Ponzetti, 2016). It is assumed that parenting skills are not instinctive. They are learned.

Parenting education programs are necessary for three major reasons: the importance of parenting to child development; the social need for parenting education; and the consistency of evidence-based programs with the rights and best interests of the child. First, as established in longitudinal studies and by a large body of research, parenting is of vital importance to children (Munro, 2009; Sanders, 2012; Smith et al., 2015). How children are parented has a significant impact on their development and on outcomes such as education, health, and behaviour. Children who are not well parented are more likely to drop out of school, have health problems, become involved in criminal and anti-social behaviour, and come into contact with the child welfare and youth justice systems. But when parents are warm and supportive of their children, when they are involved in their child's education, when they use non-violent and appropriate discipline, when they are attentive to their child's health, and when they serve as positive role models for their children, the prospects for healthy child development are greatly enhanced. Children are not endlessly resilient. For better or worse, they are affected by how they are parented.

Second, there is a social need for parenting education (Munro, 2009; NREPP, 2015; Sanders, 2012). Parents face challenges on a variety of fronts. For many parents, there is the stress of living in difficult circumstances (e.g., poverty, ill health, spousal conflict, lack of affordable daycare), which can adversely affect parenting. There is the problem of greater economic mobility and less connection with and support from extended family members, which again can affect parenting. There is the difficulty of parenting in the age of the mass media and social media, which pose more problems. There are additional challenges for specific groups of parents. Many Indigenous parents in Canada, for example, have had their parenting skills impaired by the historical experience of residential schools. Teen parents are challenged by their relative lack of maturity and confidence. Single parents are more likely to be in difficult circumstances and to lack social support. Foster parents face the major challenges of parenting children who may have experienced maltreatment and have often lived in multiple foster homes. And in addition to all these challenges, there sometimes is a lack of important information for parents. For example, there is expanding knowledge about child development, especially during the early years, which is not always known to parents. There is the evolution of law and complications in law affecting parenting, which also is not always known to parents.

In the face of such conditions and challenges, parents need support. But it is not only support in forms such as income assistance, child care, and health services. Parents also need to know how best to cope with the challenges and how best to provide for their child's best interests. They need education. It is true that education does not guarantee that parents will provide for their children's best interests. For example, despite education, some mothers still smoke or drink during pregnancy, and some parents still practise corporal punishment. But research shows that effective programs of education can have an important impact on parental attitudes and behaviour (Smith, Perou, & Lesesne, 2002). With education on healthy pregnancies, for example, overall rates of maternal smoking and drinking during pregnancy have declined over time in Canada, particularly when accompanied by smoking-cessation strategies (Covell, Howe, & Blokhuis, 2018). And with education on non-violent discipline, especially if it includes information on the negative impact of corporal punishment and the value of alternative discipline, parental use of corporal punishment has been reduced (Durrant et al., 2014).

Not all agree there is need for parenting education. Advocates for parents' rights argue that parents, not experts, know best how to raise their children because parents know best about the particular needs and circumstances of their children (Ramaekers & Suissa, 2012). Besides, they argue, the information provided by parent educators varies and is not always accurate. Parenting is simply not a science. In response to this argument, it is important to keep in mind that the purpose of parenting education is not to replace parents with experts. Rather, it is to assist parents by providing them with information about best practices in parenting, which is known not only through research but also through the experience of other parents. Input from parents, as well as from facilitators and group leaders, is a common part of parenting education sessions. It is also important to keep in mind that many parents, realizing they lack knowledge about how children grow and develop, seek more knowledge about parenting (Matusicky & Russell, 2009; Munro, 2009). Parenting education is a means of supplying this knowledge. It is true that parenting is not a science as physics is a science. But when programs of parenting education are properly evaluated, they provide the best available knowledge of best practices at a given time. And as with research findings and scientific knowledge more generally, information is constantly evolving. Knowledge about parenting may be imperfect and incomplete, but as long as it is based on careful research rather than on hunches or gut feelings or intuition, it is the best that is available.

Third, parenting education programs need to be implemented as part of the broader requirement for governments to undertake measures consistent with the rights and best interests of the child. According to the UN Committee on the Rights of the Child, in line with Article 18 of the Convention, governments have a duty to advise and educate parents on their responsibilities to act in their child's best interests (Hodgkin & Newell, 2007, pp. 233–234). To carry out this duty, governments need to invest in parenting programs that give parents a deeper appreciation of their roles and obligations, a greater understanding of child development, better parenting skills, more sensitivity to the problems of children, and more awareness of the importance of parental involvement in the lives of their children. Governments also need to invest in programs because they are a valuable means of tackling challenges—such as poverty, economic pressures, and family breakdown—that can adversely affect parenting. In addition, noted the committee, it is important that the programs work to increase parental understanding of children's rights and to emphasize the equal responsibilities of both parents in raising their children. In short, the value of parenting education is that it assists parents in fulfilling their responsibilities and, in doing so, furthers the goal of providing for the best interests of the child.

At the same time, explained the committee, parenting education is a valuable means of advancing children's rights more directly. For example, in advancing the child's right to protection from harm (articles 19, 33, and 34 of the Convention), parenting education is a means of helping parents guard against threats such as child maltreatment, drug abuse, and sexual exploitation. With greater understanding of the issues and more awareness of the dangers, parents are better positioned to shield their children from harm. In implementing the child's right to provision of basic needs (articles 24 and 27), educating parents makes success more likely. With greater awareness of needs such as appropriate health care and nutrition, parents are better able to ensure their children's needs are met. Finally, in putting into effect children's participation rights (articles 12, 13, and 14), parenting education is vital to assuring children a voice in matters affecting them and to furthering the child's freedom of expression and thought, subject to reasonable guidance. According to the committee, programs of parenting education are needed to encourage parenting styles respectful of children's voices, increase parental understanding of the child's right to participate, and help parents appreciate the importance of building mutual respect by listening to children.

EVIDENCE-BASED PROGRAMS

In support of the committee's commentary, research around the world has shown parenting education programs to be an effective or promising means of achieving favourable outcomes in parenting and child well-being. There are many examples. One is of programs to educate separated and divorcing parents on the importance of co-operation and joint supportive parenting during and after family breakdown. Studies have found that well-implemented programs of parenting education are a promising means of lessening parental conflict and promoting positive outcomes for both parents and children (Fackrell, Hawkins, & Kay, 2011; Pollett & Lombreglia, 2008). Evaluations also have been favourable for many other programs, including the following: education on prenatal care and childbirth (Nolan, 2017); the care of special-needs children (Jackson et al., 2016); and the raising of children with autism (Farmer & Reupert, 2013).

However, evaluations are not uniformly positive. In the area of child welfare, for example, there is little evidence of effective programs. A common response to parents who maltreat their children—except in extreme cases—is to have the parents enrol in classes on parenting. The aim is to change their behaviour, improve their parenting skills, and restore healthy parent–child relations. However, research has found little evidence of success (Jaffee & Christian, 2014; McWey et al., 2015). Many parents drop out of classes, lack engagement, and lack motivation to succeed. A major reason is the continuing effects on the parents of risk factors such as lack of social support, stress, mental health problems, alcohol or substance abuse, and domestic violence. Against these risk factors, it is difficult for programs to be effective—patterns of abusive parenting are very difficult to modify. Research has found some programs with an intensive therapy component—for example, Parent Management Training (Oregon Model), Incredible Years, and Triple P (Positive Parenting Program)—to be somewhat promising (NREPP, 2015). But this is a therapeutic rather than educational intervention. In any case, without effective and widespread parenting education, it is not surprising that there are high rates of parental recidivism and the repeated involvement of families in child welfare systems (Jaffee & Christian, 2014). This is far from being in the best interests of the child.

Parenting education is much more likely to be successful *before* rather than *after* maltreatment has occurred, and before a pattern of problematic parenting has developed. This is shown in the positive evaluations of well-implemented early prevention and head start programs that focus on educating parents, particularly parents at risk, with very young children (Farrington & Welsh, 2007; Karoly, Kilburn, & Cannon, 2005, NREPP, 2015). Three kinds of programs have been shown to be particularly effective. First are programs of home visitation where nurses or public health professionals visit mothers and parents on a weekly or monthly basis to provide support and education on healthy pregnancies, child health, and positive parenting practices. The Nurse Family Partnership program is a leading example of success. Second are programs of parent training or management—such as the Incredible Years and Triple P programs—where professionals meet with groups of parents for daily sessions over the course of four to six months. The aim is to educate parents on appropriate care and discipline and to build healthy child–parent relations. Third are programs of intensive parent education in combination with early childhood education. Early Head Start and the Chicago Child–Parent Center program are successful American examples. The goal here is to build good parenting skills while, at the same time, to improve the social, language, and cognitive skills of the children involved. Overall, in varying degrees, evaluations have shown all of these programs to have positive effects in improving parenting knowledge and skills, preventing child maltreatment, and promoting healthy child development. This clearly is in the best interests of the child.

Finally, that early prevention programs are important does not mean that later programs of prevention are unimportant (Munro, 2009; Samuelson, 2010). As children get older, parents need information and guidance about dealing with issues such as sexuality, school, discipline, use of drugs, and use of social media. Because of this, programs of parenting education have been developed for the parenting of children at different ages and developmental milestones. Evaluations have shown programs such as Incredible Years to be effective in educating parents of older as well as young children (Forgatch, Patterson, & Gewirtz, 2013; NREPP, 2015). It is important to note also that evaluations have been favourable not only for programs targeted at families at risk but also universal programs aimed at parents in general. A case in point is the positive evaluation of Triple P in South Carolina, implemented on a statewide basis, which showed a reduction in incidents of child maltreatment (Sanders, 2012). Although universal programs may result in small changes, small changes for many parents and for many children have a greater impact on the whole population than do major improvements on small populations (Munro, 2009). So there is great worth in universal as well as targeted programs.

In summary, international research shows the value of well-implemented programs of parenting education, especially in the area of prevention. Consistency with the Convention requires that policy-makers in Canada move forward with this evidence and invest in the creation and implementation of strong programs across the country. Policy-makers also need to be mindful that evaluation is an ongoing process. Circumstances may change over time, the demographic characteristics of families may become different, the findings of a long-term evaluation may be different from a short-term study, and what works in one jurisdiction or community may not work in another. Successful implementation therefore requires that there be ongoing evaluations and, it is hoped, longitudinal studies.

IMPLEMENTATION IN CANADA

Parenting education has a long history in Canada, dating back to the late 1800s (Skrypnek, 2002). The earliest programs were introduced as part of home economics classes in schools, public health initiatives in hospitals and health clinics, home visits by nurses, and parent programs in nursery schools. The emphasis was on hygiene, nutrition, and infant health. From the 1960s to the 1990s, influenced by the discipline of psychology, programs were developed that gave attention not only to basic health but also child development and parent–child relations. Programs such as Systemic Training for Effective Parenting provided education to small groups of parents, in sessions facilitated by trained group leaders, about problem solving and effective communication with children. Since the 1990s, with increased levels of support from federal, provincial, and territorial governments, the programs multiplied. There is now a wide assortment of government-supported programs, including ones as part of health care, child welfare, family supports, early prevention and Head Start programs such as Aboriginal Head Start, and general prevention and support programs such as Triple P and Nobody's Perfect. There are also online programs, and a wide variety of specialized programs, including ones for immigrant parents, single parents, fathers, gay and lesbian parents, and parents with children who have special needs.

The question arises: Do efforts by Canadian governments to provide for parenting education measure up with their obligations to support parents and advance children's rights, consistent with the Convention and the recommendations of the UN Committee on the Rights of the Child? On the positive side, much progress has been made since Canada ratified the Convention. Governments at all levels have become more active in funding and supporting programs. Aboriginal Head Start, for example, which started in 1995 as a small federally funded program for Indigenous families off-reserve, expanded to include families on-reserve and then was made available to greater numbers of families across the country. Triple P, which originated in Australia, was adopted for use in Manitoba in 2005 and then other provinces and First Nations communities. And Nobody's Perfect, a community-based program that originated in Atlantic Canada in the 1980s with leadership from the Public Health Agency of Canada, was expanded across the entire country. With such growth in programs, children's rights have advanced. For example, the child's right to health care has been more fully realized as a result of parent education programs on prenatal care, childbirth, and infant care. Through the Canada Prenatal Nutrition program, launched in 1995, and through various provincial and territorial health programs, most mothers now receive education in hospitals or health clinics on healthy pregnancies, nutrition, and breastfeeding. This has contributed to several important long-term health outcomes for children at risk such as declining rates of infant mortality, preterm birth, and low birth weight, and increasing rates of breastfeeding and use of vitamins (Muhajarine et al., 2012).

However, there are serious shortcomings in implementation. First, in relation to the growing need and to the growing number of parents who seek parenting education, the programs suffer from inadequate coverage (Matusicky & Russell, 2009). They reach too few families and often provide too little information. For example, although there has been a growth of prenatal and postnatal programs and—to a lesser extent—programs for older infants and toddlers, most attention is on childbirth, medical subject matter, and problems such as crying or misbehaviour. As Matusicky and Russell (2009) point out, relatively little attention is given to the fundamentals of parenting and building positive parent–child relations. Moreover, much of the information is superficial. Most programs are of short duration (e.g., one-hour weekly meetings over six to eight weeks), which means too little time for serious learning about parenting and child development. Furthermore, the majority of programs are limited to particular groups of parents, usually low-income parents, young mothers with young children (up to age five or six), and parents at risk. For example, Nobody's Perfect, one of Canada's leading programs, is offered mainly to parents who are young, single, socially isolated, or of low socio-economic status (Skrypnek & Charchun, 2009). Aboriginal Head Start is available for many families, but not in proportion to the large demand, as reflected in long waiting lists (Public Health Agency of Canada, 2012). And in the area of child welfare, although some education is provided to parents involved in the system, little is available for parents who provide regular foster care (Scott, 2014). Overall, parenting education is available only to a small minority of parents in Canada.

Behind the inadequate coverage is inadequate funding. Canada's failure to invest in comprehensive programs of parenting education is consistent with failures in other areas of family policy. According to data from the OECD, among the wealthy OECD countries of the world, Canada ranks at the low end of government spending on programs and benefits for families and children (OECD Family Database, 2017). Among 35 countries, Canada ranks 29th for spending as a percent of gross domestic product on family supports in areas such as parental leave, early childhood education, family services, child benefits, and income support. Only countries such as the United States and Mexico spend less. Canada spends much less than the OECD average and less than half the amount of countries like the United Kingdom, Denmark, France, and Sweden, so the underfunding and underdevelopment of parenting education in Canada is not surprising. It is part of a larger pattern.

Consistency with the Convention requires Canadian policy-makers to change course and make serious investments in strong and comprehensive programs. Ideally, this means that federal, provincial, and territorial governments will collaborate and develop a national strategy to ensure programs are put in place across the country. At the very least, it means that governments strengthen existing programs, especially prevention programs such as Nobody's Perfect and Aboriginal Head Start. It also means that governments support innovative universal programs that reach a broad range of parents. As reported by Covell (2005), models are available on the successful use of free newsletters and other materials. As one example, in Quebec during the 1990s, user-friendly newsletters were developed for new parents that provided information on child development, health, safety, parenting strategies, and community resources for parents. The initiative was successful in reaching a large number of parents who found the information beneficial. As another example, in Manitoba during the early 2000s, materials and a video were developed on how best to protect infants from shaken baby syndrome. This also was successful. Initiatives such as these could be models for developing cost-effective and comprehensive universal programs across Canada, which could easily be delivered through existing programs such as child benefits or as an online service. Because they are aimed at a large population of parents and children, universal programs are in keeping with the principle of the best interests of the child, which looks to positive outcomes for all children, not only children at risk.

A second major shortcoming is that parenting programs are not sufficiently evaluated. As pointed out by the UN Committee, child-impact assessments are a valuable way of determining what programs—as well as what policies and laws—work and do not work to advance the best interests of the child. Independent assessments and formal evaluations are important because the results provide information on outcomes and on the cost effectiveness of different programs. Without evaluations, which governments can obtain through commissioning research studies or providing grants to independent researchers, policy-makers are left in the dark about which programs to invest in and where to concentrate resources. Unfortunately, in Canada, programs are inadequately evaluated, leaving policy-makers without important information to help guide implementation.

Some evaluations have been done in Canada. For example, a research study by Bacon and McKenzie (2004) found that parent education programs for separated and divorcing parents were modestly effective in increasing parental co-operation during family breakdown and in improving conditions for children. Although the programs were found to be less helpful when conflict between parents was high, the programs were reasonably effective when conflict was at low or medium levels. On the other hand, in the area of child welfare, a research study by MacMillan and her colleagues (2005) found education programs to be of little value. They evaluated home visitation programs by nurses in Canada and found them to have limited effectiveness in preventing the recurrence of child abuse and neglect. Although a negative finding, this is valuable information, confirming the message from international research, as discussed previously, that parenting programs are more beneficial in preventing rather than responding to cases of child maltreatment. But further research is needed to assess other parenting programs in the child welfare system.

Some evaluations also have been done in the key area of prevention. Triple P, for example, has been frequently assessed. It is a distinctive program that is offered at five levels of increasing intensity—basic information, short consultations, skills training, in-depth skills training, and therapy—depending on the needs of parents. Numerous international studies have found the program to be effective (Sanders, 2012; Smith et al., 2015). However, some studies have reported no convincing evidence of its long-term effectiveness (NREPP, 2015). In Canada, evaluations of Triple P also have been mixed. In a qualitative study by Houlding and her colleagues (2012), Indigenous parents in northern Ontario reported the program to have positive effects on parenting skills and child outcomes. But research by McConnell, Breitkreuz, and Savage (2012) found no evidence of positive effects for families at risk in Alberta. They assessed the impact of two levels of Triple P—consultations and skills training—and found that in comparison with the usual services, they made little difference in outcomes for parents and children. This suggests the need for more study to gain a more complete picture of the impact and value of Triple P.

Nobody's Perfect also has received evaluation. A flexible and parent-centred program (rather than expert-centred), its objectives are fivefold: increase parents' knowledge of their children's development; promote positive change in parental behaviour; improve parental confidence in parenting; improve parental coping skills; and increase self-help and mutual support among parents (Kennett & Chislett, 2016). According to a major national evaluation completed in 2009, the program achieved most of its objectives, particularly in promoting a greater parental use of positive disciplinary strategies, improving problem solving, and increasing parental perceptions of social support (Skrypnek & Charchun, 2009). Parents reported a high level of satisfaction with the program and the evidence showed improvements in many areas of parenting. However, a limitation of the study is that it did not show improvements in all areas of parenting and it did not show a direct link between the program and better outcomes for children. This would require a comprehensive longitudinal study, which has yet to be undertaken.

Finally, Aboriginal Head Start also has received some evaluation. Funded by the Public Health Agency of Canada (2012), Aboriginal Head Start was designed as a culturally appropriate program, involving parents and local communities in its implementation. Its primary goals were to improve children's health outcomes, school readiness, and social, language, and academic skills, and, at the same time, to improve parenting skills. An assessment of the impact of the program in urban and northern communities was conducted in 2012 by Evaluation Services of the Public Health Agency of Canada (2012). There was evidence of positive effects on children's health, school readiness, and social and academic skills. However, because the parenting education component of the program was not assessed, it is not known if it had a positive impact. Moreover, because it was not a longitudinal study, it is not known if the program has positive long-term effects on children's health and educational outcomes. Finally, because there has been no formal national evaluation of outcomes on reserves, it is not known if the effects here are positive and lasting. In summary, like other prevention programs, more evaluation is needed.

A third major shortcoming is that the programs are largely silent on the rights of the child. Descriptions and explanations of programs rarely reference the Convention or children's rights and, in some cases, even children. Discussions of their objectives and rationales often refer to the need to support parents. If children are given attention, the rationale is to promote children's health or well-being. Seldom mentioned is the deeper principle of the rights of the child, to which governments in Canada are officially committed to (Covell, Howe, & Blokhuis, 2018). There is a notable exception. In the program of Positive Discipline in Everyday Parenting, developed by Joan Durrant (2011, 2016) and Save the Children, parenting education is justified on the basis of children's rights. Parents in the program learn about matters such as setting goals in their parenting, providing warmth and structure, and responding to children with appropriate and non-violent discipline. But what they learn is framed in terms of the Convention and the rights of children, including their participation rights. Parents learn the importance not only of protecting and guiding children but also of facilitating their participation in matters that affect them. Most fundamentally, parents learn that children are persons with rights in the here and now, not possessions or objects to be moulded. The Positive Discipline program has been evaluated and found promising in its impact. Preliminary data indicate that it has positive effects such as lowering parental approval of physical punishment and strengthening a belief among parents in their effectiveness as parents (Durrant et al., 2014). But more evaluation is needed to assess long-term effects.

Apart from the Positive Discipline program, virtually all parenting programs in Canada ignore the rights of the child. Consistency with the Convention requires that programs embrace the child's rights and incorporate the Convention into educational materials. Parents need to know that the health and well-being of children is desirable not simply out of compassion or charity but because children have rights. This is a foundational principle that has been officially endorsed by Canada and one that should not be dismissed or ignored. Parents need to appreciate this principle and understand the full range of children's rights and the relationship between these rights and parental responsibilities. They need to understand that the rights of children include not only rights of provision and protection but also rights of participation. It is important that parents appreciate that children are subjects in their development and that they have the right to express their views in all matters affecting them. In turn, parents need to understand they have the responsibility to facilitate participation, listen, and give their children's views due weight in accord with their evolving capacities. This signifies respect for children and contributes to their well-being. It is well established in research that authoritative or democratic parenting is associated with many positive child outcomes, including better decision-making skills, an increased sense of self-efficacy, increased self-esteem, and the development of democratic values (Covell, Howe, & Blokhuis, 2018). Such outcomes are in the best interests of the child, which, under the Convention, are to be a basic concern of both parents and governments.

Yet the participation rights of children are rarely mentioned in parenting education programs. Few programs explain why participation is beneficial to children and families, and few discuss parenting approaches that are consistent with participation and other children's rights. Moreover, contrary to the Convention, few programs include the views of children in the design and development of educational materials and subject matter. Nobody's Perfect, for example, prides itself on being parent-centred. The subject matter in discussion sessions, for example, is largely generated by parents. But the program would be more consistent with the Convention if it was also child-centred, allowing for child participation. Children do have important things to say about parenting, having experienced its effects. In the study *Seen, Heard and Believed*, children across Canada report on the effects of a variety of improper parenting behaviours ranging from abuse and neglect to poor role modelling, inappropriate dependency on children, and failure to listen to children (Covell, 2006). Their insights are consistent with findings in the research literature and would be valuable in the development of education materials. So in the design and development of Nobody's Perfect and other parenting programs, it is important that room is made for children's participation. This could easily be done through periodic consultations with children or their involvement on advisory bodies or committees.

Current programs in Canada also fail to spread awareness about the rights of the child. According to Article 42 of the Convention, governments have the responsibility "to make the principle and provisions of the Convention widely known, by appropriate and active means, to adults and children alike." Yet few adults, few parents, and few children in Canada have knowledge and understanding of the rights of the child (Covell, Howe, & Blokhuis, 2018). This reflects a failure by schools, educational institutions, and professional training programs to spread awareness. It also reflects a failure by parenting education programs, contrary to what the UN Committee on the Rights of the Child has recommended. A contribution to disseminating knowledge could be made by those responsible for funding, designing, and administering programs of parenting education. If this were done, to the extent that programs reach parents and are well implemented, parents would understand that children have inherent rights and that parents have responsibilities to provide for the rights and best interests of children. And through their parents, children would understand that they have the status of persons with human rights. This would be an important contribution to fulfilling Article 42 of the Convention and building a children's rights–respecting culture in Canada. But policy-makers, parent educators, and the designers of parenting education programs have yet to make this contribution.

WHY THE FAILURE?

Prior to the late 1800s, it would have been almost unthinkable for governments in Canada to support programs of parenting education. This is not surprising. Because children were seen as the property and responsibility of their parents, it was not expected that governments would provide parents with supports, including in the area of parenting education. But this view began to change as the status of children began to improve. From the late 1800s onwards, influenced by a rising tide of sentimentality toward children,

children increasingly were seen as a vulnerable class of persons, sometimes in need of paternalistic protection by the state. Although parents remained primarily responsible for the raising of their children, in circumstances where the welfare of children was threatened by parental abuse or harmful conditions, governments now had the obligation to intervene in order to protect and support children. This view led to the creation of new protective laws, policies, and programs, including programs of parenting education and support.

After World War Two, the status of children again began to change. From objects of paternalistic concern, children came to be seen as persons with rights, a conception officially embraced with Canada's ratification of the UN Convention on the Rights of the Child. With children given such elevated status, it would be expected that programs of parenting education would be elevated as well. Governments would ensure strong and comprehensive programs—with a focus on prevention—to promote positive parenting and healthy child development. The programs would be evidence-based to make certain they are working for children's best interests. And they would be infused with the rights of the child. Parents would be educated about the Convention, the full range of children's rights, the importance of child participation, and parental responsibilities in relation to the rights and best interests of the child. Parents would learn not only about appropriate parenting and child development but also the status of children as independent persons and bearers of rights, not parental possessions or objects to be moulded.

Unfortunately, programs of parenting education in Canada remain underdeveloped, inadequately evaluated, and largely silent on the rights of the child. This reflects a serious problem. Although children have the official status of persons with rights, this goes unrecognized in programs of parenting education. Governments and those responsible for designing and administering programs continue to see children as objects of welfare, to be given a helping hand when there is a need and when resources permit. They fail to appreciate that children are entitled to the best possible conditions for their development not out of compassion or charity but out of their status as persons with rights. Regrettably, this is unlikely to change in the near future.

QUESTIONS FOR DISCUSSION

1. Relatively few parents in Canada are enrolled in programs of parenting education. Why do you think this is the case?
2. Critics of government programs for families say that parents, not experts or parent educators, know best about good parenting. How do you respond?
3. The rights of the child are rarely mentioned in Canadian programs of parenting education. Why do you think this is? Does it matter?

REFERENCES

Alston, P. (1994). The best interests principle: Toward a reconciliation of culture and human rights. *International Journal of Law and the Family, 8*(1), 1–25.

Bacon, B., & McKenzie, B. (2004). Parent education after separation/divorce: Impact of the level of parental conflict on outcomes. *Family Court Review, 42*(1), 85–98.

Covell, K. (2005). *United Nations secretary-general's study of violence against children: Violence against children in North America*. Toronto: UNICEF Canada.

———. (2006). *Seen, heard and believed: What youth say about violence*. Toronto: UNICEF Canada.

Covell, K., Howe, R. B., & Blokhuis, J. (2018). *The challenge of children's rights for Canada*. Waterloo, ON: Wilfrid Laurier University Press.

Detrick, S. (1999). *A commentary on the United Nations Convention on the Rights of the Child*. The Hague: Martinus Nijhoff.

Durrant, J. (2011). *Positive discipline—what it is and how to do it*. Save the Children Sweden. Retrieved from https://resourcecentre.savethechildren.net/sites/default/files/documents/6757.pdf

———. (2016). *Positive discipline in everyday parenting*. Stockholm: Save the Children Sweden.

Durrant, J., et al. (2014). Preventing punitive violence: Preliminary data on the Positive Discipline in Everyday Parenting (PDEP) program. *Canadian Journal of Community Mental Health, 33*(2), 109–125.

Fackrell, T., Hawkins, A., & Kay, N. (2011). How effective are court-affiliated divorcing parents education programs? A meta-analytic study. *Family Court Review, 49*(1), 107–119.

Farmer, J., & Reupert, A. (2013). Understanding autism and understanding my child with autism. *Australian Journal of Rural Health, 21*(1), 20–27.

Farrington, D., & Welsh, B. (2007). *Saving children from a life of crime*. New York: Oxford University Press.

Forgatch, M., Patterson, G., & Gewirtz, A. (2013). Looking forward: The promise of widespread implementation of parent training programs. *Perspectives on Psychological Science, 8*(6), 682–694.

Freeman, M. (2007). Article 3: The best interests of the child. In A. Alen, J. Lanotte, E. Verhellen, F. Ang, E. Berghmans, & M. Verheyde (Eds.), *A commentary on the United Nations Convention on the Rights of the Child (pp. 1–79). Leiden: Martinus Nijhoff.

Hodgkin, R., & Newell, P. (2007). *Implementation handbook for the Convention on the Rights of the Child.* New York: UNICEF.

Houlding, C., et al. (2012). The perceived impact and acceptability of group Triple P Positive Parenting Program for Aboriginal parents in Canada. *Children and Youth Services Review, 34*(12), 2287–2294.

Howe, R. B., & Covell, K. (2013). *Education in the best interests of the child: A children's rights perspective on closing the achievement gap.* Toronto: University of Toronto Press.

Jackson, A., et al. (2016). Parent education programmes for special health care needs children. *Journal of Clinical Nursing, 25*(11/12), 1528–1547.

Jaffee, S., & Christian, C. (2014). The biological embedding of child abuse and neglect. *Social Policy Report, 28*(1), 3–36.

Karoly, L, Kilburn, M. R., & Cannon, J. (2005). *Early childhood interventions: Proven results, future promise.* Santa Monica, CA: Rand.

Kennett, D., & Chislett, G. (2016). Nobody's Perfect program. In J. Ponzetti (Ed.), *Evidence-based parenting education: A global perspective* (pp. 293–307). New York: Routledge.

MacMillan, H., et al. (2005). Effectiveness of home visitation by public-health nurses in prevention of the recurrence of child physical abuse and neglect. *The Lancet, 365*(9473), 21–23.

Matusicky, C., & Russell, C. (2009). Best practices for parents: What is happening in Canada? *Paediatrics and Child Health, 14*(10), 664–665.

McConnell, D., Breitkreuz, R., & Savage, A. (2012). Independent evaluation of the Triple P Positive Parenting Program in family support service settings. *Child and Family Social Work, 7,* 43–54.

McWey, L., et al. (2015). Retention in a parenting intervention among parents involved with a child welfare system. *Journal of Child and Family Studies, 24*(4), 1073–1087.

Muhajarine, N., et al. (2012). Understanding the impact of the Canada prenatal nutrition program, *Canadian Journal of Public Health, 103*(7 Suppl. 1), S26–31.

Munro, C. (2009). *Planning for parenting education and support in BC.* Report prepared for the BC Parenting Vision Working Group.

Nolan, M. (2017). Planning, implementing and evaluating a parent education programme. *Primary Health Care, 27*(4), 19–25.

NREPP (US National Registry of Evidence-based Programs and Practices). (2015). *Literature review: Parent training programs.* Retrieved from http://www.nrepp.samhsa.gov/Docs/Literatures/NREPP%20Learning%20Center%20Lit%20Review_Parent%20Training%20Programs.pdf

OECD (Organisation for Economic Co-operation and Development) Family Database (2017). *Public spending on family benefits.* 2013, updated 2017. Retrieved from https://www.oecd.org/els/soc/PF1_1_Public_spending_on_family_benefits.pdf

Pollet, S., & Lombreglia, M. (2008). A nationwide survey of mandatory parent education. *Family Court Review, 46*(2), 375–394.

Ponzetti, J. (2016). Overview and history of parenting education. In J. Ponzetti (Ed.), *Evidence-based parenting education: A global perspective* (pp. 3–11). New York: Routledge.

Public Health Agency of Canada. (2012). *Evaluation of the Aboriginal Head Start in urban and northern communities program at the Public Health Agency of Canada.* Retrieved from http://www.phac-aspc.gc.ca/about_apropos/evaluation/reports-rapports/2011-2012/ahsunc-papacun/summary-resume-eng.php#Toc319941118

Ramaekers, S., & Suissa, J. (2012). *The claims of parenting.* Dordrecht: Springer.

Samuelson, A. (2010). *Best practices for parent education and support programs.* Retrieved from http://fyi.uwex.edu/whatworkswisconsin/files/2014/04/whatworks_10.pdf

Sanders, M. (2012). Development, evaluation, and multinational dissemination of the Triple P—Positive Parenting Program. *Annual Review of Clinical Psychology, 8,* 345–379.

Scott, J. (2014). Foster parents' experiences and withdrawal considerations. *Electronic thesis and dissertation repository.* University of Western Ontario. Retrieved from http://ir.lib.uwo.ca/cgi/viewcontent.cgi?article=3358&context=etd

Skrypnek, B., & Charchun, J. (2009). *An evaluation of the Nobody's Perfect parenting program.* Ottawa: Canadian Association of Family Resource Programs.

Skrypnek, B. (2002). Parent education in Canada: Yesterday, today, and tomorrow. *Canadian Home Economics Journal, 51*(2), 5–14.

Smith, C., Perou, R., & Lesesne, C. (2002). Parent education. In M. Bornstein (Ed.), *Handbook of parenting: Vol. 4* (pp. 389–410). Mahwah, NJ: Lawrence Erlbaum.

Smith, P., et al. (2015). Supporting parenting to promote children's social and emotional well-being. *Canadian Journal of Community Mental Health, 34*(4), 129–142.

Chapter 4
Promising Policies, Ambiguous Practices
An Exploration of the Status of Children in Canadian Health Care Settings

Cheryl van Daalen-Smith, Brenda LeFrançois, and Devon MacPherson-Mayor

> *I strive to give voice to the silent agents that are the objects of [adults'] decisions: morally aware youthful subjects living their own moral experiences.*
> —Pediatric nurse ethicist Dr. Franco Carnevale

INTRODUCTION

Canada is known, for the most part, for commendable family-centred pediatric health care, facilities, and research.[1] Boasting multiple pediatric tertiary care centres, and chairs in pediatric nursing, medicine, and illness research, in many ways Canada provides exemplary pediatric health care. But to what degree is family centredness truly child-centred? What role do children and youth play in the decision making pertaining to their health care? To what degree are they involved in treatment decisions? Upon what standard do practitioners and institutions base their policies and/or practices regarding the participation of young persons in health care decision making? Covell and Howe (2001) advocate for Canada's children and youth to be permitted full citizenship reflected in their full participatory status and full provision of the rights outlined in the UN Convention on the Rights of the Child (1989) (hereafter the UNCRC). Rather than affording young people a mere protectionist status, where outdated and adultist lenses, coupled with paternalistic approaches, deny young persons their capacity and voice, a participatory status would ensure the right to have a say when engaged with health care professionals or institutions. At this point in Canada, despite many promising policies, there remains widespread confusion surrounding young people's right to refuse or consent, leading to ambiguity in practice.

In 2012, at the 61st session of the United Nations Committee on the Rights of the Child (UNCRC), Canada was described as having "inadequate mechanisms for facilitating meaningful and empowered child participation in legal, policy, environmental issues, and administrative procedures that impact children" (UN, 2012a, para. 36). As a follow-up, in 2013 the UN Committee on the Rights of the Child developed a General Comment on the right of the child to the enjoyment of the highest attainable standard of health (UN, 2013, p. 8). Acknowledging the indivisibility and interdependence of children's rights, the UN argues that the best interest of the child, the right of the child to be heard, *and* the evolving capacities and the life course of the child are to be viewed as equally important. The UN stressed that the notion of "best interest" of the child *may* mean the provision, withholding, or termination of treatment. Article 12—highlighting the importance of a young person's right to express his or her views and to have such views seriously considered—is central in the UN's discussion of Article 24. "This includes their views on all aspects of health provisions, including, for example, what services are needed, how and where they are best provided, barriers to accessing or using services, the quality of the services and the attitudes of health professionals, how to strengthen children's capacities to take increasing levels of responsibility for their own health and development and how to involve them more effectively in the provision of services. States are encouraged to conduct regular participatory consultations, which are adapted to the age and maturity of the child, and research with children, and to do this separately with their parents" (UN, 2013, p. 8). Additionally, this UN Committee explicitly identified the notion of *evolving capacity* when considering the involvement of young persons and their role in health care decision making. In so doing, they discourage arbitrary and assumptive age-based consent practices inviting, rather, ongoing evaluations related to a capacity to comprehend, consent to, or refuse treatment. By proactively employing an intersectional and power-based analysis, the committee highlighted which young people are enabled to assert their right to have a say, and who are denied this right, stating: "The committee also notes that there are often serious discrepancies regarding such autonomous decision-making, with children who are particularly vulnerable to discrimination often less able to exercise this autonomy. In other words, who the child is continues to impede full citizenship and participatory rights. It is therefore essential that supportive policies are in place and that children, parents and health workers have adequate rights-based guidance on consent, assent and confidentiality" (p. 7).

The lens(es) through which we seek to explore the status of young persons' status in health care are important to distinctly name and define. For example, the lens through which parents and "good" parenting are evaluated matters. The lens through which attempts to present or embrace Article 12 in health care matters. As do the lenses pertaining to notions of capacity through which well-intentioned health care professionals view children and childhood. Perhaps even more importantly are the often-unacknowledged lenses applied when determining the autonomy of diversely situated young persons, for not all children and youth share the same assumed capacity and therefore the right to have a say regarding their health care. In order to best unpack and analyze the status of children and youth when they interface with the health care system in Canada, there are several factors to consider. Adultism (LeFrançois, 2013a), including developmentalist assumptions surrounding consent and capacity, paternalism, as well as powerful systems that impede parents' capacities to afford more say regarding health care to their children and youth, and the litigiousness of health care in general are but a few examples of the factors that ultimately bar young people's full participation.

PRESENT IN PRINCIPLE

In this section of the chapter we will explore the policies, practices, and laws at play in Canadian health care focusing on the ways in which they impact young people's status.

Policies

We reached out to and researched various pediatric health centres to determine if there were standing policies regarding the involvement of young persons in health care decisions. The result was that for the most part, there are no consistent policies across the country, across provinces or territories, nor shared across health centres that explicitly address a young person's right to consent to *or* refuse treatment. For example, one chief ethicist at the BC Children's Hospital stated that the hospital does not have a policy on child and youth involvement in decision making as everyone is directed to follow the BC *Infant's Act* (1996) in this regard (i.e., engage patients to the extent they are able in their decision making). According to this act, anyone under 19 years of age can consent (agree) to their own medical care—if they are deemed capable. The law considers children to be capable if they understand the need for medical treatment and the consequences of refusing such treatment. It does not, however, explicitly state that they can refuse treatment.

Canadian Association of Pediatric Health Centres. The Canadian Association of Pediatric Health Centre's (CAPHC) mandate is to "improve and promote health service delivery for (not with) children and youth across the continuum of care." Their role is to unify Canada's tertiary care centres in that they strive to develop national child and youth health care standards and identify and promote "best practices." In 2017, CAPHC hosted a conference with the central theme of "Engaging children, youth and families: Are you ready to move beyond good intentions?" The conference's goal was to encourage attendees—including CEOs, CFOs, senior administrators, physicians, clinical directors, multidisciplinary practitioners, policy-makers, researchers, families, and youth (not children)—to "take the necessary steps towards making family and patient *engagement* a reality and a priority" (CAPHC, 2017). An exploration of the conference's papers and keynote addresses, aside from Dr. Cindy Blackstock's moving keynote address regarding Indigenous children's rights in health care settings, outlining Jordan's Principle and the situation behind it, reveals no mention of the UNCRC and no explicit mention of child and youth involvement in decision making. We contacted CAPHC asking if there was a policy document developed or in the works for practitioners regarding involving young persons in health care decision making and discovered sadly that the answer was no.

Canadian Medical Protective Association. The Canadian Medical Protective Association (CMPA) is an organization whose main goal is to protect the professional integrity of physicians while promoting safe medical care in Canada (CMPA, 2018). In their brief, answering the question "Can a child provide consent?" (2016), their first point is that physicians *must always act in their patients' best interest.* "While physicians' responsibilities do not vary according to a patient's age, there are medico-legal considerations to keep in mind when treating children" (CMPA, 2016). According to the CMPA, between 2007 and 2012, of the 452 complaints to regulatory authorities involving child patients, consent and communication issues factored prominently (CMPA, 2016). They advise Canada's physicians that "the legal age of majority has become largely irrelevant in determining when a young person may consent to his or her medical treatment. The concept of maturity has replaced chronological age, except in Quebec, where the age of consent is 14 years and older" (CMPA, 2016). The brief then explains that pediatric patients do not need to reach any age of majority in order to give consent but rather the determining factor in a child's ability to "provide or refuse consent" (the presence of the word "refuse" is important here) is whether the young person's physical, mental, and emotional status allows for a full appreciation of the nature and consequences of the proposed treatment or lack of treatment. When the physician determines that the child has the capacity, parental consent is not required. In such circumstances, "the physician must obtain consent from the child, even when the child is accompanied by a parent or other delegated adult" (CMPA, 2016).

Law

Canadian law generally recognizes that decision-making capacity is not tied strictly to age. For example, while the New Brunswick *Medical Consent of Minors Act* assures that minors (16+ years) have the same right to refuse or to consent to medical treatment as adults do, it stipulates that a young person under the age of 16 can make decisions about medical treatment if two medical practitioners are of the opinion that the minor is capable of understanding the nature and consequences of the medical treatment, and that the treatment and procedures are in the best interests of the minor and his or her continued health and well-being (Government of New Brunswick, 1976/2016). In Quebec, the Quebec Civil Code (1991) allows a 14-year-old to consent to care, unless the procedure is not deemed medically necessary and is thought to have associated risks, thus enshrining an out for health care professionals. Ontario (2017), Alberta (2015), British Columbia (1996), Manitoba (2004), and Saskatchewan (2017) do not identify an age at which "minors" may exercise independent consent for health care, deferring rather to a "mature minor" doctrine, which allows physicians to make a determination of capacity to consent for a child just as they would for an adult.

In its culminating efforts to expand children's participation rights in Canada, the Government of Canada and Department of Justice argue that "In the health law context, commentators have suggested moving away from consent to treatment decisions based on age toward *presumed capacity* to consent for all" (Government of Canada & Department of Justice, 2017). The Department of Justice states that this is already the law in Ontario, Prince Edward Island, and the Yukon, with Ontario's *Health Care Consent Act* (1996) serving as a legal exemplar. The Health Care Compliance Association (HCCA) outlines multiple responsibilities of health care professionals regarding consent, *does not* stipulate an age of consent, and requires a process to determine capacity to engage in decision making concerning health treatments. Despite the Canadian Department of Justice's efforts, awareness of young persons' rights and capacity remains problematic. Justice for Children and Youth (JCY) provides cross-Canada legal advice and support for young persons under 18 and for de-housed youth up to the age of 25. Over the years of their service, they found that young persons *and* their care providers needed to be made aware of their rights when engaged with health care. To that end, JCY published the *Guide to Health Care Rights for Children and Youth* (2012) wherein they explicitly instruct children and youth reading the booklet that their "consent or refusal for each treatment must be both *voluntary* and *informed*" (p. 2). In general, JCY explains, persons under the age of 18 have the legal right to make their own health care decisions, stating: "These decisions can include dental care, surgery, substance addiction treatment, etc. The law presumes that minors are capable of understanding the treatment, the treatment process, as well as the risks and benefits associated with the treatment. It is up to the healthcare practitioner (i.e. doctors, nurses, therapists, etc.) to make the decision regarding the minor's capabilities. If the doctor finds that the minor is not capable of understanding the proposed treatment, a substitute decision-maker must act on the minor's behalf; and the minor has a legal right to challenge the finding of incapacity" (JCY, 2012, p. 2).

JCY explains further that according to Ontario's *Health Care Consent Act*, all medical treatments must *not* be administered until consent has been acquired. Young persons are instructed that "in Ontario, at any age, you are *presumed to have the capacity* to make decisions with respect to your healthcare treatment. However, this right can be taken away from you by the health practitioner; and you can challenge the practitioner's decision" (p. 3). Of particular interest to JCY are the rights of young people undergoing psychiatric treatment. This will be discussed later in the chapter.

Practice

The Canadian Institute for Child Health. In 1980, the Canadian Institute for Child Health (CICH) developed and distributed a poster outlining the "Rights of the Hospitalized Child" to be made readily available and visible in Canada's tertiary care centres. Subsequent to the 1989 ratification of the UNCRC in Canada, the CICH revised the poster and developed a corresponding pamphlet now including *The Rights of the Child in the Health Care System*. In this pamphlet, children's rights in relation to the health care system are named and linked to relevant articles found in the UNCRC (see table 4.1).

This table, on the surface and taken alone, represents a strong commitment to realizing children's participation rights within health care practice. However, when considering this list along with the companion document, which expands on its intended meaning, a different discourse emerges. For example, of central importance to questions concerning the status of children in Canadian health care settings is the sixth and eighth identified right. Not only does the expanded description of these rights include an assertion that children and youth have the right to make their views known in decisions that affect them (Article 12), it states further that "As I grow up, my views should be taken more and more into account," and that young people have the right to information even if parents are trying to protect or shield them. While this

Table 4.1 The Rights of the Child in the Health Care System (CICH, 2002) and Relevant UNCRC Articles

1. I have the right to live and to have my pain and suffering treated, regardless of my age, gender or income. Articles 3, 6, 24
2. I have the right to be viewed first as a child, then as a patient. Article 3
3. I have the right to be treated as a unique individual with my own abilities, culture and language. Articles 2, 23, 24, 30
4. I have the right to be afraid and to cry when I feel hurt. Article 12
5. I have the right to be safe in an environment that is unfamiliar to me. Articles 9, 19, 24, 25
6. I have the right to ask questions and receive answers that I can understand. Articles 12, 13
7. I have the right to be cared for by people who perceive and meet my needs even though I may be unable to explain what they are. Articles 3, 5
8. I have the right to speak for myself when I am able and to have someone speak on my behalf when I am unable. Articles 12, 13, 14
9. I have the right to have those dear to me close by when I need them. Articles 3, 9, 31
10. I have the right to play and learn even if I am receiving care. Articles 28, 29, 31
11. I have the need to have my rights fulfilled. Article 42

type of nationwide statement is helpful in ensuring child-centred care that is rights-based, in the seventh right, the CICH document states that a child's rights "are interconnected with the obligations of my parents or guardians who have many important responsibilities in safe guarding my health and well-being...." In so stating, the document can be seen as shifting the focus back to a protectionist lens toward children and worse, for parents reading it, serves as a reminder that they're being closely surveilled for their compliance with said implied protectionist approach. In addition, this contradicts the third identified right for some children, and in particular for Indigenous children in Canada, who may have been raised within traditional cultural understandings of children, childhood, and parent–child/adult–child relations that do not include protectionism or an undervaluing of young people's abilities and contributions. These contradicting rights expose the many ways that ambiguity is born, despite promising principles or policies. Together with unacknowledged white Euro-Western-centredness, this regretfully derails any progress made toward child-centredness that realizes diverse children's participation rights in practice within health care.

Nursing. Since 1954, the Canadian Nurses Association, as the national regulatory body for Canada's registered nurses, has developed and enacted a code of ethics, which includes strict expectations regarding the role of nurses in ensuring informed consent. A key component of ethical nursing practice is and remains promoting and respecting informed decision making. Honouring dignity, promoting justice, and being accountable are equally important and related expectations of Canadian nurses. "Registered nurses are to ensure the rights of capable persons to direct their own health care" (the code states "person" and does not stipulate a requisite age), stating further that "Nurses advocate for persons receiving care if they believe the health of those persons is being compromised by factors beyond their control, including the decision-making of others" (CNA, 2017, p. 11). The College of Nurses of Ontario bases its Practice Guideline concerning consent (2017) on the aforementioned HCCA, stipulating that "there is no minimum age for giving consent. Health care practitioners and evaluators should use professional judgment, taking into account the circumstances and the client's condition, to determine whether the young client has the capacity to understand and appreciate the information relevant to making the decision" (p. 6).

Canada's Pediatric Nurses. On a positive note, there is recent movement in Canadian pediatric nursing, with the establishment of the *Canadian Paediatric Nursing Standards* (2017), which include explicit mention of the UNCRC, children's rights, and Article 12. Following an intensive nation-wide consultation process, the resultant standards are boldly clear in the overt requirement for Canadian pediatric nurses to both respect and partner *with* young persons and to build capacity in them so that young people may self-advocate. Pediatric nurses are expected to be competent in both child *and* family-centred care. Some key components of the standards include:

- Respects the **child** and family in goal setting and **decision-making**
- Communicates with both **child** and family as **partners** in care
- Supports the **child** and family to navigate the health care system
- Engages with **child** and family in **all care decisions** and plan of care in a respectful non-judgmental, culturally safe manner (CAPN, 2017, pp. 6–10)

This new document also identifies key competency requirements, with the following having direct relevance to promoting the status of children as full participants in their care:

- Understanding the United Nations' Conventions on the Rights of the Child
- **Child** and Family-Centred Care
- **Child** and family **capacity building** (CAPN, 2017)

Included at the end of this document is a glossary of terms, where rather than providing a separate definition of child-centred nursing, it is re-tethered under a definition of family-centred care adapted from the Institute for Patient and Family-Centred Care, stating:

> Family Centred Care (also Child and Family Centred Care) is an approach to the planning, delivery, and evaluation of health care that is grounded in mutually beneficial partnerships among health care providers, patients, and families. It redefines the relationships in health care. It recognizes the vital role that families play in ensuring the health and well-being of infants, children, adolescents, and family members of all ages. They acknowledge that emotional, social, and developmental support are integral components of health care. Child and family centered care is an approach to health care that shapes policies, programs, facility design, and staff day-to-day interactions. (CAPN, 2017, p. 13)

However, by combining the definition of child and family-centredness, the acknowledgement of children's specific role, including their full participation, risks being subsumed and/or erased, as seen in the second-last sentence above where the central and overt role of children and youth is absent when considering the *"vital role that families play* in ensuring the health and well-being of infants, children, adolescents...." The group overseeing these new standards now embarks on wide dissemination with the goal of integrating these standards into daily practice for nurses in policy, curriculum, practice, and research.

Pediatricians. The Canadian Paediatric Society (CPS) is a voluntary professional association representing more than 3,000 Canadian pediatricians. Its mission is to "work together to advance the health of children and youth by nurturing excellence in health care, advocacy, education, research and support of its membership" (CPS, 2018). In 2004 the CPS's Bioethics Committee, led by Dr. Christine Harrison, developed a position statement pertaining to "Treatment decisions regarding infants, children and adolescents." Reaffirmed in 2016, this important position statement asserts that "children and adolescents should be appropriately involved in decisions affecting them. Once they have sufficient decision-making capacity, they should become the principal decision maker for themselves" (Harrison, 2004, p. 100; emphasis added). Proactively, the CPS acknowledges how a practitioner's lens can impact how young patients and families are treated and calls for physicians working with children to therefore be highly reflective. In explaining best practices, they advocate for Canada's pediatricians to involve children and youth in their health care decision making, and address the issue of consent further by exploring the relevant aspect of *capacity*, stressing that "capacity is not age or disease-related, nor does (capacity) depend on the decision itself, but is a cognitive and emotional process of decision making relative to the medical decision" (Harrison, 2004, p. 102). Indefensibly, however, the document further states that "the majority of children will not have decision making capacity and will require a proxy to make decisions for them" (Harrison, 2004, p. 102). In one fell swoop, what appeared to be progress in relation to children's participation rights is then taken away by an adultist and assumptive statement, which gives an out for practitioners and parents who are either resistant or hesitant to "allow" a child or a youth a say regarding their health care. This out is another example of how ambiguity in practice continues.

CROSS COUNTRY CHECK-IN

To ground this chapter in real time and grassroots analyses, we reached out to and consulted with young people, provincial child advocates, and pediatric bioethicists associated with some of Canada's pediatric tertiary care centres. To that end, we asked:

- In their experience, what status do young people enjoy when engaged with the Canadian health care system?
- What issues arise pertaining to the right to have a say regarding health care treatments?
- What do they think enables or blocks young persons' full involvement in treatment decisions?

Advocates

Many provinces and territories have their own child advocate and it is often this office that discovers or receives notification of rights breaches. One key issue faced by the various advocates across the country remains the inequitable access to health care for young persons. Many advocates receive calls from young persons and families who cannot get the help their child needs, especially concerning mental health support. A second issue is that while they thought it would be young persons who most needed to be apprised of their rights—especially their rights in health care—it is, in fact, the health care service providers who appear most needing to be educated. The Ontario Office of the Provincial Advocate for Children and Youth (OPACY) works with young people in the child welfare, youth justice custody settings, or children's mental health systems and, when consulted, reported receiving calls from young people about their health-care rights and being denied personal health and treatment information, raising the following concerns that children and youth:

- feel coerced into unwanted treatment;
- have limited to no involvement in treatment decisions;
- are unable to access desired health and treatment services;
- experience difficulty advocating for health rights;
- are presumed incapable of making or informing decisions;
- have several layers of caregivers, live in residential care, and may be disconnected from natural advocates, families, and communities.

In response to these issues, the OPACY created the *I Do Care Project* (2013) with a tag line of *Inform, Decide, Consent*. Informed by seven interactive focus groups across Ontario, plus an advisory group of young people, they established a social media presence with online surveys for youth and service providers. The resultant document is an impressive overview of young people's rights when engaged with health care providers. For example, the *I Do Care* project booklet explains that "There is no age of consent. If you can understand the treatment information and what might happen if you take or don't take the treatment, you can make your own decision. You can change your mind about your decisions. There should be no discrimination. If your doctor thinks you can't make a decision but you think you can, you can complain to the consent and capacity board" (OPACY, 2013, pp. 4–6).

In consulting with service providers, the OPACY discovered that many are unclear regarding young people's rights to have a say regarding their health care treatments or to be involved in decision-making processes. According to Irwin Elman, Ontario's child advocate, service providers explained that the three most central barriers to involving young persons in decision making included: (1) fears of harm to young people; (2) concerns that young people do not understand health decisions; and (3) worries of complicating the process if children are involved. Outreach by the Ontario Office of the Provincial Advocate for Children and Youth's office to service providers has commenced, and the development of this 80-page guide is meant to clarify the process. We remain hopeful that this detailed guide will support service providers in relation to their concerns around children's participation in their health care; however, we also suggest that without a shift in the culture of care within health institutions and a shift in how (predominantly white Western) adults understand both children's abilities and the importance of their contributions, breaking down these barriers may remain a struggle.

Issues in relation to how consent plays out were also a concern for some of the child and youth advocates. They stressed that consent is a process rather than a static or a one-time thing. For example, Ontario's child advocate, Irwin Elman, stated, "consent is built in a relationship—it's a dialogue built in trust and in relationship" (October 2017, personal communication). In Ontario, the *Health Care Consent Act* (1996) governs consent practices and he added that while there is no age in terms of capacity, and the document refers to "persons," he wondered out loud how many practitioners understand that this actually means young people too. In his experience, most practitioners believe they know what is in children's *best interest*, while at the same time assuming that either there is an age of consent or that because they are minors, they are not permitted to have a role. He highlighted that health care professionals in particular have a "we know best" attitude and instead of getting consent from children and youth, they tend to make decisions for them, then invite them to go along with the plan. Elman remains hopeful, however, that the newly revised *Child and Family Services Act* (2017) will have a real impact, especially because it now "affirms and strengthens the rights of children and youth receiving services, including their right to have their views heard in decisions regarding the services they receive. Children and youth will be made aware of their rights when receiving services, and will have a voice in their service decisions. There are clear expectations for service providers on how to work with children, youth and families" (Government of Ontario, 2017). In echoing this hope, we also suggest that along with this new legislation we may very well need a promotion campaign that helps to shift adultist understandings of children's abilities in the context of participation in health care settings, in order to bring service providers' thinking in line with the spirit in which this new legislation has been written.

Pediatric Ethicists at Pediatric Tertiary Care Centres

A second component of our cross-country check-in was with various pediatric ethicists working at some of Canada's pediatric tertiary care centres, all of whom were fully aware of the components and significance of the UNCRC. The ethicists were asked if there was a policy in place regarding the involvement of young persons in their health care decision making. Some explained that widespread confusion or assumption about an age of consent was a common misconception in tertiary care. They often find their role as first educating health care providers that not only is there no magical age when a young person acquires capacity, but also to explain that it is an evolving relational process that is context-specific. They find that part of their role involves reminding clinicians that it is not about age and also that they are making capacity assessments every time they interact with a young person. Some ethicists remarked that in their experience, for more complicated issues, children are typically required to demonstrate higher levels of competence. In other words, when the perceived stakes are higher, competency requirements rise concurrently. Additionally, some ethicists conceded that in practice, they rarely see provisions for a young person to explicitly refuse consent. The BC *Infant's Act* (1996), for example, has no language in it permitting a young person to refuse treatment. While the right to refuse to participate in research is included, this same right to negative consent is not stipulated for health care situations.

The ethicists we consulted raised an alarming issue of the lack of consistent provincial/territorial or federal policies regarding the involvement of young persons in treatment decisions. In Alberta, for example, there is no legislation addressing "medical decision-making in minors," and no formal policy at the pediatric health care centre. Instead, the context for involvement in medical decision making revolves around informal consent, assent, and, more recently, *voluntariness*. An interesting situation illustrating this arose in Alberta approximately 10 years ago, when Bethany Hughes, a 16-year-old young woman diagnosed with leukemia and practising Jehovah's Witness, was assessed to be highly intelligent and in possession of all the necessary requirements to consent to treatment. As she became progressively more ill, her father reversed his stance against a blood transfusion and was reportedly excommunicated from his faith community. When subsequently interviewed by a judge regarding her capacity to make the next decision, the young woman did not, in fact, feel she was free to make a voluntary decision because of what had happened to her father. Ultimately the decision was either die or be excommunicated (Smith, 2016). This case has had substantive bearing on pediatric consent situations since and the concept of *voluntariness* now plays a more central rather than secondary or tertiary role.

For some ethicists consulted, another important issue raised was situations when parents (out of love) wanted to keep their children from knowing the truth about their situation, yet in doing so prevented them from hearing important information in order to contribute to decision making about their own health care.

Additionally, all of the ethicists we consulted noted that they didn't feel that the UNCRC is on the radar of the majority of hospitals or clinicians, but remarked that nurses were most likely to be aware that children had rights and to bring the need to hear their views forward during case conferences. The ethicists consulted uniformly made recommendations that children's participation rights be embedded in the education of all health care and allied professionals without exception.

Young Persons

A youth consultation on the right to consent and refuse treatment in Canada hosted by *The New Mentality* afforded us the opportunity to ask young people about their thoughts regarding the status of children in health care settings, and their experiences with being consulted, involved, or informed when engaged with health care. The youth we consulted had a solid understanding of the role that geography plays in whether a person is given the right to consent to his or her mental health treatment. They explained that those in rural and northern communities are often not given as much opportunity to participate in their treatment because of limited health infrastructure and education. Overcrowding and urgent bed pressures in mental health facilities or units, they explained, lead to rushed care with minimal explanations, involvement, or conversations. "My nurses never discussed my rights with me. They did mental wellness activities or brought me my food, but no, they didn't explain to me that I had a right to be involved," explained one youth.

The youth mentioned that in their experience, medical professionals would often talk to their parents or guardians about their diagnoses and treatments, typically without the youth themselves in the room. That is, they explained that many meetings occurred without their involvement and, worse, without their knowledge. When discussing discharge meetings following a mental health hospitalization, for example, our youth consultants explained that health professionals spoke first with parents and for a lengthy period of time. Following that meeting, the youth would then be brought in and the conversations would be brief and to the point—typically with directives rather than an exploratory conversation involving the young person's views, wishes, or plans. One youth stated, "After a fifty-minute meeting with my parents, and with me waiting in the lounge, when my dad came out he was kinda dazed. Then when I was brought in, there was no elaboration.... It was brief, a lot was left out. It's all pretty much filtered down." The youth felt that they should have to give consent before any information is provided to their parents or other relatives. One youth told a story about when a doctor, without her consent, revealed confidential and sensitive information to her grandma, making her grandmother very upset and the youth very uncomfortable. In their personal accounts, they explained that their parents or other adults had made decisions for them without consulting them first and that this was made possible because their right to decide who health professionals can share their medical information with was denied to them.

Although some had positive experiences with medical professionals such as psychiatrists, nurses, etc., the youth who were involved with this consultation felt intimidated by those in professional roles, making it difficult for them to ask questions and feel comfortable discussing possible treatment options. They mentioned that they have never really had their rights explained to them or been told about what is going on. "We are often shut down, right from the start. Or sometimes we are just frozen in fear and shock with what is going on all around us." The youth explained that being treated and viewed like a small child incapable of making decisions was the key factor preventing their full participation in their health care. "It was like they all thought we just were not able to make decisions."

Youth involved primarily in mental health settings identified that the focus of service providers was on "getting on the right medications" from the team's professional perspective rather than involving the youth in treatment decisions. The focus was on commencing mood-altering medications, and often in very high doses, with little or no consultation or explanations provided. The youth further explained that they were not prepared for these drugs and felt the medications were "just thrown at them." On a positive note, one of our consultants did tell us of an experience during a hospitalization when given a new medication to assist her with sleep. Although no one on the team explained the side effects of the medication prior to her taking it, the youth explained she was permitted to discontinue the drug upon her request. Unfortunately, this appears to be an unusual experience. Our youth consultants explained that fear of being wrong or getting in trouble, being forced to stay in hospital longer if they didn't go along with their service providers' plan, and not wanting to appear disrespectful to professionals all contributed to their own complicity in being denied their participation rights by the health care team.

"What needs to change?" we asked our youth consultants and we were told, similar to what we heard from the adults we consulted, that consent isn't a one-time thing. "It doesn't matter if you agreed at first—or that you were open to certain things at the time.... We should be allowed to change our minds, especially after we've been there for a while and are beginning to understand things better." Another youth said that no matter the circumstance or setting, young people must be made aware that they have a right to call or speak with an advocate. "This resource isn't taken advantage of enough. Youth actually aren't told about it at all." One scenario shared by one of our youth consultants represents the shift they call for—that rather than the young person being told minimal facts about medications, treatments, options, conversations, etc., he or she needs to be the centre and the starting point. In a rare but positive example, a child psychiatrist brought in a young person first and spent over an hour with her. Then the guardian was brought in for nearly the same amount of time, and the young person was *not* asked to leave, but rather was a full participant in a transparent conversation. After that, the health professionals were brought in, and again the young person was not only permitted to stay, but was also called upon to speak and share during that portion of the meeting. In so doing, our youth consultant explained, the psychiatrist formed a positive connection with the youth, representing a child-centred, transparent, and participatory approach.

AN EXAMPLE TO CONSIDER

Despite promising developments in policies and proclamations of belief in the virtues of children's rights in health care settings, there continues to be multiple breakdowns in practice. The following example serves as a reminder that good intentions are sometimes not enough.

Psychiatrized Children

Much has been documented about flagrant breaches of rights for children in psychiatric care, both in Canada, the United States, and the United Kingdom (Mills, 2014; LeFrançois & Coppock, 2014; Breggin, 2014; van Daalen-Smith et al., 2014). In order to best illustrate these, we provide a scenario that is an amalgamation of several cases that we have become aware of over the years, demonstrating the ways in which lack of consent to treatment in psychiatric services often plays itself out. "Michael," a 14-year-old racialized boy who was in care because of physical neglect as the result of living in poverty. He was brought into hospital by his social worker due to his intense sadness, refusal to attend school, and fears that others around him were trying to hurt him. Upon intake, he was sent to the adolescent psychiatric ward, where a nurse interviewed his social worker to get Michael's social and medical history. After a team consultation, he was presumed to be suffering from depression and paranoia, and he would be further assessed for both psychosis and general anxiety disorder. As a consequence, he was placed on three drugs: an antidepressant, an antipsychotic, and an antianxiety drug in order to commence treatment while awaiting confirmation of diagnoses. Both the diagnoses, treatment plan, and further assessment plan took place without even one consultation with Michael. After a week of taking this cocktail of drugs, Michael stated that he no longer wanted to take them due to side effects, which he stated made him feel worse than when he first arrived in hospital. He also explained that he was feeling badly upon arrival in the hospital because he was being severely bullied at school. The psychiatrist told him that he lacked insight into his illness and that he was "too disturbed" to appreciate the importance of taking the prescribed drugs or understanding the consequences if he stopped taking them. Michael's mother had visited him three times per week during this time. When after several weeks of following this treatment plan, Michael's mother became alarmed by the deterioration in his mood and behaviour, she suggested to the psychiatrist that she felt his drugs should be stopped. Michael's mother was then written up in the medical chart as being overly emotionally attached to Michael, lacking in insight herself, and a potential problem in relation to Michael's compliance with treatment. The social worker, in consultation with the medical staff, then assessed Michael's mother as a further risk to Michael, in addition to the claims of physical neglect linked to living in poverty, given that she agreed with Michael's unwillingness to follow the treatment plan and hence negatively influenced his treatment.

In this example, we see how Michael's participation rights were denied at every step from the initial consultation on his medical and social history, to the discussion of a potential diagnosis, to the decision regarding treatment with drugs, to the discussion of side effects and attempts to refuse treatment. Not only do we witness the lack of rights afforded to Michael, we see the ways in which his mother was dismissed when she attempted to advocate on his behalf and was then later deemed of questionable psychiatric stability (overly attached, lacking insight) and a child-protection risk to her child for not agreeing with the medical opinion.

DISCUSSION: IF IT'S RIGHT IN PRINCIPLE, IT'S RIGHT IN PRACTICE

In 2011, The Canadian Coalition for the Rights of Children (CCRC), known for strong monitoring reports, released a 90-page report outlining the implementation of the UNCRC in Canada entitled *Right in Principle, Right in Practice* (CCRC, 2011). To help Canada improve its performance, the CCRC collaborated with more than 30 civil society organizations and individual experts to compile a community-based analysis of progress on children's rights in Canada. The CCRC argues that systemic mechanisms must be put in place to implement children's rights across Canada and across sectors, with health care being just one. They sagely argue that if children's rights are "right in *principle*," then they are "right in *practice*"—a precise contention given the ways in which children's rights may be misunderstood, unacknowledged, or resisted across Canada. For example, as acknowledged by the Canadian Paediatric Society (2016), there is considerable variation across the provinces and territories when it comes to practices concerning young people and consent. They state: "In some provinces and territories, the age of legal majority is *presumed* to also be the age of consent. Some provinces stipulate an age of consent, while others follow a process whereby one's right to consent depends on decision-making capacity, rather than age" (CPS, 2016, p. 4). Indeed, if the participation of young people is right in principle, then it must be deemed right and enacted in practice. So why does a right to consent to or refuse health care treatments vary for citizens of different ages in Canada? Despite widespread confusion, inconsistency, and ill-informed designation of arbitrary threshold ages in a myriad of health care agencies and organizations, in Canada *there is no age of consent* when it comes to health care decision making.

In broadly conceptualizing the participatory rights of young persons, the UNCRC's Article 12 strives to ensure the participatory rights of Canadian children, and as such should *ground* and *frame* the work of pediatric health care professionals. Indeed, the provision, protection, and especially for the purposes of this chapter, the *participation* rights afforded to Canadian children in the UNCRC *fit* with the various codes of ethics of all the health professionals who work with children in Canada's health care systems.

Every code of ethics and/or standard of practice for Canadian nurses, physicians, social workers, psychologists, occupational therapists, and physiotherapists embraces the notion of the inherent rights of persons. Are young people not persons? Many, including the Canadian Association of Paediatric Nurses (2017), the Canadian Physiotherapy Association (n.d.), and the Canadian Association of Social Workers (2005), explicitly acknowledge rights, stating, for example, "respecting their rights, dignity, needs, wishes and values" (CPA, n.d., p. 2). Of central importance to all codes of ethics are strict directives concerning consent. For example, the Code of Ethics of the Canadian Psychological Association (2017) makes *no distinction regarding age* when stating that psychologists must

> provide, in obtaining informed consent, as much information as reasonable or prudent individuals and groups (e.g., couples, families, organizations, communities, peoples) would want to know before making a decision or consenting to the activity. Typically, and as appropriate to the situation and context, this would include: purpose and nature of the activity; mutual responsibilities; whether a team or other collaborators are involved; privacy and confidentiality limitations, risks and protections; likely risks and benefits of the activity, including any particular

risks or benefits of the methods or communication modalities used; alternatives available; likely consequences of non-action; the option to refuse or withdraw at any time, without prejudice; over what period of time the consent applies; and how to rescind consent if desired. (p. 14)

The Code of Ethics of the Canadian Association of Occupational Therapists (2008) serves as another example of rights-based policies or principles. Occupational therapists often work with long-hospitalized young persons, and their code stipulates that "every person can make choices about life," and directs their members to "value and respect clients' rights to be treated with respect and dignity within a safe and non-judgmental environment" (p. 3). So, if it *is* right in principle, then why are we not seeing it in practice?

WHAT IS GETTING IN THE WAY?

Given that some adults believe that children are inherently incompetent or incapable of making an informed or rational decision regarding their own health or life, children's rights to have their views considered are often denied (LeFrançois, 2008). As evidenced earlier in this chapter, adultism (LeFrançois, 2013a), including developmentalist assumptions regarding consent and capacity, paternalism, powerful systems that impede parents' capacities to advocate for their child's views to be heard, and the litigiousness of health care in general are but a few examples of the factors that ultimately bar young people's full participation. There is substantive evidence indicating wide support of young persons having participatory rights when engaged in health care treatment decisions. From the Government of Canada's Justice Department, to the various codes of ethics of health care professionals who routinely work with children, to documents put out by various child advocates, and to the approaches taken by the pediatric ethicists consulted for this chapter—indeed there has been movement regarding a young person's right to be consulted, informed, and involved in his or her health care. So why does it all unravel? And why? The ethicists say it most often has to do with high-stakes decisions—for example, in treatment decisions where life itself may be at issue. While a young person's view should be taken into account, many ethicists believe that the duty to protect—even protect a child from himself or herself—takes over. The advocates say that health care decision rights are rarely on the radar of health care professionals, especially not for children already deemed vulnerable or somehow incompetent by virtue of their involvement with child-protective services, criminal justice systems, or through being de-housed. Young people say they feel the assumption of their incapacity leads most health care professionals to filter information before it gets to them, thus preventing them from getting all the information to which they have a right. In answer to the question of *What is getting in the way?* we identify reasons in the sections that follow.

Awareness

When it comes to awareness of the UNCRC, both Justice for Children and Youth and the Canadian Coalition for the Rights of the Child (2011) assert that children and youth have not yet been substantively or consistently made aware of their rights. Additionally, when we spoke with some of Canada's child advocates, we found that health care providers also lacked awareness. Citing numerous anecdotes, the advocates affirmed that most health care professionals were unaware of the UNCRC and felt compelled to have adults determine what was in the best interest of their patients. As mentioned earlier in the chapter, Ontario's child advocate surveyed health care professionals and discovered that the reasons they opted to not involve young people were linked to fears of harm to young people, concerns that young people do not understand health decisions, and worries that children would complicate the process. And to compound this problem with lack of awareness, health care professionals across Canada continue to work with a core curriculum that does not have the UNCRC embedded in it.

Lack of Consistent or Explicit Policies

We have demonstrated that across the country and across tertiary care centres, there is no consistent policy, law, or interpretation of young people's right to have a say regarding health care decisions that affect them. Many practitioners assume that a right to agree to a predetermined plan sufficiently involves children. Aside from a lack of consistent policies or laws, there is also the problem of a lack of consistent or *explicit* policies regarding young people's right to have a say, including if that say goes against a predetermined plan said to be in their best interest.

Ambiguity in Family-Centred Care: Where Is the Young Person?

Nationally affirmed definitions of family-centred care (FCC) are different from notions of child-centred care or being child-centred. To be child-centred means to "give priority to the needs and interests of children" (Oxford Dictionaries, 2017). Family-centred care maintains the default focus on the rights of parents to have a say regarding "their" child and on the necessity of parents to protect their children. Subsuming child-centred care underneath this broad definition renders the young person invisible, perpetuates the myth that children are the property of their parents, and continues to situate the child as a component of a family, thus stripping children of their own citizenship and their own individual beingness with rights.

Parental Pressures to Conform to Parenting Norms

As viscerally evident in our example of Michael and his mother's advocacy efforts, parents are systematically oppressed and discouraged from affording their children a meaningful and informed role in their health care treatment plans. According to Sheahan, Da Silva, Czoli, and Zlotnik-Shaul (2012), a major factor impacting a young person's enablement to have a say regarding his or her health care is that parents in Canada are held legally responsible for their children. According to the Criminal Code, parents must provide their children with education and the necessities of life (Criminal Code, R.S.C. 1985 C-46). Parents who permit their child or youth to refuse treatment, for example, could be found guilty of an offence if the courts deem the child or youth's health is at risk or may be permanently "endangered" or "injured." As discussed earlier in the chapter, even the nationwide campaign to promote children's rights in hospitals, led by the Canadian Institute for Child Health, asserts that children's rights are *interconnected with the obligations of parents*. In so stating, the document pressures parents to conform to powerful parenting norms, insinuating that to do otherwise would be met with institutional if not state-initiated ramifications.

Best Interest Models Perpetuate Adult-Centred, Developmentalist Paternalism

Nurse ethicist Dr. Franco Carnevale (2012), a long-serving critical care nurse who has witnessed hundreds of pediatric patients face critical decisions, argues that *best interest* models for exploring ethical issues relating to children, including that of their right to consent to or refuse treatment, "casts the child in a highly passive role (and) the voice of the child is essentially muted" (p. 320). He argues that the reasons for this are twofold: "(1) the underestimation of the 'maturity' of children's moral reasoning, and (2) the 'adult-centredness' of the best-interests model" (p. 320). Age-based and developmentalist assumptions regarding capacity—or incapacity more specifically—continue to frame "best interest" practice approaches. This ageist bias is most profoundly evidenced in the Canadian Paediatric Society asserting that most children will *not* be found to have sufficient decision-making capacity. In stark contrast to this is the UN Committee on the Rights of the Child (2013), which discourages arbitrary and assumptive age-based consent practices, inviting a combined practice model of presumed competence and evolving capacity.

Who the Young Person Is Matters

Backed by strong directives from the UN Committee on the Rights of the Child (2013), an intersectional lens is essential in order to understand power imbalances across groups of young people where some groups are deemed to have less value, capacity, or inherent agency. Although white able-bodied middle-class children may find it difficult to be taken seriously and have their rights to informed consent to treatment realized in practice, this situation is much more tenuous for children who are further marginalized by their status as racialized, Indigenous, queer-identified, poor, in care, or regarded as physically, intellectually, or psychiatrically disabled. In short, who the young person is matters when it comes to the closing down of possibilities for participatory practice in health care situations. And who the young person is matters in terms of who practitioners tend to regard as worthy of being accorded their rights. For example, children who have been psychiatrized are seen as inherently irrational and often assumed to lack capacity to consent without engaging in an assessment of their actual abilities (LeFrançois, 2008). Incarcerated children, by virtue of their loss of liberty, are perhaps not surprisingly heavily medicated with psychiatric drugs (Findlay, 2005), and are often told that they will not get probation if they refuse to consent to this treatment, tying up their medical decision making coercively with the length of their custodial sentence. This, of course, results in neither voluntary nor informed consent. The most egregious example of this is, of course, the saga exposed by maverick CBC journalist Hana Gartner (2010) of the devastating journey of Ashley Smith, who after months of powerful psychiatric drugs and repeated, forced, and punitive solitary confinement, died by suicidal strangulation on October 19, 2007. The resultant Ontario coroner's inquest (Carlisle, 2013) exposed numerous breaches of Ashley's rights and eventually led to a nationwide policy call regarding isolation and psychiatric medications in Canada's prisons.

Children living in foster care face similar inequities and rights breaches. According to a report entitled *Looking After Children in Ontario* (Ontario Association of Children's Aid Societies, 2016), 48 percent of young people aged five to 17 in foster and group homes in Ontario are prescribed mood-altering medications without the right to refuse and without a full and impartial explanation of their impact and intent. Many of the child advocates we consulted indicated grave concern for youth once they are placed in psychiatric facilities, particularly if they are under the care of the state. According to this yearly survey conducted for the Government of Ontario and the Ontario Association of Children's Aid Societies, by the time these marginalized youth are 16 and 17, 57 percent of them are on these powerful medications. When more control is required by the carers, particularly in group home settings that are inadequately staffed and poorly trained, the percentage rises to 74 percent (Ontario Association of Children's Aid Societies, 2016). Despite widespread outcry by various advocacy groups, including the National Network for Youth in Care, this trend continues.

In addition, according to a landmark Canadian Human Rights Tribunal ruling in 2016, Indigenous children on reserves face underfunded, limited, or no service provision; a lack of access to health services; and widespread discrimination (p. 1). Further forms of systemic racism and colonial logic continue to intersect with adultist notions of which children are capable of consenting and which are not, reproducing both systemic and interpersonal forms of racism for Indigenous children (whether on or off reserve), black and racialized children (LeFrançois & Coppock, 2014) not only within health contexts, but also within the punitive child protection, juvenile justice, and psychiatric systems where they and their families remain overrepresented (LeFrançois, 2013b). Jordan's Principle attempts to address these inequities. Championed by child rights activist Dr. Cindy Blackstock, Jordan's Principle sets out to address gross health care access inequities experienced by First Nations, Métis, and Inuit (FNMI) children. "Jordan's Principle is a child-first principle to resolve jurisdictional disputes within, among and between federal and provincial/territorial governments regarding payment for First Nations children's services. It aims to ensure First Nations children can access government services on the same terms as other children so the government of first contact pays for the service and seeks reimbursement at a later stage" (First Nations Caring Society, n.d.).

Despite receiving all-party support in 2007, a lack of meaningful operationalization spurred Blackstock and the First Nations Caring Society to pursue and win a Canadian Human Rights Tribunal ruling, which found that the Canadian government's approach to FNMI's service access continued to be discriminatory. Since then, the government has enacted an application process titled Jordan's Principle, whereby applications can be made to ensure access to health care services. According to the Canadian government (2019), from July 2016 to January 2019, 214,000 requests were approved under Jordan's Principle, perhaps signalling a promise to sustainably prevent further inequity.

RECOMMENDATIONS

Nurse ethicist Dr. Franco Carnevale (2012) calls upon us all to consider the voice of the child—a simple yet profound request. Enacting this moral imperative *is* possible if the individual, institutional, and attitudinal will can be courageously championed. In 2000, a child-rights model was proposed by a UK team of child advocates, nurses, and physicians in collaboration with Child Advocacy International, the World Health Organization, the Royal College of Nursing (UK), the Royal College of Paediatrics (UK), UNICEF, and Child Health UK. Following a broad collaborative analysis spanning six countries and multiple facilities, the team discovered broad breaches of children's rights when engaged with health care practitioners and facilities. Many were due, in part, to poor infrastructure, lack of adequate training or education for staff, and an overall lack of appreciation of children as *persons* rather than property. According to Southall et al. (2000), the team developed globally applicable standards to help ensure that practices in hospitals and health centres everywhere respected children's rights. The Child-Friendly Health Care Initiative proposes several standards, each linked explicitly to several articles found in the UNCRC. Standard Five stated that "all staff should approach children as individual people with their own needs and rights to privacy and dignity, involving them in decisions affecting their care" (Southall et al., 2000, p. 1060). Southall et al. (2000) argued for systems to be put in place in order to consistently and systematically seek children's views on, and to confirm their understanding of, the care given in a language and manner that they can understand. This was linked explicitly to Article 12 and young people's right to have a say about all things affecting them.

This model and this process that engaged practitioners and organizations at the grassroots level serves as an exemplary process that Canada might consider. To date, efforts in Canada resemble a piecemeal approach of good intentions that on paper say (nearly) all the right things. In practice, however, it is difficult to assert that consistently and uniformly, pediatric health centres, units, or practitioners are grounded in a rights-informed framework.

It is clear that good intentions are not enough. As the Covell and Howe (2001) model is to serve as our yardstick for the purposes of this text, it can be argued, then, that while policies and proposed practice models are in place and have grown in popularity across Canada and while there is *no* specified age of consent in Canada, when young people interact with Canadian health care, a status of protectionist paternalism remains the default.

In order to translate well-intentioned practice guidelines and eliminate pervasive ambiguity in family-centred care or in consent practices, we offer several recommendations.

First, we call for an elimination of age-based assumptions concerning consent. This would be consistent with the Committee on the Rights of the Child's interpretation of the requirements of Article 12. This argument builds on arguments made in 2005 by the Office of Child and Family Service Advocacy (OCFSA), in its report entitled *Consent and Confidentiality in Health Services: Respecting the Child's Right to Be Heard.* Culminating in a set of unapologetic and unwavering principles to guide health care decision making (see Table 4.2), the OCFSA leaves no question as to why and how to embrace the UNCRC's Articles 12 and 13 within Canadian health care.

Second, we argue that a shift to a model of *presumed competence* is essential in ensuring that all children—no matter who they are—are accorded their rights in practice. This requires understanding children to being competent until it is proven otherwise, rather than assuming children to be "naturally" and "developmentally immature" and therefore incompetent. In addition, this presumed competence must be linked not only to children's rights to informed consent but also to their rights to refuse treatment. This would ultimately shift treatment to a child-centred approach, and aligns with Carnevale's (2012) call to "listen authentically to children where the clinician seeks a profoundly empathic attunement to the experiential perspective of the patient" (p. 325). Carnevale argues that for this to come to fruition in practice, "current standards of child *assent* be interpreted more broadly, rather that the typical approach where practitioners seek the child's willingness to accept the proposed care" (p. 325).

Third, we argue that the UNCRC must be: (1) built into all university training programs within the health professions that work directly with children; and (2) embedded into the standards of practice for all pediatric practitioners. This goes beyond the formulating of policies and codes of ethics to being fully incorporated into job descriptions, on the job training initiatives, job performance appraisals, and the daily culture of treatment and care within health care settings.

Fourth, we urge that all hospital ombudspersons and ethicists, regardless of whether it is in a pediatric tertiary care centre or a local village hospital, be trained in the UNCRC.

Fifth, a national policy mandating meaningful involvement of young people in health care settings, led by the Canadian Association of Pediatric Health Centres and ratified by every pediatric tertiary centre in Canada, is the *only* way to address the widespread inconsistency, confusion, and ambiguity. This policy would explicitly affirm young people's right to be involved in health care decision making, and would be based upon: (1) the premise of presumed competence; and (2) upon Kenny, Downie, and Harrison's

Table 4.2	OCFSA Principles to Guide Health Care Consent with Young Persons (2005)
1.	Presume that children are capable of consenting (unless there are reasonable grounds to believe otherwise), regardless of age, disability, or the administration of psychotropic drugs, although such factors may be relevant in the assessment of capacity.
2.	Ensure that children's rights to make their own health decisions are respected and that children are advised of their right to have findings of incapacity reviewed by the Consent and Capacity Board.
3.	Ensure that determinations of capacity are based on the ability of the person to understand the information that is relevant to the treatment decision and appreciate the reasonable foreseeable consequences of the decision or lack thereof.
4.	Ensure that children are given the opportunities and assistance they need to develop their competence to make health decisions.
5.	Ensure that the consent process involves an ongoing and active dialogue between the child, medical practitioner, and, in some cases, the guardian or another adult.
6.	Ensure that consent is informed, related to the treatment, voluntary, and free from misrepresentation or fraud.
7.	Ensure that children's service agencies and providers develop uniform privacy and access to information policies based upon the 10 principles of the Canadian Standards Association's Model Code for the Protection of Personal Information.

(2008) framework for "the respectful involvement of children in medical decision-making" (p. 122). They argue for the "participative assessment of

1. what the child wants to know;
2. what the child can understand;
3. the extent of the child's decision-making capacity, and
4. what the child needs to know to participate fully." (p. 124)

Such a Canada-wide explicit policy that behooves all practitioners in Canada's pediatric health centres to involve young people in health care decisions would then be widely disseminated and published on each pediatric centre's website, with signage populating the institutions' structures to enable broad and explicit awareness.

Sixth, child-centredness must be *untethered* from family-centredness, and child-centredness as its own citizenship-affirming and rights-based approach needs to be explicitly promoted widely across the Canadian Association of Pediatric Health Centres, and include a commitment to involve children and youth in decision making.

And lastly, seventh, we join the many voices across our nation calling for the establishment of a federal children's commissioner (Bendo & Mitchell, 2017; Bendo, 2017). According to the Honorable Landon Pearson, the senator responsible for Canada's ratification of the UNCRC, the establishment of an Office of the Federal Commissioner for Canada's Children and Youth would enable independent assessment, monitoring, and reporting on the services provided to children in Canada. Its initiation would enable a way to work with provincial and territorial advocates in order to address regional inconsistencies and inequities, and advocate for the rights of children and young people throughout Canada while also raising awareness of the UNCRC (Bendo, 2017).

LISTENING TO HEAR

From pediatric ethicists to provincial/territorial child advocates and to young people themselves, the experience of listening to so many wise Canadians for the purposes of this chapter was truly a privilege. Irwin Elman, Ontario's child advocate, completed a similar journey where he embarked on what he called a "listening tour" during which he met with over 400 young people in eight cities with the goal of listening to hear (#listeningtour2017) (Elman, 2017). Elman identified a long-standing gap between the "nice words" and well-meaning policies of institutions and how things actually are for young persons. Rather than being interested in discussions about policy, the young people told him that nobody asked them about anything: not about big issues and not about their own lives. His tour ended on November 20, 2017—Canada's National Child Day—a day to celebrate Canada's ratification of the UNCRC. While Elman's tour culminated in the report entitled *Reality Check* (2018), which outlines numerous and sustained breaches of children's rights to provision, participation, and protection, he ended his tour feeling optimistic and with one simple seven-word message: *Adults have to spend more time listening.*

QUESTIONS FOR DISCUSSION

1. In your future role as a child-serving professional, how can you contribute to children's participatory status in health care settings?
2. Who should be responsible for ensuring that a child knows he or she has the right to refuse treatment? What needs to change in order to better prepare these people for this role?
3. Advocates stated in the research for this chapter that health care providers require more education regarding child-centric health care practices. How could this be brought about?

NOTE

1 Shortly before this book was published, the Ontario government opted to remove the Child Advocate's Office, thus demonstrating the precarity of state support for children's rights and, in this case, further contributing to ambiguous consent practices for children engaged with health care providers.

REFERENCES

Bendo, D. (2017). An interview with Landon Pearson: On the role of a commissioner for Canada's children. *Canadian Journal of Children's Rights, 4*(1), 92–104.

Bendo, D., & Mitchell, R. C. (2017). The role of Canada's child and youth advocates: A social constructionist approach. *International Journal of Children's Rights, 25*(2), 335–358.

Breggin, P., & Mills, C. (2014). The rights of children and parents in regard to children receiving psychiatric diagnoses and drugs. *Children & Society, 28*(3), 231–241.

Canadian Association of Occupational Therapists. (2008). *Code of ethics.* Retrieved from https://www.caot.ca/document/4604/codeofethics.pdf

Canadian Association of Pediatric Health Centres. (2017). *CAPHC annual conference—engaging children, youth and families: Are you ready to move past good intentions.* Retrieved from https://caphcevents.org/conf2017/about/&lang=en

Canadian Association of Paediatric Nurses. (2017). *Canadian paediatric nursing standards: Standardizing high quality nursing care for Canada's children.* Retrieved from https://ken.caphc.org/xwiki/bin/download/Other+Resources/Canadian+Paediatric+Nursing+Standards/FINAL-Paediatric%20Nursing%20Standards.pdf

Canadian Association of Social Workers. (2005). *Code of ethics.* Retrieved from https://casw-acts.ca/en/what-social-work/casw-code-ethics/code-ethics

Canadian Coalition for the Rights of Children. (2011). *Right in principle, right in practice: Implementation of the Convention on the Rights of the Child in Canada.* Retrieved from http://rightsofchildren.ca/wp-content/uploads/2016/01/CCRC-report-on-rights-of-children-in-Canada.pdf

Canadian Human Rights Tribunal. (2016). *Decision of hearing between: First Nations Child and Family Caring Society of Canada and Assembly of First Nations (complainants) and Canadian Human Rights Commission and Attorney General of Canada (representing the Minister of Indian Affairs and Northern Development Canada) (respondents).* Retrieved from https://assets.documentcloud.org/documents/2698184/Judgement.pdf

Canadian Institute of Child Health. (2002) *The rights of the child in the health care system.* Poster and Pamphlet Campaign.

Canadian Medical Protective Association (CMPA). (2016). *Can a child provide consent? Duties and responsibilities: Expectations of physicians in practice.* Retrieved from https://www.cmpa-acpm.ca/en/advice-publications/browse-articles/2014/can-a-child-provide-consent

Canadian Medical Protective Association. (2018). *2015–2019 Strategic plan.* Retrieved from http://www.cmpa-acpm.ca/en/about/what-we-do/strategicplan

Canadian Nurses Association. (2017). *Code of ethics for registered nurses.* Retrieved from https://www.cna-aiic.ca/~/media/cna/page-content/pdf-en/code-of-ethics-2017-edition-secure-interactive.pdf?la=en

Canadian Paediatric Society. (2007). *Are we doing enough?* Retrieved from http://www.cps.ca/uploads/advocacy/StatusReport2007.pdf

Canadian Paediatric Society. (2016). *Treatment decisions regarding infants, children and adolescents.* Retrieved from https://www.cps.ca/en/documents/position/treatment-decisions

Canadian Paediatric Society. (2018). *About the Canadian Paediatric Society.* Retrieved from www.ipac2016.com/aboutcpa

Canadian Physiotherapy Association. (n.d). *Code of ethics.* Retrieved from https://physiotherapy.ca/cpa-code-ethics

Canadian Psychological Association. (2017). *Canadian code of ethics for psychologists.* Retrieved from http://www.cpa.ca/docs/File/Ethics/CPA_Code_2017_4thEd.pdf

Carlisle, Dr. J. (2013). *Coroner's inquest touching the death of Ashley Smith.* Retrieved from http://www.csc-scc.gc.ca/publications/005007-9009-eng.shtml

Carnevale, F. (2012). Listening authentically to youthful voices: A conception of the moral agency of children. In J. Storch, P. Rodney, & R. Starzomski (Eds.), *Toward a moral horizon: Nursing ethics for leadership and practice* (pp. 315–332). Toronto: Pearson Canada.

College of Nurses of Ontario. (2017). *Practice guideline on consent.* Retrieved from http://www.cno.org/globalassets/docs/policy/41020_consent.pdf

College of Physicians and Surgeons of Alberta. (2015). *Consent for minor patients.* Retrieved from cpsa.ca/wp-content/uploads/2015/08/consent-for-minor-patients.pdf

College of Physicians and Surgeons of Saskatchewan. (2017). *Informed consent and determining capacity to consent.* Retrieved from https://www.cps.sk.ca/iMIS/Documents/Legislation/Policies/POLICY%20-%20Informed%20Consent%20and%20 Determining%20Capacity%20to%20Consent.pdf

Covell, K., & Howe, R. B. (2001). *The challenge of children's rights for Canada.* Waterloo, ON: Wilfrid Laurier University Press.

Elman, I. (2017). Personal communication.

Elman, I. (2018). *Reality check: Findings from the Second Annual Listening Tour of the Ontario Provincial Advocate for Children and Youth.* Retrieved from https://www.provincialadvocate.on.careports/advocacy-reports/english-reports/Listening-Tour-Report.PDF

Findlay, J. (2005). *Snakes and ladders: A dialogue.* Retrieved from http://www.ontla.on.ca/library/repository/mon/20000/279076.pdf

First Nations Caring Society. (n.d.). *Jordan's principle.* Retrieved from https://fncaringsociety.com/jordans-principle

First Nations Child and Family Caring Society of Canada (n.d.). *Jordan's Principle.* Retrieved from https://fncaringsociety.com/jordans-principle_

Gartner, H. (Reporter) & CBC (2010, January 8). Out of control [television series episode]. *The Fifth Estate.* Toronto: CBC.

Government of British Columbia. (1996). *Infant's Act* (c.223). Retrieved from http://www.bclaws.ca/civix/document/id/complete/statreg/96223_01

Government of Canada. (1985). *Criminal code* (R.S.C. C-46). Retrieved from http://laws-lois.justice.gc.ca/eng/acts/C-46/

Government of Canada. (2019). *Jordan's Principle.* Retrieved from https://www.canada.ca/en/indigenous-services-canada/services/jordans-principle.html

Government of Canada & Department of Justice. (2017). *Article 12 of the Convention on the Rights of the Child and children's participatory rights in Canada: Expanding children's participation rights in Canada.* Retrieved from http://www.justice.gc.ca/eng/rp-pr/other-autre/Article12/p4.html

Government of New Brunswick. (1976; 2016). *Medical Consent of Minors Act* (SNB,1976), cM-6.1.

Government of Ontario. (1996). *Health Care Consent Act* (S.O.1996, C.2, Sched. A). Retrieved from http://www.e-laws.gov.on.ca/html/statutes/english/elaws_statutes_96h02_e.htm

Government of Ontario. (2017). *Child, Youth and Family Services Act* (S.O. 2017, C.14, Sched.1). Retrieved from https://www.ontario.ca/laws/statute/17c14

Harrison, C., Canadian Paediatric Society, & Bioethics Committee. (2004; 2016). Treatment decisions regarding infants, children and adolescents. *Paediatric and Child Health, 9*(2), 99–103.

Justice for Children and Youth. (2012). *Guide to health care rights for children and youth.* Retrieved from http://jfcy.org/wp-content/uploads/2013/10/Health-Care-October-2012.pdf

Kenny, K., Downie, J., & Harrison, C. (2008). Respectful involvement of children in medical decision-making. In P. Singer (Ed.), *The Cambridge textbook of bioethics* (pp. 121–126). Cambridge: Cambridge University Press.

LeFrançois, B. A. (2008). "It's like mental torture": Participation and mental health services. *International Journal of Children's Rights, 16,* 211–227.

LeFrançois, B. A. (2013a). Adultism. In T. Teo (Ed.), *Encyclopedia of critical psychology.* Berlin: Springer.

LeFrançois, B. A. (2013b). The psychiatrization of our children, or, an autoethnographic narrative of perpetuating First Nations genocide through "benevolent" institutions. *Decolonization: Indigeneity, education and society, 2*(1), 108–123.

LeFrançois, B. A., & Coppock, V. (2014). Psychiatrised children and their rights: Starting the conversation. *Children & Society, 28*(3), 165–171.

Legis Quebec. (1991). *Civil Code of Quebec.* Retrieved from http://legisquebec.gouv.qc.ca/en/showdoc/cs/CCQ-1991

Manitoba Law Reform Commission. (2004). *Substitute consent to health care* (no. 110). Retrieved from http://www.manitobalawreform.ca/pubs/pdf/archives/110-full_report.pdf

Mills, C. (2014). Psychotropic childhoods: Global mental health and pharmaceutical children. *Children & Society, 28*(3), 194–204.

Office of Child and Family Service Advocacy. (2005). *Consent and confidentiality in health services: Respecting the child's right to be heard*. Retrieved from https://www.provincial advocate.on.ca/documents/en/Consent-Confidentiality.pdf

Ontario Association of Children's Aid Societies. (2016). *Looking after children in Ontario*. Retrieved from http://www.oacas.org/wp-content/uploads/2015/03/OnLACOntario-Year-13Provincial.pdf

Ontario Office of the Provincial Advocate for Children and Youth. (2013). *I do care project*. Retrieved from https://idocareproject.files.wordpress.com/2013/02/i-do-care-booklet-english-final-for-print.pdf

Oxford Dictionaries. (2017). *Child-centred*. Retrieved from https://en.oxford dictionaries.com/definition/child-centred

Sheahan, L., Da Silva, M., Czoli, C., & Zlotnik Shaul, R. (2012). A Canadian perspective on a child's consent to research within a context of family-centered care: From incompatibility to synergy. *Journal of Clinical Research and Bioethics, 3*, 132. Retrieved from https://www.longdom.org/open-access/a-canadian-perspective-on-a-childs-consent-to-research-within-a-context-of-family-centered-care-from-incompatibility-to-synergy-2155-9627.1000132.pdf

Smith, S. (2016, October 31). Jehovah's Witnesses incapable of free, informed refusal of blood, former adherent says. *CBC*. Retrieved from http://www.cbc.ca/news/ehova/montreal/ ehovah-s-witnesses-incapable-of-free-informed-refusal-of-blood-former-adherent-says-1.3829778

Southall, D. P., Burr, S., Smith, R. D., Bull, D. N., Radford, A., Williams, A., & Nicholson, S. (2000). The child-friendly healthcare initiative (CFHI): Healthcare provision in accordance with the UN Convention on the Rights of the Child. Child Advocacy International. Department of Child and Adolescent Health and Development of the World Health Organization (WHO). Royal College of Nursing (UK). Royal College of Paediatrics and Child Health (UK). United Nations Children's Fund (UNICEF). *Pediatrics, 106*(5), 1054–1064.

UN Committee on the Rights of the Child. (2012a). *Committee on the Rights of the Child: Sixty-first section*. Retrieved from http://www2.ohchr.org/english/bodies/crc/docs/co/CRC-C-CAN-CO-3-4_en.pdf

UN Committee on the Rights of the Child. (2012b). *Concluding observations on Canada*. Retrieved from http://www2.ohchr.org/english/bodies/crc/docs/co/CRC-C-CAN-CO-34_en.pdf

UN Committee on the Rights of the Child. (2013). General comment no. 15 on the right of the child to the enjoyment of the highest attainable standard of health (Art. 24), April 17, 2013, CRC/C/GC/15. Retrieved from http://www.refworld.org/docid/51ef9e134.html

United Nations. (1989). *Convention on the Rights of the Child*. Retrieved from http://www.refworld.org/docid/3ae6b38f0.html

Van Daalen-Smith, C., Adam, S., Beggin, P., & LeFrançois, B. (2014). The utmost discretion: How presumed prudence leaves children susceptible to electroshock. *Children & Society, 28*(3), 205–217.

Chapter 5
Young People, Justice, and Children's Rights in Canada
Critical Reflections at the Edge of Abeyant Action
Shannon A. Moore

INTRODUCTION

The integration of the United Nations Convention on the Rights of the Child (UNCRC) (United Nations, 1989) into systems of youth justice holds great potential to transform how we intervene in the lives of young people living on the edge of risk and potential, perhaps most particularly young people who have engaged in behaviours in conflict with the law, both in Canada and around the globe (Moore & Mitchell, 2009, 2012). The UNCRC, serving as an umbrella treaty, has influenced the development of a majority of international juvenile justice standards, and offers basic guidance to a more coordinated implementation on the level of practice in youth justice (Denov, 2007; Moore & Mitchell, 2012). Although the UNCRC is often described as the most universally ratified human rights instrument, it is arguably the most violated (Moore & Mitchell, 2009; Muncie, 2008). Analysis of Canadian juvenile justice, similar to its American and European counterparts, shows evidence that integrating the UNCRC into juvenile justice contexts is "beset by issues of contradiction and compromise" (Muncie, 2008, p. 107), stalling meaningful translation into direct practice with young people. Even with the most noble of intentions, this abeyant action remains an artifact of juvenile justice's status as the unwanted child of the child rights movement (Abramson, 2006).

Canada may be credited with integrating principles of the UNCRC within the *Youth Criminal Justice Act* (YCJA) of 2003 (Denov, 2007; Moore, 2007). The *Youth Criminal Justice Act* was a replacement for the *Young Offenders Act*, which was criticized for its overly punitive approach to young offenders.

The YCJA was targeted to provide a "legislative framework for a fairer and more effective youth justice system" (Department of Justice Canada, 2013, p. 1). In theory, this was the intent, yet in practice a fairer rights-based approach has not been meaningfully realized. Denov (2007) reinforces this point from a Canadian perspective as she argues, "guaranteeing the rights of young offenders enables young people to exercise choices, ask questions, challenge procedures, and have the opportunity to be heard in proceedings: all this may defy assumptions about young people and the criminal justice process" (pp. 53–54). If Canada as a nation recognized that all young people have an equal birthright to experience their human rights as articulated under the UNCRC, then young offenders' views would be heard through meaningful participation in justice proceedings that impact them, and robust supports that recognize their increased vulnerability to risk due to age and context would be in place during all stages of contact with the juvenile justice system. This chapter offers an overview of the status of the UNCRC in the context of youth justice in Canada through a critical analysis of the unease in realizing a rights-based approach to youth justice; in the same instance, the chapter uncovers the potentiality of positioning Canadian youth justice toward a rights-based approach through an emphasis on rights-based restorative justice (Moore, 2007; Moore & Mitchell, 2007, 2009, 2012).

UNCRC AND YOUTH JUSTICE

Globally, the UNCRC (United Nations, 1989) could be the industry standard within youth justice programming, and is an essential instrument in any juvenile context precisely because it is legally binding at the international level and regularly evaluated by the United Nations. Further, a human rights–based approach to engaging with youthful offenders supports democratic practices that are in compliance with international law (Moore & Mitchell, 2009, 2012). Unfortunately, it remains a challenge to move principles of child rights into practice in adultist systems (Scraton, 2004), which so often abandon an appreciation of the citizenship, the innate dignity, and the increased vulnerability to risk of young offenders in favour of legitimizing power relations in paternalistic, hierarchical systems (Abramson, 2006; Clarysse & Moore, 2017; Moore & Mitchell, 2012).

CANADIAN CONTEXT OF YOUTH JUSTICE AND THE UNCRC

From 1979 to 1989, a United Nations committee composed of representatives of 42 nations drafted the Convention on the Rights of the Child (Mitchell, 2003). Canada was an early promoter of children's rights, and is credited with co-hosting the 1990 United Nations World Summit for Children in New York, which marked the inception of the UNCRC ratification process and international recognition. Canada's ratification of the UNCRC (making the Convention legally binding in Canada), was finalized in 1991 (Mitchell, 2003; Moore, 2007). In contrast to this early activity, the UNCRC has yet to be integrated into federal legislation except for the presence of UNCRC principles in the preamble of Canada's *Youth Criminal Justice Act* of 2003 (Moore, 2007; Moore & Mitchell, 2012).

The four core principles of the UNCRC are interconnected and interdependent and might be more effectively translated from legislation to policy and practice if considered holistically. Such an approach would necessarily thread the principles and provisions of the UNCRC throughout legislation rather than isolating and atomizing them into a single introductory segment, as in the case of Canada's YCJA. The four core principles of the UNCRC include the following: Article 2 "without discrimination"; Article 3 "the best interests"; Article 6 "maximum survival and development"; and Article 12 "participation." Mitchell (2003) argues for a conscientious consideration of the relationship of these articles: "When applying Article 3's 'best interests' principle with Article 12 which refers to the right of children and young people to 'express views freely in all matters ... the views being given due weight in accordance with the age and maturity of the child.' Clearly, children and youth must themselves be primary sources for information regarding adult interpretations of their 'best interests'" (p. 295).

When these the four principles of the UNCRC are translated into practice, a minimal standard for a rights-based approach is established. These four principles also provide a framework for all domestic reports to the UN Committee on the Rights of the Child (Article 42), making the principles vital to the understanding of all other provisions in the UNCRC (Mitchell, 2003), including the justice provisions contained in Articles 37 and 40. Canada's federalist governance structure further complicates translation of the UNCRC to the level of provincial and territorial governments, as within these sub-national boundaries independent decisions are made as to whether the UNCRC enters this level of regional governmental policy. One outcome of these political realities is a lack of awareness of the UNCRC among organizations and individual citizens despite national campaigns and federal endorsement (Moore & Mitchell, 2012).

As mentioned, UNCRC Articles 37 and 40 are the specific provisions for justice and these articles may be used to guide rights-based practices for juvenile justice policy-makers and practitioners. Article 37 highlights that young people, when deprived of liberty, should be treated in a manner acknowledging age-related needs for contact with family and friends, the right to play and to engage in leisure and cultural activities (see also UNCRC Articles 14, 30, 31), and the right to continue education (Articles 28 and 29). Canada has received targeted criticism from the Committee on the Rights of the Child for the government's partial acceptance of UNCRC Article 37—while accepting this article in principle, it has also reserved the right *not* to detain children separately from adults (Moore & Mitchell, 2012).

Likewise, UNCRC Article 40(1) discourages retributive responses by focusing on the need to avoid deprivation of liberty and emphasizes that young people are to be "treated in a manner consistent with the promotion of the child's dignity and worth, which reinforces the child's respect for human rights and freedoms of others and which takes into account the child's age and the desirability of promoting the child's reintegration and the child's assuming a constructive role in society" (United Nations, 1989).

Canada has egregiously failed both justice provisions expressed in Articles 37 and 40, as confirmed with the conclusion of an inquest on December 9, 2013, conducted by the chief coroner of Ontario, Canada, into the death of 19-year-old Ashley Smith (Correctional Services Canada, 2013). By way of explanation, what follows is a closer look at the life and death of Ashley Smith.

At the age of 13, Ashley Smith entered Canada's youth criminal justice system, found guilty of throwing crabapples at a postal worker, which was a breach of an earlier probation order (Richard, 2008). Ashley Smith remained in secure custody, moving from institution to institution, province to province, spending up to two-thirds of her time in solitary confinement at each institution until her death at the age of 19 (Richard, 2008). Typically, solitary confinement restricts inmates to a cell measuring nine by nine feet, allowing for just one hour outside the cell for showers and exercise. While in custody, Ashley Smith had minimal contact with others, either inside the various institutions or with the community outside secure custody, unless she was being physically restrained by guards (Richard, 2008, p. 41). At the age of 19, while in solitary confinement in Kitchener, Ontario, Canada, at Grand Valley Institution for Women, Ashley Smith tied a ligature around her neck (Ring, 2014, p. 34). Although seven guards watched as Ashley turned purple and her breathing became shallow, no one intervened and the 19-year-old died of self-asphyxiation on October 19, 2007 (Campbell, 2012, pp. 5–6). Following a 15-month trial, the chief coroner of Ontario concluded that her death was the result of homicide (Correctional Services Canada, 2013). The inquest highlighted that Correctional Services Canada demonstrated a "lack of communication, cohesiveness, and accountability" and also emphasized that "in accordance with the recommendations of the United Nations Special

Rapporteur's 2011 Interim Report on solitary confinement, indefinite Solitary Confinement should be abolished" (Correctional Services Canada, 2013, p. 1; see also Alderton, 2017).

In the context of secure custody, the freedom and liberty of young people will be restricted to some degree, yet their human rights are a birthright, something that is neither earned nor forfeited. It is clear from the findings of the coroner's inquest into the death of Ashley Smith that her inherent dignity and humanity were erased during decision-making processes while she was in secure custody. Moreover, single behaviours, devoid of context and the unique complexity of her circumstance, seemed to be the focus of the decision makers' actions.

Both UNCRC Articles 37 and 40 support the contextual analysis of youthful offences within a broader, systemic appreciation of the rights and needs of young people. To implement these principles, the Canadian government would benefit from the realization that a rights-based approach to juvenile justice creates options for intervention with young people in conflict with the law that emphasize dignity and equity. Although the *Youth Criminal Justice Act* of 2003 has principles of the UNCRC embedded in the preamble of this federal legislation, Canada's political system frequently obscures clear understanding of compliance issues related to international legal standards because these standards are differently interpreted and implemented throughout the provinces and territories. Canada's federal system holds the federal government responsible for the articulation of youth justice legislation, but each province and territory administers the federal law's most recent iteration in this area, namely the YCJA of 2003 (Moore, 2007). This process of dissemination presents challenges that are compounded by Canada's colonial history and embedded systemic discrimination within justice and social services policies and practices in every region.

Historically, Canada's retributive justice system was inherited from Europeans during colonization in the 17th and 18th centuries. The Indigenous justice systems that existed prior to colonization continued to prevail informally within First Nations communities while Canada's official system of justice began to increasingly reflect European legal and political customs. Canada's criminal law and criminal justice policy, with its central focus on retribution and punishment, was invented by Western culture within the process of colonization and the formation of Eurocentrism (Moore, 2007) and essentially denies a millennia of Indigenous peoples' history (Moore, 2007).

As this chapter is being crafted, Canada is bringing its sesquicentennial birthday to a close, an anniversary indelibly bound to the systematic cultural genocide of Indigenous populations and European colonization that have, in turn, woven the fabric of services (social, justice, health, education), the constructions of childhood, and the interpretation of human rights in this country (Moore, 2017). Cultural genocide and the manifest devastation of First Nations, Inuit, and Métis populations throughout Indigenous communities in Canada are documented clearly by the final report of the Truth and Reconciliation Commission of Canada (2015):

> For over a century, the central goals of Canada's Aboriginal policy were to eliminate Aboriginal governments; ignore Aboriginal rights; terminate the Treaties; and, through a process of assimilation, cause Aboriginal peoples to cease to exist as distinct legal, social, cultural, religious, and racial entities in Canada. The establishment and operation of residential schools were a central element of this policy, which can best be described as "cultural genocide" ... cultural genocide is the destruction of those structures and practices that allow the group to continue as a group. States that engage in cultural genocide set out to destroy the political and social institutions of the targeted group. Land is seized, and populations are forcibly transferred and their movement is restricted. Languages are banned. Spiritual leaders are persecuted, spiritual practices are forbidden, and objects of spiritual value are confiscated and destroyed. And, most significantly to the issue at hand, families are disrupted to prevent the transmission of cultural values and identity from one generation to the next. In its dealing with Aboriginal people, Canada did all these things. (p. 1)

Prior to colonization, Indigenous communities in Canada were instilled with vibrancy, spirituality, and social order (Moore, Tulk, & Mitchell, 2005) and date back at least 30 millennia (Bourgeon, Burke, & Higham, 2017) before Europeans first arrived on the shores of what is now called Canada. This truth-telling of Canada's 150-year history as a colonial nation is also a clarion call to policy-makers and practitioners to make a crucial shift toward appreciating the institutionalization of inequity that has perpetuated the silencing of minority voices, including Indigenous and black young people in Canada, who are disproportionally represented in our justice and out-of-home care systems (De Finney, Dean, Loiselle, & Saraceno, 2011; Pon, Gosine, & Phillips, 2011). Recent figures from Canada's federal Department of Justice confirm the state of structural injustice as revealed through Indigenous incarceration rates: "In 2014/2015, Indigenous youth (aged 12–17) accounted for 37% of provincial/territorial custody admissions. The proportion of Indigenous youth in provincial/territorial custody was about 5 times higher than their representation in the youth population (7%). Indigenous youth were overrepresented in provincial/territorial custody in most jurisdictions, especially British Columbia, Manitoba, and Ontario" (Department of Justice Canada, 2017, para 2). Clearly, childhood discourses that emerge in so-called post-colonial nations that deny the greatest causes of suffering also perpetuate elevated rates of expulsion from school and the overrepresentation of non-white young people in contact with mental health services, social services, and juvenile justice systems.

REALIZING RIGHTS-BASED YOUTH JUSTICE: BARRIERS AND OPPORTUNITIES

The Convention on the Rights of the Child provides an organizing framework and embedded process to assess compliance with its principles through reporting processes for countries that have ratified this convention (Mitchell, 2003; Moore & Mitchell, 2012). As the 30th anniversary of the inception of the UNCRC approaches, barriers to implementation within juvenile justice are evident throughout the international community. While the Convention on the Rights of the Child is proving to be a highly successful human rights treaty, the potential of the UNCRC is not being realized with respect to young people who are in trouble with the law. Of all the major areas covered by the Convention, juvenile justice is the most neglected (Moore & Mitchell, 2009).

Abramson's (2006) arguments regarding the unwantedness of young offenders within child rights discourses have been further developed by Moore and Mitchell (2009) and have multiple dimensions. To begin, juvenile justice is about crime, and young people in trouble with the law do not garner the same sympathy as other vulnerable young people in need of protection. Moore (2007) contends that when the social fabric of a community is torn by crime, whole communities are impacted, and this erosion of trust often produces fear. Typically, the public of any community has a huge emotional attachment to its children (White, 2003). At the same time, when youth crime reaches media headlines, politicians perpetually call for so-called get-tough measures, not penal reform or diversion programs. Juvenile justice is also multi-systemic and, in competition for resources with many child-focused services, prioritizes young people conceptualized as innocent. Further, theories of childhood that stakeholders hold to be true shape both the questions and answers formed by interventionists (Moss & Petrie, 2002), and while a dominant "ideology of childhood" expressed through the UNCRC is one of "innocence, vulnerability, helplessness, and victimization of the child ... juvenile offenders are not innocent!" (Abramson, 2006, p. 24). Abramson (2006) adds that while the UNCRC advocates for all those under 18 years of age, discussions often focus on younger children while teenagers in contact with justice officials are overlooked. Traditional approaches to justice are negative processes with a goal to punish through naming, shaming, and blaming. Although this strategy often facilitates social justice, pro-social approaches are equally required that could have much in common with a rights-based restorative justice (Moore & Mitchell, 2009, 2012) programming since their common features involve respect, dignity, and the promotion of healthy development (Mitchell & Moore, 2016). This implies an inversely reinforcing process for which an emphasis on human rights and equity for all will no doubt reduce rates of youthful offending.

Barriers to realizing rights-based youth justice are further emphasized when the UNCRC is not understood as a holistic overarching treaty. The UNCRC principles are interdependent and hold civil, political, economic, and social rights in a gestalt for which the whole is greater than the sum of the articles. By contrast, within juvenile justice contexts, young people are isolated from community and context as they are taken into custody, an act that places in jeopardy the full range of needs and rights of young people at the very moment they are the most vulnerable (Abramson, 2006; Moore & Mitchell, 2009) with respect to power relations within adultist institutions (Scraton, 2004). In response, Abramson (2006) highlights the need to address the dimension of gender given the disproportionate number of boys in contact with juvenile justice, and yet gender manifests within a complex intersection between identity, history, and power that shapes accepted forms of masculine expression within specific social worlds (Moore, 2017). This cultural artifact of gender expression impacts how verbal, physical, and relational violence manifest in society, for instance. These factors are relatively neglected in juvenile justice discourse and point to the marginalization of specific populations.

To move beyond these barriers toward realization of rights-based youth justice in Canada, it is imperative that the disproportionate rates of Indigenous and black young people in contact with justice systems are contextualized and taken into account as rights-based approaches are developed going forward. Consider the following Canadian context detailed by Goraya (2015):

> While crime rates in Canada have been declining since the early 1990s, the rate of incarceration among Aboriginal and black youth has remained largely unchanged. Put simply, minority youth have not experienced the same decline in incarceration rates as their Caucasian counterparts. The recent decline in overall youth incarceration rates in Canada has been credited to the implementation of the Youth Criminal Justice Act (YCJA) in 2003, which shifted the youth criminal justice system's formerly punitive approach to one that emphasizes community programs and rehabilitation. The success of the YCJA is largely attributed to its introduction of extra-judicial measures designed to keep youth out of the prison system. However, despite its effectiveness

in reducing overall youth crime, minority youth continue to be grossly overrepresented within the criminal justice system. (p. 1)

These arguments highlighting the Canadian context of overrepresentation of non-white young people in contact with youth justice are further buttressed with basic descriptive statistics: "While youth 12 to 17 years old who self-identified as Aboriginal represent 6 per cent of the Canadian population, in 2008/2009 they made up 24 percent of youth admitted to remand, 36 percent of youth admitted to custody, and 24% of youth that received probation.... Aboriginal youth are more likely to receive sentences that are restrictive and ... are overrepresented in custody dispositions" (Greenberg, Grekul, & Nelson, 2012, p. 234).

For Indigenous youth in Canada, and around the globe, white supremacist ideologies have contributed to post-colonial trauma. The intergenerational fallout of this is manifest in stress expressed through "addiction, depression, health problems, suicide and violence" (Greenberg, Grekul, & Nelson, 2012, p. 234). Contextualizing justice in a manner that accounts for systemic racism challenges benign and benevolent projections of Canada's social fabric as a multicultural mosaic (Reasons et al., 2016). "Race plays a role in the criminal justice system" and points to the need to emphasize "structural sources of differential treatment in the Canadian justice system" (Reasons et al., 2016, p. 75). Canada's colonial history and structural racism must be taken into account for rights-based youth justice to meaningfully manifest in Canada going forward.

Arguably, one of the central barriers to realizing rights-based youth justice in Canada may be addressed with commitment and openness to change. What is necessary is a process of truth-telling regarding our colonial national history and the role of racism in structural injustices and endemic violence impacting justice, social, and health systems. This calls for an attitude of humility on the part of adults as they hold the power of presumed expertise to shape theory, policy, and practices that impact the lives of children, young people, and families (Moore, 2007, 2017; White, 2003).

CANADA'S FUTURE POTENTIAL: RIGHTS-BASED RESTORATIVE JUSTICE

Conceptualizations of young people continue to evolve and shape how we respond within policy and practice arenas. Accordingly, the meaning attributed to behaviours perpetrated by young people in conflict with the law are socially constructed and will continue to modify as Canadians begin to more fully understand and respect young people from the perspective of human rights. Indeed, the social construction of youthful offending is frequently described as deviance, and researchers within Canada and beyond this nation's borders have begun to explore the links between this theoretical stance and retributive responses that focus on social control in the justice system. Arguably, given a move away from a focus on isolated behaviours, deviance, and a move toward understanding risk as the critical edge of potential (Moore, 2017), we may then more effectively create safety nets to support young people in conflict with the law to stay accountable and engaged in community. Such a construction of youthful offending behaviours would reflect an understanding of young people as rights bearers and full citizens responding to their unique social worlds, which may include experiences of structural and social injustice manifest in multiple nodes of inequities and violence. In this context, a rights-based approach to youth justice may aim to teach community (hooks, 2003), creating the opportunity for young people to have their dignity respected and, in turn, young people may gain tools to be increasingly accountable for the human rights of others (Moore & Mitchell, 2009, 2011, 2012; Moore, 2017). The question remains: How do we move from where we are toward a growing rights-based approach to youth justice?

In Canada, we may begin as a country to return to teachings established from a basis of Indigenous ways of knowing, which have millennia of history in this country and are demonstrated through restorative justice. In contrast to Canada's retributive system of justice, restorative justice is an approach associated with ancient Indigenous pre-colonial teachings. Restorative practice reflects the values of Indigenous or Aboriginal systems of justice in Canada (and elsewhere) and implies both a certain process and outcome. The motive behind restorative justice is practical: it aims at restoring balance back to the lives of victims of wrongdoing as well as peace within the community, while allowing offenders the chance to be accountable for their actions and develop a sense of responsibility for being the perpetrators of harm (Moore, 2007). Restorative practice focuses on disharmonies in relationships, accountability, respect, and capacity building while processes aim to decrease antagonism.

The use of the term "restorative justice" in the contemporary sense was first coined more than three decades ago in Kitchener-Waterloo, by Mark Yantzi and Dave Worth. These two Canadians advocated for community-based and social responses to violations of the law. This, in turn, sparked the establishment of Community Justice Initiatives (Waterloo region of Ontario) and formed a catalyst for the international movement found in over 100 countries around the globe today (Nyp, 2004; see also Moore, 2007). Community Justice Initiatives' roots in the Waterloo region of Ontario are linked to the Mennonite Central Committee, which also has established ties within the region. Indeed, the spiritual roots of restorative justice are evident in a broad range of faith communities, including Buddhism, Celtic, Chinese culture, Christianity, Hinduism, Islam, Judaism, and Sikhism (Hadley, 2001; Moore, 2008). In addition, the growth in the use of restorative justice over the past three decades has been supported by prison abolition movements, transformation justice initiatives, and alternative dispute resolution movements (Moore, 2004).

Restorative justice is defined by principles that focus on healthy human relationships and on healing the effects of wrongdoing through the promotion of dialogue among individuals within communities. In this way, restorative justice is context-bound and co-constructed within the social worlds of those impacted by crime, harm, and conflict (Moore, Tulk, & Mitchell, 2005; Moore, 2007). The principles of restorative justice may be summarized through five dimensions. First, the perpetration of crime and the infliction of harm are fundamentally the violation of a human being or human relationships as they rupture the well-being of individuals, communities, and societies. Second, the goals of restorative processes involve the repairing of harm done and restoring relationships between individuals and community with an aim of facilitating movement of all participants toward greater equilibrium. Third, all restorative processes must be voluntary and respect the rights of individuals to free choice. This is achieved through sensitive consideration of power relationships, and social and structural inequities within society. Fourth, victims of crime must always be of central concern and given free choice to participate in the process. Fifth, perpetrators of wrongdoing are given the opportunity to accept responsibility for the harm they have caused and a choice to participate in a restorative process. The above five aspects emphasize the importance of human interpersonal and social relationships (Moore, 2004, 2007). Restorative justice is inductive and participatory as it is shaped by the needs of the communities impacted by harm while also guided by values of empowerment, accountability, honesty, respect, engagement, volunteerism, restoration, inclusiveness, collaboration, and problem solving (Clarysse & Moore, 2017; Moore, 2007).

In contrast, retributive justice focuses on a single criminal act, is adversarial and punitive, and can increase the isolation and alienation of an offender in relation to his or her community (Moore & Mitchell, 2009, 2012). A restorative process is any process in which the victim and the offender and, where appropriate, any other individuals or community members affected by a crime participate together actively in the resolution of matters arising from the crime, generally with the help of a facilitator. In this way "crime" is also understood as a violation of human relationships or, from a rights-based perspective, crime may be similarly understood as a violation of human rights, not solely a violation of any particular legal system (Moore & Mitchell, 2009).

Notwithstanding epistemological and ontological antecedents found within Indigenous cultures over millennia (Moore, 2007), it is also true that restorative justice is still an emergent field within contemporary juvenile justice settings (Moore & Mitchell, 2009, 2012). Only in the last three decades of the 20th century was the term applied to alternative approaches within either adult or juvenile justice systems. Currently, restorative justice processes are being integrated into mainstream, correctional, and grassroots programs throughout rural and urban Canada. In fact, restorative approaches have been used in a broad range of communities through informal justice processes for over 30 years. The roots of contemporary restorative practice can be traced back to the work of Mark Yantzi in the Kitchener-Waterloo region of Ontario and Community Justice Initiatives, an organization that continues to thrive today. Community Justice Initiatives is known worldwide as having started the first restorative justice program in the contemporary sense. Restorative justice informs responses to wrongdoing in every Canadian province and territory through programs based in corrections, communities, and schools (Moore, 2007).

Canadians contributed significantly to the drafting of the UNCRC as well as to the drafting of the UN's basic principles on the use of restorative justice in criminal justice matters (United Nations Economic and Social Council, 2002). It is also a fact that the principles of the UNCRC and the United Nations basic principles of restorative justice are found within Canada's YCJA of 2003. As a result, an expansion of restorative justice community-based programming under the new *Youth Criminal Justice Act* has been evident since 2003 as public and private sector support for programs grew in tandem with educational opportunities that increased awareness (Moore, 2007).

Although on the surface this inclusion of child rights and restorative justice within the YCJA of 2003 is a hopeful movement toward a rights-based youth justice system, the fact that the principles of these two United Nations instruments are found only in the preamble of the YCJA neutralizes further UNCRC implementation in both policy and/or practices across most Canadian regions (Moore & Mitchell, 2011). Although there remains an opportunity to engage a right-based restorative practice given historic and contemporary developments in Canada as a nation-state, Canada in its totality is mired in policy and practices at the edge of abeyant action. Current frameworks have the potential and the legal mandate to support the integration of the UNCRC and the United Nations basic principles of restorative justice into systems impacting young people in Canada and globally, yet this remains largely unrealized. As Muncie (2005) argues, "the concept of globalization has gradually permeated criminology ... and widespread experimentation with restorative justice offers possibilities for rehabilitation ... epitomized by the United Nations Convention on the Rights of the Child" (p. 35). Canada's responsiveness to community-centred processes is at the heart of restorative justice and is a key factor that made Canada a world leader in restorative justice processes more than 30 years ago. Leadership is now needed that fully embraces a rights-based youth justice perspective in legislation, policy, and practice in Canada and rights-based restorative justice is one tool to move this vision forward.

Rights-based restorative justice was developed in response to the need for a framework to link the theoretically, ontologically, and methodologically congruent principles of child rights and restorative justice (Moore, 2007; Moore & Mitchell, 2007, 2009, 2011, 2012). Child rights and restorative justice practices similarly encourage the voices of victims, offenders, and young people to be heard in socially just sorts of ways through non-discriminatory, safe, authentic, and complete participation. The integration of the principles found within these two sets of United Nations instruments is the foundation of rights-based restorative justice, as summarized by Moore (2007) and Moore and Mitchell (2009):

> *Non-discrimination, Equality and Mutuality:* All young people have the same human rights regardless of social-cultural context or whether they are victims or perpetrators of harm; processes address the balance between equality and mutuality among stakeholders.
>
> *Best Interests, Well-being and Restoration:* For all young participants involved there is a concern for their best interests, their well-being and a restoration of equilibrium for all stakeholders. The aim is to heal harm done in the context of human relationships.
>
> *Survival, Development and Safety:* For young participants, there is an appropriate consideration for healthy development, especially in the context of vulnerabilities and power relations typical in circumstances of victimization. Participants must feel a sense of safety.
>
> *Participation, Voice, and Volunteerism:* All stakeholders must have an opportunity to fully participate and experience their views being meaningfully heard. All processes must be voluntarily engaged in by all stakeholders.

From the perspective of the UN Convention on the Rights of the Child, restorative justice and children's rights may be understood as theoretically congruent as they are premised from similar principles. Moreover, through their interconnection in practice, more ethical and democratic responses to young people in conflict with the law may be facilitated. Practices based on restorative justice and children's rights also may be seen to correspond with Canada's domestic and international legal commitments, including those of the UNCRC and the United Nations basic principles of restorative justice (United Nations Economic and Social Council, 2002). Both of these United Nations meta-narratives were adopted by Canada and drafted with significant Canadian input (Moore & Mitchell, 2009). Notwithstanding the potential for the theoretical and the practical application of these interconnected principles, only recently have they been linked in Canadian discourse (Moore, Tulk, & Mitchell, 2005). These principles have yet to become established in integrated practice in partnership with young people in Canada. However, movement toward such a practice and toward a fully fledged system of rights-based restorative justice is both desirable and possible for Canada, and may be informed by a limited number of international developments, as well as a Canadian model for rights-based restorative justice (Moore & Mitchell, 2012).

Rights-based restorative justice (Moore & Mitchell, 2009) as a framework for domestic policy and practice may be understood in the context of recent legislative developments in Canada and a practical focus on fair, proportionate, and democratic interventions with young people in conflict with the law. With Canada's ratification of the UNCRC in 1991, adoption of the United Nations basic principles of restorative justice (United Nations Economic and Social Council, 2002), and with the federal government's enactment of the *Youth Criminal Justice Act* in 2003, Canadian policy is committed to a system of youth justice that integrates the principles of restorative practice and children's human rights (Denov, 2007). The YCJA has emerged as a major legislative development for rights-based initiatives, notwithstanding the substantial obstacles that have to be addressed if restorative practice and children's rights are to be actualized in practice.

Further analyses of relevant UN instruments focused upon juvenile justice reveal complementary thinking to this conceptual underpinning for a rights-based restorative justice paradigm. These include: the Riyadh Guidelines (United Nations, 1990); the Beijing Rules (United Nations, 1985); the Vienna Guidelines (United Nations Economic and Social Council, 1997); and Children's Rights in Juvenile Justice (United Nations Committee on the Rights of the Child, 2007). These international instruments emphasize non-judicial interventions, and community, family, and school-based responses along with prevention strategies. Adapting such approaches could facilitate movement from an overreliance on retributive systems and partisan political responses perennially invoked to solve youth criminal justice issues in the direction of more holistic, even preventive measures.

These seeds of change toward rights-based restorative justice have recently become evident through two high-profile processes within Canada.

The principles and process of restorative justice are the basis of the truth and reconciliation processes, which Canada has recently concluded in response to the cultural genocide experiences of Indigenous peoples in Canada during processes of colonization (Truth and Reconciliation Commission of Canada, 2015) and discussed earlier in this chapter. Restorative justice principles also inform Canada's National Inquiry into Missing and Murdered Indigenous Women and Girls (2017), which is ongoing at the time of writing, and is guided by three goals: finding the truth; honouring the truth; and giving life to the truth as a path to healing (p. 5). This Inquiry states an intention to find the truth by "Gathering many stories from many people. These truths will weave together to show us what violence really looks like for Indigenous women and girls in Canada. The work of the National Inquiry is not to hear one single truth, but many truths. This will help us understand the far-reaching effects of violence, as well as solutions to end it" (p. 5).

These processes of inquiry have aided Canadians in documenting the ongoing, multi-generational effects of colonization and cultural genocide and uncovering the direct links between acts of structural injustice and the disproportionately high representation of Indigenous peoples (First Nations, Métis, and Inuit) within Canada's child welfare and criminal justice systems as both victims and offenders (Senate of Canada Standing Committee on Human Rights, 2007; Moore & Mitchell, 2009).

Indigenous young peoples are described by researchers, policy-makers, and advocates as the "most vulnerable group of children and youth in Canada today, and in the future" (Finlay, Parker-Loewen, & Mirwald, 2005, p. 10). Testifying during the Senate human rights hearings, Finlay et al. (2005) noted that Indigenous peoples in Canada are more "likely to be born into poverty, suffer health problems, be victims of maltreatment, be placed away from their families and communities in provincial and territorial child welfare systems or be incarcerated in youth correctional facilities" (p. 10). The increased risk for Indigenous young peoples to be involved in the justice system is evidenced by incarceration rates eight times higher than for non-Indigenous youth. It is also evident that young people in contact with the welfare system often "cross-over" into justice systems (Finlay, Parker-Loewen, & Mirwald, 2005, p. 10). These authors further argue that increased states of risk faced by Indigenous young peoples are indicative of "an element of racism—if the same circumstances existed for non-aboriginal people I am wondering if we would be as tolerant" (p. 10). A rights-based restorative justice framework has the potential to transcend binary notions of right-doing and wrongdoing, to consider community context and our shared histories, and to account for the underlying drivers of racism, distributive, and structural injustices that are the greatest causes of harm, suffering, and risk for Indigenous young peoples in our society. This process of acknowledging the benefits of a comprehensive approach to restorative justice has recently been evidenced by the Government of British Columbia as they made a commitment to enact a province-wide restorative justice system (Bailey, 2017), which could clear the way for other provinces and territories in Canada to engage in similar legislative action.

In light of Canada's international commitments to the UNCRC (United Nations, 1989) and the United Nations basic principles of restorative justice (United Nations Economic and Social Council, 2002), the lens provided by rights-based restorative justice could provide an effective standard of practice for rights-based youth justice. Certainly, viewing restorative practice in the context of children and young people's rights reveals several links between these constructs. Similar to human rights, restorative justice is not a new concept: both have roots that may be traced through the millennia, notwithstanding their recent appearance in discourses influencing how we relate and create space for children and young people in mainstream society (Moore, Tulk, & Mitchell, 2005). In Canada, this is demonstrated through community-based initiatives, provincial restorative justice programs, and the YCJA that reflects an openness to seriously engage restorative justice processes (Moore, 2007). Similarly, an interest in rights-based policy and practice has slowly evolved across service sectors in Canada over the past decade. Globally, restorative justice principles are evident in Indigenous and ancient cultures the world over, not only in North America but also in ancient Celtic traditions (Moore, 2008) as well as in practices in various regions of Africa and Asia (Moore, 2007). Through recognition of the complexity of justice within the context of our history, politics, and power relations, we will more likely realize a rights-based approach that is responsive to the challenges of equality and structural injustice within systems of youth justice. Further, youth justice stakeholders have a responsibility to ensure ethical practice with everyone, perhaps most especially individuals who have been victimized or are vulnerable, including young people, Indigenous peoples, individuals living with disabilities, and LGBTQ+ community members.

QUESTIONS FOR DISCUSSION

1. Describe why it could be considered important to contextualize rights-based youth justice within Canadian contexts specifically rather than solely focusing on international instruments that shape children's rights and juvenile justice?

2. How might adult attitudes and constructions of youth at risk and young offenders impact development of rights-based approaches within juvenile justice systems?

3. In Canada, what opportunities do we have nationally and sub-nationally that could facilitate positioning this country to be a leader in rights-based youth justice?

REFERENCES

Abramson, B. (2006). Juvenile justice: The "unwanted child"—Why the potential of the Convention on the Rights of the Child is not being realized, and what we can do about it. In E. Jensen & J. Jepsen (Eds.), *Juvenile Law Violators, Human Rights, and the Development of a New Juvenile Justice System* (pp. 15–38). Oxford: Hart.

Alderton, E. L. (2017). *The Death of Ashley Smith in Relation to the United Nations Convention on the Rights of the Child.* (Unpublished bachelor of arts honours thesis). Brock University, St. Catharines, ON.

Bailey, I. (2017, July 30). B.C. NDP government seeks restorative justice system. *The Globe and Mail.* Retrieved from https://www.theglobeandmail.com/news/british-columbia/bc-ndp-seeks-restorative-justice-system-for-some-offences/article35840730/

Bourgeon, L., Burke, A., & Higham, T. (2017). Earliest human presence in North America dated to the last glacial maximum: New radiocarbon dates from Bluefish Caves, Canada. *PLoS ONE, 12*(1), 1–15.

Campbell, A. (2012). *A place apart: The harm of solitary confinement.* (Master's thesis). University of Toronto, Toronto, ON.

Clarysse, L. B., & Moore, S. A. (2017). Restorative justice, peacebuilding practices, and educational praxis: Critical analysis of Canadian and United Kingdom discourses. *Journal of Leadership, Accountability and Ethics, 14*(5).

Correctional Services Canada. (2013). *Coroner's inquest touching the life of Ashley Smith.* Ottawa: Government of Canada. Retrieved from http://www.csc-scc.gc.ca/publications/005007-9009-eng.shtml

De Finney, S., Dean, M., Loiselle, E., & Saraceno, J. (2011). All children are equal, but some are more equal than others: Minoritization, structural inequities, and social justice praxis in residential care. *International Journal of Child, Youth and Family Studies, 2*(3/4), 361–384.

Denov, M. (2007). Youth justice and children's rights. In R. B. Howe & K. Covell (Eds.), *A question of commitment: Children's rights in Canada* (pp. 153–178). Waterloo, ON: Wilfrid Laurier University Press.

Department of Justice Canada. (2013). *The Youth Criminal Justice Act: Summary and background*. Ottawa: Minister of Justice and Attorney General of Canada. Retrieved from http://www.justice.gc.ca/eng/cj-jp/yj-jj/tools-outils/pdf/back-hist.pdf

Department of Justice Canada. (2017, January). Indigenous people overrepresented as homicide victims and accused. In *Research on Justice Issues, Just Facts* (para. 2). Ottawa: Author. Retrieved from http://www.justice.gc.ca/eng/rp-pr/jr/jf-pf/2017/jan02.html

Finlay, J., Parker-Loewen, D., & Mirwald, J. (2005, February). Submission to the Senate Standing Committee on Human Rights, February 21, 2005. Ottawa: Canadian Council of Provincial Child and Youth Advocates.

Goraya, J. (2015, March 9). The overrepresentation of minority youth in Canada's criminal justice system. *The Public Policy and Governance Review*. Toronto: University of Toronto Press. Retrieved from https://ppgreview.ca/2015/03/09/the-overrepresentation-of-minority-youth-in-canadas-criminal-justice-system/

Greenberg, H., Grekul, J., & Nelson, R. (2012). Aboriginal youth crime in Canada. In J. Winterdyk & R. Smandych (Eds.), *Youth at risk and youth justice: A Canadian overview* (pp. 228–252). Don Mills, ON: Oxford University Press.

Hadley, M. (Ed.). (2001). *The spiritual roots of restorative justice*. Albany: State University of New York Press.

hooks, b. (2003). *Teaching community. A pedagogy of hope*. New York: Routledge.

Jensen, E., & Jepsen, J. (Eds.). (2006). *Juvenile law violators, human rights, and the development of new juvenile justice systems* (pp. 15–38). Oxford: Hart.

Mitchell, R. C. (2003). Ideological reflections on the DSM-IV-R (or pay no attention to that man behind the curtain, Dorothy!). *Child and Youth Care Forum, 32*(5), 281–298.

Mitchell, R. C., & Moore, S. A. (2016). Restorative justice and transdisciplinary praxis: A framework for moving forward health promotion. In R. J. Waller (Ed.), *Mental health promotion in schools: Special topics, special challenges, an e-series: Vol. 2* (pp. 3–29). Sharjah, UAE: Bentham Science Publishers.

Moore, S. A. (2004). Towards an integrated perspective: Restorative justice, cross-cultural counselling and school-based programming. In M. H. France, M. C. Roderiguez, & G. G. Hett (Eds.), *Diversity, culture and counselling: A Canadian perspective* (pp. 347–355). Calgary, AB: Detselig.

Moore, S. A. (2007). Restorative justice. In R. B. Howe & K. Covell (Eds.), *A question of commitment: Children's rights in Canada* (pp. 179–208). Waterloo, ON: Wilfrid Laurier University Press.

Moore, S. A. (2008). *Rights based restorative practice evaluation toolkit*. Minneapolis: Center for Human Rights, University of Minnesota. Retrieved from http://hrlibrary.umn.edu/links/RBRJ%20toolkit.pdf

Moore, S. A. (2017). Restorative justice education, policy & practice: Transdisciplinary reflections on mental health implications. In L. Evans (Ed.), *Restorative and transitional justice: Perspectives, progress and considerations for the future* (pp. 1–24). New York: Nova Science.

Moore, S. A., & Mitchell, R. C. (2007). Rights based restorative justice: Towards critical praxis with young people in conflict with the law. In A. Ang, I. Delens-Ravier, M. Delplace, C. Herman, D. Reynaert, V. Staelens, R. Steel, & M. Verheyde (Eds.), *The UN Children's Rights Convention: Theory meets practice* (pp. 549–563).

Proceedings of the International Interdisciplinary Conference on Children's Rights, May 18–19, 2006. Ghent, Belgium: Intersentia.

Moore, S. A., & Mitchell, R. C. (2009). Rights-based restorative praxis: Promoting compliance with international standards. *Youth Justice: An International Journal, 9*(1), 27–43.

Moore, S. A., & Mitchell, R. C. (2011). Theorising rights-based restorative justice: The Canadian context. *International Journal of Children's Rights, 19*(1), 81–105.

Moore, S. A., & Mitchell, R. C. (2012). Rights-based restorative justice in Canada: From silence to citizenship. In M. Freeman (Ed.), *Oxford Law and Childhood Studies Current Legal Issues, 14,* 202–218). Oxford: Oxford University Press.

Moore, S. A., Tulk, W., & Mitchell, R. C. (2005). Qallunaat crossing: The southern–northern divide and promising practices for Canada's Inuit young people. *First People's Child and Family Review, 2*(1), 117–129.

Moss, P., & Petrie, P. (2002). *From children's services to children's spaces: Public policy, children and childhood.* London: RoutledgeFalmer.

Muncie, J. (2005). The globalization of crime control: The case of youth and juvenile justice: Neo-liberalism, policy convergence and international conventions. *Theoretical Criminology, 9*(1), 35–64.

Muncie, J. (2008). The "punitive turn" in juvenile justice: Cultures of control and rights compliance in Western Europe and the USA. *Youth Justice, 8*(2), 107–121.

National Inquiry into Missing and Murdered Indigenous Women and Girls. (2017). *Interim report: Our women and girls are sacred.* Ottawa: Government of Canada. Retrieved from http://www.mmiwg-ffada.ca/files/ni-mmiwg-interim-report-en.pdf

Nyp, G. (2004). *Pioneers of peace: The history of community justice initiatives in the Waterloo Region 1974–2004.* Kitchener, ON: Pandora.

Pon, G., Gosine, K., & Phillips, D. (2011). Immediate response: Addressing anti-native and anti-black racism in child welfare. *International Journal of Child, Youth and Family Studies, 2*(3/4), 385–409.

Reasons, C., Hassan, S., Ma, M., Monchalin, L., Bige, M., Paras, C., & Arora, S. (2016). Race and criminal justice in Canada. *International Journal of Criminal Justice Sciences, 11*(2), 75–99.

Richard, B. (2008). *The Ashley Smith report: A report of the New Brunswick Ombudsman and Child and Youth Advocate on the services provided to a youth involved in the youth criminal justice system.* Fredericton, NB: Office of the Ombudsman & Child and Youth Advocate.

Ring, J. (2014). Incorrigible while incarcerated: Critically analysing mainstream Canadian news depictions of Ashley Smith. *Canadian Graduate Journal of Sociology and Criminology, 3*(1), 34–53.

Scraton, P. (Ed.). (2004). *Childhood in crisis?* London: Routledge.

Senate of Canada Standing Committee on Human Rights. (2007). *Children: The silenced citizens.* Final Report on Effective Implementation of Canada's International Obligations with Respect to the Rights of Children. Ottawa: Author. Retrieved from https://sencanada.ca/content/sen/committee/391/huma/rep/rep10apr07-e.htm

Truth and Reconciliation Commission of Canada. (2015). *Honouring the truth, reconciling the future.* Summary of the Final Report of the Truth and Reconciliation

Commission of Canada. Winnipeg, MB: Author. Retrieved from http://nctr.ca/assets/reports/Final%20Reports/Executive_Summary_English_Web.pdf

United Nations. (1985). *United Nations standard minimum rules for the administration of juvenile justice: The Beijing rules.* New York: Author.

United Nations. (1989). *Convention on the Rights of the Child.* New York: Author.

United Nations. (1990). *United Nations guidelines for the prevention of juvenile delinquency: The Riyadh guidelines.* New York: Author.

United Nations Committee on the Rights of the Child. (2007). *Convention on the Rights of the Child, General comment no. 10: Children's rights in juvenile justice.* Geneva: Office of the United Nations High Commissioner for Human Rights.

United Nations Economic and Social Council. (1997). *United Nations resolution 1197/30: Administration of juvenile justice. The Vienna guidelines.* Geneva: Author.

United Nations Economic and Social Council. (2002). *United Nations basic principles on the use of restorative justice programmes in criminal matters.* New York and Geneva: Author. Retrieved from http://www.unodc.org/pdf/crine/terrorism/2002/19eb.pdf

White, B. (2003). A world fit for children? *Children and youth in development studies and policy, 51st Dies Natalis address.* The Hague: Institute of Social Studies.

Chapter 6
Child Welfare and the Status of Children Requiring Support and Care
Thomas Waldock

INTRODUCTION

Children requiring the support and services of the child welfare system are among the most marginalized children in the country. Unfortunately, this has been the case throughout Canada's history. This marginalization complicates the evolution of these children's place in Canada's history. If the general evolution of conceptualizations of children has portrayed them as objects or property, as sacred trusts and "not-yets" under the authority of adults and the state, and increasingly as subjects and bearers of rights, at every stage marginalized children's status has been lived and experienced as "lesser than" the general population. Certain disadvantaged groups have been particularly vulnerable—notably Indigenous children and youth—and, unfortunately, at times child welfare has played a central role in their marginalization. So the challenge for Canada in an area like child welfare is immense, attempting to turn the tide of a less than admirable history in an effort to meet the demands of the progressive standards of the United Nations Convention on the Rights of the Child (UNCRC), and treat children requiring the support and care of child welfare as rights-bearing citizens, respecting their dignity as fully human persons in their own right.

Meeting the challenge in this area is especially important because of the stakes involved. History reveals a strong correlation between the status of children and their vulnerability to abuse and violence. By failing to recognize the full humanity of others, defining them in lesser terms than fellow citizens, the stage is set. As conveyed by Freeman (noted in the "Introduction"), to accord rights is to respect dignity; to deny rights is to cast doubt on humanity and integrity. Historically, the denial of rights is associated with susceptibility to abuse and violence, and in the most extreme instances, life itself can hang in the balance (Freeman, 2007). Marginalized children are even more likely to be devalued in terms of their status, and this makes them particularly susceptible. Canada is committed under international law to the UNCRC, and has agreed to incorporate the Convention's Principles and Articles into policy and practice, including in the area of child welfare. Because rights are entitlements and allow for demands to be made, the UNCRC can be employed in the battle to secure recognition. In short, children and those advocating on their behalf can make demands of child welfare, and Canada needs to meet its obligations and rise to the child welfare challenge.

In what follows, a UNCRC framework is employed to assess Canada's record in the area of child welfare, with a particular focus on whether or not the dignity and integrity of marginalized children requiring the care and support of child welfare have been respected. This requires an assessment of the extent to which the country has fulfilled its obligations in relation to the provision, protection, and participation rights of these children. The first section outlines the relevant principles and articles of the UNCRC; generally this section provides a framework of analysis by which to judge Canada's record in the child welfare area. The second section identifies a central challenge for child welfare in Canada related to discrimination and marginalized children, with a focus on Indigenous children. In the sections that follow, the decision has been made—since child welfare is a vast area of interrogation—to focus on three relevant subject matters, rendered here as questions for critical reflection:

1. To what extent has child welfare actually adopted the UNCRC as its guiding framework, notably in relation to the existing model of social work practice in the field and whether it is consistent with UNCRC dictates?

2. Have child welfare systems of care and the quality of caregiving in the field been consistent with requirements under the UNCRC, especially as these relate to the recovery and reintegration of these children in an environment that fosters health, self-respect, and dignity?

3. To what extent have participation rights—so important for empowerment and also indicative of status and recognition as rights-bearing citizens (stage 3 in Howe and Covell's template of analysis)—been incorporated into child welfare legislation and practice?

In relation to the first question, it will be demonstrated that Canada has much more to do in terms of adopting the UNCRC as a guiding framework for child welfare policy and practice. Despite some recent progress on the legislative front, which will be highlighted, historically child welfare has been plagued by a lack of consensus around the proper orientation for the field, with pendulum-like swings between child-centred and family-centred approaches to the state's role in the child welfare enterprise. Moreover, these swings have taken place within the confines of the Anglo-American child welfare model, which comparatively speaking is limited in nature and not the model most aligned with the UNCRC. Secondly, systems of care in child welfare are deficient in many respects, and have yet to come close to being in line with the standards of the UNCRC in this regard; fundamental reforms in this area are required, particularly since nowhere is the marginalization of children in care more apparent. Lastly, it will be argued that some tangible progress has been made in the area of participation rights for children in care, even if many challenges still remain. While progress in this area signifies some movement in the direction of children being regarded as right bearers, it falls far short of what is required if Canada is to enhance the voice of marginalized children requiring the care and support of the child welfare system.

UNCRC "STANDARDS" AND CHILD WELFARE

All of the UNCRC's general principles certainly relate to child welfare: non-discrimination (Article 2), the best interests of the child (Article 3), the right to survival and development (Article 6), and child participation (Article 12). Other relevant UNCRC rights fall under Hammarberg's (1990) three categories—provision, protection, and participation rights—keeping in mind that Convention rights are interrelated, and at times, rights cross over these categories and relate to more than one of them. For example, UNCRC rights related to child welfare can simultaneously call for the protection of children while emphasizing the need to provide supportive services to children and families. In terms of relating this theoretical emphasis to the functions of the child welfare enterprise, protection, provision, and participation rights should all be prioritized by child welfare systems.

Article 2 calls on states to respect the rights set forth in the Convention to each child without discrimination of any kind. Of course, there are many forms of discrimination, including those based on race, age, and class, and, unfortunately, marginalized children and families—especially those requiring the care and services of child welfare—have experienced discrimination throughout Canada's history (Strong-Boag, 2002, 2011; Waldock, 2012). Particular groups of children have been especially vulnerable. The next section focuses on the situation of Indigenous children in relation to child welfare.

Discrimination can also relate to geographic location in a country with a federal system. Child welfare in Canada is a provincial and territorial responsibility, and given the propensity for federal systems to generate inequities in services, coordinating mechanisms would be necessary, as well as common theoretical and legal frameworks.

In Canada, coordination largely has been informal—for example, meetings between federal, provincial, and territorial directors of service—and provincial and territorial jurisdictions have their own child welfare legislation. While legislation across the country shares common features to some degree, it also varies in important respects. For example, the UNCRC is incorporated into child welfare legislation in only four jurisdictions: the Yukon (Preamble), Ontario (Preamble) more recently, the Northwest Territories (Principles), and Nunavut (Principles) (Birdsell & Chan, 2017). Suffice to say that while the UNCRC could provide a common theoretical and legal framework for child welfare across the country, for the most part, it has not been incorporated into provincial/territorial child welfare legislation to the extent that it could be; certainly other countries—for example, Belgium and Norway (see Chapter 1: "Introduction")—have achieved far more progress in this regard. Without sufficient coordinating mechanisms and common theoretical and legal frameworks, disparities between the provinces and territories in child welfare policy and practice continue to exist. The failure to institute a national children's commissioner (see Hunter's Chapter 13) at the federal level also has not been helpful in this regard.

One of the ways to empower children in their families and communities is through education about the UNCRC (mandated under Article 42), and in particular through emphasizing that children are rights bearers. They are not objects or property, or simply passive benefactors dependent on the goodwill of adults, but rather, they are individuals with agency deserving of dignity and respect as rights-bearing citizens. At times, the child welfare system has been counterproductive in terms of children's status in families and communities, and it has contributed to the marginalization of children. For example, for the most part, the field continues to employ inappropriate language that objectifies children and solidifies stigma. Children in care are referred to as "clients," "cases," "placements," and "runaways." Terms and phrases like "apprehension," "custody," "ward of the state," "intake," "visits," and "records"—associated with institutional settings like prisons—are employed (Waldock, 2007). Youth in care have identified stigmatization as a central concern (National Youth in Care Network, 2005). In this regard, such terminology is objectifying and dehumanizing (Wharf, 2000), and while it may suit bureaucratic processes like classification and categorization, it is not child-centred, nor does it accord with empowerment or the full citizenship status of the UNCRC. In so far as it objectifies children, it relegates children to stage 1 status ("objects"), but at best it reflects a paternalistic (stage 2) approach to interacting with children.

The good news is that some progress on this front has been made. For example, Ontario's new *Child, Youth, and Family Services Act* (in force on April 30, 2018) (Government of Ontario, n.d.) has addressed terminology issues to some degree. For example, the term "ward" is no longer employed; and the new Act does not refer to children as "runaways" or being "abandoned." These changes are more in line with Article 2 of the UNCRC. For especially marginalized children defined as "lesser-thans"—children requiring the care and support of child welfare—such progress is particularly significant, even if more remains to be done.

UNCRC Article 3 makes the bests interests of the child "a primary consideration" in all policy and practice areas concerning children. The "best interests of the child" has been a cornerstone concept of child welfare in the Canadian context for over a century. Article 3's emphasis highlights the child-centred philosophical foundation of the Convention, rooted in the conceptualization of children as rights bearers, and in this regard, also incorporates the child's own views (Article 12). At the same time, UNCRC articles also reflect the importance of families, communities, and cultures to a child's overall well-being, and thus to their best interests. The child has the right "as far as possible ... to know and be cared for by his or her parents" (Article 7). They can "not be separated from his or her parents against their will, except when competent authorities subject to judicial review determine ... that such separation is necessary for the best interests of the child" (Article 9). And in terms of the Convention incorporating the significance of broader environments, Article 30 provides a central example in this regard. It emphasizes a child's right to "enjoy his or her own culture, to profess and practice his or her own religion, or to use his or her own language."

A hallmark of the UNCRC is in fact the extent to which the child's environments are acknowledged—from parents and families through to communities and cultures—and it is clear that supportive contexts are viewed as crucial to meeting the requirements of another foundational principle, that the survival and development of the child be ensured to the maximum extent possible (Article 6). But the Convention goes beyond simply acknowledging the environments themselves as significant developmental contexts. It requires states to provide supports to parents, families, and communities for the sake of children's well-being, and the emphasis in this regard is proactive, preventative policies and programs. This emphasis has implications for approaches to social welfare generally, but also for child welfare specifically. For example, at the same time that Article 27 (on poverty) references the right of every child to a "standard of living adequate for the child's physical, mental, spiritual, moral and social development," it also emphasizes the need to provide parents and other caregivers with "material assistance and support programmes." Mitigating the stress on families by dealing with issues such as poverty in a proactive, preventative way is supportive of the child welfare enterprise. Article 19, which is directly associated with child welfare, follows the same pattern. States are to protect children from all forms of abuse and neglect while in the care of "parent(s), legal guardians, or any other person who has the care of the child," but at the same time, they are to provide "support for the child and for those who have the care of the child." Protection is prioritized, but so is prevention through the provision of support for those responsible for children.

States are obligated, then, to provide preventative, proactive child and family supports through their social welfare policies and programs. At the same time, when violence against children does occur in the context of families and communities, the child also has the right to alternative care (Article 20). Again, the child is an individual with rights (a rights bearer), and sometimes in their best interests, alternative placements are required. The field of child welfare is front and centre in this regard, with responsibilities related to the provision of foster care. These responsibilities require care to be available—a sufficient "quantity" of care—but also require that care should be of sufficient "quality." It must be able to meet the needs of abused and neglected children. Article 39 increases the standards of care in this regard because it addresses the "rehabilitative" function of fostering systems. Alternative care is supposed to "promote physical and psychological recovery and social reintegration" of such children in "an environment which fosters the health, self-respect and dignity of the child." In short, the UNCRC also provides normative standards by which to judge systems of care, something that we will turn to shortly.

As noted above, the last section of the chapter focuses on the extent to which participation rights have been incorporated into child welfare. Again, the UNCRC provides the normative standards by which to judge the field. Article 12 is a fundamental principle of the Convention, and provides the child "who is capable of forming his or her own views the right to express those views freely in all matters affecting the child, the views of the child being given due weight in accordance with the age and maturity of the child." Article 12 includes more detail in this regard that is relevant to child welfare, such as "the opportunity to be heard in any judicial and administrative proceedings affecting the child." While the age and maturity of the child can be considered, the fundamental principle applies. The acknowledgement and recognition of participation rights for children largely defines the transition between stage 2 and stage 3 of the Howe and Covell framework.

Voice and agency rights are necessary if children are to be conceptualized as rights-bearing citizens.

MARGINALIZATION AND CHILD WELFARE: A FOCUS ON INDIGENOUS CHILDREN

Certain disadvantaged groups of children have been particularly vulnerable, and unfortunately at times child welfare has played a major role in their marginalization. In this regard, some chapters of Canadian history have been particularly egregious. The experience of the so-called "Home children" (sent to Canada between 1869 and 1939), which coincided with the earliest stages of child welfare legislation, policy, and practice—and with authorities finding "placements"—is a case in point. These children were rounded up in Britain and sent to Canada in a misplaced emigration scheme, and often ended up being exploited as cheap labour in the colony; many experienced various forms of neglect and abuse (Bagnell, 2001; Waldock, 2012). Moreover, they were discriminated against based on their status in the community and culture, with many citizens viewing them as "lesser-thans," as Britain's cast-offs and "waifs" (one of the labels applied to them). If intersections of age and class-based discrimination characterized this chapter of Canadian history, race also has been a profound factor in terms of government intervention in the lives of children and families. Indigenous children and families continue to be affected by the legacy of residential schools (19th to the late 20th century) (TRCC, 2015), and more directly related to the role of child welfare, the so-called Sixties Scoop (between the 1950s and 1980s) saw thousands of Indigenous children removed from their families and placed primarily in white foster families.

Concerns about racial discrimination continue to plague Canadian society in general and child welfare in particular. More recent attention has been paid, for example, to discrimination against black children as this relates to their overrepresentation in care (OHRC, 2018). While beyond the scope of this chapter, there is a need for more focus on racial and ethnic discrimination in child welfare. Here, the focus is the most egregious example of this discrimination, both historically and ongoing up to the present day. It has been noted that there are more Indigenous children in care now than at the height of residential schools (Blackstock, 2003, p. 331). The statistics for 2016 reveal that, despite being only 7.7 percent of the population of children across the country, Indigenous children make up over 50 percent of the children in care. This overrepresentation of Indigenous children exists across virtually every province. In Ontario, for example, Indigenous children make up 4.1

percent of all children, but approximately 30 percent of the children in care (OHRC, 2018). Figures climb to even higher levels in the western provinces: in British Columbia, Indigenous children make up less than 10 percent of all children, but over 60 percent of the children in care (BC Representative for Children and Youth, 2017); and levels in Manitoba reach staggering proportions, with approximately 90 percent of children in care being Indigenous, while they make up less than 30 percent of all children (Sinha, Trocmé, Blackstock, MacLaurin, & Fallon, 2011; Barrera, 2017). The situation has become so dire that the phrase "Millennium Scoop" was coined to emphasize a time frame for the crisis well beyond that suggested by the Sixties Scoop (CBC Radio, 2018); indeed, as already noted, the vastly disproportionate number of Indigenous children in care continues to exist right up until the present time. Even Jane Philpott, the then federal minister of Indigenous Services, referred to the situation as a humanitarian crisis (Barrera, 2017).

The reasons for the overrepresentation of Indigenous children in care are complex, but poverty and intergenerational trauma certainly are factors. As noted in an Ontario Human Rights Commission Report dealing with the overrepresentation of both Indigenous and black children in care, concerns also have been raised about discrimination in the child welfare sector with regard to policies, practices, and organizational culture (OHRC, 2018). Particularly problematic is that some studies suggest that even after controlling for other variables (risk factors and case characteristics), a child's Indigenous identity or background may affect child welfare decision making, resulting in the greater likelihood of Indigenous children being placed in care (Fallon et al., 2013). In terms of racial bias, such concerns extend to legal decision making associated with child removal (Sinclair, 2016). Moreover, it also has been demonstrated that with regard to Indigenous children, overrepresentation is driven by neglect cases (Sinha et al., 2011, p. 319), which at times can be related to poverty and living conditions. Given Canada's colonial legacy and the disruption of Indigenous communities, combined with a child welfare paradigm that doesn't emphasize supportive services for families—the focus of the next section—a very disturbing picture emerges.

Compounding such concerns is the reality of underfunding for Indigenous children on reserves. In 2007, the First Nations Child and Family Caring Society (FNCFCS) and the Assembly of First Nations (AFN) filed a complaint with the Canadian Human Rights Commission (CHRC), claiming that this underfunding constituted discriminatory treatment of these children. In 2016, after a long and onerous process with a time frame extending to almost a decade (FNCFCS, n.d.), in which the federal government fought the case at every turn, the Canadian Human Rights Tribunal issued a landmark ruling. The Canadian government is discriminating against on-reserve Indigenous children by underfunding on-reserve child welfare services, an important effect of which is inadequate funding for preventive services (CHRT, 2016). Indeed, on-reserve funding is up to 38 percent lower than funding elsewhere, where services are provided by provincial and territorial governments. In the aftermath of the ruling, Carolyn Bennett, the government's minister of Crown-Indigenous Relations, appeared to agree with the decision and committed to come up with solutions. But as Cindy Blackstock, executive director of FNCFCS, rightly reflected, "Why did we have to bring the government of Canada to court to get them to treat First Nation children fairly? Little kids.... Why would it ever be OK to give a child less than other children?" (Fontaine, 2016). After two years and numerous compliance orders being issued because of a failure to follow through on the initial ruling to address the inequities, the government recently announced new funding to address the need for immediate relief (Ballingall, 2018). This is helpful, but considering the record, at this point the most that can be said is that there is "work in progress," the results of which largely remain to be seen.

In terms of both the past and the present, not just child welfare but Canadian society in general has failed Indigenous peoples. In particular, Indigenous children have been treated as somewhere between objects of control and manipulation (stage 1 status) and incomplete beings requiring paternalistic intervention (stage 2 status), never as rights-bearing citizens. The child welfare system has played a central role in terms of state intervention into the lives of Indigenous children and families. The ongoing and wide-ranging violations of the UNCRC are numerous, but would relate to all of the principles (Articles 2, 3, 6, and 12), articles having to do with prevention and family supports (for example, Article 27), and Article 30, the right to culture and language.

THE UNCRC AND CHILD WELFARE MODELS

A good deal of scholarship has focused on the relationship between cultural contexts and child welfare policy and practice models. The focal point of such analyses has tended to be the work of Esping-Andersen as it relates to cultural contexts, and Gilbert's categorization of child welfare models based on this cultural framework (Esping-Andersen, 1990; Gilbert, Parton, & Skivenes, 1997, 2011). The Esping-Andersen typology outlines cultural contexts corresponding to three welfare state classifications: liberal, conservative, and social democratic. "Liberal" states (for example, Canada, the United States, and England) are characterized by minimal state intervention and an emphasis on individual responsibility. Generally, social welfare benefits are relatively limited, and tend to be reactive rather than proactive or preventative. Both

"Conservative" (for example, Germany, France, and Italy) and "Social Democratic" (for example, the Nordic countries of Denmark, Sweden, Finland, and Norway) states acknowledge the state's responsibility for social welfare (collective responsibility), and generally pursue a proactive, preventative policy and practice approach, with the main distinction being the extent of their reliance on private versus public service delivery; Social Democratic welfare states are more likely to emphasize governmental responsibility (public) for social welfare services.

Gilbert employs these cultural and welfare state classifications to situate child welfare policy and practice models (Gilbert et al., 1997, 2011), distinguishing between "child protection" and "family service" paradigms. In "Liberal" states like Canada, the United States, and England, the cultural context spawns child protection systems (the Anglo-American model). With a preference for minimal state involvement and an emphasis on individual responsibility, these states are not prone to countenance intrusion into family life and interference with the autonomy of the family. As a result, there is a more limited focus on child protection concerns. From a critical standpoint, such states fail to provide a supportive environment for children and families by not providing benefits and supports in a proactive, preventative way.

Social Democratic states provide the most pronounced contrast in this regard. In the Nordic countries in particular, the cultural context engenders family service systems. This model of child welfare is more holistic in nature, with child welfare as a "field" situated within a supportive cultural environment characterized by a societal commitment (policies and practices) to the well-being of children, families, and communities. Supportive social welfare policies, and proactive, preventative child and family policies—such as advanced systems of developmental daycare, and extensive parental leave—mitigate family stress, and enhance the welfare of children and families; this is reflected in research focused on comparative outcomes between welfare states—for example, lower poverty rates, and higher scores on measures of child well-being (Alcock & Craig, 2009; Andersen, Guillemard, Jensen, & Pfau-Effinger, 2005; OECD, 2016; UNICEF Office of Research, 2017). Within this context, a family service philosophy characterizes the child welfare system itself, with its emphasis on preventative, proactive approaches and the provision of extensive support to families.

The Esping-Andersen/Gilbert classifications have been very instructive for child welfare scholarship focused on comparative models of child welfare. In theorizing child welfare, this author has outlined the strengths and weaknesses of these classifications as manifested in some of the literature (Waldock, 2016). Suffice to say that such scholarship has played an important role in terms of allowing for critical reflection on the child protection model of child welfare, comparing and contrasting this model with potential alternatives. The Anglo-American model has been widely criticized for its narrow focus on protection, and for an inadequate emphasis on sufficient supports for children and families (Gilbert, 1997; Gilbert et al., 2011; Cameron, Coady, & Adams, 2007; Hetherington & Nurse, 2006). Common criticisms often relate to its "child saving" history and orientation that has led to significant historical wrongs—for example, the Sixties Scoop—and ongoing issues today, such as child welfare's treatment of Indigenous children and families. Other concerns abound, among them the following: the lack of focus on preventative and proactive approaches (corresponding to its reactive nature); its focus on individual responsibility and neglect of collective responsibility (and accountability); its punitive nature, especially in relation to parents and mothers in particular; its investigative orientation and preferencing of risk assessment approaches; and its propensity to employ the formal, adversarial legal system rather than more family-friendly approaches.

At the same time, such scholarship sometimes fails to correctly incorporate children's rights into the comparative analysis of child welfare models. The reality is this: supportive cultures with a family service child welfare model also embrace children's rights. Social welfare states (for example, the Nordic countries) have demonstrated a far greater commitment to children's rights and the UNCRC than liberal welfare states. As noted by Covell and Howe (2009), these cultures "embrace a positive role for government ... and children as bearers of rights" (p. 195). The stronger commitment to children's rights is apparent; Norway, for example, amended its child welfare act for the purpose of giving the UNCRC direct application (Howe & Covell, 2007, p. 9). By contrast, liberal welfare states have not demonstrated the same level of commitment. For the most part, Canada has not directly incorporated the UNCRC into child welfare legislation across the country, and the United States hasn't even ratified the Convention (Waldock, 2016).

In terms of the evolving status of children and the framework employed in this text (three stages), it is in fact liberal welfare states with child protection models of child welfare that are more likely to be beholden to earlier conceptualizations of children either as the "property" of parents, or as objects and "not-yets" in need of paternalistic protection. Only over the past few decades has the view of children as subjects with rights come to the fore, an evolution in the conceptualization of children that is still in process, and it is the social democratic states with family service child welfare models that are leading the charge.

The UNCRC (a children's rights framework) supports a family service model of child welfare with a child-centred children's rights focus. The best interests of children (Article 3), including their right to protection from abuse and neglect (Article 19), require a wide array of preventative, proactive social welfare supports for children, families, and communities (e.g., Article 27). At the same time, a family service model does not imply that the best interests of children as individuals with rights shouldn't be prioritized. Nor does it mean that a child-centred focus is a secondary consideration. Scholarship within the Nordic context is instructive in this regard, and relates to the complexities of child welfare; without due diligence, family service orientations can lead to a child-centred focus not being a priority in some circumstances, particularly with regard to decision making (Heimer, Nasman, & Palme 2018; Heimer & Palme, 2016; Waldock, 2016). Assuming a blanket identity of interests between children, families, and communities is not justified. In this regard, children also have a right to quality, alternative placements (Articles 20 and 39) when required. But even in this situation, the UNCRC incorporates the tensions and helps to define the balance (Waldock, 2016). A family service or inclusive approach to foster care (Kufeldt, 1994) would be most in line with the Convention, with parents and children both receiving support in the context of a system of care that is not anti-family.

A Swinging Pendulum within an Anglo-American Model

If a family service model with a child-centred, children's rights focus is most in line with a UNCRC framework for child welfare and a view of children as independent, rights-bearings citizens, Canada's child protection system (Anglo-American model) needs significant reform. In this regard, reforms would relate not just to child welfare, but also to the Canadian welfare state generally. To date, Canada's reform efforts have never constituted anything resembling a paradigm shift. Rather, there have been shifts of emphasis that have taken place within the dominant, Anglo-American model.

Historically, with regard to the prospect of intervention in the lives of children and families, the pendulum of child welfare has swung back and forth from a family-centred to a child-centred approach, but always within the confines of the dominant Anglo-American model. With the lessons of the child-saving past having been learned to some degree—and the experience of the Sixties Scoop fresh in mind—a family preservation approach dominated from the 1980s through to the mid-1990s. By that point, the deaths of some children in relatives' care led to child mortality inquests and extensive media attention, with the focus on children sometimes being left in at-risk situations. Within this time frame, "neglect" also was added to some child welfare legislation (Ontario, for example), broadening the grounds for intervention. These developments resulted in the adoption of a child-centred approach in the mid-1990s. This led to increasing numbers of children coming into care, which in turn generated budgetary concerns. From the early 2000s onward, the dominant approach incorporated a policy of differential response combined with an emphasis on kinship care and adoption. Potential placement with kin (extended family or significant others) or adoption became the main priority. These reforms represent to some degree a shift back to a family-centred approach (Waldock, 2007). While this last swing of the pendulum has held until today, concerns have been expressed about compromises being made to facilitate kinship care, something that will be addressed in the next section.

An examination of these pendulum swings could lead to the conclusion that child welfare is governed by knee-jerk reactions to currents events and media coverage. But it may be the case that in the absence of an overarching philosophical and legal framework, which the UNCRC could provide, a kind of identity crisis is understandable, as the field grapples with its raison d'être. Conflicting understandings of priorities can be emboldened by the lack of consensus around governing principles, which could be a driving factor in the swinging pendulum of child welfare. But regardless, these shifts of emphasis within the Anglo-American child protection model are insufficient; what is required is a paradigm shift toward a family service paradigm with a children's rights focus.

CHILD WELFARE AND SYSTEMS OF CARE

The UNCRC requires that alternative placements be available (Article 20) when required for the best interests of children, and that these placements contribute to the recovery and reintegration of such marginalized children (Article 39). Having a system in place that has sufficient placement options for children requiring alternative care is essential since ideally, child welfare agencies should be matching children and placements based on children's needs and rights. On the ground, often agencies simply are finding a bed. This has been the case for decades, because systems of care and caregivers have not been substantial priorities. The ongoing crisis of care in many jurisdictions—exemplified by the occasional use of motel rooms as placements (Waldock, 2007)—threatens to deepen in nature over the coming decades as aging caregivers leave the system.

For child welfare, a major focus of reform priorities should be the quality of the foster care system and the competency level of caregivers. For children requiring care and support, this is where they live. As priorities have shifted to kinship care, the traditional foster care system itself has not been the focus of concern, or the subject matter of reform discussions. Of course, pursuing kinship care makes sense; potential kinship placements are important options when they are available, and when they are in the best interests of children. For Indigenous children in particular, such placements are viewed as more culturally appropriate; the recruitment of Indigenous caregivers—kinship or traditional—is an important priority. Yet even in the early days of the trend toward kinship care, it was never suggested that it would be a solution for the majority of children requiring the care and support of child welfare agencies; one study suggested an estimate of around 20 percent of children (Trocmé et al., 2005). While a specific accounting of kinship usage is difficult given definitional variations in kinship care across the country, the use of kinship care is on the rise, and percentages likely are higher and climbing (Schwartz et al., 2014). Whether or not compromises are being made to facilitate the strategy is considered more below. But suffice to say that a quality foster care system needs to be a priority. Simply put, having placement options is in the best interests of children requiring alternative care (Article 3).

When it comes to the system of care, concerns about governments and agencies not acting in accordance with children's rights continue to be raised, and this can relate to two factors in the present environment. First, in order to facilitate kinship care, compromises may be made and corners cut. Kinship care is a priority today, and financial considerations are part of the equation (Waldock, 2007). To be sure, there are advantages if such placements are available and in the best interests of children; for example, research has highlighted the benefits of continuity of care (Connolly, 2003). But vigilance is still warranted, especially since research also has supported concerns like intergenerational aspects of child abuse and neglect, and poor parenting practices across generations (Connolly, 2003). Unfortunately, the history of child welfare is rife with examples that confirm the following: a family connection is no guarantee that a particular caregiver is in the best interests of a child. It is disturbing, then, that concerns continue to be raised about compromises being made to facilitate the strategy, like insufficient screening practices and training prior to placements occurring. Mary Ellen Turpel-Lafonde, the former BC children's advocate, provided a comprehensive report concerning kinship care detailing "shortcuts" that compromised children's safety and well-being (BC Representative for Children and Youth, 2010).

The second factor militating against placements being in the best interests of children isn't just related to the present environment, since it has been a reality for a long time. The system of care has been in crisis for decades, with a shortage of caregivers and homes for children requiring care. At times, overcrowding within systems has been the result (Bernstein, 2009), with some governments and agencies overriding regulations in order to find a bed. In many provinces across the country—despite how detrimental it is to the best interests of children—motel rooms have been employed (Waldock, 2007), with children being placed under worker supervision. Sadly, it is difficult to conclude that this occurs only in "exceptional circumstances," when the practice has been employed for decades, and continues to this day (Stueck, 2017). This practice violates the basic dignity of children requiring care, not just requirements under the UNCRC to provide alternative care (Article 20) that promotes recovery and reintegration needs (Article 39). When simply finding a bed becomes the dominant priority, children's rights to appropriate placements, and quality alternative care, can be violated.

The potential significance of caregivers in the lives of children requiring alternative care is clear. Caregivers can be an immediate and significant presence in the lives of these children, perhaps the adult connection emphasized in resilience research (Flynn, Dudding, & Barber, 2006). The competencies of caregivers, their abilities to advocate for marginalized children, and the extent to which caregivers themselves are supported in their role are all key variables affecting the quality of care that children receive. It is important to emphasize that the standard here requires that caregivers contribute to the recovery and reintegration of children who may have complex needs. Given the significance of the role, and the nature of the obligations, one might assume that reform efforts in child welfare would have made the system of care a major priority, especially when confronted with the ongoing crisis situation. But aside from some initiatives in the 1990s—more on this below—that has not been the case. Band-aid type "solutions" have been the norm (Waldock, 2007, 2011).

As noted in the previous main section, consistency with a UNCRC framework requires a family service approach with a child-centred, children's rights focus. There are approaches to foster care that are consistent with Convention requirements in this regard, where caregivers not only provide care and support to the children in their home, but also work with their parents and families. Two inclusive foster care programs were piloted in the 1990s at two Toronto, Ontario, Children's Aid Societies, and then were sustained for the better part of a decade. The role of caregivers was enhanced, with a greater level of competency required. If children had to come into care, the need for protection could be ensured, while at the same time operating with a family service orientation; the goal of agencies and caregivers was to provide parents with the supports necessary to facilitate the child's return home. To the extent possible, parents stayed involved with their children throughout the process (Waldock, 2007). With the shrinking mandates of child welfare agencies in the late 1990s, this approach to foster care was abandoned.

Since this time, there has been no serious attempt to reform the system of traditional foster care. Kinship care has been pursued, and this has diverted some children away from traditional foster care. But this has little to do with improving traditional foster care itself, a system that is required and serves children in social welfare states regardless of the particular child welfare model of practice. In the meantime, the status quo continues and the system remains in crisis. What is particularly revealing—and speaks to the extent of children's marginalization in child welfare—is that there doesn't even seem to be much motivation to fix this system, in a context where the general public is aware of issues, and media portrayals generally are unflattering.

Two recent developments are revealing in terms of highlighting the need to improve the system of care. In the first instance, criminal charges (negligence) were laid against a former Children's Aid Society director in Ontario for overseeing an agency that placed children in a foster home with caregivers who later ended up being convicted of abuse (Charles, 2018). And the second development concerns the recent certification of a class-action lawsuit brought by former Crown wards (between January 1, 1966, until March 30, 2017), alleging that the Ontario government systematically failed to take all necessary steps to protect the legal rights and claims of children in its care (OACAS, 2017).

In the final analysis, the system of care needs substantial reform if children requiring the care and support of child welfare are to be treated with dignity and respect in accordance with their rights to alternative placements (Article 20) that meet their recovery and reintegration needs (Article 39). Authorities and practitioners in child welfare should make reforms of this system a major priority.

PARTICIPATION RIGHTS: SIGNS OF PROGRESS?

The incorporation of participation rights into the UNCRC marked a historical turning point in the evolution of children's rights, and for our purposes here, a transition in conceptualizations of children from being viewed as incomplete adults ("not-yets") to being seen as independent rights bearers and citizens. First and foremost, children requiring the care and support of child welfare need to have their own voices heard; they have the right to participate, in accordance with their age and maturity, in all decisions affecting them (Article 12). Because of the extent of their vulnerability and marginalization, this right to participate needs to be supported by adults and advocates. In terms of the Howe and Covell framework, then—and assessing whether or not there are signs of progress in child welfare toward the children's rights stage (stage 3)—there would have to be evidence both of opportunities to participate, as well as the provision of substantial advocacy support. The latter could be provided through a variety of formal channels—provincial advocates offices, for example—but advocacy support also would be required in their day-to-day lives. In this regard, incorporating "embedded advocacy" (Waldock, 2007) may be the biggest challenge for child welfare.

Only through an understanding of the marginalization of children in care is it possible to gain a full appreciation of the need for participation rights and voice, as well as the extent of the advocacy support required. As noted in this chapter, marginalization and discrimination based on the discourse of child welfare has been problematic, although there are signs of improvement in this regard. In the case of discrimination based on age, class, race, and ethnicity, the marginalization is pronounced. In particular, nowhere is marginalization more evident than in the situation of Indigenous children and families. Generally speaking, children in care are in care in their homes, in the child welfare system, in their schools and communities, and "in" the culture. Within these environments, problems might be individualized and not put into context. Children might be labelled in various contexts, and not just in child welfare. They might be treated as outsiders. They might be affected by discriminatory school suspension policies. Access to health care might be an issue, with doctors at times not taking new patients, and paperwork requirements for children in care being a disincentive in this regard. There might be an excessive or inappropriate use of psychotropic medications (Waldock, 2007, 2011). This list of challenges could be expanded. Participation (voice) and advocacy support are especially important for children requiring the care and support of the child welfare system.

Are there positive signs when it comes to participation rights? To some degree there are, even if many challenges remain. As previously pointed out, the UNCRC has not been incorporated into child welfare legislation across the country to the extent that it should be, although there are some signs of progress (Ontario—Preamble) in this regard. But it should be pointed out that most provincial/territorial child welfare legislation does accord rights to children, and participation rights often are highlighted. More coordination is required across provinces and territories because there are considerable variations; for example, there are differences in terms of age requirements and the extent to which children are able to participate. Jan Hancock covers many of the variations between provinces in detail in Chapter 12. The same is true of other advocacy services; there are variations across the country in the roles and responsibilities of children's lawyers, child advocates, and ombudsmen (Howe, 2001). Here as elsewhere—aside from more formal incorporation of the UNCRC—a national children's commissioner is required in order to formalize and increase levels of coordination and avoid geographical inconsistency and discrimination.

But irrespective of the above observations and concerns, the fact remains that participation rights are included in child welfare legislation across the country. For example, Part 4 of British Columbia's *Child, Family, and Community Services Act* (CFCSA) outlines the rights of children in care, including the right "to be consulted and to express their views, according to their abilities, about significant decisions affecting them" (Government of British Columbia, n.d.). And in Ontario, the participation rights accorded to children are the most extensive and explicit, covered in Part 2 (sections 3 and 8) of the *Child, Youth and Family Services Act* (CYFSA) (Government of Ontario, n.d.). Children have the right to participate in decisions affecting them, and their views are to be "given due weight, in accordance with their age and maturity," mirroring the wording of Article 12 of the UNCRC. Despite the shortcomings, then, in relation to more formal incorporation of the UNCRC and issues of coordination and consistency, there are signs of progress in relation to participation rights. To be clear, in no way does this suggest adherence to the children's rights stage of the evolutionary framework (status of children); it simply suggests some light on the horizon.

A similar analysis applies to provincial and territorial children's advocates, charged with supporting children and advocating on their behalf. Again, the challenges around coordination and consistency, and the lack of a national children's advocate, are apparent. M. Theresa Hunter covers these variations and challenges in detail in Chapter 13, including the observation that the UNCRC is embedded in Provincial Advocate for Children and Youth legislation only in Yukon, Nunavut, and Ontario (Hunter's Chapter 13). But again, there has been some evidence of progress that pertains to advocacy for marginalized youth in the area of child welfare. Many advocates have been extremely active in lobbying for positive change and providing critical reports in the area of child welfare. But from the point of view of children themselves being engaged in constructive activism, the Ontario example is a good one. With a legislative mandate to "partner" with children to bring issues forward, follow UNCRC's principles (which includes Article 12), and be an "exemplar for meaningful participation" (Government of Ontario, Provincial Advocate for Children and Youth Act, n.d.), the advocate has facilitated youth—in or from care—participation that has been very effective in influencing the provincial government. The closure of that office (2018) (Hunter's Chapter 13), then, is a definite setback and all the more disappointing given the headway that it had made under the advocate at the time (Irwin Elman).

Given the extent of their marginalization, and conditions that undermine the ability to participate, the need to support children in care is pronounced. At times these children require independent advocacy (child advocates) in their dealings with caregivers, agencies, governments, and others. While this type is advocacy is very important, it is not sufficient. It is bureaucratic in nature, and somewhat removed from children's everyday lives. Marginalized children need advocacy embedded in their day-to-day lives. Social workers are not present on a daily basis, and regardless, with paperwork and other bureaucratic demands, their advocacy role for children in care has been declining (Boylan & Ing, 2005). Family may not be present either, and even if they are involved, they may not be a position to provide this support.

Children in care need their voices amplified, and caregivers are in the best position to provide this type of advocacy because it can be "immediate and informed, built upon the experience of sharing lives and struggles, and witnessing first-hand a child's interaction with workers, agencies, teachers, schools, and communities" (Waldock, 2007, p. 309). Caregivers with strong advocacy skills and the ability to navigate complex systems (child welfare, educational, and perhaps legal) are required in a society and culture that discriminates against marginalized populations (Waldock, 2007, 2011). But this recognition simply requires us to circle back to a system of care (previous section) that is in dire need of reform. Just as the quality of that system compromises the ability to meet UNCRC requirements to provide protection and quality care (Articles 20 and 39) for victims of neglect and abuse, so too does it undermine the participatory rights (Article 12) of children in care by not ensuring that caregivers have the competencies required to support and empower the voice of children in their care. With regard to participation and voice, the failure to provide embedded advocacy for children in care is the Achilles heel of the child welfare system in Canada.

Given the extent of children's marginalization in the child welfare context, and thus the pronounced need for participation (voice) and advocacy support, the progress to date is inadequate. The best that can be said is that progress in the area of participation rights does represent a glimmer of light on the horizon and a movement in the right direction.

CONCLUSION

If Canada were to advance a children's rights agenda, substantial reform of the child welfare system would be required. The following interrelated priorities have been highlighted: address the situation of marginalized groups of children, particularly Indigenous children, and increase funding to address existing inequities, especially those affecting preventative services; incorporate the UNCRC into all child welfare legislation across the country, and institute a national children's commissioner to help facilitate more coordination and consistency moving forward; move to a family service paradigm of policy and practice with a children's rights focus in the context of an overall commitment to proactive, preventative child and family policies; vastly improve systems of care (for example, inclusive foster care) and the competencies of caregivers; and amplify the voice of children in care by coordinating advocacy services and ensuring embedded advocacy.

Children requiring the care and support of child welfare deserve to be treated with dignity and respect. Child welfare should be leading the way in terms of addressing the conditions of their marginalization, and facilitating their status as rights-bearing citizens.

QUESTIONS FOR DISCUSSION

1. What does it mean to say that children requiring the care and support of the child welfare system are marginalized? How might this marginalization affect their day-to-day lives?

2. In your view, what are the most significant criticisms of the Anglo-American child protection model of practice? How should the critique of this model inform reform priorities?

3. What is the solution to the crisis of care in child welfare?

REFERENCES

Alcock, P., & Craig, G. (2009). *International social policy: Welfare regimes in the developing world* (2nd ed.). Basingstoke: Palgrave Macmillan.

Andersen, J. G., Guillemard, A., Jensen, Per H., & Pfau-Effinger, B. (2005). *The changing face of welfare: Consequences and outcomes from a citizenship perspective.* Bristol: Policy.

Bagnell, K. (2001) *The little immigrants: The orphans who came to Canada.* Toronto: Dundurn Group.

Ballingall, A. (2018, February 1). Ottawa commits to new First Nations child welfare funding. *The Star.* Retrieved from https://www.thestar.com/news/canada/2018/02/01/ottawa-commits-to-new-first-nations-child-welfare-funding.html

Barrera, J. (2017, November 2). Indigenous child welfare rates creating "humanitarian crisis" in Canada, says federal minister, *CBC News.* Retrieved from https://www.cbc.ca/news/indigenous/crisis-philpott-child-welfare-1.4385136

BC Representative for Children and Youth. (2017). *Delegated Aboriginal agencies: How resourcing affects service delivery.* Victoria, BC: Office of the Representative for Children and Youth.

BC Representative for Children and Youth. (2010). *No shortcuts to safety: Doing better for children living with extended family.* Victoria, BC: Office of the Representative for Children and Youth.

Bernstein, M. (2009). *A breach of trust: An investigation into foster home overcrowding in the Saskatoon Service Centre.* Saskatchewan Children's Advocate.

Bernstein, M. (2016). Honouring the twenty-fifth anniversary of the United Nations Convention on the Rights of the Child: Transforming child welfare in Canada into a stronger child rights-based system. In H. Montgomery, D. Badry, D. Fuchs, & D. Kikulwe (Eds.), *Transforming child welfare: Interdisciplinary practices, field education, and research* (pp. 3–26). Regina, SK: University of Regina Press.

Birdsell, M., & Chan, E. (2017). *Application of the UNCRC in Canadian law—children's participation in justice processes: Finding the best way forward.* Retrieved from http://findingthebestwaysforward.com/Materials/4B%20PPt%20CRC%20and%20Charter%20-%20Birdsell%20Chan.pdf

Blackstock, C. (2003). First Nations child and family services: Restoring peace and harmony in First Nations communities. In K. Kufeldt & B. McKenzie (Eds.), *Child welfare: Connecting research, policy and practice* (pp. 331–342). Waterloo, ON: Wilfrid Laurier University Press.

Boylan, J., & Ing, P. (2005). Seen but not heard—young people's experience of advocacy. *International Journal of Social Welfare, 14*(1), 2–12.

Cameron, G., Coady, N., & Adams, G. (2007). *Moving toward positive systems of child and family welfare.* Waterloo, ON: Wilfrid Laurier University Press.

Canadian Human Rights Tribunal (CHRT). (2016, January 26). *First Nations Child and Family Caring Society of Canada et al. v. Attorney General of Canada,* 2016 CHRT 2. Retrieved from https://decisions.chrt-tcdp.gc.ca/chrt-tcdp/decisions/en/item/127700/index.do

CBC Radio. (2018, January 30). The Current: *The millennium scoop: Indigenous youth say care system repeats horrors of the past.* Retrieved from https://www.cbc.ca/radio/thecurrent/a-special-edition-of-the-current-for-january-25-2018-1.4503172/the-millennium-scoop-indigenous-youth-say-care-system-repeats-horrors-of-the-past-1.4503179

Charles, R. (2018, July 5). Negligence charges for former child welfare official after kids abused in foster care. *CBC News.* Retrieved from https://www.cbc.ca/news/canada/prince-edward-county-foster-care-abuse-negligence-charges-1.4723516

Connolly, M. (2003). *Kinship care: A selected literature review.* Wellington, New Zealand: Department of Child, Youth and Family.

Conway, J. (2003). *The Canadian family in crisis.* Toronto: James Lorimer & Company.

Covell, K., & Howe, R. B. (2009). *Children, families and violence: Challenges for children's rights.* London: Jessica Kingsley.

Esping-Andersen, G. (1990). *The three worlds of welfare capitalism.* London: Polity Press.

Fallon, B., Chabot, M., Fluke, J., Blackstock, C., MacLauren, B., & Tonmyr, L. (2013). Placement decisions and disparities among Aboriginal children: Further analysis of the Canadian incidence study of reported child abuse and neglect, Part A: Comparisons of the 1998 and 2003 surveys. *Child Abuse and Neglect, 37*(1), 47–60.

First Nations Child and Family Caring Society (FNCFCS). (n.d.). i am a witness: Canadian Human Rights Tribunal hearing—*Tribunal timeline and documents.* Retrieved from https://fncaringsociety.com/tribunal-timeline-and-documents#2007

Flynn, R. J., Dudding, P. M., & Barber, J. G. (2006). *Promoting resilience in child welfare.* Ottawa: University of Ottawa Press.

Fontaine, T. (2016, January 26) Canada discriminates against children on reserves, tribunal rules. *CBC News*. Retrieved from https://www.cbc.ca/news/indigenous/canada-discriminates-against-children-on-reserves-tribunal-rules-1.3419480

Freeman, M. (2007). Why it remains important to take children's rights seriously. *International Journal of Children's Rights, 15*(1), 5–23.

Gilbert, N. (Ed.). (1997). *Combatting child abuse: International perspectives and trends*. Oxford: Oxford University Press.

Gilbert, N., Parton, N., & Skivenes, M. (Eds.). (2011). *Child protection systems: International trends and orientations*. Oxford: Oxford University Press.

Government of British Columbia. (n.d.). *Child, Family and Community Service Act* (CFCSA). Retrieved from http://www.bclaws.ca/civix/document/id/complete/statreg/96046_01#section70

Government of Ontario. (n.d.). *Child, Youth and Family Services Act* (CYFSA). Retrieved from https://www.ontario.ca/laws/statute/17c14

Government of Ontario. (n.d.). *Provincial Advocate for Children and Youth Act*. Retrieved from https://www.ontario.ca/laws/statute/07p09#BK19

Hammarberg, T. (1990). The UN Convention on the Rights of the Child—and how to make it work. *Human Rights Quarterly, 12*(1), 97–105.

Heimer, M., Nasman, E., & Palme, J. (2018). Vulnerable children's rights to participation, protection, and provision: The process of defining the problem in Swedish child and family welfare. *Child and Family Social Work, 23*(2), 316–323.

Heimer, M., & Palme, J. (2016). Rethinking child policy post–UN Convention on the Rights of the Child: Vulnerable children's welfare in Sweden. *Journal of Social Policy, 45*(3), 435–452.

Hetherington, R., & Nurse, T. (2006). Promoting change from "child protection" to "child and family welfare": The problems of the English system. In N. Freymond & G. Cameron (Eds.), *Towards positive systems of child and family welfare* (pp. 53–83). Toronto: University of Toronto Press.

Howe, R. B. (2001). Implementing children's rights in a federal state: The case of Canada's child protection system. *International Journal of Children's Rights, 9*(4), 361–382.

Howe, R. B., & Covell, K. (Eds.). (2007). *Children's rights in Canada: A question of commitment*. Waterloo, ON: Wilfrid Laurier University Press.

Kufeldt, K. (1994). Inclusive foster care: Implementation of the model. In B. McKenzie (Ed.), *Current perspectives on foster family care for children and youth* (pp. 84–100). Toronto: Wall and Emerson.

National Youth in Care Network. (2005). *Current themes facing youth in state care*. Backgrounder Series #3. Ottawa, ON: National Youth in Care Network

Ontario Association of Children's Aid Societies (OACAS). (2017, December 5). *Class action lawsuit on behalf of Crown wards*. Retrieved from http://www.oacas.org/2017/12/class-action-lawsuit-on-behalf-of-crown-wards/

OECD. (2016). *Society at a glance 2016: OECD social indicators*. Paris: OECD Publishing. Retrieved from http://dx.doi.org/10.1787/9789264261488-en

Ontario Human Rights Commission (OHRC). (2018). *Interrupted childhoods: Over-representation of Indigenous and black children in Ontario child welfare*. Toronto, ON: Ontario Human Rights Commission.

Ploug, N. (2012). The Nordic child care regime—history, development and challenges. *Children and Youth Services Review, 34*(3), 517–522.

Schwartz, C., Waddell, C., Barican, J., Gray-Grant, D., Dickson, S., & Nightingale, L. (2014). Kinship foster care. *Children's Mental Health Research Quarterly, 8*(3), 1–16. Vancouver: Children's Health Policy Centre, Faculty of Health Sciences, Simon Fraser University.

Sinclair, R. (2016). The Indigenous child removal system in Canada: An examination of legal decision-making and racial bias. *First Peoples Child and Family Review, 11*(2), 8–18.

Sinha, V., Trocmé, N., Blackstock, C., MacLaurin, B., & Fallon, B. (2011). Understanding the overrepresentation of First Nations children in Canada's child welfare system. In K. Kufeldt & B. McKenzie (Eds.), *Child welfare: Connecting research, policy and practice* (2nd ed.) (pp. 307–322). Waterloo, ON: Wilfrid Laurier University Press.

Smith, R. (2018). Reconsidering value perspectives in child welfare. *British Journal of Social Work, 48*(3), 616–632.

Strong-Boag, V. (2002). Getting to now: Children in distress in Canada's past. In B. Wharf (Ed.), *Community work approaches to child welfare* (pp. 29–46). Peterborough, ON: Broadview Press.

Strong-Boag, V. (2011). *Fostering nation? Canada confronts its history of childhood disadvantage*. Waterloo, ON: Wilfrid Laurier University Press.

Stueck, W. (2017, February 8). Lack of foster homes spurs rise in costly contract care for province. *Globe and Mail*. Retrieved from https://www.theglobeandmail.com/news/british-columbia/lack-of-foster-homes-spurs-rise-in-costly-contract-care-for-province/article33961974/

Trocmé, N., Fallon, B., MacLaurin, B., Daciuk, J., Felstiner, C., Black, T., Tonmyr, L., Blackstock, C., Barter, K., Turcotte, D., & Cloutier, R. (2005). *Canadian incidence study of reported child abuse and neglect—2003: Major findings*. Gatineau, QC: Minister of Public Works and Government Services Canada.

Truth and Reconciliation Commission of Canada (TRCC) (2015). *Honouring the Truth, Reconciling for the Future: Summary of the Final Report of the Truth and Reconciliation Commission of Canada*. Retrieved from http://www.trc.ca/websites/trcinstitution/File/2015/Findings/Exec_Summary_2015_05_31_web_o.pdf

UNICEF Office of Research. (2017). Building the future: Children and the sustainable development goals in rich countries. *Innocenti Report Card 14*. Florence: UNICEF Office of Research.

United Nations General Assembly. (2010). *Guidelines for the alternative care of children*. Document a/res/64/142. New York: United National General Assembly.

Waldock, T. (2007). The rights of children in care: Consistency with the Convention? In R. B. Howe & K. Covell (Eds.), *Children's rights in Canada: A question of commitment*. Waterloo, ON: Wilfrid Laurier University Press.

Waldock, T. (2011). Enhancing the quality of care in child welfare: Our obligation under the UN Convention on the Rights of the Child, *Relational Child and Youth Care Practice, 24*(3), 50–61.

Waldock, T. (2012). Apologize ... for goodness sake: Canada's "home children" and our history of discrimination against marginalized children. *Relational Child and Youth Care Practice, 25*(2), 69–75.

Waldock, T. (2016). Theorising children's rights and child welfare paradigms. *International Journal of Children's Rights, 24*(2), 304–329.

Wharf, B. (2000). Cases or citizens: Viewing child welfare through a different lens. *Canadian Social Work, 2*(2), 132–136.

Chapter 7
Assessing the Rights and Realities of War-Affected Refugee Children in Canada

Myriam Denov and Maya Fennig

THE IMPORTANCE OF CONTEXT: THE REALITIES OF WAR-AFFECTED REFUGEE CHILDREN

The realities of armed conflict are increasingly impacting the lives of children and families around the globe. The increase in armed conflict in countries like Syria, Democratic Republic of the Congo, Iraq, South Sudan, and Afghanistan represents the highest level of human suffering since World War Two. Exposure to armed violence has been shown to be a key risk factor on children's psychological functioning (Fazel, Reed, Panter-Brick, & Stein, 2012). War ruptures healthy child development, causes injury, illness, severs familial and social networks, and breaks down the structures that provide preventive, curative, and ameliorative care (Devakumar, Birch, Osrin, Sondorp, & Wells, 2014). The United Nations estimates that over 60 million people worldwide are currently displaced by war, armed conflict, or persecution. In fact, flight as a result of armed conflict is at a 20-year high, while the number of internally displaced persons is at its highest level in 50 years (Miller & Rasmussen, 2017). Children comprise 51 percent of the 65.3 million forcibly displaced by war worldwide (UNHCR, 2016a).

Children and families who flee violence and persecution and resettle in other countries often endure great psychosocial challenges during displacement and continue to suffer major challenges after their arrival in a new context (Fazel et al., 2012). Flight may expose refugees to serious injury, rape, imprisonment, torture, and combat situations (Ee et al., 2013). In their study of unaccompanied minors who fled war situations, Denov and Bryan (2012) highlight the ways in which flight frequently involved not only navigating escapes from violence and warfare, but also profound experiences of famine, drought, and travelling on foot over long distances in their attempts to seek refuge. For half of the world's refugees, flight also means remaining in "protracted situations" within unstable and insecure locations, often in refugee camps in deplorable conditions with minimal services and rights (Shakya et al., 2014).

While flight from armed violence presents profound challenges, so does resettlement to a new country and context. Indeed, research has shown that post-migration stressors profoundly impact the mental health and well-being for both adults and children. In fact, it has been shown that *post-migration stressors predict distress as powerfully as war exposure* (Miller & Rasmussen, 2017). Post-migration stressors, which have been shown to worsen the physical and mental health of refugees (Shakya et al., 2014), include social isolation resulting from loss of social networks (Denov & Bryan, 2014; Priebe, Burns, & Craig, 2013); loss of home and homeland (Ee, Sleijpen, Kleber, & Jongmans, 2013); unemployment due to lack of skill or to host society restrictions on permission to work (Miller & Rasmussen, 2017); poverty (Rasmussen et al., 2010); perceived discrimination (Ellis, MacDonald, Lincoln, & Cabral, 2008; Fazel et al., 2012; Denov & Bryan, 2010); increased family violence (Betancourt et al., 2012); and challenges navigating uncertain legal status and immigration procedures (Miller & Rasmussen, 2017; Fazel et al., 2012; Denov & Bryan, 2014; Lacroix & Sabbah, 2011).

Ultimately, research has consistently shown that the mental health impact of armed conflict is compounded or alleviated by contexts of migration and resettlement. In this sense, the mental health of refugees is powerfully influenced by war-related violence and loss *combined with* the conditions they encounter en route to and within their host countries (Miller & Rasmussen, 2017, p. 129).

War is a global phenomenon yet is intimately linked to children and families living in Canada. Each year, thousands of children enter Canada, fleeing war zones (Stewart, 2011). Canada receives between 25,000 and 35,000 refugees every year. This represents about 10–12 percent of the roughly 250,000 permanent residents who settle in Canada annually (Immigration, Refugees and Citizenship Canada, 2015). Compared to 2015, the 2016 resettlement level reflects a striking 133 percent increase. This is due in part to the success of Canada's humanitarian transfer of Syrian refugees carried throughout 2016 with UNHCR's support. The United Nations High Commissioner for Refugees (UNHCR, 2017b) praised Canada for providing solutions to the plight of a record 62,000 refugees through their resettlement to Canada in 2016 (IRCC, 2017a). This is the largest number of refugees admitted in a year since the implementation of the 1976 *Immigration Act*. On average, about 11,000 refugees come as "sponsored refugees" under the Refugee and Humanitarian Resettlement Stream: 7,500 as government-assisted refugees; and 3,500 as privately sponsored refugees. An estimated 12,000–19,000 come to Canada through the "in-Canada Asylum" stream in which people apply as refugee claimants upon entering Canada and then become "permanent residents" once their claim process is approved by the Immigration and Refugee Board. The remaining 5,000 resettle in Canada as family dependents of people who have come as refugees (IRCC, 2015).

Between January 2015 and May 2017, a total of 34,360 resettled refugee children (17 years old and under) were admitted to Canada (IRCC, 2017). Out of these, an estimated total of 10,750 were from Syria (IRCC, 2017). Of the 46,702 refugees resettled in 2016, 46 percent are minors (UNHCR, 2017a). According to the Canada Border Services Agency, refugee claims filed for minors 17 years old or younger have increased from 2,011 in 2015 to 3,400 in 2016 (Kalaichandran, 2017). According to researchers and clinicians working in the Canadian context, child refugees are at risk for a variety of mental health challenges that depend upon their age and developmental stage, particularly when there are pre- and post-trauma risks (Measham et al., 2014). Although there is a growing literature on war-affected refugee children in Canada (Pacione, Measham, & Rousseau, 2013; Rousseau et al., 2013b), our understanding of their lived realities, their flight and resettlement experiences, and service provision needs once in Canada deserves greater attention.

This chapter examines the rights and realities of war-affected refugee children and its implications for Canada. We focus on Article 38(4) and Article 39 of the United Nations Convention on the Rights of the Child (UNCRC), which are of particular relevance to war, postwar, and resettlement experiences. To further substantiate and authenticate the points raised in the literature, we highlight the voices and experiences of 22 war-affected youth currently living in Canada who fled contexts of armed violence as children. The participants, interviewed in 2013 by the first author and colleagues, are part of a larger study exploring the reintegration experiences of war-affected youth living in Canada (Denov & Blanchet-Cohen, 2016; Blanchet-Cohen & Denov, 2015). These participants help to articulate and give voice to the key issues facing this unique population living in Canada. We examine Canada's response to war-affected refugee children, particularly as they relate to the unique situation of unaccompanied refugee minors, children in detention, family reunification responses, and refugee children's access to education and health services.

THE RIGHTS OF WAR-AFFECTED REFUGEE CHILDREN: EXPLORING THE PROVISIONS IN THE UNCRC

Article 38 of the UNCRC

Article 38 of the UNCRC establishes that children have the right to be protected during times of war and that governments must do everything they can to prevent child recruitment into armed groups, and to protect and care for children affected by war. Article 38(4) outlines that: "In accordance with their obligations under international humanitarian law to protect the civilian population in armed conflicts, State Parties shall take all feasible measures to ensure protection and care of children who are affected by an armed conflict."

Despite the UNCRC's provisions under Article 38, as well as the Optional Protocol on the Involvement of Children in Armed Conflict, which prohibit the recruitment of children under 18 into armed groups, children across the globe continue to be implicated in armed conflict. It has been well documented in the literature that children, both boys and girls, living in conflict zones contend with overwhelming rights violations and experiences of victimization, and insecurity on multiple levels (Denov, 2010; Wessells, 2006). Globally, nearly 87 million children have been growing up in conflict zones in devastating conditions of violence and deprivation that can hinder their development and long-term well-being (Mis, 2016). Children lack access to adequate food and nutrition, education, health care, and often live in dire poverty. In cases where children are separated from their families and communities, and recruited into armed groups, the security and survival of traditional communities, cultures, and values are put severely at risk. Moreover, children's personal and physical security is constantly threatened through acts of torture, violence, and abuse—whether physical, sexual, or psychological.

Participants interviewed reported witnessing and/or directly experiencing severe and unimaginable violence and upheaval in their countries of origin. The following participants describe the context in which they lived, which was characterized by ongoing violence, insecurity, and poverty: "Where there is war, there is no peace, there is no safety, there is no stability, so there are always problems, day and night. It affected a lot: it affected us physically, it affected us psychologically, it affected us morally, it affected us in every possible way ... the disgust, not even feelings, to feel not at home, in your own country. It's just too much.... We lived like that, we grew up like that, in constant peril, threats from left to right."

Etched in their memories, participants vividly recalled key wartime events and circumstances. This male participant from Democratic Republic of

Congo recalled the pervasive feelings of fear and insecurity: "It was around ... three in the afternoon. The weather, during the war ... you can also feel there is a difference. It was a clear sunny day, even the birds weren't singing. Even the sun wasn't ... shining the way it should."

The glaring rights violations of the young people are revealed not only in the profound lack of protections provided to them during armed violence, but also in the significant losses of loved ones. The violent and senseless murders of family members and close friends profoundly marked participants' lives:

> They did come after me. I was hiding ... I stayed in the forest, [in the] bush for months, yeah two months, because I was hiding, so that they won't kill me. They had killed all my family members, and they were looking [for me]. Because, it's like, your neighbours, they know everybody at home. They know they have already killed this and that, this and that, and this one is remaining. Yeah, they knew I was still there, and they were looking for me.... They don't want anyone to remain. So, like I think they had a list of people.... They put a check[mark], this one is killed. This one is remaining, question mark. Where is this person? And they start searching for you.... I lost my entire family ... the entire family. Sisters, brothers, father, mother, grandparents, aunts, uncles.

The above narratives provide a snapshot of the intensity of young people's experiences where war ravaged their livelihoods, families, and in multiple ways truncated their childhoods. The participants' poignant narratives reveal the continued breach of their rights. Indeed, the obligation to provide "protection and care" to children was infringed upon repeatedly and violently.

Article 39 of the UNCRC

In relation to the postwar and resettlement context, Article 39 articulates that:

> States Parties shall take all appropriate measures to promote physical and psychological recovery and social reintegration of a child victim of: any form of neglect, exploitation, or abuse; torture or any other form of cruel, inhuman or degrading treatment or punishment; or armed conflicts. Such recovery and reintegration shall take place in an environment that fosters the health, self-respect and dignity of the child.

According to Article 39, once resettled in Canada, provincial and federal governments have an obligation to promote the physical and psychological recovery and social reintegration of children who have been affected by war.

In the following section, we address the realities of unaccompanied refugee minors, detention, family reunification, school integration, and access to quality services in the realms of education and health, all of which are integral to understanding the resettlement experiences of war-affected refugee children in Canada.

UNACCOMPANIED REFUGEE MINORS

Representing between 360,000 and 900,000 children globally (2–5 percent of the approximate 18 million refugees worldwide) (Montgomery, Rousseau, & Shermarke, 2001), an unaccompanied minor is defined as "a person who is under the age of eighteen years, unless, under the law applicable to the child, majority is attained earlier and who is separated from both parents and is not being cared for by an adult who by law or custom has the responsibility to do so" (UNHCR as cited in Ayotte, 2001, p. 6). These children often flee their countries of origin as a result of war, forced military recruitment, abandonment, poverty, ethnic or political persecution, and other human rights abuses (Mann, 2001). Given that parents and other supportive adults often mediate or buffer the effects of difficult experiences in a child's life, unaccompanied children may face greater risk than other refugee children because of the interplay between traumatic experiences and separation from significant emotional relationships (Rousseau, Said, Gagné, & Bibeau, 1998; Sourander, 1998). Although most of these children live in refugee camps or spontaneously self-settle in the developing world, a small proportion arrive in industrialized countries, including Canada, which has experienced a gradual increase in the number of unaccompanied child refugee claimants (Ali, Taraban, & Gill, 2003).

While data on the issue are scarce, in 2007, the number of independent child migrants arriving in Canada rose by 18 percent compared with 2006 (CIC, 2018). While boys continue to be overrepresented, the number of female child asylum seekers arriving in Canada has also increased (CIC, 2018). In Canada, it is estimated that approximately 300 separated children arrive each year. These young people represent one of two principle categories of separated refugee children in Canada. Like other asylum seekers, they request asylum upon arrival in Canada, either at the border or inland. And while this is their right (as mandated by both Canadian and international refugee protection law), their legal status and standing in Canada is tenuous, contingent upon a successful refugee determination process and mediated largely by the supportive services they are able to access (or not). The second group of unaccompanied children are those who arrive via the Government-Assisted Refugee (GAR) program. These young people arrive as refugees and, as such, are permanent Canadian residents with the rights and privileges thereof. Since 2001, however, a moratorium has restricted the settlement of separated children who do not have family in Canada. Both groups face considerable challenges upon arrival, and while the former must contend with the inconsistencies and contradictions of Canadian refugee protection, both must navigate the precarious terrain of resettlement and integration into a new culture and context.

In 1996, the federal government established a loose set of protocols intended to standardize the treatment of unaccompanied children throughout the determination process, as well as guarantee their rights as children. Nonetheless, a cohesive *federal* policy concerning their protection has yet to materialize. Moreover, formal Canadian integration programs and services are designed to address the needs of adults rather than children (Wouk et al., 2006). Similarly, child welfare services may be ill-equipped to deal with these children (Denov & Bryan, 2012). This situation is, in part, the result of jurisdictional precedent that designates immigration as a primarily federal responsibility and child welfare as a provincial responsibility. As a result, there are considerable inconsistencies in terms of the services available to unaccompanied children across the country.

Upon arrival, unaccompanied children often live in temporary group residences for refugees or youth. If extended family is present, the child may be placed with a family member. In some cases, unaccompanied children in Canada may be detained (Canadian Council for Refugees, 2004). This may occur when the child's identity or age is in question, or, in cases where trafficking is suspected, for the child's protection. In accordance with the 1996 protocols, once a claim for asylum has been made, a designated representative is appointed to assist the child through the process. Despite recommendations for expedited determination processes for children, unaccompanied children can wait for several years for the outcome of their claim (Bryan & Denov, 2011). Importantly, however, not all unaccompanied children are granted asylum. When this happens, there are avenues available for recourse; for example, the child can apply for permanent residency under humanitarian and compassionate grounds. In rare cases, children may be deported. The barriers experienced by unaccompanied children may resemble the needs of other immigrant children. However, these children appear to face additional challenges of coping with loss and trauma, profound isolation, limited educational opportunities, and financial hardship.

The trauma associated with flight, separation from family, and resettlement in a new context cannot be underestimated or oversimplified. Although commonalities exist, the experiences of unaccompanied children vary depending largely upon gender, age, social location in the country of origin, family structure, status in receiving states, and the complexity of events leading to flight, flight, and available supports in Canada. Practitioners must be cognizant of these differences, and the reality that unaccompanied children may be fearful and wary of discussing issues of flight.

Detention

Every year, thousands of migrants are placed in detention in Canada. In 2013, a total of 7,300 people were detained. A third of these individuals were put in provincial jails alongside inmates facing criminal charges or serving sentences (Canadian Human Rights Commission, 2017). The remaining were distributed between Canada's three immigration holding centres in Montreal, Toronto, and Vancouver, run by Canada Border Services Agency, which is responsible for carrying out immigration detention.

While living in detention is never in the best interest of children, and detention should therefore be avoided—a principle is firmly established in international law—Canada continues to hold children in detention. According to official statistics provided by Canada Border Services Agency (2017), between 2014 and 2017, a total of 595 children were detained in immigration holding centres (IHC), 43 of which were unaccompanied refugee minors. Importantly, however, the true number of detained children is likely to be higher, as the above figures do not account for children who are themselves not under formal detention orders, but are accompanying parents who are (Gros, 2017). These children are de facto detained, but have been invisible to statistics (Gros & Song, 2016). According to figures obtained by the International Human Rights program through access to information requests between 2011 and 2015, an average of at least 48 Canadian children stayed in the Toronto immigration holding centre for some period of time (Gros, 2017).

Children are likely to be detained in Canada for three principal reasons: (1) a child's identity is being confirmed (most often in the case of asylum seekers); (2) an officer deems a child unlikely to appear for a meeting or hearing (thus deemed a flight risk); and (3) a child is considered a danger to the public. According to Kronick, Rousseau, and Cleveland (2017), between 2010 and 2014 fewer than five children per year have been held for alleged dangerousness.

Detention facilities are profoundly detrimental to children. Immigration holding centres (IHCs) are medium-security facilities where children are subject to constant surveillance, searches, and restricted mobility. In IHCs, men and women are held in separate wings, with a special range for children detained with their mothers (Silverman & Molnar, 2016). Family separation within the facilities inherently limits children's contact and interaction with key family members, particularly fathers. Children held within these facilities have limited educational opportunities that have been deemed inconsistent in terms of quality and frequency, and where opportunities for recreation and social interaction with other children are severely curtailed. Instead, under-stimulation, boredom, and a sense of powerlessness may prevail (Gros & Song, 2016).

Research has demonstrated that living in immigration detention causes serious psychological harm to children. Children who have lived in detention experience increased symptoms of depression, anxiety, post-traumatic stress, and suicidal ideation. Many children also experience developmental delays and behavioural issues (Mares, 2016; Lorek et al., 2009; Robjant, Hassan, & Katona, 2009). These mental health consequences often persist long after the children have been released, affecting their adjustment to life post-detention (Kronick et al., 2017).

Canada's current practices relating to immigration detention of children are in violation of its international and legal obligations (Gros & Song, 2016). In fact, the United Nations Committee on the Rights of the Child has repeatedly admonished and chastised Canada for its practice of child detention. In its 2012 report, the UN Committee expressed that it is "deeply concerned that the frequent detention of asylum-seeking children is being done without consideration for the best interests of the child" and urged Canada to use detention only as a measure of last resort.

The foundational principle of the best interests of the child—enshrined in the Convention on the Rights of the Child—should become a primary consideration in all detention-related decisions affecting children. Currently, the best interests of the child are inadequately protected. The use of detention speaks to Canada's proclivity toward security and immigration control and illuminates the contradictory rhetoric of children's rights and protection on the one hand, and security and immigration control on the other (see Bryan & Denov, 2011).

The following participants articulated the fear and loss of dignity that they experienced upon arrival to Canada:

> And so they [immigration] put me in this room.... And it was just an empty room with like you know those concrete cinder blocks, just painted.... Just a hard bench, and there was nothing else in the room. Maybe a couple of posters. You know, like, "Welcome to Canada" posters. And I remember seeing these posters of all these happy faces of people coming to Canada. And there was this juxtaposition of my misery just sitting in there, you know, and thinking to myself, "These guys

really don't care." A certain part of my dignity had been lost, because as far as these guys [immigration] are concerned this is just another refugee coming into Canada trying to seek political asylum.

[Coming from Sierra Leone] I never knew where the ship was going. I just saw the ship ... we boarded the vessel [illegally] ... we hid in a container. When I think about the way we came here, it makes me cry. Because it was too tough. It's too tough. Only God who saved us from that journey.... It really was tough.... I arrived at the Montreal seaport. But we never knew where we were.... When we arrived [in Montreal immigration] they handcuffed me.... I was afraid, for sure.... That was my first time in my life [to be handcuffed].... I was afraid, really.

Family Reunification

Children's rights to family, including the prevention of separation and the preservation of family unity, is recognized and protected in the UNCRC. Article 9 states that "States Parties shall respect the right of the child who is separated from one or both parents to maintain personal relations and direct contact with both parents on a regular basis, except if it is contrary to the child's best interests." The committee advises on this right in both their General Comments No. 6 and No. 14. The committee explicitly notes in General Comment No. 14 (2013) that "When the child's relations with his or her parents are interrupted by migration (of the parents without the child, or of the child without his or her parents), preservation of the family unit should be taken into account when assessing the best interests of the child in decisions on family reunification." In Canada, the prominence of family reunification has been acknowledged in two of the main stated objectives of the *Immigration and Refugee Protection Act* (IRPA) with respect to immigration: "to see that families are reunited in Canada" and, with respect to refugees, "to support the self-sufficiency and the social and economic well-being of refugees by facilitating reunification with their family members in Canada."

These objectives are supported by research findings that highlight the crucial role family unity plays in the mental health and well-being of refugees (Nickerson, Bryant, Steel, Silove, & Brooks, 2010). A recent systematic review on the mental health of displaced and refugee children emphasized the protective role of family and social support (Fazel et al., 2012), whereas extended separation from family members has been found to serve as a major barrier to children's mental health and well-being (Rousseau, Mekki-Berrada, & Moreau, 2001). Children's ability to reunite with their families has been repeatedly highlighted as a major concern for refugee groups (Luster, Qin, Bates, Johnson, & Rana, 2008). In a recent study conducted by Choummanivong, Poole, and Cooper (2014), 85 percent of participants reported family reunification issues as the principal obstacle to their effective resettlement. In Canada, studies have consistently highlighted the negative effects of family separation on the child's well-being and the significant stress they encounter upon reunification (Rousseau et al., 2001; Rousseau, Rufagari, Bagilishya, & Measham, 2004).

The importance of family reunification is also acknowledged by the Canadian government through its allocation of up to 80,000 places annually for reuniting families (Mas, 2016). Moreover, recently Immigration, Refugees and Citizenship Canada amended the Immigration and Refugee Protection Regulations, changing the definition of dependent child in the Regulations from "less than 19 years of age" to "less than 22 years of age." When publicizing the proposed change, the IRCC (2017b) stated that "when immigrant and refugee families are able to remain together, their integration into Canada and their ability to work and contribute to their communities improve." This increase will hopefully allow thousands of young adult children the opportunity to reunite with their families.

Yet important disparities in policies regarding family reunification persist. Currently, Canadian law does not provide avenues by which separated refugee children can be reunited with their parents and siblings who are outside the country. Under the *Immigration and Refugee Protection Act* (IRPA) and the *Immigration and Refugee Protection Regulations* (IRPR), adult refugees can apply to reunite with family members living abroad by applying for permanent residence and include their spouse and dependent children on the application. However, minors who are found to be refugees in Canada can apply for permanent residence only for themselves and cannot sponsor their parents or other family members (Immigration, Refugees and Citizenship Canada, 2014).

Family reunification often suffers from excessive delays that considerably prolong family separations. Citizenship and Immigration Canada's statistics on processing times show that the average time for refugee dependants ("DR2s") to be processed is 38 months—over three years of separation—and there is no guarantee of success (Canadian Council for Refugees, 2016; Rousseau et al., 2004). These delays are particularly alarming when considering that parents often leave behind family members, including children, in dangerous or precarious situations (Canadian Council for Refugees, 2016). Moreover, studies have indicated that the longer the period of separation, the greater the symptom severity of children in terms of mental health and the greater the conflict when parent and child are reunited (Suarez-Orozco, Bang, & Kim, 2011).

An additional controversial policy that has raised great concern regarding the best interest of the child is the 2004 Canada–US Safe Third Country Agreement. Under the Agreement, refugee claimants who request protection at a US–Canada land port of entry are denied access to the refugee determination process in Canada, with a few exceptions, including if the claimant is an unaccompanied minor or has a relative in Canada (Amnesty International Canada & Canadian Council for Refugees, 2017). Advocates have warned that the Agreement separates children from their parents and encourages asylum-seeking families to take long, riskier routes to enter Canada (Grabish, 2017; Kassam, 2017). Delaying family reunification goes against the spirit of the UNCRC.

ACCESS AND QUALITY OF SERVICES

Health

It is generally agreed today that governments ought to play a role in facilitating the right of refugee children to health. This right, which entitles refugee children to access national health services on the same grounds as nationals of the resettlement country, has been enshrined in multiple human rights instruments endorsed by Canada, including the Universal Declaration of Human Rights (United Nations General Assembly, 1948), the 1951 United Nations Convention relating to the Status of Refugees, the International Covenant on Economic, Social and Cultural Rights (1966), and the United Nations Convention on the Rights of the Child (UNCRC) (United Nations General Assembly, 1989). The right to health care contained in Article 24 of the UNCRC clearly states that "States Parties recognize the right of the child to the enjoyment of the highest attainable standard of health and to facilities for the treatment of illness and rehabilitation of health. States Parties shall strive to ensure that no child is deprived of his or her right of access to such health care services."

Access to health care for war-affected refugee children is of special concern due to their high medical and psychosocial needs (Guruge & Butt, 2015). Recent guidelines for Canadian physicians highlighted that both pre- and post-migration stressors such as displacement, poverty, and limited proficiency in English or French increase the risk of a decline in health among refugees (Pottie et al., 2011). Inadequate care may lead to a deterioration in children's health and have long-term consequences for their development (Fazel et al., 2012). However, in Canada, access to health care for refugee children has fluctuated within the last decade with a great variation in entitlements.

The creation of the Interim Federal Health Program (IFHP) in 1957 provided funding for refugees and refugee claimants for basic health care and a range of supplemental services (Government of Canada, Department of Justice, 2012). However, drastic changes made by the federal government to the program in June 2012 excluded refugees and their children—except those who were government-sponsored and victims of human trafficking—from accessing publicly funded medical care unless it was deemed to be "urgent" or essential" (Olsen, El-Bialy, Mckelvie, Rauman, & Brunger, 2016). For a portion of refugee claimants, such as families whose refugee claims have been rejected and those from designated countries of origin (countries the government deemed to be "safe" and therefore not in need of protection), even essential medical care was denied, with treatment being provided only if "needed to prevent or treat a disease that is a risk to public health or to treat conditions of public safety concern" (Government of Canada, Department of Justice, 2012).

Studies assessing the impact of these cuts on refugees in Canada found that it led to a confusion about entitlements among health care providers (Ruiz-Casares, Cleveland, Oulhote, Dunkley-Hickin, & Rousseau, 2016), a drastic reduction of access to health care services for many war-affected children (Evans, Caudarella, Ratnapalan, & Chan, 2014), and a delay in seeking medical care, making health problems worse and leading to an overrepresentation of uninsured children in high-acuity emergency triage (Rousseau et al., 2013a). In 2014, a federal court decision declared that the IFHP cuts violated the Canadian Charter of Rights, especially as it related to children and termed them "cruel and unusual" (Payton, 2014). Almost two years later, in April 2016, the Liberal government fully restored public health care coverage for all refugee and refugee claimants to pre-2012 levels (Government of Canada, 2016).

The recent policy changes are promising and the restoration of the IFHP has already allowed many previously uninsured children to obtain necessary medical treatment (Chen, Gruben, & Liew, 2018). However, focusing solely on the entitlement of war-affected refugee children—for example, the formal right enshrined in law and policy to receive a certain range of services—may tell us little about their lived experiences and realities "on the ground" (Watters, 2011). To truly understand if war-affected refugee children's health rights are being upheld, we must examine how the laws and policies established by the state are implemented and interpreted at a local level (Ruiz-Casares, Rousseau, Derluyn, Watters, & Crépeau, 2010). For example, Chen and Liew (2017) argue that despite the policy change, many newly arrived refugees continue to be left without adequate access to health care. After conducting a series of interviews with health providers in Ottawa, they found that the IFHP remains plagued by "a legacy of confusion." They reported that many clinics, pharmacies, and health care specialists did not accept refugee patients based on the false assumption that they are not covered by the program or because they wanted to avoid complicated paperwork and time delays in processing for reimbursement (Chen, Gruben, & Liew, 2018). This finding was reiterated in an earlier study, which found that refugees covered by the IFHP were frequently refused essential services or referred to particular clinics known to accept refugees (ter Kuile, Rousseau, Munoz, Nadeau, & Ouimet, 2007).

Indeed, entitlement in itself is of little value if refugees cannot access treatment or if the treatment received is not appropriate for their needs. In a recent study examining the use of health care services among newly arrived Syrian refugees in Toronto, nearly half of the respondents reported unmet health care needs (Oda et al., 2017). Some of the main reasons reported were lengthy wait times, unavailability of services at the time required, and cost of services (Oda et al., 2017). An additional study on the health status of newly arrived Syrian refugees reported gaps and delays in receiving health care due to delays in finding permanent housing for government-sponsored refugees as well as local challenges in health delivery (Hansen, Maidment, & Ahmad, 2016). Further studies found that refugee children encountered numerous barriers to accessing services, including communication difficulties due to a lack of professional interpretation services, a shortage of primary care providers, restrictive attitudes of practitioners toward entitlement, a lack of culturally appropriate services, and difficulties accessing services due to location and transportation issues (Hassan, Ventevogel, Jefee-Bahloul, Barkil-Oteo, & Kirmayer, 2016; Campbell et al., 2014; Ruiz-Casares et al., 2013).

Immigration status has been found to be the "single most important factor affecting both an individual's ability to seek out healthcare and her experiences when trying to access healthcare" (Campbell, Klei, Hodges, Fisman, & Kitto, 2014, p. 1). Children and families whose refugee claims have been refused and continue to reside in Canada while they appeal lose their eligibility for public insurance, either provincial or federal (Caulford & Vali, 2006). These uninsured youth often forestall or avoid seeking out health care altogether due to fear of authorities and deportation or the lack of financial means to pay (Ruiz-Casares et al., 2010).

With the exception of newly arrived Syrians, children who are new permanent residents are subject to a three-month waiting period in Ontario, Quebec, British Columbia, and New Brunswick—whose populations include close to 90 percent of Canada's newcomers—before being able to access provincial care (Wayland, Community Foundations of Canada, & Law

Commission of Canada, 2006). Since health care options during this period are limited, many families whose children become ill turn to emergency rooms and walk-in clinics, which often result in expensive out-of-pocket medical bills, and inconsistent and inappropriate care (Chen, Gruben, & Gruben, 2018).

It seems that while the Canadian health care system is widely praised for its universality, Canadian policies and their interpretation and implementation on the ground continue to restrict access to health care for many war-affected refugee children. These restrictions often translate into poorer health outcomes in a population that is already extremely marginalized and vulnerable (Guruge & Butt, 2015).

Education

Access to education for children and youth from refugee families is widely recognized as a universal right and has been enshrined in the 1949 UN Declaration on Human Rights, the 1951 Convention Relating to the Status of Refugees, and the 1989 Convention on the Rights of the Child. The United Nations' Sustainable Development Goals (SDG), which have been adopted by world leaders in 2015, highlight that education is key to achieving many other SDGs and explicitly urges governments and civil societies to ensure inclusive and equitable quality education for all and to promote lifelong learning opportunities (United Nations Development Program, 2016). In Canada, refugee children's rights to receive education is secured both in the Canadian Charter of Rights and Freedoms as well as the "best practice" guidelines for separated children in Canada prepared by the International Bureau for Children's Rights. These guidelines contain the following statement: "Separated children, irrespective of their immigration status, should have access to the same statutory education as national children. Separated children should have full access to all services within schools, including the services of school social workers and counsellors" (International Bureau for Children's Rights, p. 30, as cited in Watters, 2008).

For refugee children arriving in Canada, schools offer both tremendous educational opportunities—the acquisition of knowledge and learning of skills—as well as a significant means of social inclusion and integration into the communities they and their families have joined (Brenner & Kia-Keating, 2016). Schools play a key role in helping refugee children adapt and integrate in Canadian society (Wilkinson, 2002). They are particularly important for children who have experienced war and displacement as they provide a safe and stable environment, serve as a site for rebuilding peer relationships and social networks, address psychosocial needs, enhance their positive developmental trajectories, and often serve as the main access point to mental health services (Tyrer & Fazel, 2014; Rousseau & Guzder, 2008). Indeed, a perceived sense of safety and belonging at school has been shown to protect against the development of mental health disorders such as post-traumatic stress disorder, depression, and anxiety (Fazel et al., 2012). Schools are not only crucial for the healthy development of children, they may also serve as an important link between the local community and families (Morantz, Rousseau, & Heymann, 2012). Schools are social hubs where refugee parents who often suffer from isolation can socialize and share experiences. They may also hold a key to the enhancement of the family's economic stability and well-being by equipping children with degrees and increasing their opportunities in the labour market (Watters, 2008).

However, despite its crucial role and its formal recognition in international conventions, the fundamental right to education is often not extended to refugee children and youth. Recent reports indicate that refugee children worldwide experience multiple obstacles and disruptions to their education (UNHCR, 2016b). School enrolment of refugee children falls far below those of other children globally, with refugee children and adolescents being five times more likely to be out of school than their non-refugee peers (UNHCR, 2016b).

These prior schooling experiences have significant implications for post-resettlement education in Canada. Refugee children may have significant gaps in skills and knowledge due to disrupted schooling as a result of outbreak of war or violence or inadequate schooling within under-resourced refugee camps. They often lack proficiency in the official language of instruction (English or French in Canada), resulting in difficulties in academic advancement (Dryden-Peterson, 2016). In a Canadian study of Southeast Asian refugee youth, refugee students commonly reported having difficulty adjusting to school due in part to limited English fluency, which contributed to academic difficulties and feelings of stress, low self-confidence, and estrangement (Hyman, Vu, & Beiser, 2000).

Furthermore, refugee children entering the Canadian school system may find themselves having difficulty adjusting and understanding the educational and cultural environments of their new school, resulting in a renegotiation of their identities (Collet, 2007). Discrimination and racism may also be a challenge, particularly for visible minorities, as reported in a year-long study examining educational barriers of African refugee students in Manitoba (Kanu, 2008). In Kanu's study, participants commonly reported experiencing prejudice, marginalization, and racism from peers, teachers, and school personnel, which often impacted their academic achievement and adversely affected their self-confidence and well-being (Kanu, 2008). These challenges are often compounded by war-related trauma exposure and post-migration stresses, significantly affecting refugee students' learning or ability to function well within the school environment (Stermac, Clark, & Brown, 2013). As one participant stated, "I was able to go to school, but I did not study well as I would be before.... Yeah, [the genocide] affects my studies, because, sometimes it's like I remember, my memory goes back [to the genocide]. And then I feel I don't want to study. Sometimes I say, oh, why do I have to study? My father studied, but where is he? [Deceased as a result of the genocide] ... Yeah. Sometimes I feel like I don't want to study."

Unfortunately, Canadian schools are often ill-equipped to meet the educational needs of refugee children and teachers may lack the professional development training to adapt their curriculum and instructional practices to refugee children's unique learning, cultural, and psychosocial needs (Blanchet-Cohen & Denov, 2015; Stewart, 2011; Kanu, 2008). The diversity in lived experiences could easily result in misunderstandings. Comments made at school by teachers—some involving violent imagery—which were intended to be "jokes," were interpreted very differently by participants:

> When we were working, we did practical exercises. One of the people who was in charge there just said one little phrase: "I'll tear your head off if you answer yes or no. I need an explanation!" "Yes," I said. "Wow!" I had to answer yes or no, but he meant it as a joke. But for me, the joke went directly into my brain: "Oh! They're going to rip our heads off! Wow! Oh! It's normal!" Because I experienced things where, like, people's heads were being ripped off. And I said to myself, "That guy too, he could rip our heads off. Wow!" That's what I understood, given the situation I experienced.... But for him, ripping off someone's head, he sees it on TV. He has never been involved in anything where people's heads are getting ripped off. Okay, so he thinks it's a joke. But for me it was really hard.... So I withdraw a little, and I say to myself, "What's going on here? Where am I? Where did I end up?" It took a while before anyone explained all this to me—these things, the circumstances we went through.

Some promising programs and services, such as the LEAD program (Miles & Bailey-McKenna, 2017) and the use of educational cultural brokers (Yohani, 2013), do exist in pockets throughout the country. However, researchers and civil society organizations stress that critical policy gaps persist. One important policy gap is the lack of sufficient funding to support school boards and schools receiving these children (Shakya et al., 2012).

Teacher unions and boards across Canada have complained about the lack of provincial and federal funding, which precludes schools from providing Syrian refugee children the support they need (Alphonso & Chiose, 2017). As a result, many school boards are forced to pay expenses from their own budgets to assist their students (Alphonso & Chiose, 2017).

Another important policy gap that disproportionately affects refugee youth is the cut-off age of free public secondary education (Wilkinson, 2002). While in Canada's public school system there are no school fees for all children, in most provinces this is true only for children of school age. After this, youth must finance their own secondary education. However, refugee youth with disrupted education and low official language fluency are more likely to be placed in grade levels much lower than their age, making it highly unlikely for them to complete high school before the prescribed age of 19 (Wilkinson, 2002).

When examining educational policies, it is important to look beyond refugee children and examine policies targeting their parents. Studies have consistently stressed the crucial role that parents play in the educational performance of their children, particularly refugee children (McBrien, 2011). A recent study conducted by Hou and Bonikowska (2016) for Statistics Canada examined the educational and labour market outcomes of children of immigrants to Canada by admission class. It found that "unlike the pattern observed for the family class and live-in caregivers parents' education, language and source region accounted for most of the gap in the educational attainment of government-assisted and privately sponsored refugee children" (Hou & Bonikowska, 2016, p. 35). Consequently, researchers in Canada highlight the pressing need to involve Syrian and other refugee parents more fully in their children's education in culturally respectful and responsive ways (Cranston & Labman, 2016; McBrien, 2011).

IMPLICATIONS FOR CANADIAN POLICY AND PRACTICE

As a signatory to the Convention on the Rights of the Child, the Government of Canada has accepted the obligation to respect, protect, and fulfill *all* children's rights. However, Canada has yet to fully incorporate these rights into immigration and refugee legislation, policies, programs, and practices. Ensuring that the rights of war-affected refugee children are protected requires placing priority first and foremost on the best interests of the child. Too often, anti-terrorism and security concerns are put at the forefront of migration policy at the expense of refugee children's rights (Crépeau, Nakache, & Atak, 2007; Bryan & Denov, 2011). This is especially true when it comes to unaccompanied and separated children who are particularly vulnerable to becoming victims of human rights abuses and are in need of specific support to ensure their healthy development (Bryan and Denov, 2011; Fazel et al., 2012).

Providing safe and developmentally appropriate alternatives to the detention of children and their caregivers, prioritizing and speeding up reunion of children with families, and ensuring access to and quality of public services are only some of the much-needed policy amendments that have been highlighted in this chapter and must continue to be pushed to the forefront of Canada's agenda. Further, a cohesive federal policy concerning refugee children's protection must be made a priority. In its latest review of Canada, the UN Committee on the Rights of the Child (2012) noted that "the absence of such overall national legislation has resulted in fragmentation and inconsistencies in the implementation of child rights across the State party, with children in similar situations being subject to disparities in the fulfilment of their rights depending on the province or territory which they reside in" (p. 2). Greater interagency communication and coordination can ensure that no child has fallen through the cracks and been denied equal treatment.

Moreover, it is important to recognize that protecting refugee rights does not stop at legislation. As demonstrated in the passages above, the manner in which policies are carried out by different actors on the ground significantly impacts the rights of refugee children and the services they receive. In order for the standards and principles articulated in the Convention to be materialized, all institutions that provide services for children—refugee determination boards, welfare services, schools, clinics, and policy-makers at all levels of government—must be provided with appropriate training that sensitizes them to the rights and specific needs of refugee children and enhances their capacity to work with this unique population.

It is vital to recognize that war and migration do not simply affect individual children, but the entire family system. Families are often displaced from their homes and separated from one another, and the associated emotional stress may impair the ability of adults to provide care and nurturance to young children (Betancourt et al., 2015). The mental health of parents remains intimately connected to children and vice versa. Mental health issues, affecting a family's ability to function, can persist long after the conflict has ended. Betancourt et al. (2015) have argued that given the vital role that family plays in shaping children's mental health in post-conflict settings, policy-makers and service providers must not only understand and take into consideration the war exposure histories and mental health of children and adolescents, but also the mental health of their adult caregivers. Moreover, family stressors such as socio-economic background, precariousness of status, employment opportunities, and official language ability have all been linked to higher rates of child mental health problems and long-term developmental problems (Fazel et al., 2012), as well as lower educational outcomes (Hou & Bonikowska, 2016). Policy-makers, health providers, community organizations, and social workers dealing with refugee claimants should therefore design services that automatically consider not only the children's needs but also the needs of their parents and family. Family-centred solutions must replace the narrow, individualized paradigm of current immigration and social policies in order to keep the detrimental consequences of war and resettlement to a minimum.

Honouring and promoting children's rights, voices, and perspectives throughout these processes will be of paramount importance. In supporting this endeavour, it will be crucial for adults, governments, and international organizations to attend to and transform dominant attitudes and assumptions concerning children's agency and competence. Adults and other authority figures hold power over children and often minimize children's capacity to understand and voice their concerns, interests, needs, and experiences (Lansdown, 2001). Children affected by armed conflict in particular are presumed to be too vulnerable, traumatized, naive, unknowledgeable, and irrational to contribute to decision-making processes (McMullin, 2011). Children must have a voice in all decisions affecting them. Moreover, policy and program development initiatives must be increasingly grounded in the ways young people, in different contexts, define themselves for themselves, including their unique needs, capacities, realities, and ways of knowing.

This chapter has highlighted that when it comes to war-affected refugee children in Canada, much work lies ahead to ensure the treatment and status of this population as rights bearers and full citizens. An analysis of Canada's responses to unaccompanied refugee minors, children being held in detention, family reunification practices, and access to quality services in the realms of health and education shows that Canada falls short. Not only are there instances of a failure to protect, and a neglect of the best interest of the child (as seen in relation to detention), but also there are few instances and spaces where refugee children have the ability to participate in key decision making, and where refugee children's agency, competence, and voice can be clearly articulated. By protecting and promoting refugee children's rights and participation, Canada will demonstrate leadership as a human rights defender, and uphold its humanitarian tradition of reuniting families and providing protection and rights to refugee children who have enormous capacity and ability as future leaders and contributors to Canadian society.

QUESTIONS FOR DISCUSSION

1. How can the tension between Canada's obligation to respect and protect the rights of war-affected refugee children and its right to ensure national security be successfully negotiated to the benefit of children and young people?

2. How can Canada translate the rhetoric of human rights into practical measures/effective programs and policies?

3. What mechanisms are necessary to ensure that policy and program development initiatives are grounded in the ways young people define themselves?

REFERENCES

Ali, M. A., Taraban, S., & Gill, J. K. (2003). *Unaccompanied/separated children seeking refugee status in Ontario: A review of documented policies and practices.* CERIS Working Paper No. 27. Toronto, Ontario: CERIS.

Alphonso, C., & Chiose, S. (2017, November 12). The big picture: How education can be a lifeline for Syrian families. *The Globe and Mail.* Retrieved from https://www.theglobeandmail.com/news/national/syrian-refugees-to-canada-and-education/article33237207/

Amnesty International Canada & Canadian Council for Refugees. (2017). *Contesting the designation of the US as a safe third country.* Retrieved from www.amnesty.ca/sites/amnesty/files/Contesting%20the%20Designation%20of%20the%20US%20as%20a%20Safe%20Third%20Country.pdf

Ayotte, W. (2001). *Separated children seeking asylum in Canada.* Ottawa: United Nations High Commissioner for Refugees. Retrieved from http://ccrweb.ca/sites/ccrweb.ca/files/static-files/separated.PDF

Betancourt, T. S., Abdi, S., Ito, B. S., Lilienthal, G. M., Agalab, N., & Ellis, H. (2015). We left one war and came to another: Resource loss, acculturative stress, and caregiver-child relationships in Somali refugee families. *Cultural Diversity and Ethnic Minority Psychology, 21*(1), 114–125.

Betancourt, T. S., Newnham, E. A., Layne, C. M., Kim, S., Steinberg, A. M., Ellis, H., & Birman, D. (2012). Trauma history and psychopathology in war-affected refugee children referred for trauma-related mental health services in the United States. *Journal of Traumatic Stress, 25*(6), 682–690.

Blanchet-Cohen, N., & and Denov, M. (2015). War-affected children's approach to resettlement: Implications for child and family services. *Annals of Anthropological Practice, 39*(2), 120–133.

Brenner, M. E., & Kia-Keating, M. (2016). Psychosocial and academic adjustment among resettled refugee youth. In A. W. Wiseman (Ed.), *Annual review of comparative and international education 2016, Vol. 30* (pp. 221–249). Bingley, UK: Emerald Group Publishing.

Bryan, C., & Denov, M. (2011). Separated refugee children in Canada: The construction of risk identity. *Journal of Immigrant and Refugee Studies, 9*(3), 242–266.

Campbell, R. M., Klei, A. G., Hodges, B. D., Fisman, D., & Kitto, S. (2014). A comparison of health access between permanent residents, undocumented immigrants and refugee claimants in Toronto, Canada. *Journal of Immigrant and Minority Health, 16*(1), 165–176.

Canada Border Services Agency. (2017). *Arrests, detentions and removals: Detention statistics.* Retrieved from www.cbsa-asfc.gc.ca/security-securite/detent-stat-eng.html

Canadian Council for Refugees. (2004). *Impacts on children of the Immigration and Refugee Protection Act.* Retrieved from http://ccrweb.ca/sites/ccrweb.ca/files/children.pdf

Canadian Council for Refugees. (2016). *Family reunification: Submission to the Standing Committee on Citizenship and Immigration.* Retrieved from http://ccrweb.ca/sites/ccrweb.ca/files/family-reunification-submission-nov-2016.pdf

Canadian Human Rights Commission. (2017). *People first: The Canadian Human Rights Commission's 2016 annual report to Parliament.* Retrieved from www.chrcreport.ca/assets/pdf/CHRC-Annual-2016-EN-web.pdf

Canadian Immigration and Citizenship. (2018). *Asylum claimants processed by Canada Border Services Agency (CBSA) and Immigration, Refugees and Citizenship Canada (IRCC) offices, January 2011–February 2018.* Retrieved from https://www.canada.ca/en/immigration-refugees-citizenship/services/refugees/asylum-claims/processed-claims.html

Caulford, P., & Vali, Y. (2006). Providing health care to medically uninsured immigrants and refugees. *Canadian Medical Association Journal, 174*(9), 1253–1254.

Chen, Y. Y., Gruben, V., & Liew, J. C. Y. (2018). "A legacy of confusion": An exploratory study of service provision under the Reinstated Interim Federal Health Program. *Refuge: Canada's Journal on Refugees/Refuge: revue canadienne sur les réfugiés, 34*(2), 94–102.

Choummanivong, C., Poole, G. E., & Cooper, A. (2014). Refugee family reunification and mental health in resettlement. *Kotuitui: New Zealand Journal of Social Sciences Online, 9*(2), 89–100.

Collet, B. A. (2007). Islam, national identity and public secondary education: Perspectives from the Somali diaspora in Toronto, Canada. *Race, Ethnicity and Education, 10*(2), 131–153.

Cranston, J., & Labman, S. (2016, October 23). Refugee parents must be involved in children's education, experts say. *CBC News.* Retrieved from www.cbc.ca/news/canada/manitoba/refugee-school-students-parents-opinion-1.3814322

Crépeau, F., Nakache, D., & Atak, I. (2007). International migration: Security concerns and human rights standards. *Transcultural Psychiatry, 44*(3), 311–337.

Denov, M. (2010). *Child soldiers: Sierra Leone's Revolutionary United Front.* New York: Cambridge University Press.

Denov, M., & Blanchet-Cohen, N. (2016). Trajectories of violence and survival: Turnings and adaptations in the lives of two war-affected youth living in Canada. *Peace and Conflict: Journal of Peace Psychology, 22*(3), 236–245.

Denov, M., & Bryan, C. (2010). Unaccompanied refugee children in Canada. *Settlement of Newcomers to Canada, 12*(1), 67–75.

Denov, M., & Bryan, C. (2012). Tactical maneuvering and calculated risks: Independent child migrants and the complex terrain of flight. In A. Orgocka & C. Clark-Kazak (Eds.), *Independent child migration—insights into agency, vulnerability, and structure* (pp. 13–27). San Francisco: Wiley Publishing.

Denov, M., & Bryan, C. (2014). Social navigation and the resettlement experiences of separated children in Canada. *Refuge: Canada's Journal on Refugees, 30*(1), 25–34.

Devakumar, D., Birch, M., Osrin, D., Sondorp, E., & Wells, J. C. (2014). The intergenerational effects of war on the health of children. *BMC Medicine, 12*(57), 1–15.

Dryden-Peterson, S. (2016). Refugee education: The crossroads of globalization. *Educational Researcher, 45*(9), 473–482.

Ee, E., Sleijpen, M., Kleber, R. J., & Jongmans, M. J. (2013). Father-involvement in a refugee sample: Relations between posttraumatic stress and caregiving. *Family Process, 52*(4), 723–735.

Ellis, B. H., MacDonald, H. Z., Lincoln, A. K., & Cabral, H. J. (2008). Mental health of Somali adolescent refugees: The role of trauma, stress, and perceived discrimination. *Journal of Consulting and Clinical Psychology, 76*(2), 184–193.

Evans, A., Caudarella, A., Ratnapalan, S., & Chan, K. (2014). The cost and impact of the Interim Federal Health Program cuts on child refugees in Canada. *PloS one, 9*(5), 1–5.

Fazel, M., Reed, R. V., Panter-Brick, C., & Stein, A. (2012). Mental health of displaced and refugee children resettled in high-income countries: Risk and protective factors. *Lancet, 379*(9812), 266–282.

Government of Canada. (2016). *Notice—Changes to the Interim Federal Health Program*. Retrieved from www.cic.gc.ca/english/department/medianotices/2016-04-11.asp

Government of Canada, Department of Justice. (2012). *Order respecting the Interim Federal Health Program (SI/2012-26)*. Retrieved from http://laws-lois.justice.gc.ca/eng/regulations/SI-2012-26/FullText.html

Grabish, A. (2017, February 13). U.S.-Canada pact could split kids from families fleeing to Canada: Refugee group. *CBC News*. Retrieved from www.cbc.ca/news/canada/manitoba/families-separated-safe-third-country-agreement-1.3979364

Gros, H. (2017). *Invisible citizens: Canadian children in immigration detention*. Toronto: International Human Rights Program, University of Toronto, Faculty of Law.

Gros, H., & Song, Y. (2016). *No life for a child: A roadmap to end immigration detention of children and family separation*. Toronto: International Human Rights Program, University of Toronto, Faculty of Law.

Guruge, S., & Butt, H. (2015). A scoping review of mental health issues and concerns among immigrant and refugee youth in Canada: Looking back, moving forward. *Canadian Journal of Public Health, 106*(2), e72–e78.

Hansen, L., Maidment, L., & Ahmad, R. (2016). Early observations on the health of Syrian refugees in Canada. *Canada Communicable Disease Report, 42*(S2), S8–S10.

Hassan, G., Ventevogel, P., Jefee-Bahloul, H., Barkil-Oteo, A., & Kirmayer, L. J. (2016). Mental health and psychosocial wellbeing of Syrians affected by armed conflict. *Epidemiology and Psychiatric Sciences, 25*(2), 129–141.

Hou, F., & Bonikowska, A. (2016). *Educational and labour market outcomes of childhood immigrants by admission class*. Statistics Canada. Retrieved from www.statcan.gc.ca/pub/11f0019m/11f0019m2016377-eng.htm

Hyman, I., Vu, N., & Beiser, M. (2000). Post-migration stresses among Southeast Asian refugee youth in Canada: A research note. *Journal of Comparative Family Studies, 31*(2), 281–293.

Immigration and Refugee Protection Act, SC 2001, c 27, ss 4(2)(a)-(c), 7 [IRPA].

Immigration, Refugees and Citizenship Canada. (2014). *Evaluation of the Family Reunification Program*. Retrieved from www.cic.gc.ca/english/pdf/pub/e4-2013-frp.pdf

Immigration, Refugees and Citizenship Canada. (2015). *Facts & figures 2015: Immigration overview—permanent residents—annual IRCC updates*. Retrieved from https://open.canada.ca/data/en/dataset/2fbb56bd-eae7-4582-af7d-a197d185fc93?_ga=2.134124172.349822579.1521896008-1893943906.1499794295

Immigration, Refugees and Citizenship Canada. (2017a). *2017 annual report to Parliament on immigration*. Retrieved from https://www.canada.ca/en/immigration-refugees-citizenship/corporate/publications-manuals/annual-report-parliament-immigration-2017.html

Immigration, Refugees and Citizenship Canada. (2017b). *Canada to benefit economically and socially by increasing the age of dependents*. Retrieved from https://www.canada.ca/en/immigration-refugees-citizenship/news/2017/05/canada_to_benefiteconomicallyandsociallybyincreasingtheageofdepe.html?wbdisable=true

Immigration, Refugees and Citizenship Canada. (2017c). *Resettled refugees—monthly IRCC updates*. Retrieved from www.cic.gc.ca/english/resources/statistics/index.asp

Immigration, Refugees and Citizenship Canada. (2017d). *Syrian refugees—monthly IRCC updates*. Retrieved from www.cic.gc.ca/english/resources/statistics/index.asp

Kalaichandran, A. (2017, March 16). Advocates concerned about unaccompanied minors seeking asylum in Canada. *The Canadian Press*. Retrieved from http://www.nationalnewswatch.com/2017/03/16/advocates-concerned-about-unaccompanied-minors-seeking-asylum-in-canada-2/#.WYiS4cYZOgQ

Kanu, Y. (2008). Educational needs and barriers for African refugee students in Manitoba. *Canadian Journal of Education, 31*(4), 915–940.

Kassam, A. (2017, July 6). Activists challenge "unsafe" US-Canada pact that prompts refugees to flee by foot. *The Guardian*. Retrieved from www.theguardian.com/world/2017/jul/06/canada-us-refugees-safe-third-country-agreement-border-crossing

Kronick, R., Rousseau, C., & Cleveland, J. (2017). Refugee children's sandplay narratives in immigration detention in Canada. *European Child & Adolescent Psychiatry, 27*(4), 423–437.

Kuile, S., Rousseau, C., Munoz, M., Nadeau, L., & Ouimet, M. (2007). The universality of the Canadian health care system in question: Barriers to services for immigrants and refugees. *International Journal of Migration, Health and Social Care, 3*(1), 15–26.

Lacroix, M., & Sabbah, C. (2011). Posttraumatic psychological distress and resettlement: The need for a different practice in assisting refugee families. *Journal of Family Social Work, 14*(1), 43–53.

Lansdown, G. (2001). *Promoting children's participation in democratic decision-making*. Florence, Italy: Innocenti Research Center, UNICEF.

Lorek, A., Ehntholt, K., Nesbitt, A., Wey, E., Githinji, C., Rossor, E., & Wickramasinghe, R. (2009). The mental and physical health difficulties of children held within a British immigration detention center: A pilot study. *Child Abuse & Neglect*, 33(9), 573–585.

Luster, T., Qin, D. B., Bates, L., Johnson, D. J., & Rana, M. (2008). The lost boys of Sudan: Ambiguous loss, search for family, and reestablishing relationships with family members. *Family Relations*, 57(4), 444–456.

Mann, G. (2001). *Networks of support: A literature review of care issues for separated children*. Stockholm: Save the Children Sweden.

Mares, S. (2016). Fifteen years of detaining children who seek asylum in Australia—evidence and consequences. *Australasian Psychiatry*, 24(1), 11–14.

Mas, S. (2016, March 8). Liberals shift immigration focus to family reunification, refugee resettlement. *CBC News*. Retrieved from www.cbc.ca/news/politics/liberals-immigration-levels-plan-2016-1.3479764

McBrien, J. L. (2011). The importance of context: Vietnamese, Somali, and Iranian refugee mothers discuss their resettled lives and involvement in their children's schools. *Compare*, 41(1), 75–90.

McMullin, J. (2011). Reintegrating young combatants: Do child-centred approaches leave children—and adults—behind?. *Third World Quarterly*, 32(4), 743–764.

Measham, T., Guzder, J., Rousseau, C., Pacione, L., Blais-McPherson, M., & Nadeau, L. (2014). Refugee children and their families: Supporting psychological well-being and positive adaptation following migration. *Current Problems in Pediatric and Adolescent Health Care*, 44(7), 208–215.

Miles, J., & Bailey-McKenna, M. C. (2017). Giving refugee students a strong head start: The LEAD Program. *TESL Canada Journal*, 33(10), 109–128.

Miller, K. E., & Rasmussen, A. (2017). The mental health of civilians displaced by armed conflict: An ecological model of refugee distress. *Epidemiology and Psychiatric Sciences*, 26(2), 129–138.

Mis, M. (2016). *Nearly 87 million children under seven live in conflict zones, brains not developing*. UNICEF. Retrieved from www.yahoo.com/news/nearly-87-million-children-live-conflict-zones-brains-003309969.html?ref=gs

Montgomery, C., Rousseau, C., & Shermarke, M. (2001). Alone in a strange land: Unaccompanied minors and issues of protection. *Canadian Ethnic Studies Journal*, 33(1), 103–124.

Morantz, G., Rousseau, C., & Heymann, J. (2012). The divergent experiences of children and adults in the relocation process: Perspectives of child and parent refugee claimants in Montreal. *Journal of Refugee Studies*, 25(1), 71–92.

Nickerson, A., Bryant, R. A., Steel, Z., Silove, D., & Brooks, R. (2010). The impact of fear for family on mental health in a resettled Iraqi refugee community. *Journal of Psychiatric Research*, 44(4), 229–235.

Oda, A., Tuck, A., Agic, B., Hynie, M., Roche, B., & McKenzie, K. (2017). Health care needs and use of health care services among newly arrived Syrian refugees: A cross-sectional study. *CMAJ Open*, 5(2), E354–E358.

Olsen, C., El-Bialy, R., Mckelvie, M., Rauman, P., & Brunger, F. (2016). "Other" troubles: Deconstructing perceptions and changing responses to refugees in Canada. *Journal of Immigrant and Minority Health*, 18(1), 58–66.

Pacione, L., Measham, T., & Rousseau, C. (2013). Refugee children: Mental health and effective interventions. *Current Psychiatry Reports*, 15(2), 341–357.

Payton, L. (2014, July 4). Federal government to appeal ruling reversing "cruel" cuts to refugee health. *CBC News*. Retrieved from www.cbc.ca/news/politics/federal-government-to-appeal-ruling-reversing-cruel-cuts-to-refugee-health-1.2696311

Pottie, K., Greenaway, C., Feightner, J., Welch, V., Swinkels, H., Rashid, M., & Hassan, G. (2011). Evidence-based clinical guidelines for immigrants and refugees. *Canadian Medical Association Journal, 183*(12), E824–E925.

Priebe, S., Burns, T., & Craig, T. K. (2013). The future of academic psychiatry may be social. *British Journal of Psychiatry, 202*(5), 319–320.

Rasmussen, A., Nguyen, L., Wilkinson, J., Vundla, S., Raghavan, S., Miller, K. E., & Keller, A. S. (2010). Rates and impact of trauma and current stressors among Darfuri refugees in eastern Chad. *American Journal of Orthopsychiatry, 80*(2), 227–236.

Robjant, K., Hassan, R., & Katona, C. (2009). Mental health implications of detaining asylum seekers: Systematic review. *British Journal of Psychiatry, 194*(4), 306–312.

Rousseau, C., & Guzder, J. (2008). School-based prevention programs for refugee children. *Child and Adolescent Psychiatric Clinics of North America, 17*(3), 533–549.

Rousseau, C., Laurin-Lamothe, A., Rummens, J. A., Meloni, F., Steinmetz, N., & Alvarez, F. (2013). Uninsured immigrant and refugee children presenting to Canadian paediatric emergency departments: Disparities in help-seeking and service delivery. *Paediatrics & Child Health, 18*(9), 465–469.

Rousseau, C., Measham, T., & Nadeau, L. (2013). Addressing trauma in collaborative mental health care for refugee children. *Clinical Child Psychology and Psychiatry, 18*(1), 121–136.

Rousseau, C., Mekki-Berrada, A., & Moreau, S. (2001). Trauma and extended separation from family among Latin American and African refugees in Montreal. *Psychiatry: Interpersonal & Biological Processes, 64*(1), 40–59.

Rousseau, C., Rufagari, M. C., Bagilishya, D., & Measham, T. (2004). Remaking family life: Strategies for re-establishing continuity among Congolese refugees during the family reunification process. *Social Science & Medicine, 59*(5), 1095–1108.

Rousseau, C., Said, T. M., Gagné, M. J., & Bibeau, G. (1998). Resilience in unaccompanied minors from the north of Somalia. *Psychoanalytic Review, 85*(4), 615–637.

Ruiz-Casares, M., Cleveland, J., Oulhote, Y., Dunkley-Hickin, C., & Rousseau, C. (2016). Knowledge of healthcare coverage for refugee claimants: Results from a survey of health service providers in Montreal. *PloS one, 11*(1), 1–11.

Ruiz-Casares, M., Rousseau, C., Derluyn, I., Watters, C., & Crépeau, F. (2010). Right and access to healthcare for undocumented children: Addressing the gap between international conventions and disparate implementations in North America and Europe. *Social Science & Medicine, 70*(2), 329–336.

Ruiz-Casares, M., Rousseau, C., Laurin-Lamothe, A., Rummens, J. A., Zelkowitz, P., Crépeau, F., & Steinmetz, N. (2013). Access to health care for undocumented migrant children and pregnant women: The paradox between values and attitudes of health care professionals. *Maternal and Child Health Journal, 17*(2), 292–298.

Shakya, Y. B., Guruge, S., Hynie, M., Akbari, A., Malik, M., Htoo, S., Khogali, A., Mona, S. A., Murtaza, R., & Alley, S. (2012). Aspirations for higher education among newcomer refugee youth in Toronto: Expectations, challenges, and strategies. *Refuge, 27*(2), 65–78.

Shakya, Y. B., Guruge, S., Hynie, M., Htoo, S., Akbari, A., Jandu, B. B., & Forster, J. (2014). Newcomer refugee youth as "resettlement champions" for their families: Vulnerability, resilience and empowerment. In L. Simich & L. Andermann (Eds.), *Refuge and Resilience: Promoting resilience and mental health among resettled refugees and forced migrants* (pp. 131–154). Dordrecht: Springer.

Silverman, S. J., & Molnar, P. (2016). Everyday injustices: Barriers to access to justice for immigration detainees in Canada. *Refugee Survey Quarterly, 35*(1), 109–127.

Sourander, A. (1998). Behavior problems and traumatic events of unaccompanied refugee minors 1. *Child Abuse & Neglect, 22*(7), 719–727.

Stermac, L., Clark, A. K., & Brown, L. (2013). Pathways to resilience: The role of education in war-zone immigrant and refugee student success. In C. Fernando & M. Ferrari (Eds.), *Handbook of resilience in children of war* (pp. 211–219). New York: Springer.

Stewart, J. (2011). *Supporting refugee children: Strategies for educators*. Toronto: University of Toronto Press.

Suárez-Orozco, C., Bang, H. J., & Kim, H. Y. (2011). I felt like my heart was staying behind: Psychological implications of family separations and reunifications for immigrant youth. *Journal of Adolescent Research, 26*(2), 222–257.

ter Kuile, S., Rousseau, C., Munoz, M., Nadeau, L., & Ouimet, M. J. (2007). The universality of the Canadian health care system in question: Barriers to services for immigrants and refugees. *International Journal of Migration, Health and Social Care, 3*(1), 15–26.

Tyrer, R. A., & Fazel, M. (2014). School and community-based interventions for refugee and asylum seeking children: A systematic review. *PLoS ONE, 9*(2), 1–12.

UNHCR. (2016a). *Forced displacement in 2015*. Retrieved from http://www.unhcr.org/news/latest/2016/6/5763b65a4/global-forced-displacement-hits-record-high.html

UNHCR. (2016b). *Missing out: Refugee education in crisis*. Retrieved from www.unhcr.org/57d9d01d0

UNHCR. (2017a). *Canada resettlement facts*. Retrieved from www.unhcr.ca/newsroom/publications/

UNHCR. (2017b). *Canada's 2016 record high level of resettlement praised by UNHCR*. Retrieved from http://www.unhcr.org/news/press/2017/4/58fe15464/canadas-2016-record-high-level-resettlement-praised-unhcr.html

United Nations Committee on the Rights of the Child. (2012, October 5). *Consideration of reports submitted by states parties under article 44 of the Convention. concluding observations: Canada*. Retrieved from www2.ohchr.org/english/bodies/crc/docs/co/CRC-C-CAN-CO-3-4_en.pdf

United Nations Committee on the Rights of the Child. (2013, May 29). *General comment no. 14 (2013) on the right of the child to have his or her best interests taken as a primary consideration (art. 3, para. 1)*. Retrieved from www2.ohchr.org/English/bodies/crc/docs/GC/CRC_C_GC_14_ENG.pdf

United Nations Development Program. (2016). *Sustainable development goals*. Retrieved from www.undp.org/content/undp/en/home/sustainable-development-goals.html.

United Nations General Assembly. (1948). *Universal Declaration of Human Rights* (217 [III] A). Paris.

United Nations General Assembly. (1989, November 20). *Convention on the Rights of the Child*, United Nations, Treaty Series, vol. 1577, p. 3. Retrieved from http://www.refworld.org/docid/3ae6b38f0.html

Watters, C. (2008). *Refugee children: Towards the next horizon*. London: Routledge.

Watters, C. (2011). Towards a new paradigm in migrant health research: Integrating entitlement, access and appropriateness. *International Journal of Migration, Health and Social Care, 7*(3), 148–159.

Wayland, S. V., Community Foundations of Canada, & Law Commission of Canada. (2006). *Unsettled: Legal and policy barriers for newcomers to Canada: Literature review*. Ottawa: Law Commission of Canada.

Wessells, M. G. (2006). *Child soldiers: From violence to protection*. Cambridge, MA: Harvard University Press.

Wilkinson, L. (2002). Factors influencing the academic success of refugee youth in Canada. *Journal of Youth Studies, 5*(2), 173–193.

Wouk, J., Yu, S., Roach, L., Thomson, J., & Harris, A. (2006). Unaccompanied/separated minors and refugee protection in Canada: Filling information gaps. *Refuge, 23*(2), 125–139.

Yohani, S. (2013). Educational cultural brokers and the school adaptation of refugee children and families: Challenges and opportunities. *Journal of International Migration and Integration, 14*(1), 61–79.

CHILDREN AND THE LAW

Chapter 8
The Supreme Court of Canada and the Convention
J. C. Blokhuis

Over the past quarter century since its ratification, the United Nations Convention on the Rights of the Child has been invoked in 20 decisions by the Supreme Court of Canada as an interpretive guide to the rights of children under the Charter, along with federal and provincial legislation.[1] These decisions illustrate how judicial recognition of the Convention has helped to advance children's rights in Canada in the absence of implementing legislation. In this chapter, we review 14 of the 20 decisions to date in which the Supreme Court has invoked the Convention in support of the "best interests of the child" principle.

ADOPTING THE CONVENTION

When it ratified the Convention in 1991, Canada made a commitment to recognize the rights of children outlined within its provisions. Because states are sovereign unto themselves, because individuals lack standing at international law, and because enforcement mechanisms against sovereign states at international law are limited, it would have been overly simplistic at that point to say that children in Canada had rights because the Convention said so. When it was first made available for signature, the Convention represented a moral commitment by states to safeguard and promote the welfare and developmental interests of children, but signatory states were essentially making that commitment to each another, not to children per se. To be sure, moral rights are correlates of moral duties, including duties assumed by states (Hohfeld, 1914; Cowden, 2016, pp. 27–33). But *legal* rights are institutionally contingent in ways that moral rights are not. There must be an institutional structure—courts of law—within which rights claims may be raised, recognized, and enforced (Blokhuis, 2015, p. 76).

In the absence of federal or provincial implementing legislation, Canadian courts could not immediately recognize the Convention as a source of legal rights for children following its ratification (see Lundy, Kilkelly, & Bryne, 2013). Moreover, neither children nor their parents had standing at international law or recourse to the UN except through the Canadian government. What would have happened if a well-informed twelve-year-old who did not want to be taken to church by her parents each week insisted that she had religious freedoms under the Convention in 1991? Her parents might have laughed. They might have been angered. Either way, they would probably not have taken her rights claim seriously.

As it happens, Article 14(1) of the Convention requires signatory states to "respect the right of the child to freedom of thought, conscience and religion." But neither this right nor the corresponding obligations for Canada are unqualified. Under Article 14(2), Canada also promised to "respect the rights and duties of the parents ... to provide direction to the child in the exercise of his or her right in a manner consistent with the evolving capacities of the child." The duties associated with the Convention are those of the state, not those of the parents of our precocious twelve-year-old, and Canada had promised to recognize and balance children's rights with the responsibilities of their parents and guardians. As a minor, our twelve-year-old had few avenues for legal recourse other than through her parents. If a signatory state reneges on its commitments under the Convention, there is no international court in which another signatory state or intergovernmental organization could sue Canada. Moreover, other states are unlikely to impose penalties through trade sanctions or restrictions on capital mobility should a state party fall short on its commitments under the Convention.

According to legal philosopher H. L. A. Hart (2012, p. 84), "rules are conceived and spoken of as imposing obligations when the general demand for conformity is insistent and the social pressure brought to bear upon those who deviate or threaten to deviate is great." Perhaps this is why, under Article 42, Canada and other signatory states have agreed "to make the principles and provisions of the Convention widely known, by appropriate and active means, to adults and children alike." Article 43 of the Convention establishes a Committee on the Rights of the Child to review reports of states parties in implementing the Convention and make recommendations for progress. Although the committee cannot compel implementation, it can bring pressure for change. The reports are publicly available and highlight shortcomings in implementation. Thus there are mechanisms for "naming and shaming" states that have failed to fulfill their commitments under the Convention (see Hafner-Burton, 2008).

ENFORCING THE CONVENTION

In order to have a *legal* right, one must have standing to raise a valid claim in court. Rights to which one cannot make a claim are imperfect at best (Feinberg, 1970, p. 251), and rights claims that are not enforceable in the courts are mere interests, hopes, or wishes. In order for the Convention to be enforceable in Canadian courts, its terms had to become part of domestic law. This happens automatically when some countries sign treaties, but in Canada and other parliamentary democracies on the Westminster model, ratification of treaties and conventions is generally done with a bill before Parliament explicitly implementing the treaty or convention, or by a bill incorporating some or all of its provisions into existing legislation by reference. Canada has yet to implement the Convention, in part due to separation of powers concerns. While the federal government is responsible for international relations, immigration, criminal law, and divorce, the provinces are individually responsible for social welfare, marriage, health, and education (Noël, 2015). Because the Convention deals with so many areas that fall within provincial jurisdiction, each province and territory would have to incorporate its provisions into its own legislation for children across the country to have comparable rights to provision, protection, and participation (see White, 2014). Canada still has a long way to go in this respect.

THE CHARTER AND THE CONVENTION

When Canada ratified the Convention in 1991, a legal revolution was already under way. Before the Charter, "Canadian law was primarily concerned with the regulation of economic, commercial and property affairs, and with the control of deviant personal behaviour by means of the criminal law," observed Nicholas Bala (2004, p. 4). With the advent of the Charter, "the role of law in Canadian society has changed dramatically. Law has become an important social policy tool, affecting virtually every aspect of Canadian public policy." For the first time, Canadians found themselves in "an increasingly 'rights-based' society ... in which individuals [could] look to the courts to address a broad range of concerns" (Bala, 2004, p. 5). Among these concerns were the limits of the *parens patriae* doctrine, historically exercised to safeguard the welfare and developmental interests of children. In a new rights-based legal landscape in which all persons were constitutionally entitled to equality before and under the law, could Canadian courts continue to prioritize the interests of children? Where would Canadian courts look for guidance in interpreting Charter rights? The United States has had ample experience with its own Bill of Rights, but American constitutional jurisprudence since

1972 has prioritized the interests of parents over the interests of children (Blokhuis, 2010).

The Supreme Court of Canada began using international agreements to interpret the Charter almost immediately after it came into full force and effect. In *Re Public Service Employee Relations Act*, [1987] 1 S.C.R. 313, Chief Justice Brian Dickson observed that "the similarity between the policies and provisions of the Charter and those of international human rights documents attaches considerable relevance to interpretations of those documents by adjudicative bodies" (paragraph 58). In 1993, two years after Canada ratified the Convention, a pair of custody disputes made their way to the Supreme Court of Canada from British Columbia and Quebec. Decided concurrently, the cases involved Charter challenges to the application of the "best interests of the child" principle. Here, for the very first time, the Supreme Court turned to the Convention as an interpretive aid.

Because the Supreme Court is the highest court in the land, its majority decisions must be followed across Canada as authoritative and definitive statements of the law. Dissenting opinions may have no formal legal weight, but they can (and often do) influence future majority decisions (van Geel, 2009, p. 11). When the Supreme Court finds federal or provincial legislation unconstitutional or inadequate, the legislation must be revised. Thus, as we shall see, the invocation of the Convention by the Supreme Court has, in a slow and piecemeal way, helped to fulfill the promise of children's rights under the Convention.

In *Young v. Young*, [1993] 4 S.C.R. 3, the British Columbia Supreme Court had granted Irene Young custody of her three daughters, while James Young was granted access subject to the condition that he not discuss his faith with the children, take them to religious services, or include them in door-to-door canvassing activities. This was largely because the two older children did not share their father's identity as a Jehovah's Witness. At the Supreme Court, James Young claimed that *his* freedom of religion, *his* freedom of expression, *his* freedom of association, and *his* equality rights under ss. 2(a), (b), (d) and s. 15 of the Charter had been infringed by the conditions imposed by the court. He also claimed that the "best interests of the child" standard was unconstitutionally vague.

Five of the seven Supreme Court justices who heard the appeal issued separate opinions agreeing in whole or in part with one another. One point on which there was general agreement was Justice Claire L'Heureux-Dubé's characterization of custody as the right of the child: "The power of the custodial parent is not a 'right' with independent value granted by courts for the benefit of the parent," she wrote. "Rather, the child has a right to a parent who will look after his or her best interests and the custodial parent a duty to ensure, protect and promote the child's best interests." Unless separating spouses made reasonable arrangements in the best interests of their children, the courts, acting in a *parens patriae* capacity, would continue to do so. "[I]n those rare cases where parents cross the line and engage in ... 'indoctrination, enlistment or harassment', courts have a duty to intervene in the best interests of children," she concluded. In her view, parents were not the only parties whose freedom of religion and expression were at stake in custodial disputes: "Freedom of religion is not an absolute value. Here, powerful competing interests must also be recognized, not the least of which, in addition to the best interests of the children, are the freedoms of expression and religion of the children themselves."

Justice L'Heureux-Dubé found that the "best interests of the child" principle was "completely consonant with the articulated values and underlying concerns of the Charter, as it aims to protect a vulnerable segment of society by ensuring that the interests and needs of the child take precedence over any competing considerations in custody and access decisions" (paragraph 83). She strongly denied that the "best interests" principle was unconstitutionally vague. "[T]he need to make the best interests of the child [a] primary consideration in all actions concerning children, including legal proceedings, is specifically recognized in international human rights documents such as the United Nations Convention on the Rights of the Child" (paragraph 910).

P. (D.) v. S. (C.), [1993] 4 S.C.R. 141, decided concurrently with the *Young* case, involved a couple who had lived together for three years following the birth of their child. They then signed a separation agreement ratified by the Quebec Superior Court giving the mother (C. S.) custody and the father (D. P.) access privileges. After D. P. became a Jehovah's Witness, C. S. asked the court to bar him from discussing his faith or engaging in door-to-door proselytizing during his access visits. The Superior Court recognized D. P.'s "religious fanaticism" as a source of anxiety for the child and granted C. S's application. Although *parens patriae* doctrine does not apply in Quebec (Morin, 1990), the Civil Code permits courts within the province to exercise comparably broad discretion in the best interests of the child. The Quebec Court of Appeals upheld the ruling.

For a unanimous Supreme Court, Justice L'Heureux-Dubé again defended the "best interests of the child" standard under the Charter and the Convention. "The right to custody of a very young child includes that of educating and instructing it in accordance with its best interests having regard to its moral, intellectual and physical development," she wrote. "A court has a clear duty to observe and apply this principle, and this has nothing to do with a violation of judicial neutrality or failure to respect the constitutional guarantee of freedom of religion." As in the *Young* case, Justice

L'Heureux-Dubé invoked the Convention as clear evidence that the "best interests of the child" standard was anything but vague: "This criterion has also been applied for decades by courts in Quebec and abroad, giving rise to a large body of case law. This indicates the universal and lasting value of the criterion, as well as the fact that its content is significant" (paragraph 101).

Three years later, the Supreme Court heard a third custody dispute. *Gordon v. Goertz*, [1996] 2 S.C.R. 27 involved a custodial parent, Janet Gordon, who planned to move from Saskatchewan to Australia with her child. Her former spouse, Robin Goertz, sought custody or an order barring the move. The Saskatchewan courts had dismissed his application and varied his access order to allow for visits in Australia only. The Supreme Court unanimously agreed that as the custodial parent, Janet Gordon could relocate as she saw fit. Robin Goertz could have access visits in both Canada and Australia. While there was no presumption in favour of the custodial parent seeking to relocate, her views and those of the child were to be taken into account. Writing for a majority on the Court, Justice Beverly McLachlin described the best interests principle as "an eloquent expression of Parliament's view that the ultimate and only issue when it comes to custody and access is the welfare of the child whose future is at stake" (paragraph 20). Concurring on this point, Justice L'Heureux-Dubé found that under the *Divorce Act*, "All decisions as to custody and access must be made in the best interests of children, assessed from a child-centred perspective" (paragraph 143) and in accordance with the Convention (paragraph 87): "International awareness of children's rights is illustrated by various international documents [including] the United Nations Convention on the Rights of the Child ... which recognizes the need to make the best interests of the child the primary consideration in all actions concerning children, including legal proceedings."

As the highest court in the land, the Supreme Court of Canada agrees to hear appeals from across the country in all areas of law, especially where there is uncertainty or inconsistency in the interpretation or application of law among the lower courts. In the same year as *Young v. Young* and *P. (D.) v. S. (C.)*, the Supreme Court heard an appeal from Manitoba on the constitutionality of s. 715.1 of the Criminal Code, which permits videotaped testimony from child victims of sexual assault to protect them from the trauma of testifying in open court (and in full view of their abusers). In *R. v. L. (D. O.)*, [1993] 4 S.C.R. 419, a man charged with sexually assaulting a nine-year-old girl argued that videotaped testimony violated *his* rights under sections 7 and 11(d) of the Charter. Citing the Convention, Justice L'Heureux-Dubé concurred with her colleagues in rejecting these claims. "I find that the inclusion of all children up to the age of 18 under the protections afforded by s. 715.1 of the Criminal Code is required by the continued need for such protection and is in conformity with international and domestic instruments," she concluded (paragraph 69).

A watershed for judicial recognition of the Convention occurred six years later in *Baker v. Canada* [1999] 2 S.C.R. 817. Mavis Baker was a Jamaican citizen who had arrived in Canada on a tourist visa in 1981. A deportation order was issued against her in 1992. The following year, she sought a ministerial exemption to apply for permanent residency from within Canada on humanitarian and compassionate grounds, arguing that she and her four Canadian-born children would suffer emotional hardship if they were separated. Significantly, she also argued that the Convention required immigration officials to prioritize the best interests of her children when making a decision in her case.

At the Federal Court, Trial Division, Justice Sandra Simpson dismissed Baker's application for judicial review and denied her Convention claim. In her view, because the Convention had not been implemented, it was not part of domestic law and could not give rise to a legitimate expectation on Baker's part that her children's interests would be a primary consideration in the circumstances. The Federal Court of Appeals agreed and referred the following question to the Supreme Court: "Given that the *Immigration Act* does not expressly incorporate the language of Canada's international obligations with respect to the Convention on the Rights of the Child, must federal immigration authorities treat the best interests of the Canadian child as a primary consideration in assessing an applicant under s. 114(2) of the *Immigration Act*?"

At the Supreme Court, Justices Frank Iacobucci and Peter Cory agreed with the lower courts, answering the question from the Federal Court of Appeals in the negative. "It is a matter of well-settled law that an international convention ratified by the executive branch of government is of no force or effect within the Canadian legal system until such time as its provisions have been incorporated into domestic law by way of implementing legislation," wrote Justice Iacobucci. "I do not agree with the approach adopted by my colleague, wherein reference is made to the underlying values of an unimplemented international treaty in the course of the contextual approach to statutory interpretation and administrative law," he continued, "because such an approach is not in accordance with the Court's jurisprudence concerning the status of international law within the domestic legal system" (paragraph 79).

Justice Iacobucci was referring to the approach taken by Justice L'Heureux-Dubé, whose decision in *Baker* was supported by a majority on the Court. She answered the question from the Federal Court of Appeals in the affirmative. "Another indicator of the importance of considering the interests of children when making a compassionate and humanitarian decision is the ratification by Canada of the Convention on the Rights of the Child," she wrote, "and the recognition of the importance of children's rights and the best interests of children in other international instruments ratified by Canada." She acknowledged that the Convention had not been implemented by statute. Nevertheless, she concluded that "the values reflected in international human rights law may help inform the contextual approach to statutory interpretation and judicial review" (paragraphs 69–70), citing a tenet of statutory interpretation (Sullivan, 1994, p. 330; see also Beaulac & Côté, 2007) that "the legislature is presumed to respect the values and principles enshrined in international law, both customary and conventional.... In so far as possible, therefore, interpretations that reflect these values and principles are preferred."

"Because the reasons for this decision do not indicate that it was made in a manner which was alive, attentive, or sensitive to the interests of Ms. Baker's children, and did not consider them as an important factor in making the decision," concluded Justice L'Heureux-Dubé, "it was an unreasonable exercise of the power conferred by the legislation, and must, therefore, be overturned." Mavis Baker would be allowed to remain in Canada with her children and apply for permanent residency.

This was a victory for Mavis Baker and her children, but also for the Convention as a touchstone for children's rights in Canada. Following *Baker*, the federal government amended the *Immigration and Refugee Protection Act*, S.C. 2001, c. 27. Under s. 25(1), immigration officials must now consider the best interests of a child directly affected by decisions made on humanitarian and compassionate grounds. Consistent with Article 3 of the Convention, which stipulates that the best interests of the child shall be *a* primary consideration rather than *the* primary consideration, the federal government maintains that "the best interests of a child is only one of many important factors that the decision maker needs to consider when making an H&C decision that directly affects a child" (Government of Canada, 2016).

The following year, the Supreme Court upheld the constitutionality of provisions within the *Manitoba Child and Family Services Act* allowing for the warrantless apprehension of a child in a non-emergency. *Winnipeg Child and Family Services v. K. L. W.* [2000] 2 S.C.R. 519 involved a woman whose two older children had been taken into care due to neglect and intoxication. Having reasonable and probable grounds to believe her newborn third child was also in need of protection, social workers apprehended the baby. K. L. W. alleged this violated *her* section 7 Charter right to "life, liberty and security of the person and the right not to be deprived thereof except in accordance with the principles of fundamental justice." Writing for a majority on the Supreme Court, Justice L'Heureux-Dubé observed that "From the child's perspective, state action in the form of apprehension seeks to ensure the protection, and indeed the very survival, of another interest of fundamental importance: the child's life and health." Citing the protection of children from harm as "a universally accepted goal" under the Convention (paragraph 73), and "because children are vulnerable and cannot exercise their rights independently, particularly at a young age, and because child abuse and neglect have long-term effects ... the State has assumed both the duty and the power to intervene to protect children's welfare" (paragraph 75).

In a notorious case from the British Columbia Court of Appeal the following year, a majority on the Supreme Court recognized certain types of pornographic writings as forms of expression protected under section 2(b) of the Charter. In *R. v. Sharpe*, [2001] 1 S.C.R. 45, the criminal charges associated with John Sharpe's possession of *written* child pornography were dismissed, while the charges associated with his possession of *graphic* child pornography would stand. In a searing dissent, Justice L'Heureux-Dubé objected to the protection of *any* form of child pornography under the Charter, citing Articles 2, 19, 9, 16, 32, 33, 35, 37, and 34 of the Convention, which had at that time been signed by 191 states (paragraph 171) and the Optional Protocol to the Convention on the Sale of Children, Child Prostitution and Child Pornography, which had at that time been signed by 69 states (paragraph 178). "The possession of child pornography has no social value; it has only a tenuous connection to the value of self-fulfillment underlying the right to free expression," she concluded. "As such, it warrants only attenuated protection. Hence, increased deference should be accorded to Parliament's decision to prohibit it" (paragraph 186).

Another setback for children's rights and the Convention occurred three years later, when the Supreme Court agreed to hear an appeal from Ontario on the constitutionality of Canada's so-called "spanking law" in *Canadian Foundation for Children, Youth and the Law v. Canada*, [2004] 1 S.C.R. 76. Striking another person is a form of assault. Section 43 is a statutory defence that may be invoked by parents and schoolteachers charged with assault under the Criminal Code. Section 43 of the Criminal Code, R.S.C., 1985, c. C-4, provides as follows: "Every schoolteacher, parent or person standing in the place of a parent is justified in using force by way of correction toward a pupil or child, as the case may be, who is under his care, if the force does not exceed what is reasonable under the circumstances." It is important to note that while teachers who use corporal punishment may invoke section 43 if they are charged with criminal assault, it is of absolutely no use to them if they are sued for battery in a civil proceeding, or if they are stripped of their licence for violating professional standards of conduct and school policies.

The Canadian Foundation for Children, Youth and the Law argued that corporal punishment violates children's section 7 (security of the person), 12 (cruel and unusual punishment), and 15 (equal protection) rights under the Charter, along with Canada's commitments under the Convention, including Article 3 (best interests of the child); Article 19 (protection from all forms of physical or mental violence by parents or others in positions of authority); Article 28 (school discipline and human dignity); and Article 37 (degrading treatment). The attorney general for Canada successfully defended section 43 of the Criminal Code with the assistance of a number of well-financed intervenors, mostly US-based parental rights organizations (including Focus on the Family and the Home School Legal Defense Association). The section 43 defence had been invoked successfully in numerous cases involving corporal punishment against children of all ages by parents and teachers by 2004, and in its report on Canada's compliance with the Convention the preceding year, the UN Committee on the Rights of the Child expressed "deep concern" that Canada had taken "no action to remove section 43 of the Criminal Code" (Committee on the Rights of the Child, 2003; cited by Justice Louise Arbour at paragraph 188).

Writing for a majority on the Supreme Court, Chief Justice Beverly McLachlin found that section 43 of the Criminal Code did *not* violate children's section 7 Charter rights. In her view, the "best interests of the child" is not a principle of fundamental justice, and laws affecting children need not be in their best interests. Noting that children's interests are represented in criminal trials by the Crown as *parens patriae*, she found there were adequate procedural safeguards for children under section 43. Whether corrective force is "reasonable in the circumstances," according to the chief justice, should be understood in light of Canada's international treaty obligations (paragraphs 31–32). But by her account, "Neither the Convention on the Rights of the Child nor the International Covenant on Civil and Political Rights explicitly require state parties to ban all corporal punishment of children" (paragraph 33). "Without s. 43, Canada's broad assault law would criminalize force falling far short of what we think of as corporal punishment," she concluded. "The decision not to criminalize such conduct is not grounded in devaluation of the child, but in a concern that to do so risks ruining lives and breaking up families—a burden that in large part would be borne by children and outweigh any benefit derived from applying the criminal process" (paragraph 62).

In a vigorous dissent, Justice Louise Arbour accused the chief justice of rewriting section 43 in order to validate its constitutionality (paragraph 139). In her view, section 43 violated the Charter rights of children because, among other things, the "reasonable in the circumstances" criterion had been interpreted differently across the country in dozens of cases. Thus section 43 violated the principle of fundamental justice that laws be clear. "A vague law violates the principles of fundamental justice because it does not provide 'fair warning' to individuals as to the legality of their actions," she noted (paragraph 177). In addition, she found that the degree of protection to which children are entitled under the Charter had to be informed by the rights of protection under the Convention (paragraph 186).

Justice Marie Deschamps penned a separate dissenting opinion finding that section 43 violates children's rights under both the Charter and the Convention. "[Children] have been recognized as a vulnerable group time and again by legislatures and courts. Historically, their vulnerability was entrenched by the traditional legal treatment of children as the property or chattel of their parents or guardians," she wrote. "Fortunately, this attitude has changed in modern times with a recognition that children, as individuals, have rights, including the right to have their security and safety protected by their parents, families and society at large" (paragraph 225). However, she continued, "s. 43 appears to be a throwback to old notions of children as property."

Given Chief Justice Beverly McLachlin's defence of section 43 of the Criminal Code and its "reasonable in the circumstances" standard in 2004, her opinion in a youth justice case from Nova Scotia the following year was somewhat surprising. *R. v. R.C.* [2005] 3 S.C.R. 99 involved a youth who stabbed his mother in the foot with a pen and punched her in the face after she yelled at him to get out of bed and go to school. R. C. pleaded guilty to assault with a weapon. Under section 487.051(1)(a) of the Criminal Code, courts must authorize the taking of DNA samples from persons accused of assault unless the accused person establishes that the impact of such an order on his or her privacy and security interests under s. 7 of the Charter "would be grossly disproportionate to the public interest in the protection of society and the proper administration of justice."

Writing for the majority, the Chief Justice found that "[t]he taking and retention of a DNA sample constitutes a grave intrusion on a person's right to personal and informational privacy" (paragraph 39). "While no specific provision of the youth criminal justice legislation modifies s. 487.051, Parliament clearly intended that this legislation would be respected whenever young persons are brought within the criminal justice system." Citing the Convention, she added, "Parliament has recognized their heightened vulnerability and has sought to extend enhanced procedural protections to them, and to interfere with their personal freedom as little as possible" (paragraph 41). In her view, the trial court's decision not to order a DNA test was reasonable in the circumstances and should not have been set aside by the Court of Appeal" (paragraph 70).

It may have been difficult for observers to understand how spanking a child for corrective purposes could be considered "reasonable in the circumstances" and constitutional in *Canadian Foundation for Children, Youth and the Law*, while the taking of DNA with a mouth swab could be considered "unreasonable in the circumstances" and unconstitutional in *R. v. R.C.* The Chief Justice's apparent about-face may have been related to the coming into force on April 1, 2003, of the *Youth Criminal Justice Act* [YCJA], S.C. 2001, c. 1, replacing the *Young Offenders Act*. Hailed as "the most systematic attempt in Canadian history to structure judicial discretion regarding the sentencing of juveniles" (Roberts & Bala, 2003, p. 396; cited by Justice Louise Charron at paragraph 19), the YCJA was a significant piece of legislation because, for the first time, Parliament explicitly incorporated Canada's commitments under the Convention into its Preamble by reference: "WHEREAS Canada is a party to the United Nations Convention on the Rights of the Child and recognizes that young persons have rights and freedoms, including those stated in the Canadian Charter of Rights and Freedoms and the Canadian Bill of Rights, and have special guarantees of their rights and freedoms...."

The effects were readily apparent in the next two decisions from the Supreme Court of Canada. The first decision concerned appeals from Manitoba and British Columbia consolidated as *In R. v. B. W. P. and R. v. B. V. N.*, [2006] 1 S.C.R. 941. B. W. P. was a 15-year-old who pleaded guilty to manslaughter in the death of 22-year-old Chya Saleh. The sentencing judge held that general deterrence was not applicable under the YCJA and sentenced him to one day in open custody and 15 months under conditional supervision in the community. The Manitoba Court of Appeal affirmed this decision. B. V. N. was a 16-year-old who pleaded guilty to aggravated assault for punching and kicking a 42-year-old heroin addict. The sentencing judge issued a nine-month closed custody and supervision order to ensure his participation in rehabilitation programs. The British Columbia Court of Appeals upheld the sentence, affirming that while general deterrence was a permissible factor under the YCJA, it had not increased the length of B. V. N's sentence. General deterrence is a principle by which lengthier sentences may be imposed to deter other people from committing similar crimes, essentially using the convicted person as an example. "It is quite clear in considering the Preamble and the statute as a whole that Parliament's goal in enacting the new youth sentencing regime was to reserve the most serious interventions for the most serious crimes and thereby reduce the over-reliance on incarceration for non-violent young persons," wrote Justice Louise Charron for a unanimous

Supreme Court (paragraph 35). In keeping with the Convention, she found that "Parliament deliberately excluded general deterrence as a factor of youth sentencing" (paragraph 34).

The second decision concerned an appeal from Ontario. In *R. v. D. B.*, [2008] 2 S.C.R. 3, 17-year-old D. B. had pleaded guilty to manslaughter after an altercation with a friend in a shopping mall led to his death. Under the YCJA, an adult sentence was presumptively applied in offences including manslaughter, with the onus on the accused to convince the court to apply a youth sentence. D. B. argued that this reverse onus violated his s. 7 Charter rights. Writing for a majority on the Supreme Court, Justice Rosalie Abella agreed with D. B. "The presumption of an adult sentence in the onus provisions is inconsistent with the principle of fundamental justice that young people are entitled to a presumption of diminished moral culpability throughout any proceedings against them," she wrote (paragraph 69). "The legislative history of the youth criminal justice system in Canada confirms that the presumption of diminished moral culpability for young persons is a long-standing legal principle [that] ... also finds expression in Canada's international commitments, in particular the UN Convention on the Rights of the Child" (paragraphs 59–60).

While the statutory age of majority for particular purposes in each province or territory is categorical, marking the point at which legal presumptions of competence shift, competence itself evolves over time as a child matures. Thus children have an interest in making more and more choices for themselves as they mature. In the next decision by the Supreme Court of Canada, in *A. C. v. Manitoba*, [2009] 2 S.C.R. 181, this approach was found to be consistent with children's rights under the Convention. Fourteen-year-old A. C. was admitted to hospital with gastrointestinal bleeding due to Crohn's disease. In keeping with her family's beliefs as Jehovah's Witnesses, she had earlier signed a directive declining the blood transfusions. Child and Family Services apprehended her as a child in need of protection, and sought a treatment order under section 25(8) of the Manitoba *Child and Family Services Act* (CFSA). A judge ordered the transfusions, concluding that for a child under 16, *parens patriae* authority could be exercised in the best interests of the child. A. C. and her parents argued that this infringed her rights under sections 2(a), 7, and 15 of the Charter. The Manitoba Court of Appeal upheld the constitutionality of the CFSA and of the blood transfusion order.

"The extent to which [input from the child] affects the 'best interests' assessment is as variable as the child's circumstances, but one thing that can be said with certainty is that the input becomes increasingly determinative as the child matures," wrote Justice Abella in her majority opinion at the Supreme Court (paragraph 88; citing Eekelaar, 1992, and Eekelaar,

1994). "This is true not only when considering the child's best interests in the placement context, but also when deciding whether to accede to a child's wishes in medical treatment situations" (paragraph 92). "The Convention ... describes 'the best interests of the child' as a primary consideration in all actions concerning children (Article 3)," she continued. "It then sets out a framework under which the child's own input will inform the content of the 'best interests' standard,' with the weight accorded to these views increasing in relation to the child's developing maturity" (paragraph 93). Because sufficiently mature children under 16 can rebut the statutory presumption of incompetence to make medical treatment decisions, Justice Abella found the Manitoba CFSA did not violate section 7. Nor did it violate section 15 of the Charter because capacity to consent to medical treatment is a function of *maturity*, not age.

Three years later, in an appeal from Nova Scotia concerning a pervasive social toxin for young people across Canada, the Supreme Court found that the privacy interests of children are a function of age, not maturity. In *A. B. v. Bragg Communications*, [2012] 2 S.C.R. 567, the issue was whether the privacy interests of a victim of cyberbullying trumped freedom of the press. Through her father, 15-year-old A. B. had asked the Nova Scotia courts to compel her Internet service provider to release the IP address and identity of the person who had created a fake Facebook profile with A. B.'s photo, negative comments about her appearance, and some sexually explicit references. Bragg Communications was not opposed to disclosing the information. However, the *Halifax Herald* and *Global Television* opposed A. B.'s request to proceed anonymously and for a publication ban on the proceedings, arguing that this would impair freedom of the press. The trial court agreed with the media companies and awarded costs against A. B. The Court of Appeal upheld the decision, primarily because A. B. had not shown real and substantial harm to her that would justify a publication ban.

For a unanimous Supreme Court, Justice Abella granted the appeal. "[A. B.'s] privacy interests in this case are tied both to her age and to the nature of the victimization she seeks protection from. It is not merely a question of her privacy, but of her privacy from the relentlessly intrusive humiliation of sexualized online bullying" (paragraph 14). In her view, the protection of children from cyberbullying outweighed both open court and free press principles. The lower courts should have recognized that as a child, A. B., was inherently vulnerable: "Recognition of the inherent vulnerability of children has consistent and deep roots in Canadian law. This results in protection for young people's privacy under the Criminal Code, the *Youth Criminal Justice Act* and child welfare legislation, not to mention international protections such as the Convention ... all based on age, not the sensitivity of the particular child," wrote Justice Abella (paragraph 17). "As a result, in an application involving sexualized cyberbullying, there is no need for a particular child to demonstrate that she personally conforms to this legal paradigm. The law attributes the heightened vulnerability based on chronology, not temperament."

In the most recent case of those examined in this chapter, the Supreme Court heard an appeal from the Federal Court of Appeals that was similar in some respects to the watershed *Baker* case in 1999. The legal landscape had changed, however, as the best interests of the child principle was incorporated into section 25(1) of the *Immigration and Refugee Protection Act* in the wake of *Baker*. This created a statutory obligation to take into account the best interests of any child directly affected by an IRB decision, in accordance with Canada's commitments under the Convention. In *Kanthasamy v. Canada*, [2015] 3 S.C.R. 909, 16-year-old Jeyakannan Kanthasamy claimed refugee protection based on his fear that he would be arrested if returned to Sri Lanka. The Immigration and Refugee Board denied his claim. The following year, Kanthasamy filed an application for humanitarian and compassionate relief under section 25(1). Although Kanthasamy was diagnosed with post-traumatic stress disorder and depression, the board determined that his return to Sri Lanka would not result in "unusual and undeserved or disproportionate" hardship, and the Federal Court of Appeals upheld that decision.

For a majority on the Supreme Court, Justice Abella granted the appeal. In her view, because children were "rarely, if ever, deserving of any hardship, the concept of unusual or undeserved hardship was presumptively inapplicable to the assessment" of a child's application for humanitarian and compassionate relief (paragraph 41). Kanthasamy's status as a child under the Convention should have triggered the requirement that his best interests be taken into account (paragraph 59). "It is difficult to see how a child can be more directly affected than where he or she is the applicant," concluded Justice Abella (paragraph 41). Kanthasamy would be allowed to remain in Canada and to apply for permanent residency.

CONCLUSION

"[Children] have been recognized as a vulnerable group time and again by legislatures and courts. Historically, their vulnerability was entrenched by the traditional legal treatment of children as the property or chattel of their parents or guardians," wrote Justice Marie Deschamps in *Canadian Foundation for Children, Youth and the Law*. "Fortunately, this attitude has changed in modern times with a recognition that children, as individuals, have rights, including the right to have their security and safety protected by their parents, families and society at large" (paragraph 225). Taken together, the Supreme Court decisions in which the Convention has been invoked illustrate how judicial recognition has helped to advance children's rights in Canada.

Ultimately, children can enjoy the substance of their rights only when they are recognized and respected as rights holders. In this sense, rights are both socially and institutionally contingent. "Enjoyment of the substance of a right is socially guaranteed," writes philosopher Henry Shue (1980, p. 75), "only if all social institutions, as well as individual persons, avoid depriving people of the substance of the right and some provide, if necessary, aid to anyone who has nevertheless been deprived of the substance of the right." The halting and piecemeal recognition of the Convention by the Supreme Court has achieved in part what implementing legislation and widespread children's rights education would surely achieve more fully. Much remains to be done if children are actually to enjoy the substance of their rights under the Convention in Canada.

QUESTIONS FOR DISCUSSION

1. If Canada were to implement the Convention, would children instantly enjoy the substance of their rights? What else would have to happen?

2. How does the lack of implementing legislation in Canada illustrate the institutional contingency of Convention rights?

3. Why can't children make rights claims under the Convention in Canadian courts?

NOTES

The author wishes to thank Katherine Covell, R. Brian Howe, and Wilfrid Laurier University Press for permission to reprint some of his contributions to Chapter 4 in Katherine Covell, R. Brian Howe, & J. C. Blokhuis, *The challenge of children's rights for Canada* (2nd ed.).

1   In six Supreme Court decisions, the Convention was invoked but not relevant to their disposition: *M. M. v. United States of America*, [2015] S.C.J. No. 62; *Kazemi Estate v. Islamic Republic of Iran*, [2014] S.C.J. No. 62; *R. v. C. D.* and *R. v. C. D. K.*, [2005] S.C.J. No. 79; *Trinity Western University v. British Columbia College of Teachers*, [2001] S.C.J. No. 32; *United States of America v. Burns*, [2001] S.C.J. No. 8; and *V. W. v. D. S.*, [1996] S.C.J. No. 53.

REFERENCES

Bala, N. (2004). Child welfare law in Canada: An introduction. In N. Bala, M. K. Zapf, R. J. Williams, R. Vogl, & J. P. Hornick (Eds.), *Canadian child welfare law: Children, families and the state* (2nd ed.). Toronto: Thompson.

Beaulac, S., & P.-A. Côté (2007). Driedger's "modern principle" at the Supreme Court of Canada: Interpretation, justification, legitimization. *Revue Juridique Thémis*. Retrieved from https://papers.ssrn.com/sol3/papers2.cfm?abstract_id=987199

Blokhuis, J. C. (2010). Whose custody is it, anyway? Homeschooling from a *parens patriae* perspective. *Theory and Research in Education, 8*(2), 199–222.

Blokhuis, J. C. (2015). Student rights and the special characteristics of the school environment in American jurisprudence. *Journal of Philosophy of Education, 49*(1), 65–85.

Committee on the Rights of the Child. (2003). Consideration of reports submitted by state parties under article 44 of the Convention, 34th session, CRC/C/15/Add. 215. Retrieved from http://repository.un.org/handle/11176/384083

Covell, K., Howe, R. B., & Blokhuis, J. C. (2018). *The challenge of children's rights for Canada* (2nd ed.). Waterloo, ON: Wilfrid Laurier University Press.

Cowden, M. (2016). *Children's rights: From philosophy to public policy*. Basingstoke, UK: Palgrave Macmillan.

Eekelaar, J. (1992). The importance of thinking that children have rights. *International Journal of Law and the Family, 6*(1), 221–235.

Eekelaar, J. (1994). The interests of the child and the child's wishes: The role of dynamic self-determinism. *International Journal of Law and the Family, 8*(1), 42–61.

Feinberg, J. (1970). The nature and value of rights. *Journal of Value Inquiry, 4*(4), 243–257.

Government of Canada. (2016). Humanitarian and compassionate assessment: Best interests of a child. Ottawa: Immigration, Refugees and Citizenship Canada. Retrieved from https://www.canada.ca/en/immigration-refugees-citizenship/corporate/publications-manuals/operational-bulletins-manuals/permanent-residence/humanitarian-compassionate-consideration/processing/assessment-best-interests-child.html

Hafner-Burton, E. M. (2008). Sticks and stones: Naming and shaming the human rights enforcement problem. *International Organization, 62*(4) (2008), 689–716.

Hart, H. L. A. (2012). *The concept of law* (3rd ed.). New York: Oxford University Press.

Hohfeld, W. N. (1914). Some fundamental legal conceptions as applied in judicial reasoning. *Yale Law Journal, 23*(1), 16–59.

Lundy, L., Kilkelly, U., & Bryne, B. (2013). Incorporation of the United Nations Convention on the Rights of the Child in Law: A comparative review. *International Journal of Children's Rights, 21*(3), 442–463.

Morin, M. (1990). La compétence *parens patriae* et le droit privé québécois: Un emprunt inutile, un affront à l'histoire. *Revue du Barreau, 50*(5), 827–923.

Noël, J.-F. (2015). *The Convention on the Rights of the Child*. Ottawa: Department of Justice. Retrieved from http://www.justice.gc.ca/eng/rp-pr/fl-lf/divorce/crc-crde/conv2a.html

Roberts, J. V., & Bala, N. (2003). Understanding sentencing under the Youth Criminal Justice Act. *Alberta Law Review, 41*(2), 395–423.

Shue, H. (1980). *Basic rights*. Princeton, NJ: Princeton University Press.
Sullivan, R. (1994). *Driedger on the construction of statutes* (3rd ed.). Toronto: Butterworths.
van Geel, T. R. (2009). *Understanding Supreme Court opinions* (6th ed.). New York: Longman.
White, L. A. (2014). Understanding Canada's lack of progress in implementing the UN Convention on the Rights of the Child. *International Journal of Children's Rights, 22*(1), 164–188.

Chapter 9
More Than a Symbol
Canada's Legal Justification of Corporal Punishment of Children
Joan Durrant

In 1979, Sweden became the first country to unequivocally prohibit all corporal punishment of children. This was the first time in world history that children's rights to full protection were enshrined in law. The Swedish law states: "Children are entitled to care, security and a good upbringing. Children are to be treated with respect for their person and individuality and may not be subjected to corporal punishment or other injurious or humiliating treatment" (Chapter 6, Section 1, Parenthood and Guardianship Code).

Sweden's law was highly significant for several reasons. First, it erased the hypothetical line between "punishment" and "abuse." All corporal punishment was prohibited, no matter how "light." Second, it ended the presumptive distinction between corporal punishment administered by parents and that administered by others in their lives. All corporal punishment was prohibited. Third, the law was written from the perspective of children. Its intent was to protect children from harm, rather than to protect adults from being held accountable should they harm them. Finally, Sweden's law recognized children as independent rights bearers, entitled not only to protection from violence, but to a standard of care. It enshrined children's rights to dignity as persons, with identities separate from those of the adults who care for them and, by implication, with an autonomous voice. (For more information on the history and outcomes of this law, see Durrant, 1999, 2000, 2003; Durrant & Janson, 2005; Durrant & Olsen, 1997.)

Covell and Howe (2001) have set out three stages of legal evolution, proceeding from social laissez-faire, in which children are seen primarily as "objects of parental authority" (p. 16), through paternalistic protection, in which children are viewed as in need of state protection when mistreated, to the stage of children's rights, in which children are recognized as independent bearers of rights and the state is viewed as having an obligation to fulfill those rights. In this third stage, "children are entitled to have their needs provided for not because parents have obligations or because the state has a paternalistic duty to children, but because children have fundamental rights to having their basic needs fulfilled" (p. 19). Sweden's law is the embodiment of stage 3 law.

Since Sweden passed its historic law, 57 countries have followed its lead. These countries are located in almost all regions of the world.[1] While most of their laws are based on children's rights to full protection, some also recognize children's rights to dignity and/or redress for violations of their rights.

- In Bulgaria: Every child has a right to protection against all methods of upbringing that undermine his or her dignity; against physical, psychical, or other types of violence; against all forms of influence which go against his or her interests (Article 11.2, *Child Protection Act*, 2000).

- In Latvia: A child shall not be treated cruelly, tortured or physically punished, and his or her dignity or honour shall not be violated (Law on Protection of the Rights of the Child, 1998).

- In Liechtenstein: (1) Children and young people have the rights outlined in the Convention on the Rights of the Child and to the following measures: (a) protection notably against discrimination, neglect, violence, abuse, and sexual abuse; (b) education/upbringing without violence: corporal punishment, psychological harm, and other degrading treatment are not accepted.... (2) Children can address the Ombudsperson when they believe their rights have been violated (Article 3, *Children and Youth Act*, 2008).

- In Mongolia: Children have the right to be protected from crime, offences, or any forms of violence, physical punishment, psychological abuse, neglect, and exploitation in all social settings (Article 7.1, Law on the Rights of Children).

- In Paraguay: All children and adolescents have the right to good treatment and for their physical, psychological, and emotional integrity to be respected. This right includes the protection of their image, their identity, their autonomy, their thoughts, their feelings, their dignity, and their values. Corporal punishment and humiliating treatment of children and adolescents is prohibited as a form of correction or discipline, especially when it is imparted by parents, tutors, guardians, or anyone responsible for their education, care, guidance, or treatment of any kind. Children and adolescents are especially entitled to receive guidance, education, care, and discipline by implementing guidelines for positive parenting.... State institutions ... must provide resources to ... guarantee the full exercise of the rights of the child or adolescent at all levels and public agencies (Articles 1 and 5, Law on Promotion of Good Treatment, Positive Parenting and Protection of Children and Adolescents against Corporal Punishment or Any Type of Violence as a Method of Correction or Discipline, 2016).

- In South Sudan: Every child has the right: ... f) to be free from corporal punishment and cruel and inhuman treatment by any person including parents, school administrations and other institutions (Article 17.1, Transitional Constitution of the Republic of South Sudan, 2011).

The only continent on which no child has full legal protection is North America. Unlike the 58 prohibitions that are written from the perspective of children, Canada's law was written to protect "persons in authority": "Every school teacher, parent or person standing in the place of a parent is justified in using force by way of correction toward a pupil or child, as the case may be, who is under his care, if the force does not exceed what is reasonable in the circumstances" (Section 43, Criminal Code).

This is Canada's law in 2019.

CHILDREN'S RIGHTS AND CORPORAL PUNISHMENT IN CANADA

Canada enjoys a positive reputation internationally with regard to its human rights record. In reality, however, Canada has many human rights challenges, including the detention of immigrant children in prison-like institutions, lack of access to clean drinking water for many Indigenous children, the inequitable provision of child welfare services to First Nations children—and the government's failure to provide children with full legal protection from physical assault (First Nations Child and Family Caring Society of Canada, 2014; Gros & Song, 2016; Human Rights Watch, 2016; Watkinson, 2012). Among Western industrialized countries, Canada is rapidly becoming an anomaly with respect to its law on corporal punishment. For example, in 2004, the Parliamentary Assembly of the Council of Europe called for full prohibition of corporal punishment of children across Europe (Parliamentary Assembly, 2004, paragraph 7). By September 2019, 70 percent of the council's member states (33 of 47 States) and 82 percent of the European Union's member states (23 of 28 states) have prohibited all corporal punishment of children.

This progress is not limited to Europe. For example, as of September 2019, eight countries in Africa have implemented full prohibitions and at least another 18 have made a clear commitment to doing so.[2] The Inter-American

Commission on Human Rights (2009) has called on all member states of the Organization of American States (OAS) to prohibit and eliminate all corporal punishment of children. Eight years later, out of 19 Latin American countries, 10 have implemented full prohibitions and another seven have publicly committed to doing so. This global progress continues while Canada retains a law that was codified in 1892.

THE HISTORY OF CANADA'S LAW

Canada's corporal punishment defence has ancient roots—in an edict issued by the Roman emperors Valentinian and Valens (McGillivray & Durrant, 2012). Under the ancient Roman law of *patria potestas*, the eldest male member of the household had complete power over all members of his family, as well as his slaves and freedmen, including the power to execute them. In AD 365, Valentinian and Valens issued a decree granting "the power of punishing minors to their elder relatives," but they withdrew "the right to inflict extremely severe castigation for the faults of minors" (Scott, 1939, Digest, Book 9, Title 15). This early child protection law provided the foundation for the current concept of "reasonable force" found in section 43 of the Criminal Code.

The legal route from Ancient Rome to Canada travelled by way of English common law. Many early English judges and scholars were educated in Roman law, and were heavily influenced by it. Those ancient legal concepts entered their judgments, became part of the common law, were integrated into the laws of English colonies, and remain part of Canada's law today. For example, the famous treatise by Henry de Bracton, a common-law scholar, reflected elements of Roman law. In 1250, he wrote: "whippings ... are not punishable if imposed by a master or parent (unless they are immoderate) since they are taken to be inflicted to correct not injure, but are punished when one is struck in anger by a stranger" (de Bracton, 1968, vol. 2, p. 299).

Five hundred years later, another common-law scholar, Blackstone, incorporated Roman law concepts into his treatise, *Commentaries on the Laws of England*: "The ancient Roman laws gave the father a power of life and death over his children.... The power of a parent by our English laws is much more moderate; but still sufficient to keep the child in order and obedience. He may lawfully correct his child, being under age, in a reasonable manner; for this is for the benefit of his education" (Blackstone, 1872, Book 1, Chapter 16, paragraph 452; originally published 1765).

Then, in 1860, the concept of "reasonable force" was entrenched in the common law by a judicial decision that became the prototype for section 43.

Reginald Cancellor, a 14-year-old student at Eastbourne School in England, was perceived by his teachers as "uneducable" (Moore, 2008). The schoolmaster, Thomas Hopley, believed that he could "subdue his obstinacy" through corporal chastisement using a skipping rope and a walking stick. Hopley flogged the boy so severely that he died. Hopley was charged with his death. This case provided a platform for distinguishing "reasonable" from "unreasonable" punishment. Justice Cockburn convicted Hopley of manslaughter, stating: "by the law of England, a parent or a Schoolmaster ... may for the purpose of correcting what is evil in the child inflict moderate and reasonable corporal punishment, always, however, with this condition, that it is moderate and reasonable" (Freeman, 1999).

Hopley's decision was enacted as a defence in Canada's first Criminal Code—in 1892: "It is lawful for every parent, or person in the place of a parent, schoolmaster or master, to use force by way of correction towards any child, pupil or apprentice under his care, provided that such force is reasonable under the circumstances" (section 55, Criminal Code, 1892).

In 1955, this defence was amended to exclude masters of apprentices from its protection. The amended defence became section 43, which has remained unchanged and continues to provide protection to parents, teachers, and persons in loco parentis from charges when assault has been deemed "corrective."

It is interesting to note the parallel between the history of corporal punishment of children and that of wives. In 753 BC, the Roman Law of Chastisement granted husbands the absolute right to physically punish their wives. During the later Roman period, this power was curtailed, but the concept of "reasonable" correction of wives entered common law. In 1765, Blackstone wrote:

> The husband, by the old law, might give his wife moderate correction. For, as he is to answer for her misbehaviour, the law thought it reasonable to intrust him with this power of restraining her, by domestic chastisement, in the same moderation that a man is allowed to correct his apprentices or children; for whom the master or parent is also liable in some cases to answer. But this power of correction was confined within reasonable bounds; and the husband was prohibited to use any violence to his wife other than lawfully and reasonably pertains to the husband for the rule and correction of his wife. The civil law gave the husband the same, or a larger, authority over his wife; allowing him, for some misdemeanors, to beat his wife severely with whips and sticks, for others, only with moderate punishment. (Blackstone, 1872, Book 1, Chapter 15, paragraph 444)

In 1829, the right of a husband to chastise his wife was abolished in England, so the right of a man to strike his wife never entered Canadian law. The right of adults to strike children, however, was enshrined in the Criminal Code, where today it is the sole law to be found under the heading, "Protection of Persons in Authority."

IN WHAT STAGE IS CANADA'S LAW?

According to Covell and Howe's (2001) framework, section 43 itself is clearly a stage 1 law. It conceives of children as objects of adult authority. Parents are given broad latitude in child rearing; teachers are given a free hand in discipline. The only bound on the infliction of pain on children is that it be "reasonable under the circumstances," which, of course, is defined solely by adults. Under section 43, children's rights are not only invisible, they are negated. In a unanimous decision, Canada's Supreme Court ruled in 1984 that "Section 43 is ... a justification. It exculpates a parent, schoolteacher or person standing in the place of a parent who uses force in the correction of a child, because it considers such an action not a wrongful, but a rightful, one" (Ogg-Moss v. R., [1984] 2 S.C.R. 173).

Thus, section 43 is not merely a defence for an otherwise illegal assault. It does not provide an excuse for poor judgment or weak impulse control. It "justifies" the infliction of pain on a child as punishment. It considers such an act the "right" thing to do.

However, the matter is not quite as simple as classifying section 43 into stage 1. While the text of the law clearly does not meet the test of providing basic protection to children, this law has undergone scrutiny in recent decades and its interpretation has evolved to some extent.

Legislative Efforts to Move Canada into Stage 2

During the latter half of the 20th century, societal support for harsh punishment began to decline, seen most clearly in correctional system reforms focused on rehabilitation, better training of prison staff, and some protection of prisoners' rights (Correctional Service Canada, 2014; Fauteux, 1956). The last recorded administration of corporal punishment in penitentiaries took place in 1968 (Correctional Service Canada, 2015).[3] Whipping was abolished as a judicial sentence in 1972; the death penalty was abolished in 1976. Section 44 of the Criminal Code, which protected ships' officers who used corporal punishment to maintain "good order and discipline," was repealed in 2001.

During this same period, legislative efforts were undertaken to repeal section 43, which came "under study" by the Federal Department of Justice in 1976 (Robertshaw, 1994, pp. 48–49). Over the ensuing five years, repeal was recommended almost annually, as shown in Table 9.1. However, the government took no action.

Given the government's inaction, individual members of Parliament (MPs) and senators began to introduce private members' bills[4] to get the issue onto the government's agenda. The first private member's bill to repeal section 43 was introduced in the House of Commons by New Democratic Party (NDP) MP Svend Robinson in 1989. This bill did not go beyond First Reading. The private members' bills that have subsequently been introduced in the House of Commons and the Senate are shown in Table 9.2. All failed, regardless of the governing political party.

In 1993, Canada had a brush with repeal. The government had ratified the Convention on the Rights of the Child (UNCRC) in 1991. Two years

Table 9.1 Recommendations for the Repeal of Section 43, 1977–1981

YEAR	SOURCE	RECOMMENDATION
1977	Ontario Human Rights Commission	Discussion be initiated "aimed at eliminating such discriminatory provisions from the Criminal Code" (p. 68).
1978	Federal Department of Justice	Section 43 "be done away with ... and that the Code should make it clear that an adult may not use physical force upon a child under any circumstances" (p. 48).
1980	Canadian Commission for the International Year of the Child	"Section 43 of the Criminal Code be immediately examined in depth by the Minister of Justice with the object of eliminating discrimination against children" (p. 116).
1980	Senate Standing Committee on Health, Welfare and Science	Section 43 and similar provincial and territorial legislation be "reconsidered by Federal, Provincial and Territorial Governments in view of the sanction which this type of provision gives to the use of violence against children" (p. 58).
1981	House of Commons Standing Committee on Health, Welfare and Social Affairs	"Section 43 of the Criminal Code be repealed immediately" (p. 20:19).

later, Kim Campbell, the federal justice minister, prepared a bill (C-126) that would repeal section 43. But that same year, Prime Minister Brian Mulroney announced his retirement and Campbell replaced him. Campbell's successor as justice minister, Pierre Blais, considered repeal to be "too controversial" and removed it from the bill (McGillivray & Milne, 2011). Despite increasingly strenuous recommendations by the United Nations Committee on the

Table 9.2   Private Members' Bills Introduced to Repeal or Amend Section 43

YEAR BILL WAS INTRODUCED	BILL'S TITLE	BILL'S SPONSOR	SPONSOR'S PARTY AFFILIATION[a]
1991, House of Commons	C-245	MP Svend Robinson	NDP
1994, House of Commons	C-296	MP Svend Robinson	NDP
1996, Senate	S-14	Sen. Sharon Carstairs	Liberal
1996, House of Commons	C-305	MP Svend Robinson	NDP
1997, House of Commons	C-276	MP Libby Davies	NDP
1998, House of Commons	C-368	MP Tony Ianno	Liberal
1999, House of Commons	C-273	MP Libby Davies	NDP
2001, House of Commons	C-329	MP Libby Davies	NDP
2004, Senate	S-21	Sen. Céline Hervieux-Payette	Liberal
2006, Senate	S-207	Sen. Céline Hervieux-Payette	Liberal
2007, Senate	S-209	Sen. Céline Hervieux-Payette	Liberal
2009, Senate	S-209	Sen. Céline Hervieux-Payette	Liberal
2010, Senate	S-204	Sen. Céline Hervieux-Payette	Liberal
2012, Senate	S-214	Sen. Céline Hervieux-Payette	Liberal
2013, Senate	S-206	Sen. Céline Hervieux-Payette	Liberal
2015, Senate	S-206	Sen. Céline Hervieux-Payette	Liberal

a   As of December 2019, 20 political parties are registered in Canada. However, only two have governed at the federal level—the Liberal Party of Canada and the Progressive Conservative Party of Canada (renamed the Conservative Party of Canada in 2003).

Rights of the Child (1995, 2003, 2012) that Canada fully prohibit all corporal punishment of children, no subsequent justice minister has considered repeal of section 43.

Another opportunity for repeal recently came before the Senate. Following its documentation of the experiences of Indigenous children who attended the Indian residential schools, the Truth and Reconciliation Commission (TRC; www.trc.ca) issued 94 Calls to Action, the sixth of which was to repeal section 43. The chair of the TRC, Justice Murray Sinclair, was subsequently appointed to the Senate of Canada, where he sits as an Independent senator without party affiliation. In 2017, Senator Sinclair assumed sponsorship of Bill S-206, which had received first reading in December 2015. The bill subsequently passed second reading and was referred to the Standing Senate Committee on Legal and Constitutional Affairs in May 2018, but died on the order paper when a federal election was called in September 2019.[5]

In the meantime, section 43 has repeatedly failed to provide basic protection to many children. Within the last 30 years, acts considered to constitute reasonable force have included hitting children with rulers, sticks, belts, and a horse harness (*R. v. Dunfield*, 1990; *R. v. L. A. K.*, 1992; *R. v. Atkinson*, 1994; *R. v. Kootenay*, Alberta, 1995; *R. v. J. [O]*, 1996; *R. v. Morton*, 1998; *R. v. N. S.*, 1999; *R. v. Bell*, 2001; *R. v. C. [G]*, 2001), and punishment that has caused physical injury to the child (*R. v. Wheeler*, 1990; *R. v. Olsen*, 1990; *R. v. Goforth*, 1992; *R. v. K. [M]*, 1993; *R. v. V. L.*, 1995; *R. v. D. W.*, 1995; *R. v. James*, 1998; *R. v. N. S.*, 1999; *R. v. C. [G]*, 2001). Section 43 has informed such decisions as "punishment causing bruises is not necessarily excessive" (*R. v. Wheeler*, Yukon, 1990); "striking with a belt is perhaps a little distasteful but is authorized by law" (*R. v. L. A. K.*, Newfoundland, 1992); kicking, slapping, and bruising an eight-year-old boy is "well within the range of what has been accepted in this province" (*R. v. K. [M]*), Manitoba, 1993); raising welts does not amount to bodily harm (*R. v. N. S.*, Ontario, 1999); and hitting a child with a belt is a legally accepted form of punishment (*R. v. C.[G]*, Newfoundland, 2001).

In 1994, a Manitoba judge acquitted a foster mother who hit three toddlers with a belt because he did not have enough information about the belt. "Was it the kind of belt normally used to keep a person's pants up, or was it a different kind of belt? Was it made of leather as many belts are, or of some other material such as plastic, vinyl or cloth? Was there a buckle on the belt, and if so what kind, or was there some other type of decorative accent such as metal studs? Clearly some description of the belt used is relevant in assessing whether the use of the belt was unreasonable and excessive in the circumstances" (*R. v. Atkinson*, 1994, 9WWR 485, Manitoba).

A stepfather who ordered a 12-year-old girl to remove her pants and underpants and spanked her bare buttocks was acquitted of sexual assault. His acquittal was upheld on appeal in 1995 on the basis that spanking was "simply discipline." In 2000, a boy who ignored instructions not to kick a volleyball in gym class and continued his "horseplay" was grabbed by the arm and throat by his teacher and pushed against a wall. The teacher was acquitted because he showed "incredible restraint" (*R. v. Skidmore* Unreported No. 8414/99 June 27, 2000, Ontario).

The clear reluctance of Canada's government to repeal section 43, even in the face of its failure to protect children, eventually led to a constitutional challenge in the courts. This challenge, which took five years, ended in a new interpretation of section 43 that arguably moved Canada's law into stage 2 of Covell and Howe's framework.

THE CONSTITUTIONAL CHALLENGE TO SECTION 43

In 1978, the Liberal government of Pierre Trudeau launched the Court Challenges program, which provided funding to help citizens litigate language rights cases in the courts.[6] When the Charter of Rights and Freedoms (the Charter), part of Canada's Constitution, came into effect in 1985, the Court Challenges Program was expanded to support nationally significant test cases based on equality rights. Under this program, a citizen could apply to argue in court that a law "unreasonably restricts or denies a right or freedom protected by the Charter" (McGillivray & Durrant, 2012, p. 106). If section 43 were successfully challenged, the courts would have the power to strike it down. In 1995, Dr. Ailsa Watkinson, a professor of social work at the University of Regina, received funding to support such a challenge. She chose the Canadian Foundation for Children, Youth and the Law (the Foundation) to initiate the challenge in the Ontario Superior Court of Justice.

The Foundation argued that section 43 violates three sections of the Charter: section 7 (the right to life, liberty, and security of the person); section 12 (the right not to be subjected to cruel and unusual treatment or punishment); and section 15 (the right to equal protection and equal benefit of the law without discrimination based on ... age ...). The Foundation also argued that section 43 violates four articles of the UNCRC: Article 3(1) (the best interests of the child principle); Article 18(1) (the best interests of the child will be the basic concern of those with the primary responsibility for bringing up a child); Article 19(1) (the right to protection from all forms of violence); and Article 28(2) (school discipline must respect the child's human dignity). Thus, the Foundation argued for full repeal of section 43 based on children's fundamental rights to protection and dignity.

The decision of the Ontario Superior Court did not uphold children's rights. In 2000, Mr. Justice McCombs ruled that section 43 does not violate the Charter, dismissing the challenge (Canadian Foundation for Children, Youth and the Law v. Canada [Attorney General], 2000). He explicitly rejected the argument that the law discriminates against children:

> Parliament's purpose in enacting s. 43 was to recognize that parents and teachers require reasonable latitude in carrying out the responsibility imposed by law to provide for their children, to nurture them and to educate them. Parliament decided that these responsibilities cannot be carried out unless parents and teachers have a protected sphere of authority. That sphere of authority is intended to allow a defence to assault within a limited range of physical discipline, while at the same time ensuring that children are protected from child abuse (p. 2).... Section 43 did not infringe principles of fundamental justice by denying children fair procedure and equal benefit and protection of the law. The interests of children are adequately represented by the Crown, which prosecutes the case. Moreover, procedural fairness to children must be weighed against the entitlement of accused persons to procedural fairness to protect them from unwarranted denials of liberty by the state. (p. 4)

Thus, the court perpetuated the putative dichotomy between "discipline" and "abuse"; affirmed the belief that children cannot be provided for, nurtured, or educated without corporal punishment; placed the onus on children to claim their protection rights; and established that adults' protection from criminal charges should supersede children's rights to protection, dignity, and personhood.

The Foundation appealed this ruling to the Ontario Court of Appeal whose three judges unanimously upheld the lower court's decision (Canadian Foundation for Children, Youth and the Law v. Canada [Attorney General], 2002): "The s. 7 issue presented by s. 43 is not about whether physical punishment of children is good or bad. The government has clearly and properly determined that it is bad.... The object of s. 43 is to permit parents and teachers to apply strictly limited corrective force to children without criminal sanctions so that they can carry out their important responsibilities to train and nurture children without the harm that such sanctions would bring to them, to their tasks and to the families concerned" (paragraphs 52, 59).

Therefore, the Ontario Court of Appeal established that physical punishment is "bad," yet considered it one of parents' responsibilities. Once again a Canadian court protected adults who carry out this "bad" behaviour against children; affirmed the concept of "non-abusive physical punishment" (paragraph 62); and confirmed that such punishment "can achieve correction" (paragraph 62), yet noted that "it is clear the federal government does not advocate any form of physical punishment" (paragraph 19). The court ruled that "s. 43 infringes the child's security of the person only to the extent of decriminalizing the limited application of force to the child in circumstances where the risk of physical harm is modest" (paragraph 49). Repealing section 43 would "hinder parental and teacher efforts to nurture children" (paragraph 50). Thus, placing a child at modest risk of harm was viewed by the court as nurturance. With its dismissal of the constitutional challenge, its statement that the best interests of the child is not a principle of fundamental justice (paragraph 37), and its acceptance of moderate risk to children, the Ontario Court of Appeal failed to uphold children's most basic rights to protection. Following this decision, the Foundation obtained leave to appeal the case to the Supreme Court of Canada (Canadian Foundation for Children, Youth and the Law v. Canada [Attorney General], 2004).

The Decision of the Supreme Court of Canada

In 2004, in a 6–3 decision,[7] the Supreme Court upheld the decision of the Ontario Court of Appeal:

> Section 43 protects parents and teachers, not children.... [T]o deny equality relief to children in this case is premised on the view that the state has good reason for treating children differently because of the role and importance of family life in our society (p. 79).... To deny children the ability to have their parents successfully prosecuted for reasonable corrective force under the Criminal Code does not leave them without effective recourse. It just helps to keep the family out of the criminal courts (p. 80).... Section 43 permits conduct toward children that would be criminal in the case of adult victims (para. 50).... Parliament's choice not to criminalize this conduct does not devalue or discriminate against children, but responds to the reality of their lives by addressing their need for safety and security in an age-appropriate manner (para. 51). Section 43 is not arbitrarily demeaning. It does not discriminate. Rather it is firmly grounded in the actual needs and circumstances of children. (para. 68)

Thus, the Supreme Court's decision retained section 43. However, the Supreme Court also did something unusual; it set out criteria for defining "reasonable force" that, going forward, judges should apply in corporal punishment cases. The court's intent was to "delineate a sphere of non-criminal conduct within the larger realm of common assault" (paragraph 19) by limiting section 43's applicability as follows:

1. Only parents may use corporal punishment. Teachers may use reasonable force only to "remove a child from a classroom or to secure compliance with instructions, but not merely as corporal punishment" (paragraph 40).
2. Only children aged two and older, but not yet teenagers, may be corporally punished.
3. Force may be used only on children "capable of benefiting from the correction" (paragraph 25). A child may be incapable of learning from force "because of disability or some other contextual factor" (paragraph 25).
4. The force used must be "minor corrective force of a transitory and trifling nature" (paragraph 40).
5. The force may not involve "the use of objects or blows or slaps to the head" (paragraph 40).
6. The force may not be "degrading, inhuman or harmful" (paragraph 40).
7. The force may not stem "from the caregiver's frustration, loss of temper or abusive personality" (paragraph 40).
8. The question of what is reasonable "must be considered in context and in light of all the circumstances of the case" but "the gravity of the precipitating event is not relevant" (paragraph 40).

These limits provide more protection to children than was previously the case. As of 2004, Canada no longer allows the corporal punishment of infants, teenagers, and children with disabilities; or hitting children on the face or head, or with objects. But these protections are completely arbitrary. There is no evidence to indicate that a 24-month-old child is less vulnerable than a 23-month-old child, or that a slap to the face is more harmful than a slap anywhere else on the body. The Court decontextualized and negated the experience of corporal punishment for a child. Throughout her decision, the chief justice referred to "the perspective of a reasonable person" (paragraphs 53, 54, 68, 223) as the basis for deciding whether section 43 is discriminatory or violates children's dignity. That "reasonable person" is, of course, a hypothetical adult—the person with the most to gain if the law is upheld (Watkinson, 2012). That "reasonable person" remains protected should he or she strike a child aged two to 12, below the chin, while calm.

Justice Binnie, whose opinion dissented from that of the majority, viewed section 43 from the perspective of a child: "With all due respect to the majority of my colleagues, there can be few things that more effectively designate children as second-class citizens than stripping them of the ordinary protection of the assault provisions of the Criminal Code. Such stripping of protection is destructive of dignity from any perspective, including that of a child. Protection of physical integrity against the use of unlawful force is a fundamental value that is applicable to all."

Justice Deschamps, who also dissented, recognized the discrimination embodied in section 43.

> On its face, as well as in its result, s. 43 creates a distinction between children and others which is based on the enumerated ground of age. Moreover, the distinction or differential treatment under s. 43 constitutes discrimination. The government's explicit choice not to criminalize some assaults against children violates their dignity.... S. 43 perpetuates the notion of children as property rather than human beings and sends the message that their bodily integrity and physical security is to be sacrificed to the will of their parents, however misguided. Far from corresponding to the actual needs and circumstances of children, s. 43 compounds the pre-existing disadvantage of children as a vulnerable and often-powerless group whose access to legal redress is already restricted. (pp. 82–83)

In her dissenting opinion, Justice Arbour explicitly addressed the rights of children: "Section 43 of the Criminal Code infringes the rights of children under s. 7 of the Charter. The phrase 'reasonable under the circumstances' in s. 43 violates children's security of the person interest and the deprivation is not in accordance with the relevant principle of fundamental justice" (p. 81).

IN WHAT STAGE IS THE SUPREME COURT'S INTERPRETATION OF SECTION 43?

While the text of section 43 remains firmly planted in stage 1 (Covell & Howe, 2001), the Supreme Court's decision might push the legal status of corporal punishment into stage 2—paternalistic protection. Covell and Howe (2001) describe this stage as characterized by a view of children as vulnerable and in need of state protection, but also by a view of family privacy as being of "pivotal importance, with parental rights not to be intruded upon by the state except when absolutely necessary" (p. 18).

Children's Rights to Protection

The Supreme Court's concept of protection was not based on universal human rights standards. It did not recognize in any way the inherent rights of children. Rather, it bestowed a greater level of protection on some children, but not others, based on arbitrary criteria—namely age, ability, and the part of the body struck.

The increased protection that the Supreme Court envisaged in its decision was based solely on subjective speculation through an adult lens, not on the realities of children's lives. In fact, the Supreme Court's definition of reasonable force describes most cases of substantiated child maltreatment in Canada. Among a nationally representative sample of substantiated cases of physical maltreatment (Durrant, Trocmé, Fallon, Milne, & Black, 2009): 90.6 percent of the perpetrators were parents; 68.9 percent of the children were between two and 12 years of age inclusive; 87.3 percent of the children had no learning impairments; the force used was "minor" in 53.7 percent of cases; objects were not used in 81.2 percent of cases; and the act was intended to be corrective in 76.8 percent of cases. In 23.8 percent of substantiated cases of physical maltreatment, none of the court's limits on reasonable force was exceeded. These findings were replicated on a provincially representative sample of physical maltreatment cases in Ontario (Durrant, Fallon, Lefebvre, & Allan, 2017).

The Supreme Court's decision has not put an end to acquittals of adults who harm children. For example, a father who held a hot cigarette lighter to his seven-year-old child's arm to teach him about fire was acquitted (*R. v. Earl* [2006] NS 626). The court ruled that the resulting injury was unintentional and the act was "part of an education process" (paragraph 9).[8] A driver of a bus for children with special needs, and former teacher, tied a six-year-old boy's wrists together with surgical tape and taped a sock in his mouth. The boy had been in foster care for the previous two months and was seeing a psychologist. The bus driver was acquitted: "it cannot be said in the context of this case that the force or technique used by the accused was excessive.... Only when it seemed necessary in the circumstances ... did the accused take the step of taping his hands and gagging him" (*R. v. Morrow* [2009] ABPC 114, paragraph 45).

A mother who hit her 13-year-old daughter on the face for giving her "the silent treatment" and not turning off the television when told to do so, engaged in legal acrobatics to determine whether a slap to the head could be reasonable, despite the Supreme Court's prohibition of such acts:

> Only those slaps to the head which amount to "corporal punishment" or "discipline" are not covered by section 43. There are other types of slaps to the head which, although they are assaults, are covered by section 43 because they do not amount to "corporal punishment" or "discipline" and they are "minor corrective force of a transitory and trifling

nature" (para. 33). In my view, it is apparent that the slap delivered by [the mother] falls into this second category. It cannot be properly said that the light slap which did not hurt [the child] amounted to "corporal punishment" or "discipline" and, as I previously found, the slap was an instance of "minor corrective force of a transitory and trifling nature." From this it follows that section 43 does justify this use of force by [the mother], and she will accordingly be found not guilty. (*R. v. Kaur* [2004] O.J. 4676, paragraph 34)

Adults' Rights to Protection

The Supreme Court's decision strongly endorsed the precedence of adult protection over child protection. For example,

> The force permitted is limited and must be set against the reality of a child's mother or father being charged and pulled into the criminal justice system, with its attendant rupture of the family setting, or a teacher being detained pending bail, with the inevitable harm to the child's crucial educative setting (para. 68).... A stable and secure family and school setting is essential to this growth process (para. 58).... Introducing the criminal law into children's families and educational environments in such circumstances would harm children more than help them (para. 59).... [The criminal law] is a blunt instrument whose power can also be destructive of family and educational relationships. (paragraph 60)

The court did not provide any evidence that repealing section 43 would destroy families, nor did they show any creativity in thinking about how such situations could be prevented. They referred to hypothetical scenarios in which a parent placed a scarf around a child's neck (paragraph 117) or placed "an unwilling child in a chair for a five-minute 'time-out'" (paragraph 62). But they did not ask themselves why early childhood educators, youth workers, nurses working with people with dementia, and others who must frequently restrain, move, or impose upon other people do not have section 43 protection. Clearly, there are other defences available for such situations (Stuart, 2014). In Canada, the Criminal Code excuses assaults committed to defend oneself or another person (section 34), to defend property (section 35), and to prevent the commission of an offence (section 27). In addition, cases could be considered under the common law defence of necessity (Stuart, 2014). "The common law defence of necessity has always been available to parents in appropriate circumstances and would continue to be available if the s. 43 defence were struck down" (Arbour in Canadian Foundation for Children, Youth and the Law v. Canada [Attorney General], 2004, paragraph

199). Finally, for a criminal prosecution to proceed, two criteria must be satisfied: (1) the evidence must demonstrate a reasonable likelihood of conviction; and (2) the prosecution must be in the public interest. The notion that a parent would be charged for putting a scarf on a child is absurd. Early childhood educators dress thousands of children every day and are never charged with assault, yet they do not have section 43 protection.

WHAT COULD BE DONE TO MOVE CANADA INTO STAGE 3?
Step 1: Repeal Section 43

Clearly, the first step toward a truly rights-based law in Canada is the repeal of section 43. In Sweden, as in most countries that have subsequently prohibited corporal punishment of children, the first step has been to remove the criminal defence for adults who intentionally hurt children as discipline. Would this make corporal punishment of children a criminal act? Yes. The Ontario Court of Appeal incorrectly concluded that "no country in the world has criminalized all forms of physical punishment of children by parents" (Canadian Foundation for Children, Youth and the Law v. Canada [Attorney General], 2002, paragraph 21). In fact, in virtually every country with a corporal punishment ban, the criminal defense was struck down before, or simultaneously with, the implementation of an explicit prohibition.[9] In every country with a prohibition, an assault of a child has the same legal status as an assault of an adult. Yet, in each of these countries, there has been no surge of parents into courtrooms or prisons. Unfortunately, the Supreme Court justices assumed that protection is a zero-sum game; that full protection for children equates to a complete loss of protection for parents. In fact, police and prosecutors have discretionary powers. Charges are not laid in every violation of the law, nor is every person charged also prosecuted. Acts that legally constitute assault between adults may be addressed through "public education and workplace policies, or not addressed at all" (Barnett, 2016, p. 4). Even so, Canada could take specific measures to minimize the chances that parents would be charged in trivial cases.

Develop a National Charging Protocol. Although section 43 clearly refers to "corrective" (i.e., punitive) force,[10] protocols could be developed by police and prosecutors to ensure that adults are not charged for using non-corrective force (for example, putting a scarf on a child, placing a child in a car seat). In cases where corrective force has been used but prosecution would not be in the best interests of the child, cases could be diverted to the child protection system. Watkinson (2012) provides the example of the *Youth Criminal Justice Act*, which provides for diversion of young offenders out of the justice system and into, for example, family group conferencing to determine what the family needs to support the safety and security of the child. There are many other examples across Canada of collaborations among the criminal justice, child protection, and family systems (Department of Justice Canada, 2013). Such collaborations could not only prevent unnecessary and unjust charges, but could move our entire system toward a more restorative model that could help, rather than harm, families.

Expand the De Minimis Defence. The common-law principle of de minimis non curat lex translates to "the law does not concern itself with trifles." According to this principle, judges will not hear cases of very minor legal transgressions, preventing convictions for trivial violations of the law. Justice Arbour, who dissented from the majority of Supreme Court justices, made the following suggestion (Canadian Foundation for Children, Youth and the Law v. Canada [Attorney General], 2004):

> The common law defence of de minimis, as preserved under s. 8(3) of the Code, is sufficient to prevent parents and others from being exposed to harsh criminal sanctions for trivial infractions (para. 206). I am of the view that an appropriate expansion in the use of the de minimis defence—not unlike the development of the doctrine of abuse of process—would assist in ensuring that mere technical violations of the assault provisions of the Code that ought not to attract criminal sanctions are stayed. In this way, judicial resources are not wasted, and unwanted intrusions of the criminal law in the family context, which may be harmful to children, are avoided. Therefore, if s. 43 were to be struck down, and absent Parliament's re-enactment of a provision compatible with the constitutional rights of children, parents would be no more at risk of being dragged into court for a "pat on the bum" than they currently are for "tasting" a single grape in the supermarket. (paragraph 207)

Step 2: Implement a Prohibition of All Corporal Punishment

When Sweden repealed its equivalent of section 43 in 1957, the government assumed that adults would now understand that all assaults are equal, and that children have the same protection from assault as adults. But a case of serious physical abuse came before the courts in the 1970s, and the father who had beaten the child was acquitted. The public outrage that was expressed over this decision led to the appointment of a Commission on Children's Rights, which ultimately proposed that an explicit statement be added to the Parenthood and Guardianship Code (a civil code) that corporal punishment is not permitted. This became the Swedish corporal punishment ban (for more information, see Durrant, 1999). Therefore, the second step in Sweden's initiative to eliminate punitive violence was not to create a new crime of corporal punishment, with judicial sanctions attached to it. Rather, it was to make a clear statement to educate adults that children may no longer be hit or hurt as punishment. In the public education brochure that was widely distributed following the ban's passage, the Ministry of Justice (1979) stated: "Should physical chastisement meted out to a child cause bodily injury or pain which is more than of very temporary duration it is classified as assault and is an offence punishable under the Criminal Code ... although as before trivial offences will remain unpunished, either because they cannot be classified as assault or because an action is not brought."

Most of the 58 corporal punishment prohibitions implemented around the world are, like Sweden's, in their countries' civil codes. So following the removal of the criminal defence, a civil law was enacted to explicitly state that all children have full rights to protection, without qualification. In some of these laws, children's rights to dignity and personhood are also affirmed.

As a federal state, Canada's civil laws exist at both the federal and provincial/territorial levels. For example, some aspects of marriage and divorce, custody and access, and child support fall under federal jurisdiction and others fall under provincial/territorial jurisdiction. Child protection and education legislation fall under provincial/territorial jurisdiction.[11] At this time, 11 of Canada's 13 provinces and territories have enacted corporal punishment prohibitions in their education legislation.[12] Twelve have prohibited corporal punishment in child care and six have prohibited it in foster care.[13] This inconsistency is an indicator of the lack of a child rights–based framework in Canada. Full prohibitions could be enacted in every province and territory's child protection and education legislation. This would provide consistent protection for children, regardless of where they live. It also could launch consistent public education campaigns and parent support initiatives across the country.

CONCLUSION

The legal status of corporal punishment is a powerful symbol of a country's commitment to recognizing the personhood of children. But it is also much more than symbolic. Laws that justify hurting children in order to teach them are placing children's safety and security at risk. The most recent Canadian Incidence Study of Reported Child Abuse and Neglect revealed that 17,212 investigations of physical abuse were substantiated in 2008 alone (Public Health Agency of Canada, 2010). At least 75 percent of substantiated physical maltreatment in Canada takes place in a "corrective" context; in fact, substantiated cases are more likely to be characterized by the use of spanking in the family than by each of the criteria set out by the Supreme Court (Durrant, Fallon, Lefebvre, & Allan, 2017; Durrant, Trocmé, Fallon, Milne, & Black, 2009). As long as the Canadian government maintains that adults are justified in hurting children as correction—and, therefore, that children need to be hurt—this message will undermine all educational attempts to end punitive violence. It will continue to serve as a green light to parents (Durrant, Sigvaldason, & Bednar, 2008), deter early intervention that could prevent escalation, and lead to court judgments that deny children their fundamental rights as persons.

Despite numerous recommendations from Canadian bodies, as well as the UN Committee on the Rights of the Child, Canada has dragged its feet on this issue for decades. The government's position lags far behind public attitudes. As long ago as 2003, a national survey found that 60 percent of Canadian adults would support the repeal of section 43 "if guidelines were developed to prevent prosecutions for mild slaps or spankings" (Toronto Public Health, 2003, p. 2). In 2016, a national poll found that 57 percent of Canadians view spanking a child as "always or usually morally wrong" (Angus Reid Institute, 2016). The proportion of Canadian parents who reported physically punishing their two- to five-year-old children declined from 50 percent to 30 percent between 1994 and 2008 (Fréchette & Romano, 2015). Canada's Joint Statement on Physical Punishment of Children and Youth, which calls for the same protection for children from physical assault as that given to adults, has been endorsed by more than 600 professional organizations (Durrant, Ensom, and Coalition on Physical Punishment of Children and Youth, 2004).

The Canadian government should be leading on this issue: upholding its international commitments under the UNCRC; following through on its commitment to implement the TRC's calls to action; and promoting children's health, well-being, and safety. In the words of the Committee on the Rights of the Child (2006): "It is clear that [corporal punishment] directly conflicts with the equal and inalienable rights of children to respect for their human dignity and physical integrity. The distinct nature of children, their initial dependent and developmental state, their unique human potential as well as their vulnerability, all demand the need for more, rather than less, legal and other protection from all forms of violence" (paragraph 21).

QUESTIONS FOR DISCUSSION

1. What factors account for the Canadian courts' reluctance to repeal section 43 of the Criminal Code, despite the fact that 58 other countries have prohibited the use of corporal punishment?

2. Consider the 2004 Supreme Court decision upholding section 43. In particular, do the parameters for the use of corporal punishment—the criteria for defining "reasonable force"—make sense to you?

3. What does the failure to ban the corporal punishment of children signify in terms of the status of children in Canada? In this regard—and considering the evolution of the law—to what extent is progress evident?

NOTES

I am grateful to Marvin Bernstein, BA, JD, LLM, for his comments on an earlier draft of this chapter.

1 *In Africa:* Benin, Cabo Verde, Kenya, Republic of Congo, South Africa, South Sudan, Togo, Tunisia. *In Asia and the Pacific:* Mongolia, Nepal, New Zealand. *In Europe:* Albania, Andorra, Austria, Bulgaria, Croatia, Cyprus, Denmark, Estonia, Finland, France, Georgia, Germany, Greece, Hungary, Iceland, Ireland, Kosovo, Latvia, Liechtenstein, Lithuania, Luxembourg, Malta, Montenegro, Netherlands, Norway, Poland, Portugal, Republic of Moldova, Romania, San Marino, Slovenia, Spain, Sweden, TFYR Macedonia, Turkmenistan, Ukraine. *In the Middle East:* Israel. *In Central and South America:* Argentina, Bolivia, Brazil, Costa Rica, Honduras, Nicaragua, Paraguay, Peru, Uruguay, Venezuela.
2 Details available at http://www.endcorporalpunishment.org/assets/pdfs/legality-tables/Africa%20progress%20table%20(commitment).pdf
3 In the early days of the penitentiaries, flogging was a common event. At that time, children were imprisoned with adults and subject to the same punishments. The report of the Penitentiary Commission (1849), which investigated conditions at Kingston Penitentiary in Ontario, found that many children were flogged—including an 11-year-old who, over three years, was lashed 38 times with a rawhide whip and six times with a cat-o-nine-tails for talking, laughing, and idling. Another boy of the same age was lashed 37 times in less than nine months. Some prisoners "had been flogged into a state of insanity" (Jackson, 1983, p. 29).
4 In a parliamentary system, any member of Parliament who is not a cabinet minister may introduce a bill in the House of Commons. These bills follow the same legislative process as bills introduced by the government and can become law. However, bills are chosen through a lottery system and only one hour per day is allotted to debating them. Thus, their progress through Parliament can be very slow. Further, if an election is called, any bill that has not been passed is removed from the parliamentary agenda and must be reintroduced in the next session of Parliament. Senators may also introduce private members' bills in the Senate.

5 At Second Reading, senators have their first opportunity to debate a bill. If the bill passes Second Reading with majority support, it will be referred to a Senate committee for examination. Hearings may be held and expert witnesses may be called to answer questions. The committee may suggest amendments to the bill when it reports back to the Senate, where debate resumes on the bill and the proposed amendments. The bill will then be called for a Third Reading, when it is debated again. If it passes Third Reading, it will be sent to the House of Commons, where it will go through the same stages once again.

6 Canada became an officially bilingual country under the 1969 *Official Languages Act*, which declared that "the 'equality of status' of English and French in Parliament and the Canadian public service applies to all federal departments, judicial and quasi-judicial bodies, and administrative agencies and crown corporations established by federal statute" (Historica Canada, 2015).

In 1992, the then-governing Progressive Conservative Party, under Prime Minister Brian Mulroney, cancelled the Court Challenges Program. A new Liberal government under Prime Minister Jean Chrétien reinstated the program in 1994. When Stephen Harper (Conservative) was elected prime minister in 2006, he cancelled the program though an executive order. The program was reinstated in February 2017 by Prime Minister Justin Trudeau's Liberal government.

7 The decision was written by Chief Justice Beverly McLachlin. In support were Justices Michel Bastarache, Charles Gonthier, Frank Iacobucci, Louis LeBel, and John Major. Dissenting were Justices Louise Arbour, Ian Binnie, and Marie Deschamps.

8 The father was convicted of assault with a weapon on appeal (*R. v. Earl* [2006] NSSC 52).

9 Iceland never had a corporal punishment defence.

10 Indeed, the Supreme Court ruled that section 43 requires that the force be "by way of correction" (paragraph 22) and that "obviously, force employed in the absence of any behaviour requiring correction by definition cannot be corrective" (paragraph 35).

11 The exception is child protection on First Nation reserves, which falls under the federal *Indian Act*.

12 As of May 2018, Alberta and Manitoba have not enacted corporal punishment prohibitions in their *Education Acts*.

13 Only New Brunswick has not prohibited corporal punishment in child care. Corporal punishment is prohibited in foster care in Alberta, British Columbia, Manitoba, Ontario, and Quebec.

REFERENCES

Angus Reid Institute. (2016, January 13). *Canadians say our moral values are weakening four-to-one over those who say they're getting stronger*. Retrieved from http://angusreid.org/morality

Barnett, L. (2016). *The "spanking" law: Section 43 of the Criminal Code*. Ottawa: Library of Parliament, Legal and Social Affairs Division, Parliamentary Information and Research Service.

Blackstone, W. (1872). *Commentaries on the laws of England* (2nd ed.). Chicago: Callaghan and Company. (Original work published 1765)

Canadian Commission for the International Year of the Child. (1980). *For Canada's children—National Agenda for Action*. Ottawa: Author.

Canadian Foundation for Children, Youth and the Law v. Canada (Attorney General). (2000). Ontario Superior Court of Justice. Retrieved from http://www.ontario courts.ca/search-canlii/scj/scj-en.htm

Canadian Foundation for Children, Youth and the Law v. Canada (Attorney General). (2002). Ontario Court of Appeal. C34749. Retrieved from http://www.ontario courts.ca/decisions/2002/january/canadianC34749.pdf

Canadian Foundation for Children, Youth and the Law v. Canada (Attorney General). (2004). Supreme Court of Canada. 2004 SCC 4. Retrieved from https://scc-csc .lexum.com/scc-csc/scc-csc/en/2115/1/document.do

Committee on the Rights of the Child. (2006). *General comment no. 8: The right of the child to protection from corporal punishment and other cruel or degrading forms of punishment*. Retrieved from http://tbinternet.ohchr.org/_layouts/ treatybodyexternal/Download.aspx?symbolno=CRC%2fC%2fGC%2f8&Lang=en

Correctional Service Canada. (2014). *Penitentiaries in Canada*. Retrieved from http://www.csc-scc.gc.ca/about-us/006-1006-eng.shtml

Correctional Service Canada. (2015). *Abolition of corporal punishment 1972*. Retrieved from http://www.csc-scc.gc.ca/text/pblct/rht-drt/05-eng.shtml

Covell, K., & Howe, R. B. (2001). *The challenge of children's rights for Canada*. Waterloo, ON: Wilfrid Laurier University Press.

de Bracton, H. (1968). *On the laws and customs of England*. Cambridge, MA: Harvard University Press. (Original work published ca. 1250)

Department of Justice Canada. (2013). *Making the links in family violence cases: Collaboration among the family, child protection and criminal justice systems. Report of the Federal-Provincial-Territorial Ad Hoc Working Group on Family Violence*. Ottawa: Author. Retrieved from http://publications.gc.ca/collections/ collection_2016/jus/J2-385-2013-1-eng.pdf

Durrant, J. E. (1999). Evaluating the success of Sweden's corporal punishment ban. *Child Abuse & Neglect, 23*(5), 435–448.

Durrant, J. E. (2000). Trends in youth crime and well-being in Sweden since the abolition of corporal punishment. *Youth and Society, 31*(4), 437–455.

Durrant, J. E. (2003). Legal reform and attitudes toward physical punishment in Sweden. *International Journal of Children's Rights, 11*(2), 147–174.

Durrant, J. E., Ensom, R., & Coalition on Physical Punishment of Children and Youth. (2004). *Joint statement on physical punishment of children and youth*. Ottawa: Coalition on Physical Punishment of Children and Youth. Retrieved from http:// www.cheo.on.ca/en/physicalpunishment

Durrant, J. E., Fallon, B., Lefebvre, R., & Allan, K. (2017). Defining reasonable force: Does it advance child protection? [Special issue]. *Child Abuse & Neglect, 71*, 32–43.

Durrant, J. E., & Janson, S. (2005). Law reform, corporal punishment and child abuse: The case of Sweden. *International Review of Victimology, 12*(2), 139–158.

Durrant, J. E., & Olsen, G. M. (1997). Parenting and public policy: Contextualizing the Swedish corporal punishment ban. *Journal of Social Welfare and Family Law, 19*(4), 443–461. Retrieved from http://dx.doi.org.uml.idm.oclc .org/10.1080/09649069708410210

Durrant, J. E., Sigvaldason, N., & Bednar, L. (2008). What did the Canadian public learn from the 2004 Supreme Court decision on physical punishment? *International Journal of Children's Rights, 16*(2), 229–247.

Durrant, J. E., Trocmé, N., Fallon, B., Milne, C., & Black, T. (2009). Protection of children from physical maltreatment in Canada: An evaluation of the Supreme Court's definition of reasonable force. *Journal of Aggression, Maltreatment and Trauma, 18*(1), 64–87. Retrieved from http://dx.doi.org/10.1080/10926770802610640

Fauteux, G. (1956). *Report of the committee appointed to inquire into the principles and procedures followed in the remission service of the Department of Justice of Canada.* Ottawa: Queen's Printer.

Federal Department of Justice. (1978). *Memorandum concerning section 43 of the Criminal Code.* Ottawa: Author.

First Nations Child and Family Caring Society of Canada. (2014). *The Canadian Human Rights Tribunal on First Nations child welfare (Docket: T1340/7708).* Ottawa: Author.

Fréchette, S., & Romano, E. (2015). Change in corporal punishment over time in a representative sample of Canadian parents. *Journal of Family Psychology, 29*(4), 507–517.

Freeman, M. (1999). Children are unbeatable. *Children & Society, 13*(2), 130–141.

Gros, H., & Song, Y. (2016). *"No life for a child": A roadmap to end immigration detention of children and family separation.* Toronto: International Human Rights Program, University of Toronto Faculty of Law.

Historica Canada. (2015). Bilingualism. In Bronwyn Graves (Ed.-in-Chief), *The Canadian Encyclopedia.* Toronto: Author. Retrieved from http://www.thecanadianencyclopedia.ca/en/article/bilingualism/

House of Commons Standing Committee on Health, Welfare and Social Affairs. (1981). *Response of the House of Commons Standing Committee on health, welfare and social affairs respecting the Report of the Canadian Commission for the International Year of the Child, 1979 Entitled "For Canada's children—national agenda for action."* Ottawa: Author.

Human Rights Watch. (2016). *Make it safe: Canada's obligation to end the First Nations water crisis.* New York: Author.

Inter-American Commission on Human Rights. (2009). *Report on corporal punishment and human rights of children and adolescents.* Washington, DC: Inter-American Commission on Human Rights, Organization of American States. Retrieved from http://www.cidh.org/Ninez/CastigoCorporal2009/CastigoCorporal.1eng.htm

Jackson, M. (1983). *Prisoners of isolation: Solitary confinement in Canada.* Toronto: University of Toronto Press.

McGillivray, A., & Durrant, J. E. (2012). Child corporal punishment: Violence, rights and law. In R. Alaggia & C. Vine (Eds.), *Cruel but not unusual: Violence in Canadian families* (2nd ed.) (pp. 91–118). Waterloo, ON: Wilfrid Laurier University Press.

McGillivray, A., & Milne, C. (2011). The rocky road of repeal. In J. E. Durrant & A. B. Smith (Eds.), *Global pathways to abolishing physical punishment: Realizing children's rights* (pp. 98–111). New York: Routledge.

Ministry of Justice. (1979). *Can you bring up children successfully without smacking and spanking?* Stockholm, Sweden: Author

Moore, J. (2008). Hopley, Thomas (1819–1876). In D. Cannadine (Ed.), *Oxford dictionary of national biography*. Oxford: Oxford University Press. Retrieved from http://dx.doi.org/10.1093/ref:odnb/93658

Ontario Human Rights Commission. (1977). *Life together: A report on human rights in Ontario*. Toronto: Author.

Parliamentary Assembly. (2004). *Council of Europe Recommendation 1666: Europe-wide ban on corporal punishment of children*. Retrieved from http://assembly.coe.int/nw/xml/XRef/Xref-XML2HTML-EN.asp?fileid=17235&lang=en

Penitentiary Commission. (1849). Reports of the commissioners appointed to inquire into the conduct, discipline, and management of the Provincial Penitentiary, with the documents transmitted by the commissioners. Montreal: R. Campbell.

Public Health Agency of Canada. (2010). *Canadian incidence study of reported child abuse and neglect—2008: Major findings*. Ottawa: Author.

Robertshaw, C. (1994). *Government sponsored reports concerning section 43 of the Criminal Code of Canada, 1976–1993: Eighteen years of indecision*. Unpublished manuscript.

Scott, S. P. (Ed.). (1939). *The civil law code of Justinian*. Cincinnati, OH: Central Trust.

Senate Standing Committee on Health Welfare and Science. (1980). *Child at risk*. Ottawa: Author.

Stuart, D. (2014). *Canadian criminal law: A treatise* (7th ed.). (2014). Toronto: Thomson Reuters.

Toronto Public Health. (2003). *National survey of Canadians' attitudes on section 43 of the Criminal Code*. Toronto: Author.

United Nations Committee on the Rights of the Child. (1995). *Concluding observations: Canada*. CRC/C/15/Add.37.

United Nations Committee on the Rights of the Child. (2003). *Concluding observations: Canada*. CRC/C/13/Add.215.

United Nations Committee on the Rights of the Child. (2012). *Concluding observations: Canada*. CRC/C/CAN/CO/3-4.

Watkinson, A. M. (2012). Constructing the "criminal"—deconstructing the "crime." *International Journal of Human Rights, 16*(3), 517–532. doi: http://www.tandfonline.com/doi/abs/10.1080/13642987.2011.5837

Chapter 10
A Children's Rights Perspective on "Wrongful Life" Disability Medical Negligence Cases

Sonja C. Grover

INTRODUCTION

This book considers three stages of evolution in considering children's place in the larger society and the challenges children face: social laissez-faire, paternalistic protection, and children's rights approaches. The children's rights approach is the perspective that most fully recognizes children as persons with equal human rights while also acknowledging the need for special considerations in respect of their vulnerabilities. The children's human rights perspective is informed in Canada in part by various international human rights laws, in particular the United Nations Convention on the Rights of the Child (UNCRC), which Canada ratified in December 1991. At the same time, it is clear that Canada has not come to terms with the full recognition of children's rights to agency in advancing their basic human rights as evidenced, for instance, by Canada's failure to date (at the time of writing) to sign or ratify the Optional Protocol to the Convention on the Rights of the Child on a Communications Procedure (the complaint procedure re. violations of the UNCRC). That Optional Protocol to the UNCRC allows children to bring complaints against their country for violations of their rights guaranteed under the UNCRC if that country is a state party to the UNCRC and to the Optional Protocol on a Communications Procedure.

The legal case discussed in this chapter is one that illustrates the failure of the Canadian courts to recognize the full personhood and agency of significantly disabled children in advancing their basic human rights and in exercising their rights to equal protection under the law in a particular context. The case exemplifies those instances where the born-alive child's disabilities were caused during the prenatal period by a medical practitioner and were avoidable. This is not at all a case that concerns abortion or abortion rights but rather *the legal rights of a born-alive disabled child* to compensation for permanent injury unnecessarily caused by another. Nevertheless, the abortion rights frame has often been erroneously imposed in the analysis, and this has been detrimental to the courts' realization of the basic human rights of disabled children to bring civil legal cases against others for carelessness during the prenatal period that caused the harms to the unborn that persisted postnatally. In most instances, other family members support the child's civil claim as the intention is to supplement the amount received from insurance for the long-term care of a significantly disabled child whose injuries were sustained in the first instance prenatally and persisted after live birth. As will be discussed, the Convention on the Rights of the Child addresses the rights of the child (defined as a human being under age 18 where "human bring" is not defined) to adequate prenatal care (i.e., Article 24[2] (a), (d)). In addition, the UNCRC refers to the right of the unborn to good development prenatally with continuous good development as a born-alive child (i.e., Article 6, Article 27[1], [2]), not just to survival at birth with or without severe disability.

This chapter more specifically concerns the Canadian courts' rejection of a separate claim brought by a born-alive child for legal damages in a civil lawsuit where the child's disabilities were indirectly caused through the careless acts of a medical professional prior to the child's birth. It is argued here that it is too often the case that meritorious medical negligence claims brought by disabled children are dismissed as erroneously so-called "wrongful life" cases: "Generally, courts dismiss wrongful life lawsuits because they fail to perceive that the child has suffered any legally cognizable injury: had the doctor not been negligent, the child would not exist" (Burns, 2003, pp. 807–808).

Medical professionals can predict a host of diseases and defects in the fetus through prenatal testing and often also accurately assess the approximate risk of having a child with a certain genetically based disorder or condition through genetic testing of the parents (Hanson, 1996). The estimated risks of certain drugs taken by the prospective mother prior to conception or by the pregnant woman during her child's fetal period in terms of the potential for the child being born disabled are in many cases known. In some instances, however, a misdiagnosis may occur regarding the health status of the fetus, or the wrong genetic risk information may be conveyed to the prospective parents, or misinformation may be provided to the woman regarding the risks of a fertility drug or some other medication in relation to having a disabled child. As a result, the mother may continue with the pregnancy because she was given misinformation and did not have the opportunity to consider avoiding conception or having an abortion had she become pregnant and had the correct medical information on risks to her unborn. In other cases, the prospective mother or pregnant woman may have avoided the drug prescribed for her that ultimately caused her child's disabilities, had she been given correct information about its risks.

Where the born-alive child's disabilities are indirectly linked to the medical professional's negligence in the aforementioned way and the child sues to recover compensation for his or her disabilities, the child's lawsuit is often mislabelled a "wrongful life" claim and, as a result, dismissed by the Canadian courts. The latter erroneous categorization (on the view here) occurs on the theory that: (1) since the physician or other medical professional did not directly cause the child's injury, the child cannot sue such a professional for the injuries themselves and therefore (2) the child's legal complaint must be considered to relate to the very fact of being born disabled as somehow allegedly being less desirable than not being born at all. Hence the term "wrongful life" is used in these instances to refer to the lawsuit brought by the disabled child. Such suits are deemed as non-viable given the difficulty of determining the proper amount of monetary damages for the alleged legal injury of being born disabled compared to not being born at all. In such cases (involving the minor child being born alive with significant disabilities as a result of the negligence of the medical professional that indirectly caused the birth and the injuries), a lawsuit cannot be brought through a separate claim by the child. Rather, the parent(s) must sue for "wrongful birth" regarding the injuries of their child or children negligently caused by the medical professional.

Considered in this chapter is whether such cases are properly regarded as, in part, non-actionable "wrongful life" cases or should be examined solely on the basis of the harms inflicted on the parent(s) and child for which each should be able to separately recover legal damages. What is particularly telling is that though the viability of so-called "wrongful life" claims brought by disabled children has been rejected by the Canadian courts, the notion of "wrongful birth" has been considered as legally viable. In a "wrongful birth" claim, it is the parent or parents and/or other immediate family members who bring the claim on their own behalf. For instance, the parents of the disabled child seek legal damages (monetary compensation) for having to care for a child born with such challenges due indirectly to the careless acts of a medical professional that occurred at some point prior to the child's birth. This chapter seeks to highlight that this unbalanced approach reflects: (1) a view of the child born disabled in the previously described circumstance as parental property rather than as a legal person with an autonomous basic human right to a legal remedy for the harms that he or she sustained (persisting postnatally) due to the medical professional's carelessness; (2) a failure, to some extent, to adequately provide all potential available resources for the child's post-birth basic protection and support needs as a significantly disabled person; and (3) a semantic framing of the child's separate claim in terms of "wrongful life" that is erroneous, misleading, and sidesteps the core issue of the child's independent right to a legal remedy for his or her negligently inflicted disabilities and their consequences in terms of, for instance, the child's need for costly and often long-term specialized care.

This chapter, as discussed, concerns the child's right to sue in tort; that is, to bring a civil claim for wrongful infringement of his or her rights relating to injuries that persist in some form post–live birth, but which originated pre-birth due directly or indirectly to another's careless acts. This approach is also referred to as the "tort paradigm" in a later quote. It is here argued that such a civil claim brought by the child against the harm doer in no way devalues the sanctity of the life of the disabled child or his or her basic human right to survival and to maximal support for good development. Rather, it is here contended that it is the blocking of the disabled child's right to sue the person who caused the injuries to the child post-birth (through avoidable actions that predated the child's live birth) that adversely impacts respect for the disabled child's human dignity and legal personhood with all of its correlated fundamental human rights.

These issues will be examined here in the context of the leading Canadian case, *Bovingdon et al. v. Hergott* (2006, 2008). That case involved severely disabled twins injured due to alleged medical negligence but ultimately denied the right to pursue their own separate claim for a legal remedy for their injuries. Those injuries were linked to the harms indirectly inflicted through the careless act of a physician prior to the children's conception (prescribing of a certain fertility drug to the mother that greatly increased the chances for disabilities in the future Bovingdon children). Considered here is whether in *Bovingdon* there was: (1) a physician duty of care to protect the "future children" (the twins during the fetal period as potential legal persons); (2) separate civil liability to the children once live born; and (3) a judicial duty to protect the legal rights post-birth of the injured children by allowing them to pursue their separate tort claim (civil personal injury lawsuit). It should be noted that generally in Canada, a human being is not a legal person with rights to potentially sue for injuries sustained prenatally (even where the circumstances are *not* deemed to relate to a non-viable wrongful life case) until the child is live born with disabilities and exited the birth canal whether or not the umbilical cord is yet cut. Let us begin, then, with a brief overview of the court rulings in the *Bovingdon* case.

BOVINGDON ET AL. V. HERGOTT: AN OVERVIEW

Superior Court of Ontario

The obstetrician in the *Bovingdon* case, Dr. Hergott, prescribed a fertility drug (Clomid) to help Mrs. Bovingdon ovulate as she was having, at that point, difficulty in that regard. It is important to understand, however, that Mrs. Bovingdon had been pregnant twice before without Clomid and had had one healthy child who was delivered prematurely. It cannot be ruled out, therefore, that Mrs. Bovingdon may have become pregnant had the Clomid never been prescribed.

Clomid can cause twinning, premature delivery, and developmental disabilities in children relating to that pre-maturity. Dr. Hergott gave Mrs. Bovingdon incorrect information regarding the actual risks relating to her taking Clomid and conveyed that those risks were at a significantly lower level than was in fact the case. Based on the erroneous low-risk information provided to her by Dr. Hergott, Mrs. Bovingdon decided to take the Clomid in order to increase her chances of becoming pregnant. She ultimately gave birth to premature, severely disabled twins.

The jury at trial held that Dr. Hergott had been negligent in not providing Mrs. Bovingdon the correct risk information regarding the drug Clomid, thereby negating the possibility of her making a properly informed decision as to whether she wished to take the drug given its actual risks. Mrs. Bovingdon testified that she would *not* have opted for an abortion had she known the children were to be born disabled, but would *not* have chosen to take the Clomid in the first instance were she informed by Dr. Hergott of the actual risks. Recall that there was still a chance she might have conceived without the drug. The Superior Court found in favour of the family, including the disabled twins, with regard to their legal right to recover damages in respect of the disabilities the twins suffered.

The jury found, based on Mrs. Bovingdon's testimony, which the jury found credible, that she would not have chosen to take the drug Clomid had she known the true increased risks it posed of her having twins and of one or both of the children being born disabled. Based on the jury findings, the trial judge ruled that Dr. Hergott had breached his duty of care not only to the parents but also a co-extensive duty to the twins, who were born disabled as the result of Mrs. Bovingdon having taken the drug Clomid. The court held that Mrs. Bovingdon took Clomid due to her reliance on the erroneous risk information she had been provided by her obstetrician, Dr. Hergott. The trial judge concluded thus that the twins as well as the parents were entitled to separate legal damages for the injuries the twins sustained as the result of the chain of events that Dr. Hergott put in motion. That chain of events, according to the trial judge, was triggered by the misinformation as to risk that Dr. Hergott provided, which ultimately led to the children being born prematurely and severely disabled.

The trial judge held that this was *not* a case of "wrongful life" (which is not actionable in Canada) since the jury found that the doctor was responsible not just for the children's birth but also for their severe disabilities. Therefore, the Superior Court essentially held that Dr. Hergott could not evade civil liability for the injuries caused to the children through the consequences of his prescribing the mother Clomid by framing the disabled children's lawsuit as a "wrongful life" claim: "In any event, the infant plaintiffs do not complain that they were deprived of the right to 'non-existence.' It is no answer to an action by an infant to simply say that if the physician had not been negligent the child would not have been born" (*Bovingdon et al. v. Hergott*, Ontario Superior Court of Justice, September 11, 2006, judgment at paragraph 6).

Note that in a "wrongful life" lawsuit (were such permissible in Canada) the claim technically could be brought also by the child through a litigation guardian in relation to a healthy child born alive (i.e., as in a botched abortion case where the mother had freely made an informed decision opting for abortion, but due to the negligence of the physician, the woman gave birth nevertheless to a healthy, born-alive child). In such cases the child might contend in a civil claim that, for instance, he or she suffers and suffered psychological damage due to, for example: (1) the alienation of affection from the mother, where such occurs, as the mother (or parents) never intended to have the child and/or due to (2) the child's knowledge that he or she exists only due to a botched abortion.

In the *Bovingdon* case, then, the trial judge held that the doctor was responsible for the children's severe disabilities albeit somewhat indirectly through the complex chain of events he triggered by the incorrect risk information he provided to the mother regarding Clomid. Legal damages, the court ruled, could therefore be properly awarded separately to the parents and to the disabled twins. This separate damage award to the children would then be based on the twins' disabilities and not in relation to the birth of the twins per se. The Ontario Superior Court reasoned that it was essential that the disabled children as legal persons in their own right—and not just their parents—be considered entitled to recover a separate award of legal damages: "Here it would be anomalous to allow the parents recovery for future costs of the children, but to deny that recovery to the persons injured. Recovery by the parents rather than the children may expose the children to a risk of loss of funds awarded for the cost of future care because of death, divorce or bankruptcy of the parents" (Ontario Superior Court of Justice, October 19, 2006, judgment, at paragraph 14). Further, the trial court found it was irrelevant that the careless act of the physician occurred prior to conception of the Bovingdon twins. This was the case, the court held, as it was foreseeable that if Mrs. Bovingdon was misinformed of the risk, and on that basis decided to take Clomid, that the drug could potentially cause the disabilities that the Bovingdon twins in fact suffered (*Bovingdon et al. v. Hergott*, Ontario Superior Court of Justice, October 19, 2006, judgment, at paragraph 10).

Dr. Hergott appealed the Superior Court judgment. In part, he argued that (contrary to the lower court's finding on this point) the Bovingdon parents had, on behalf of their disabled twins, in fact advanced a "wrongful life" claim (a cause of action that is not permissible given Canadian case law precedent). He thus maintained that the remedy of separate additional financial compensation to the disabled children should be reversed, but agreed that he was liable to the parents for providing incorrect drug risk information relating to the fertility drug Clomid and that the parents' "wrongful birth" claim should succeed.

The Court of Appeal of Ontario Judgment

Dr. Hergott was held by the Court of Appeal of Ontario to have owed *no* duty of care to the Bovingdon twins for a drug-free conception and not to have been responsible for the children's severe disabilities. The parents of the disabled twins, in contrast, had argued that the children's "right was to have a drug-free conception, with a reduced risk of disability, rather than a right not to be born" (*Bovingdon et al. v. Hergott*, 2008, at paragraph 62). In addition, the Court of Appeal affirmed that a mother is not under a legal obligation in Canada to act in the best interest of her unborn and that the choice, regardless of the actual or perceived risk, had been entirely Mrs. Bovingdon's to make as to whether or not to take the Clomid that potentially could cause harm to her unborn (i.e., by possibly causing twinning, premature birth, and potential correlated disability for the future children).

The Court of Appeal concluded that Mrs. Bovingdon was not acting on behalf of her future children when she took the Clomid but rather making an independent choice: "However, once she had the information, it was entirely her choice whether to take the Clomid. She was not obliged to act in the best interests of a future child or children or to make the choice they would want. She was not acting as their surrogate making a choice on their behalf. She was entitled to choose to take the risk of having twins. This is similar to a mother's right to choose whether to have an abortion. That is why the Supreme Court protected mothers from any tort liability to an unborn child ..." (*Bovingdon et al. v. Hergott*, 2008, at paragraph 64).

The Court of Appeal held that a reasonable person still may have taken the Clomid even if she had been informed of the actual risks the drug posed regarding the potential of having a disabled child or children. The court pointed out that the evidence is that most women in Mrs. Bovingdon's situation opt to take the Clomid even when given the correct risk information prior to attempting a pregnancy (*Bovingdon et al. v. Hergott*, 2008, at paragraph 67). The court held that the doctor owing a duty of care to the unborn in a case such as *Bovingdon*—where the doctor is considering prescribing a drug that is presumptively medically indicated for the mother and one that does not directly injure the unborn but poses certain potential risks for the future child—might set up a conflict of interest situation for the physician as to where his or her loyalties should lie in exercising a proper standard of duty of care and was therefore untenable.

Dr. Hergott was found by the Court of Appeal, however, to have contributed to causing the disabled twins' birth by providing erroneous risk information that led the mother to proceed with taking the drug that facilitated the pregnancy. Mrs. Bovingdon testified that she thought her risk was negligible, if not zero, of having twins or of having twins born prematurely and disabled due to her having taken Clomid. The court held that it was not unreasonable for the jury to conclude, based on the evidence, that Mrs. Bovingdon would not have taken the Clomid had she known the actual risks (*Bovingdon et al. v. Hergott*, 2008 at paragraphs 34–35). Therefore, the Court of Appeal upheld the parents' "wrongful birth" claim.

At the same time, the Court of Appeal dismissed the separate claim by the twins (brought through their litigation guardians) regarding their request for monetary compensation in respect of their disabilities and the legal injury that resulted from the disabilities. This was the ruling as the Court of Appeal held that Dr. Hergott did not owe the twins a duty of care to provide them a safe, drug-free conception and further found he was not responsible for causing the twins' injuries: "Although the Clomid was the first step in the chain of causation that led to the damage, the appellant's negligence did not cause the damage" (*Bovingdon et al. v. Hergott*, 2008, at paragraph 59). Clomid, the Court of Appeal pointed out, has no direct negative pharmacological effects and was, in its view, therefore not a contraindicated drug for Mrs. Bovingdon given her medical problem.

The Court of Appeal, since it found the doctor owed no duty of care to the twins for a drug-free conception and that he had not been negligent in prescribing Clomid, dismissed the twins' claim without deciding (1) whether or not "wrongful life" claims can be actionable in Ontario, or (2) whether the twin's lawsuit in *Bovingdon* constituted a "wrongful life" claim (*Bovingdon et al. v. Hergott*, 2008, at paragraph 72). The Court of Appeal formulated the key question in a wrongful life case as follows: "In deciding whether to recognize a 'wrongful life' claim, the key question is, if a child would not have been born at all without the doctor's negligence, can such a child sue the doctor for the value of the difference between a life burdened with physical or mental defects and no life at all?" (*Bovingdon et al. v. Hergott*, 2008, at paragraph 37). Ultimately, then, the Court of Appeal in *Bovingdon* upheld the award of monetary damages to the parents for the care of the children and calculated that care as including the period both before and after the twins reached the age of majority given their anticipated continued dependency on the parents in light of the children's severe disabilities. However, the court denied any separate monetary award to the disabled twins, stating the following:

> I also believe that a policy analysis supports the conclusion that where the standard of care requires a doctor to give a woman the information to make an informed decision about taking a drug or undergoing a procedure, the doctor cannot owe a co-extensive duty to a future child. Where the standard of care on the doctor is to ensure that the mother's decision is an informed one, a co-extensive duty of care to a future child would create a potential conflict of interest with the duty to the mother. If future children have a right to a drug-free birth, as the respondents suggest, then doctors might decide to deny women the choice of taking Clomid on the basis that providing such choice might be a breach of the doctor's duty to the unborn children. In my view, the policy of ensuring that women's choice of treatment be preserved supports the conclusion that the doctor owed no legal duty to the unborn children in this case. (*Bovingdon et al. v. Hergott*, 2008, at paragraph 71)

Subsequently the Supreme Court of Canada declined to hear the case, thus leaving the Court of Appeal's dismissal of the disabled Bovingdon children's separate claim for recovery of legal damages to stand.

ANALYSIS

It is here argued that so-called "wrongful life" claims are but the other side of the coin in respect of "wrongful birth" claims; the latter being brought by the parents or other legal guardians. Yet, as discussed, it is only the "wrongful birth" category of lawsuit brought by the child's guardian on the guardian's own behalf that is legally viable in Canada and not the misleadingly labelled "wrongful life" suit brought by the child. This is the case even though the essential facts of the case are the same in both instances. Further, the child is not suing for being born per se but for having to live with disabilities negligently indirectly caused by, for instance, the medical professional during the child's prenatal period and those disabilities persisting postnatally. This judicial approach, in the view of the current author, reflects a conceptual framework that reinforces a narrative of the unborn as property to "whom" no duty of care exists and no separate inherent right to existence, hence reinforcing Canada's decision to legalize abortion. In *Bovingdon* the mother testified, however, that she would never choose abortion, hence it is unclear how, in that particular case, it could be that the duty of care to Mrs. Bovingdon as a pregnant woman was not "co-extensive" (correlated) with a separate duty of care to her unborn. Both mother and the prospective twins in *Bovingdon* had an interest in the children being born and being born healthy. There was then no conflict of interest set up for Dr. Hergott in *Bovingdon* since Mrs. Bovingdon as a pregnant woman and her unborn had the same interests.

In contrast, in the *Cherry* (1992) case a mother wished to have an abortion and the court held that the physician in that case owed a duty of care to both mother and child to perform the abortion competently. Yet in *Bovingdon*, the same court held that the physician did not owe a separate duty of care to the children not to indirectly cause them to be born with disabilities, but did owe a duty of care to the mother not to have caused the same. It appears ironic, then, that the Court of Appeal holds that (1) in a case such as *Cherry* (1992) there was a co-extensive duty of the physician to mother and child that the abortion be performed competently so that a child is not live born (able-bodied or disabled) despite the child's interest in life, while (2) in *Bovingdon* the Court of Appeal finds no co-extensive duty of care of the physician to mother and future child where both mother and child have an interest in the child being born healthy. It may be then that the difference in the court's analysis in the two cases is that *Cherry* had to do with affirming abortion rights (ironically, also the child's hypothesized right, in the view of the court, not to be born) and in *Bovingdon* the mother expressed that she would not have had an interest in abortion whether or not her children were able-bodied.

The trial court in *Bovingdon* thus suggested such a co-extensive physician duty of care to mother and unborn existed with the separate duty of care to the unborn twins not to cause them injury being recognized legally only once they were live-born disabled. In contrast, the Court of Appeal held no such co-extensive separate duty of care existed for the physician to the twins at any point. Certainly the Convention on the Rights of the Child (UNCRC) (1990) seems to contemplate a co-extensive separate physician duty of care to the mother and the unborn at a minimum where the mother wishes to have the child. In that regard, UNCRC Article 24 sets out the unborn's right to a prenatal environment that maximizes the unborn's chances for healthy prenatal development, absence of disability, and successful, uncomplicated delivery through proper prenatal care of the mother:

1. States Parties recognize the right of the child to the enjoyment of the highest attainable standard of health ...
2. States Parties shall pursue full implementation of this right and, in particular, shall take appropriate measures:

    d) To ensure appropriate pre-natal ... health care for mothers....
    (Convention on the Rights of the Child, 1990).

Further, it is to be noted that the UNCRC at Article 1 sets out the rights of the child under age 18 (unless age of majority under the law applicable is reached earlier), thus not precluding the prenatal child from UNCRC protections, including survival, and that the UNCRC Preamble mentions the prenatal child's right to special care and protection: "Bearing in mind that, as indicated in the Declaration of the Rights of the Child, 'the child, by reason of his physical and mental immaturity, needs special safeguards and care, including appropriate legal protection, before as well as after birth' ..." (Convention on the Rights of the Child, Preamble, 1990). Broughton (2016) has reviewed the position of various states parties to the UNCRC regarding a prenatal right to survival and good development, and there are many states that endorse such a child right and hold it to be encompassed within the UNCRC.

Clearly, Dr. Hergott undermined the possibility of good prenatal development for the Bovingdon offspring by increasing the chances for twinning, pre-maturity, and developmental disabilities relating to pre-maturity. The latter occurred when he provided incorrect drug risk information that led Mrs. Bovingdon to make (for her) an ill-informed decision to take Clomid, a decision she testified she would otherwise not have made. In fact, it can be argued that Dr. Hergott deprived the mother of reproductive and treatment choice as she testified that she would not have taken the Clomid had she known the actual risks.

It is important to understand that regardless of one's position on abortion, the issue in *Bovingdon* is whether a child *post-live birth* (a legal person) should have the option in his or her own right (through a litigation guardian) to sue a physician for setting in motion a sequence of events that indirectly led to the child's disabilities. The born-alive disabled child's right to recover legal damages in tort for negligence causing post-birth injury, it is here argued, should not be impacted by policy considerations regarding abortion (Grover, 2017). The denial by the high courts in Canada of the *born-alive disabled child's right* to a civil remedy in erroneously labelled "wrongful life" cases grossly undermines the child's status as a rights holder. A child's legal capacity to sue for a remedy—a prime indicator of society's recognition of the child as an independent rights holder with legal personality—should take precedence over any unrelated general policy considerations such as pertains to abortion.

Since Mrs. Bovingdon did not want to take any risks of having a disabled child as a result of taking the drug Clomid, it can be argued (contrary to the Court of Appeal's holding) that: (1) the drug Clomid with its actual risks was, on that basis, in fact contraindicated in her case, and (2) Dr. Hergott's providing the wrong risk information was part and parcel of negligent prescribing. Mrs. Bovingdon made it clear in her testimony that had she known that the risks of twinning, premature delivery, and hence of disabilities in her children were increased due to taking Clomid, she would never have taken the drug regardless of the actual percentage increased risk of disability for her future child (children) (*Bovingdon et al. v. Hergott*, 2008, at paragraph 15).

Even in cases where a drug is deemed clearly medically contraindicated for a pregnant woman and the woman is prescribed the drug, the Court of Appeal of Ontario has held that the physician owes no separate duty of care to the future child. In *Paxton v. Ramji* (2008), for instance, the Court of Appeal of Ontario held that a physician was not separately liable for the injuries caused to a child born to a mother who was prescribed Accutane for acne prior to the child's conception and continued with the drug while pregnant even though this drug carries the significant risk of causing disability to the fetus and hence the future child. The doctor in *Paxton* (2008) prescribed the drug on the understanding that the husband had had a vasectomy several years prior and that therefore Mrs. Paxton would not become pregnant. However, the vasectomy failed and Mrs. Paxton did become pregnant while on the Accutane and gave birth to a significantly disabled child. The mother, due to faulty medical testing, had been misinformed by the physician early in her pregnancy that she was not pregnant and it was on that basis that she had continued with the Accutane while pregnant. The Court of Appeal held in that case that regardless of whether or not the child's claim was a "wrongful life" claim, the physician did not owe a duty of care to the future child. Hence the court found that there could be no medical negligence by the physician in respect of the child. This despite the doctor having prescribed the mother Accutane while she was in fact pregnant and the physician thus indirectly causing permanent disability to her born-alive child. This was the ruling then even though the drug is contraindicated for pregnant women or women planning to become pregnant: "Because I have concluded that Dr. Ramji did not owe a duty of care to the future child of Dawn Paxton, the issue whether he complied with the standard of care is moot. This court cannot properly assess the applicable standard of care when there is no duty to which the standard would be applied ..." (*Paxton v. Ramji*, 2008, at paragraph 87).

Recall that in *Bovingdon* the Court of Appeal held that Clomid was not medically contraindicated for Mrs. Bovingdon and the mother was not acting on behalf of her children when she took the drug. In the view of this author, however, contrary to the conclusion of the Court of Appeal, when Mrs. Bovingdon took Clomid she was in fact acting on behalf of her future children and in what she thought were their best interests. She thought she was facilitating the chance of having children who would be born alive and healthy as she believed the Clomid to have tantamount to zero risk relating to disabilities. On this analysis, the mother was acting as a proxy for the future children to facilitate their existence and their non-disabled existence, and therefore a separate duty of care was owed by the physician Dr. Hergott to the future children. That separate duty was co-extensive with that owed to the mother and actionable in law upon the disabled twins' live birth.

It is here contended that the failure to award separate monetary damages to the disabled children in *Bovingdon* relating to their negligently inflicted injuries violates Article 23 of the Convention on the Rights of the Child (1990). Article 23 refers to the rights of the disabled "eligible child" in addition to "those responsible for his or her care" to available resources for necessary care and a decent life, thus according the disabled child separate legal standing by implication regarding this matter:

1. States Parties recognize that a mentally or physically disabled child should enjoy a full and decent life, in conditions which ensure dignity, promote self-reliance and facilitate the child's active participation in the community.
2. States Parties recognize the right of the disabled child to special care and shall encourage and ensure the extension, subject to available resources, to the eligible child and those responsible for his or her care, of assistance for which application is made and which is appropriate to the child's condition and to the circumstances of the parents or others caring for the child ... (Convention on the Rights of the Child, 1990).

It is here contended then that Article 23 of the Convention (UNCRC) does not contemplate denying a separate award for care to the disabled child in a medical negligence case such as *Bovingdon* based on considerations relating to the domestic law pertaining to a right to abortion or any other unrelated policy consideration.

In the view here, *Bovingdon* need not be conceptualized in terms of "wrongful birth" or "wrongful life" and hence lawsuits for a legal remedy for injury in such cases do not undermine the dignity of the disabled child. Rather, the Bovingdon disabled children are, it is here contended, by suing the physician for their injuries, demanding recognition as legal persons in their own right entitled to a separate judicially articulated remedy. Both the parents and the children then, in this view, should be compensated for the medical negligence as the physician owed a duty of care to the mother and a separate duty of care to the future children and caused both the parents and the children legal injury. The physician miscalculated the risk that the Bovingdon children would be live-born disabled as a result of the chain of events he put in motion by prescribing the mother Clomid and hence he did not adequately consider also that the children could be foreseeable plaintiffs in a lawsuit for their injuries.

In *Bovingdon*, as discussed, the issue of abortion in fact did not arise as the mother was opposed to abortion. In addition, there was no conflict of interest that would have arisen if Dr. Hergott was held to have had a separate duty of care to mother and the future children since Mrs. Bovingdon would not have taken the drug had she known its actual risks and may still have conceived without the use of Clomid as she had in the past. Yet the Court of Appeal decided the case based on what it considered to be the need to remove in all cases any duty of care by a physician to future children when prescribing to the woman which drugs could be rationalized as medically indicated for the woman but which might pose a risk to her unborn. The Court of Appeal held that dismissing the Bovingdon disabled twins' separate claim served to preserve the principle of freedom of choice of the woman to take a drug with some risks attached for the future child. As discussed, however, in *Bovingdon*, the facts do not set up such conflicting duties for the physician as the duty of care to the mother also matched the interests of the future children on the particular facts in the case. Furthermore, the Court of Appeal's approach, with respect, undermines the live-born disabled child's status as a legal person by effectively denying access to the courts for a tort remedy for the disabilities suffered by the born-alive child due to another's negligence causally connected to prenatal events. The live-born child in such a scenario then is effectively considered no more than parental property that was negligently damaged for which damage the parents can recover compensation through the courts.

Furthermore, in the analysis of the current author, even a healthy, live-born child in the case of a botched abortion should be able to sue the physician for negligent harms where that child can, for instance, prove psychological injuries relating to the ramifications of knowing that but for the botched abortion, he or she would not exist and/or where there has been an adverse impact on the parent–child relationship arising out of the prenatal history of a botched abortion. This author would thus argue that the issue also in such a case is not properly formulated as relating to a "wrongful life" claim and that such a case does not require the court to decide "the value of no life versus a damaged life" (*Bovingdon et al. v. Hergott*, 2008, at paragraph 37), which one can agree is impossible. Rather, the issue in such a case is the value of a damaged life versus a non-damaged life since at that point we are dealing with a legal person (the born-alive child, i.e., potentially psychologically damaged by knowledge of the circumstances of his or her birth) who does exist and is recognized under Canadian law.

To recap then, on the view argued here, the dismissal of claims brought by the born-alive disabled child who would not be disabled but for the carelessness of a medical professional (and the chain of events that carelessness set in motion prior to the child's birth) negates the child after live birth as an autonomous and a rights-bearing person entitled to separate access to a legal remedy for the harms inflicted. At the same time, such potential civil liability in *Bovingdon* to the born-alive disabled children would not have equated to prohibiting the physician from prescribing the drug or the woman choosing to take Clomid knowing its actual risks or Mrs. Bovingdon opting to abort her disabled twins. The choice remains with the mother whether or not to take the drug.

This author would argue that it is not the child's very existence that is defined as a legal injury in a case such as *Bovingdon* via the child's claim for damages (in contrast to what is argued by Schuster, 2016) but rather the disabilities suffered postnatally by the born-alive child and their consequences for the quality of the child's life in various aspects. Burns (2003) holds that in so-called "wrongful life" cases where children are born disabled due indirectly to medical negligence relating to the careless acts of a health professional that occurred prior to the child's birth, the children should be able to recover legal damages for economic harms arising due to such injuries: "Economic considerations dictate that courts should hold doctors liable for their negligence when the result is compatible with the tort paradigm. The tort paradigm can achieve this result by construing the injury in wrongful life as economic harm to the financial condition of the child. This would allow *children* to recover medical expenses (because those expenses constitute the injury)" (Burns, 2003, p. 835; emphasis added). Burns (2003) holds at the same time, however, in contrast to this author's position, that the child should not be able to sue for pain and suffering "because those costs collide with the non-existence paradox" (Burns, 2003, p. 835). Burns holds that the disabled child not be able to sue for pain and suffering for having to live the life of a disabled person since without the medical negligence, the child would not have been born at all—the "non-existence dilemma."

In short, it is the children's disabilities as born-alive children resulting from medical negligence that are at issue. The fact is that the born-alive child is recognized as a legal person in Canadian law and therefore is someone who, on the view here, ought to have the same access to a legal remedy for medical negligence as does the parent of the disabled child in cases such as in *Bovingdon*. Instead, the children's separate tort claims in such cases are being dismissed due to the erroneous misnomer categorizing these children's claims as pertaining to "wrongful life." It is long overdue that in Canada it be considered an expression of the inherent dignity of the disabled born-alive child to be permitted to exercise his or her separate autonomous right as a legal person to access the courts and recover damages in tort (financial compensation and in addition, where warranted, also punitive damages) for the consequences he or she bears physically and/or psychologically of a health professional's medical negligence, and regardless whether those harms were inflicted through an indirect or more direct chain of events that occurred prior to the child's birth or after.

QUESTIONS FOR DISCUSSION

1. Should disabled children be able to recover separate compensatory and/or punitive legal damages for physical injuries that indirectly or directly resulted from the careless acts of a medical professional that occurred prior to the child's live birth, as well as for pain and suffering, if any, relating to those disabilities and their myriad consequences?

2. Did the Court of Appeal essentially hold the mother, Mrs. Bovingdon, responsible in part for her twins' severe disabilities by negating any separate duty of care of the obstetrician, Dr. Hergott, to the future children to provide them a drug-free conception?

3. In what way, if any, are children's rights implicated in so-called "wrongful life" and "wrongful birth" cases?

REFERENCES

Bovingdon et al. v. Hergott. (2008). Ontario Court of Appeal (ONCA) 2.
Bovingdon et al. v. Hergott. Ontario Superior Court of Justice Judgment, September 11, 2006 (Court File no.: 22711/A4).
Bovingdon et al. v. Hergott. (2006). 83 O.R. (3d) 465 (released October 19, 2006).

Broughton, F. (2016) Overstepping the mark? The UN Committee on the Rights of the Child's recommendations to decriminalise abortion in Ireland and the meaning of "child" within the Convention on the Rights of the Child. *International Journal of Children's Rights, 24*(4), 687–717.

Burns, T. A. (2003). When life is an injury: An economic approach to wrongful life suits. *Duke Law Journal, 52*(4), 807–839.

Cherry (Guardian Ad Litem) v. Borsman. (1992). 94 D.L.R. (4th) 487.

Convention on the Rights of the Child. Entry into force September 2, 1990. Retrieved from http://www.ohchr.org/EN/ProfessionalInterest/Pages/CRC.aspx

Grover, S. (2017). Maternal tort immunity, the born alive rule and the disabled child's right to legal capacity: Reconsidering the Supreme Court of Canada judgment in Dobson v. Dobson, *Special issue of* the *International Journal of Human Rights: The Notion of Maternal Immunity in Tort for Pre-natal Harms Causing Permanent Disability for the Born Alive Child: Human Rights Controversies, 21*(6), 708–742.

Hanson, F. A. (1996). Suits for wrongful life, counterfactuals and the non-existence problem. *Southern California Interdisciplinary Law Journal, 5*, 1–24.

Optional Protocol to the Convention on the Rights of the Child on a Communications Procedure. Entered into force April 14, 2014. Retrieved from https://www.institut-fuer-menschenrechte.de/fileadmin/user_upload/PDFDateien/Pakte_Konventionen/CRC/crc_op3_A__RES__66_138_en.pdf

Paxton v. Ramji. [2008] ONCA 697.

Schuster, W. R. (2016). Rights gone wrong: A case against wrongful life. *William and Mary Law Review, 57*(6), 2330–2367.

Chapter 11
The Extraordinary Cases of J. J. and Makayla Sault

J. C. Blokhuis and Amy Smoke

In January 2014, 11-year-old Makayla Sault was diagnosed with acute lymphoblastic leukemia. After 11 weeks of chemotherapy, Makayla begged her parents for traditional medicine in a scripted *YouTube* video. "This chemo I'm on is killing my body and I cannot take it anymore," she declared (*Two Row Times*, 2014a). Her parents, evangelical pastors Ken and Sonya Sault, withdrew their consent to chemotherapy. The same day, in a media interview, Sonya Sault claimed an oncologist at McMaster Children's Hospital had told her, "Anyone who says that traditional medicine works should be thrown in jail" (*Two Row Times*, 2014b).

On May 20, 2014, the local Children's Aid Society (CAS) announced its decision not to intervene in the case. "We do not have any intention of interfering with the family or apprehending Makayla or any of her other siblings. We respect Makayla's choice," said executive director Andrew Koster (Garlow, 2014a). "[I]t's going to be a disaster," cautioned pediatric oncologist Bruce Camitta. By his account, the cancer had been beaten down by 11 weeks of chemotherapy, not cured, and Makayla was "almost certainly" going to relapse. While chemotherapy would have had a 75 percent chance of success if uninterrupted, it would now have a 15 percent chance of success if resumed (Frketich, 2014a).

Koster claimed his decision was not based on medical considerations. "I'm not a medical expert. I also don't know the relative merits of traditional medicine," he said. "As child welfare professionals, we did what we felt was the right decision from a child's emotional and spiritual wellbeing" (Frketich, 2014a). Community leaders later issued a press release lauding Makayla's choice and describing her as "a very mature child, on the brink of adolescence [who] ... is legally capable of making decisions for herself concerning her medical treatment and of providing either informed consent or refusal to such treatment" (Garlow, 2014b).

On August 12, 2014, 11-year-old J. J. was likewise diagnosed with acute lymphoblastic leukemia. She began the first phase of a two-year course of chemotherapy at McMaster Children's Hospital. After 11 days, her mother, D. H., withdrew her consent. In a CBC interview, she acknowledged that she had made her decision after speaking with Brian Clement, the globe-trotting owner of the Hippocrates Health Institute, a resort-like spa in West Palm Beach, Florida. Clement had been repeatedly investigated for false claims about the curative powers of wheatgrass and enzymatic supplements, raw foods, veganism, and electromagnetic therapy. "We [at Hippocrates] have ... the highest success rate on the planet Earth of people healing cancer," he effused in a promotional talk posted on *YouTube* in 2010 (Clement, 2010). "We have dealt with mostly stage-three, stage-four catastrophic cancers—a big percentage of them, probably 25%, have been told they're going to die. We have seen thousands and thousands of those people recover" (Blackwell, 2015a).

J. J.'s oncologist immediately contacted the local Children's Aid Society: "It is with grave concern that I report on the medical neglect of [J. J.]," wrote Dr. Vicky Breakey. "We feel [her mother's] decision to terminate chemotherapy puts [J. J.'s] life at risk." She noted that J. J. had a 90 percent chance of success with chemotherapy and that she was unaware of anyone surviving pediatric leukemia without it. "Given that [J. J.] cannot make her own decisions, and that the medical team does not agree with the mother's decision, we ask that the [CAS] intervene to ensure [J. J.] gets the medicine she needs to give her the best possible chance at survival" (*Hamilton Health Sciences Corp. v. D. H.* [2014], paragraph 12).

Again, the CAS declined to intervene. On September 8, J. J. was discharged from the hospital, which promptly filed suit against the agency. On September 17, Dr. Breakey faxed another letter to the CAS: "I have found that [J. J.] is not capable of making an informed decision," she wrote. "[Her] diagnosis was explained to her in very simple terms. She did not ask questions and deferred all discussions to her mother. She lacks the maturity even of typical children her age ..." (*Hamilton Health Sciences Corp. v. D. H.* [2014], paragraph 24). Later that same day, Justice Gethin Edward ordered that J. J. remain in Ontario pending the outcome of the suit between McMaster and the CAS (*Hamilton Health Sciences Corp. v. D.H.* [2014], paragraph 25). But J. J. and D. H. had already left for Florida, where they would join Makayla and Sonya Sault for $18,000 treatments, including raw vegan diets and wheatgrass supplements, at the Hippocrates Health Institute.

❖ ❖ ❖

William Galston has observed that "[w]hile decisions of the US Supreme Court necessarily draw on the specific provisions and traditions of the US Constitution, these decisions often make claims which, if correct, have general implications for educational practices across [liberal-constitutional democracies]" (Galston, 2006, p. 413). While J. J. and Makayla Sault's cases were governed by provincial legislation and subject to the *Constitution Act* (1982) and the Canadian Charter of Rights and Freedoms, the rights asserted by their parents and communities were inspired in part by decisions of the US Supreme Court subsequently invoked in a Supreme Court of Canada decision that appeared to apply in the circumstances. *B. (R.) v. Children's Aid Society of Metropolitan Toronto*, 1 S.C.R. 315 (1995) involved a baby in danger of imminent death without a blood transfusion, but as Jehovah's Witnesses, her parents could not consent. The local CAS obtained a judicial order temporarily suspending the custodial authority of the parents and consented to the transfusions. Citing a series of favourable US Supreme Court decisions, including *Meyer v. Nebraska*, 262 U.S. 390 (1923); *Pierce v. Society of Sisters*, 268 U.S. 510 (1925); and *Wisconsin v. Yoder*, 406 U.S. 205 (1972), the parents claimed this process violated their "parental liberty" under section 7 (a counterpart in some respects to the US Fourteenth Amendment) to choose medical treatment for their child and that their religious freedoms under section 2(a) (a counterpart in some respects to the US First Amendment) had been infringed.

The Supreme Court of Canada issued four separate opinions denying these constitutional claims. Justice Gérard La Forest agreed that the liberty interests protected under section 7 include a putative right for parents "to nurture a child, to care for its development, and to make decisions for it in fundamental matters such as medical care." But he was careful to preserve a supervening role for the state: "The common law has long recognized the power of the state to intervene to protect children whose lives are in jeopardy and to promote their well-being, basing such intervention on its *parens patriae* jurisdiction," he wrote. "The protection of a child's right to life and to health is a basic tenet of our legal system ..." (B. [R.], paragraphs 83, 88, 215). Justice Peter Cory agreed: "While the right to liberty embedded in s. 7 may encompass the right of parents to have input into the education of their child ... it does not include a parent[al] right to deny a child medical treatment that has been adjudged necessary by a medical professional and for which there is no legitimate alternative." In his view, "the child's right to life must not be so completely subsumed to the parental liberty to make decisions regarding that child." Justice Cory then defended both the constitutional rights of children and the *parens patriae* role of the state (*B. [R.]*, paragraph 192):

"Parental duties are to be discharged according to the 'best interests' of the child. The exercise of parental beliefs that grossly invades those best interests is not activity protected by the right to liberty in s. 7. There is simply no room within s. 7 for parents to override the child's right to life and security of the person. To hold otherwise would be to risk undermining the ability of the state to exercise its legitimate *parens patriae* jurisdiction and jeopardize the Charter's goal of protecting the most vulnerable members of society."

Justice La Forest found the CAS had seriously infringed upon the parents' section 2(a) religious rights, but the exercise of *parens patriae* authority in the circumstances was readily justifiable under the limitations clause in section 1. Chief Justice Antonio Lamer concurred: "A parent's freedom of religion, guaranteed under s. 2(a) of the Charter, does not include the imposition of religious practices which threaten the safety, health or life of the child." Moreover, he observed, "there is an impingement on [the child's] freedom of conscience, which arguably includes the right to live long enough to make [her] own reasoned choice about the religion [she] wishes to follow as well as the right not to hold a religious belief" (*B. [R.]*, paragraph 231). This is consistent with Richard Arneson and Ian Shapiro's view (1996, p. 154) that parents "cannot pretend to speak for the child while really regarding the child as an empty vessel for [their] own religious convictions. As a fiduciary, the parent is bound to preserve the child's own future religious freedom" (cited by Galston, 2006, p. 421).

Of course, neither J. J. nor Makayla were infants. As 11-year-olds, they were quite capable of expressing their *wishes* regarding treatment. While Makayla was deemed competent to consent to treatment, J. J. was not. There has been a least one Ontario case in which a 12-year-old child's decision to stop chemotherapy was recognized and upheld by a court, but that was *because* the child's wishes were found *by the court* to be consistent with her best interests: *In Re L. D. K.*, 48 R.F.L. (2d) 164 (1985) involved a 12-year-old girl who suffered from leukemia. The CAS sought judicial consent for the chemotherapy and blood transfusions to which L. D. K and her parents—again, Jehovah's Witnesses—had objected. But in this case, chemotherapy had only a 30 percent likelihood of success, putting L. D. K.'s life in jeopardy whether she received it or not. Accordingly, Ontario Provincial Court Justice D. R. Main returned L. D. K. to the "care, custody and control" of her parents, concluding that "[she] should be given the opportunity to fight this disease with dignity and peace of mind ... by acceptance of the plan put forward by her and her parents" (*In re L.D.K.*, paragraphs 1, 33).

"Expressive liberty and political pluralism serve to limit the state's power to mold individuals into citizens. That is what it means to affirm a sphere of parental power not subject to state control. And as we saw, that is the clear meaning of *Meyer* and *Pierce*," writes Galston (2006, p. 428). By his account, there must be limits to the scope of parental rights that can be accommodated by the liberal democratic state. "No civil association can be permitted to engage in human sacrifice: there can be no free exercise for Aztecs," he writes. "Nor can a civil association endanger the basic interests of children by withholding medical treatment in life-threatening situations" (Galston, 2006, p. 425). Even in the United States, where the scope of *parens patriae* authority was diminished by the interpretation of *Meyer* and *Pierce* given by the Supreme Court in *Yoder*, the admonition of Justice Rutledge in *Prince v. Massachusetts*, 321 U.S. 158 (1944) still holds true: "Parents may be free to become martyrs themselves," he wrote. "But it does not follow they are free, in identical circumstances, to make martyrs of their children before they have reached the age of full and legal discretion when they can make that choice for themselves" (p. 170).

Philosophers may disagree on whether and to what extent parents have a duty to make decisions that will safeguard and promote their children's putative "right to an open future," as Joel Feinberg put it (2007, p. 112). A liberal democratic state may not foreclose the future options of any of its children by ascribing to them the interests and identities of the persons to whom they happened to be born. After all, the rejection of ascribed status and religious conformity has always been a hallmark of liberalism (see Curren, 2006), and it would be immoral for the state to treat children as the property of their parents or as mere means to parental or community ends. Yet over the objections of Justices Byron White and William O. Douglas in *Yoder*, a liberal democratic state consigned children born to Amish parents to an Amish future. "A State has a legitimate interest not only in seeking to develop the latent talents of its children," lamented Justice White, "but also in seeking to prepare them for the lifestyle that they may later choose, or at least to provide them with an option other than the life they have led in the past" (p. 240). Galston (2006, p. 424) insists that the liberal constitutional state "must be parsimonious in defining the realm in which uniformity must be secured through coercion."

Can constitutional claims ever trump a child's right to life-saving medical treatment or the associated duties of the state? Article 6 of the UN Convention on the Rights of the Child (the Convention), ratified by Canada (but not the United States), recognizes that "every child has the inherent right to life" and that states parties must ensure "the survival and development of the child." Under Article 24, states are to recognize "the right of the child to the enjoyment of the highest attainable standard of health and to facilities for the treatment of illness and rehabilitation of health." Moreover, states are to "strive to ensure that no child is deprived of his or her right of access to such health care services."

In most North American jurisdictions, a person who has not reached the statutory age of majority for particular legal purposes is presumptively incompetent to make medical decisions unless an individualized judicial assessment determines otherwise. A notable exception to the shifting presumption rule is in the domain of medical treatment in Ontario. Under the *Health Care Consent Act*, 1996, S.O. 1996, c. 2, Schedule A, there is no age of consent to medical treatment, so every patient is presumed competent unless a doctor has reasonable grounds to believe otherwise. In case of disagreement, individualized assessments are undertaken by a Consent and Capacity Review Board (CCRB), taking into account the complexity of the proposed treatments and whether the patient can appreciate the foreseeable consequences of his or her choices. The statutory framework for an individualized assessment by medical practitioners of each patient's capacity to consent to treatment under the *Ontario Health Care Consent Act* appears to be consistent with Article 12 of the Convention, which requires signatory states to "assure to the child who is capable of forming his or her own views the right to express those views freely in all matters affecting the child, the views of the child being given due weight in accordance with the age and maturity of the child."

Returning to the lawsuit filed by McMaster Children's Hospital (*Hamilton Health Sciences Corp. v. D. H.* [2014]), Justice Gethin Edward issued a decision on November 14, 2014. First, he found that Dr. Breakey and the medical team at McMaster were correct in concluding that J. J. "lacked capacity to make such a life-and-death decision as to the discontinuation of chemotherapy" (paragraph 39). Second, he disagreed with the position of the CAS that the case should be referred to the CCRB (paragraph 40). Third, he agreed with McMaster that D. H.'s decision to discontinue chemotherapy was a child protection matter within the court's jurisdiction (paragraph 41). Fourth, he determined that J. J. was indeed a "child in need of protection" under the *Child and Family Services Act*, section 37(2)(e) because she required "medical treatment to cure, prevent or alleviate physical harm or suffering and the child's parent or person having charge of the child does not provide, or refuses or is unavailable or unable to consent to, the treatment" (paragraph 55).

Yet Justice Edward did not consent to chemotherapy on J. J.'s behalf even though this would have been entirely consistent with the decision of the Supreme Court of Canada in *A. C. v. Manitoba*, 2 S.C.R. 181 (2009). That case involved a 14-year-old "mature minor" with Crohn's disease who had declined blood transfusions. The CAS sought judicial consent to the treatments. The court found that in such circumstances, "it is the ineffability inherent in the concept of 'maturity' that justifies the state's retaining an overarching power to determine whether allowing the child to exercise his or her autonomy in a given situation actually accords with his or her best interests" (*A. C.*, paragraph 86). In other words, the presumptive capacity of a minor to consent to medical treatment would remain subject to the supervening *parens patriae* authority of the state. Accordingly, the more urgent a particular course of medical treatment, the more likely it is that a court will authorize the treatment against the wishes of both the patient and her parents.

South of the border, the US Supreme Court has not directly addressed the question of whether adolescents may consent or withhold consent to life-saving medical treatments, although it recognized that some minors are sufficiently mature to exercise a constitutional right to have an abortion in *Planned Parenthood v. Danforth*, 428 U.S. 52 (1976). In *Bellotti v. Baird*, 443 U.S. 622 (1979), the court indicated that adolescents' constitutional rights could not "be equated with those of adults" due to "the particular vulnerability of children; their inability to make critical decisions in an informed, mature manner; and the importance of the parental role in child rearing" (p. 634; cited in *A. C.*, paragraph 65). *In Parham v. J. R.*, 442 U.S. 584 (1979), the court held that "[m]ost children, even in adolescence, simply are not able to make sound judgments concerning many decisions, including their need for medical care or treatment" (p. 603; cited in *A. C.*, paragraph 65). Indeed, the US Supreme Court has consistently rejected claims that the constitutional rights of minors should be co-extensive with those of adults since Justice Scalia declared in *Vernonia School District 47j v. Acton*, 515 U.S. 646 (1995) at 654–656: "Traditionally at common law, and still today, unemancipated minors lack some of the most fundamental rights of self-determination— including even the right of liberty in its narrow sense, i.e., the right to come and go at will. They are subject, even as to their physical freedom, to the control of their parents or guardians."

Since *Vernonia*, the US Supreme Court has deployed the phrase "custodial and tutelary" in cases in which constitutional or statutory rights claims have been raised by or on behalf of minors in public schools. Thus, for children in the United States, where the prospects for ratification of the Convention remain dim, there can be no unqualified presumption in favour of rights for minors co-extensive with those of adults in any context, including consent to treatment cases.

Having added the Six Nations as respondents on his own motion in *Hamilton Health Sciences v. D. H.*, Justice Edward then accepted their claim that subsection 35(1) of the *Constitution Act*, 1982 should apply in the circumstances of the case. He then observed that subsection 35(1), which recognizes and affirms "the existing aboriginal and treaty rights of the aboriginal peoples of Canada," falls outside the Canadian Charter of Rights and Freedoms, and is thus not subject to the limitations clause under section 1 (paragraph 82). Relying on the testimony of an Indigenous studies professor at McMaster University, Justice Edward concluded that traditional medicine has remained an integral part of Six Nations culture and identity from before European contact to the present. Thus D. H.'s decision to pursue traditional medicine for her daughter was within her rights as an Indigenous person. "I cannot find that J. J. is a child in need of protection when her substitute decision-maker has chosen to exercise her constitutionally protected right to pursue their traditional medicine over [McMaster's] stated course of treatment of chemotherapy," concluded Justice Edward, himself a member of the Six Nations (paragraph 83). If the federal government had implemented the Convention, he might also have invoked Article 30, which provides that a child "who is indigenous shall not be denied the right, in community with other members of his or her group, to enjoy his or her own culture ..."

"This is monumental for our people all across the country," exulted Chief Ava Hill after the ruling. "Without treatment, this child has no chance of survival," mourned Dr. Peter Fitzgerald, president of McMaster Children's Hospital. "I'm glad out of a tragic situation we have certain rights confirmed," added Andrew Koster of the CAS. J. J.'s family claimed they'd always known the case "was going to have much broader effects than on our individual rights" when the hospital turned to the "courts to have Canadian law ... judge our very existence as valid or invalid" (Frketich, 2014b).

The hue and cry in the popular press was immediate: "First Nations parents can now kill their kids," fumed Rosie DiManno (2014) of the *Toronto Star*. Terry Glavin (2014) of the *Ottawa Citizen* denounced "an aboriginal right to impose a death sentence on a cancer-ridden child." The Indigenous press had been equally vociferous in the weeks and months leading up to the ruling: "[We] have always cared for our children ... despite the disastrous interventions from outsiders and their tragic results," read a press release from the Mississaugas of New Credit First Nation. "Residential schools, the Sixties Scoop, and more recent interference with our families and children, purportedly in their 'best interests', have caused and continue to cause irreparable harm" (Garlow, 2014b).

For First Nations families and communities across North America, the *parens patriae* doctrine is hardly benign. Since their implementation in the second half of the nineteenth century, non-Indigenous parents have been subject to compulsory schooling laws requiring them to share custody of their children with state-certified teachers for six hours a day. Indigenous parents, by contrast, were forced to surrender custody of their children indefinitely in an excessive and wrongful expansion of the *parens patriae* authority of the settler state into the territory and lives of nations sovereign unto themselves. "Aboriginal children were the only children in Canadian history who, over an extended period of time, were statutorily designated to live in institutions primarily because of their race. Large numbers of school-aged Aboriginal children, at times up to one-third of them, were sent to residential schools," noted the president of the Law Commission of Canada (Des Rosiers, 2001; cited by Bezeau & Hoskins, 2007). Over 150,000 children attended, and over 4,000 died in residential schools, the last of which closed in 1996. Thousands more Indigenous children were removed from their homes from the 1960s to the 1980s and placed with non-Indigenous families.

By some accounts, residential schools were policy tools designed to further the interest of the Canadian state in consolidating its control over the land and its resources. "What do Whites want? The answer is quite simple," writes Thomas King (2012, p. 216). "Land. Whites want land." Children were strategic assets in the battle for control of the land and resources of the continent. "[T]he Indians would regard them [their children] as hostages, given to the whites and would hesitate to commit any hostile acts that might endanger their children's wellbeing," wrote Edgar Dewdney, Indian commissioner of the Northwest Territories, to the Macdonald government in 1885. "It is unlikely that any Tribe or tribes would give trouble of a serious nature to the Government whose members had children completely under [its] control," wrote Indian Agent J. A. Macrae in 1886 (Milloy, 2006, p. 32; cited by Bezeau & Hoskins, 2007). "We're never going to allow another agency ever to do that to us again, where they remove our children from their community, from their culture, from their traditions," said Chief Bryan LaForme. "We are not going to let foreign governments come in and apprehend [our] children.... We are a sovereign nation" (Blackwell, 2014).

The media firestorm reached a crescendo after Makayla Sault died on January 19, 2015—two months and five days after Justice Edward had issued his ruling. "The Canadian constitution has killed an 11-year-old child," declared Douglas L. Martin (2015) of the *National Post*. "Makayla might be alive if she had been white," thundered Terry Glavin (2015) of the *Ottawa Citizen*. A letter writer to the *Two Row Times* castigated the "slew of mainstream media taking aim at the people of Six Nations/New Credit and our 'aboriginal right' to use indigenous medicines to treat our children," calling it "nothing short of a resurgence in the residential school era attitude toward indigenous people ..." (*Two Row Times*, 2015). "This is about indigenous people reclaiming their wholeness as a people," wrote Dr. Karen Hill. "This isn't about religion; it isn't about choice. It's about being who we are" (Eggertson, 2015).

The Sault family "continue[d] to support Makayla's choice to leave chemotherapy" (Garlow, 2015). Andrew Koster expressed admiration at how "eloquently [Makayla had] exercised her indigenous rights as a First Nations person and those legal rights provided to her under Ontario's *Health Care Consent Act*" (Alamenciak, 2015). A political science professor published an opinion piece in the *Toronto Star*, claiming that "aboriginal rights empower their holders with a unique legal and moral basis to protect their traditional and evolving cultures, customs and internal constitutional orders," and that "the death of Makayla Sault very accurately reflects a legal and political reality that is consistent with Canada's approach to human rights" (Alcantara, 2015).

Medical ethicists and legal scholars strenuously disagreed. "This is the only case in Canadian history involving the life or death of a child in which the court has not placed the best interests of the child as the factor that trumps everything else," said Arthur Schafer, director of the Centre for Professional and Applied Ethics at the University of Manitoba. "[It] is not a triumph for First Nations rights," he added. "The child welfare authorities ... haven't fulfilled their duties," said Margaret Somerville, director of the Centre for Medicine, Ethics and Law at McGill University. "When the life of a child is at stake, that is one of the clearest situations in which other rights should not prevail. Society has an obligation to protect those unable to protect themselves, and that's particularly true with respect to children." "Every Canadian child is protected against the wildly unreasonable decisions of their parents except for First Nations children now," added Schafer (Frketich, 2015).

Public pressure mounted on the provincial government to make a reference to the Ontario Court of Appeal. "[This is] a matter of such public importance, and the constitutional issues are so important, and the institutional issues are so important, that it should be decided at a higher level," said Lorraine Weinrib, an expert on constitutional law at the University of Toronto. Cheryl Milne, executive director of the David Asper Centre for Constitutional Rights at the University of Toronto, added that another issue was "the role of individual rights in the context of the collective rights under Section 35. Very little is mentioned in the decision about the child's rights ..." (Alamenciak, 2014). "Children should always be involved to the greatest extent possible and so should their family—but if the stakes are very high and the risks are very great ... that's the point at which children need to be protected," added Arthur Schafer. "Once you become an adult, you can throw away your own life; it's your call" (Alamenciak, 2015).

It is true that Aboriginal rights under section 35 of the *Constitution Act* are not subject to the limitations clause under section 1 of the Charter. But in *R. v. Van der Peet*, 2 S.C.R. 507 (1996), the Supreme Court of Canada's decision on which Justice Edward relied in finding traditional medicines integral to Indigenous identity, there was a clear limit on the scope of such claims. "Any right, aboriginal or other, by its very nature carries with it the obligation to use it responsibly. It cannot be used, for example, in a way which harms people, aboriginal or non-aboriginal" (Glavin, 2015).

In the end, a most extraordinary thing happened—by some accounts unprecedented in Canadian jurisprudence (Blackwell, 2015c). With the agreement of all parties, the attorney general of Ontario invited Justice Edward to "clarify" his ruling. In a special proceeding on April 24, 2015, Justice Edward added, "[I]t does no mischief to my decision to recognize that the best interests of the child remains paramount" (paragraph 4) before adding three new paragraphs to his previous decision (*Hamilton Health Services Corp. v. D. H.* [2015] O.J. No. 2214):

[83] ... I cannot find that J. J. is a child in need of protection when her substitute decision-maker has chosen to exercise her constitutionally protected right to pursue their traditional medicine over the applicant's stated course of treatment of chemotherapy.

[83a] But, implicit in this decision is that recognition and implementation of the right to use traditional medicines must remain consistent with the principle that the best interests of the child remain paramount....

[83b] In law as well as in practice, then, the Haudenosaunee have both an aboriginal right to use their own traditional medicines and health practices, and the same right as other people in Ontario to use the medicines and health practices available to those people. [...]

J. J. suffered a relapse of her cancer and resumed chemotherapy shortly before Justice Edward's clarification. "The fact that the parents have agreed to chemotherapy, along with traditional Haudenosaunee medicine, means that the child has a chance to live," said Juliet Guichon, a bioethicist and legal scholar at the University of Calgary. J. J.'s health care team would include both a pediatric oncologist *and* a Haudenosaunee chief (Blackwell, 2015b).

AFTERWORD

Amy Smoke

As a First Nations woman, mother, student, and activist I speak only for myself, but when asked to contribute some thoughts regarding these two young Indigenous children and their complex decisions regarding traditional medicine versus Western medical treatment, I was humbled. I looked inward. I questioned every decision I have had to make for my children and their health and well-being. Have I been a good parent? In whose eyes?

In these cases, so many questions arise: Who decides whether they (my children) are legally capable of making this choice? Who decides that I (the parent) am not qualified to make that choice? The Canadian courts or the child welfare services? These have all been created and maintained on these lands for the benefit and privilege of settler Canadians. Decisions made for First Nations families in the past regarding mandatory Eurocentric education (residential schools) allowed for the deaths of thousands of Indigenous children. The mistreatment of the 150,000+ survivors of residential schools under the guise of their "best interests" was not a decision made by First Nations parents. And the shocking numbers of babies apprehended from First Nations families by the governing bodies of each province tells me these are not "laws" in my best interests or designed for every "Canadian." I am by no means a legal scholar, but I know that "Aboriginal rights are inherent rights, grounded in Indigenous legal traditions" (Fitzgerald & Schwartz, 2017, p. 4).

Current colonial laws would not stop me from going to the ends of the earth for my child's right to her people's cultural beliefs and the ability to practise them *and* to seek all knowledge available on any helpful Western medical practice. My children are not political pawns; they are human beings and deserve the same rights as any other "Canadian." It is appropriate for the Onkwehonwe to assert our sovereign right to raise and protect our children in our own ways.

QUESTIONS FOR DISCUSSION

1. Subsection 35(1) of the *Constitution Act* recognizes and affirms "the existing aboriginal and treaty rights of the aboriginal peoples of Canada," while Article 30 of the Convention provides that "a child ... who is indigenous shall not be denied the right, in community with other members of his or her group, to enjoy his or her own culture...." Should constitutional or cultural rights trump a child's right to life-saving medical treatment?

2. Article 12 of the Convention requires signatory states to "assure to the child who is capable of forming his or her own views the right to express those views freely in all matters affecting the child, the views of the child being given due weight in accordance with the age and maturity of the child." Should children be allowed to decline life-saving medical treatment?

3. Do you agree with Justice Edward's "clarification" in *D. H. v. Hamilton Health Services*? If you had been the judge in this case, would you have made a different decision?

REFERENCES

Alamenciak, T. (2014, December 10). Ruling on aboriginal medicine for girl with leukemia needs to be clarified, constitutional experts say. *Toronto Star*. Retrieved from https://www.thestar.com/news/gta/2014/12/10/ruling_on_aboriginal _medicine_for_girl_with_leukemia_needs_to_be_clarified_constitutional _experts_say.html

Alamenciak, T. (2015, January 21). Ontario law allows children to determine medical care. *Hamilton Spectator*. Retrieved from https://www.thespec.com/ news-story/5267386-ontario-law-allows-children-to-determine-medical-care/

Alcantara, C. (2015, January 28). Why Makayla was allowed to die. *Toronto Star*. Retrieved from https://www.thestar.com/opinion/commentary/2015/01/27/ why-makayla-sault-was-allowed-to-die.html

Arneson, R., & Shapiro, I. (1996). Democratic autonomy and religious freedom: A critique of *Wisconsin v. Yoder*. In I. Shapiro (Ed.), *Democracy's place*. Ithaca, NY: Cornell University Press.

Bezeau, R. N., & Hoskins, J. R. (2007). *The fallen feather: Indian industrial residential schools and Canadian Confederation* [video recording]. Surrey, BC: Fallen Feather Productions.

Blackwell, T. (2014, June 6). Makayla Sault's parents say they have no regrets. *National Post*. Retrieved from http://news.nationalpost.com/news/canada/makayla-saults-parents-say-they-have-no-regrets-over-girls-decision-to-opt-for-holistic-cancer-treatment

Blackwell, T. (2015a, February 21). Questions about Hippocrates. *National Post*. Retrieved from http://news.nationalpost.com/news/questions-about-hippocrates-complaint-filed-against-clinic-that-treated-first-nations-girl-pulled-out-of-chemo

Blackwell, T. (2015b, April 25). First Nations girl who used alternative treatment back on chemotherapy after leukaemia returns. *National Post*. Retrieved from http://news.nationalpost.com/health/first-nations-girl-who-sought-alternative-cancer-treatments-back-on-chemotherapy-after-leukaemia-returns

Clement, B. (2010, April 28). Brian Clement Q & A: Raw food, cancer & more. *YouTube*. Retrieved from https://www.youtube.com/watch?v=E-3m1fOqtck

Curren, R. (2006). Developmental liberalism. *Educational Theory, 56*(4), 451–468.

Des Rosiers, N. (2001, August 15). *Moving forward with dignity—the report of the Law Commission of Canada and its aftermath*. Remarks delivered at the Moving Forward conference in Sydney, Australia. Retrieved from http://www.turtleisland.org/news/news-residential2.htm

DiManno, R. (2014, November 15). First Nations parents can now doom their sick children. *Toronto Star*. Retrieved from https://www.thestar.com/news/gta/2014/11/15/first_nations_parents_can_now_doom_their_sick_children_dimanno.html

Eggertson, L. (2015, March 17). Doctors should collaborate with traditional healers. *Canadian Medical Association Journal, 187*(5), 153–154.

Feinberg, J. (2007). The child's right to an open future. In R. Curren (Ed.), *Philosophy of education: An anthology* (pp. 112–123). Malden, MA: Blackwell.

Fitzgerald, O., & Schwartz, R. (2017). Introduction. In *UNDRIP implementation: Braiding international, domestic and Indigenous laws* (Special Report). Waterloo, ON: Centre for International Governance Innovation.

Frketich, J. (2014a, May 24). Halting chemo: A child's life in the balance. *Hamilton Spectator*. Retrieved from https://www.thespec.com/news-story/4538643-halting-chemo-a-child-s-life-in-the-balance/

Frketich, J. (2014b, November 15). Aboriginal family describes stress of precedent-setting case. *Hamilton Spectator*. Retrieved from https://www.thespec.com/news-story/5031049-aboriginal-family-describes-stress-of-precedent-setting-case/

Frketich, J. (2015, January 23). Medical ethicists decry death of Aboriginal girl. *Hamilton Spectator*. Retrieved from http://www.thespec.com/news-story/5272164-medical-ethicists-decry-death-of-aboriginal-girl-who-refused-chemo/

Galston, W. (2006). Church, state, and education. In R. Curren (Ed.), *A companion to the philosophy of education* (pp. 412–429). Malden, MA: Blackwell.

Garlow, N. (2014a, May 20). CAS closes case on Ojibwe child. *Two Row Times*. Retrieved from https://tworowtimes.com/news/cas-closes-case-on-ojibwe-child-we-respect-makaylas-choice/

Garlow, N. (2014b, October 6). Mississaugas of New Credit assert they will protect all their children. *Two Row Times*. Retrieved from https://tworowtimes.com/news-release/media-release-makayla-sault-member-mississaugas-new-credit-first-nation/

Garlow, N. (2015, January 19). Makayla Sault, Ojibwe child who refused chemo, dies from stroke. *Two Row Times*. Retrieved from https://tworowtimes.com/news/makayla-sault-ojibwe-child-refused-chemo-dies-stroke/

Glavin, T. (2014, November 19). Junk law, junk science is not what Aboriginal rights are about. *Ottawa Citizen*. Retrieved from http://ottawacitizen.com/opinion/columnists/glavin-junk-law-in-aid-of-junk-science-is-not-what-aboriginal-rights-are-about

Glavin, T. (2015, January 22). Would Makayla be dead if she had been a white girl? *Ottawa Citizen*. Retrieved from http://ottawacitizen.com/opinion/columnists/would-makayla-be-dead-if-she-had-been-a-white-girl

Hamilton Health Sciences Corp. v. D. H. [2014] O.J. No. 5419.

Hamilton Health Sciences Corp. v. D. H. [2015] O.J. No. 2214.

King, T. (2012). *The inconvenient Indian: A curious account of Native people in North America*. Toronto: Anchor.

Martin, D. L. (2015). Makayla Sault didn't have to die. *National Post*. Retrieved from http://news.nationalpost.com/full-comment/todays-letters-makayla-sault-didnt-have-to-die

Milloy, J. S. (2006). *A national crime: The Canadian government and the residential school system, 1879 to 1986*. Winnipeg: University of Manitoba Press.

Two Row Times. (2014a, May 13). *Child refuses chemo, wants traditional medicine instead*. Retrieved from https://www.youtube.com/watch?v=NrF5wWQ4hIU

Two Row Times. (2014b, May 13). Anyone who says that traditional medicine works should be thrown in jail. *Two Row Times*. Retrieved from https://tworowtimes.com/news/physician-tells-ojibwe-family-anyone-who-says-that-traditional-medicine-works-should-be-thrown-in-jail/

Two Row Times. (2015, January 28). As Haudenosaune people, we are aware that it is our first priority to love one another. *Two Row Times*. Retrieved from https://tworowtimes.com/editorial/haudenosaune-people-aware-first-priority-love-one-another/

PARTICIPATION RIGHTS, STATUS, AND RECOGNITION

Chapter 12
Participation Rights of the Child
At the Crossroads of Citizenship
Jan Hancock

INTRODUCTION

Facilitating and encouraging the appropriate participation of the child in deciding important matters in his or her life is vital for nurturing the cognitive, emotional, and social development of the child. For this reason, the United Nations Convention on the Rights of the Child (UNCRC) included child participation as a fundamental guiding principle alongside the best interests of the child, non-discrimination, and the survival and development of the child (Hodgkin & Newell, 2007). The UNCRC (1989) went on to codify a list of substantive participation rights that now constitute a new generation of children's rights distinct from protection and provision rights. While protection and provision rights envision children as beneficiaries of support, participation rights are unique in conceptualizing and empowering children as agents of decision making.

Child participation rights refer to communication processes between children and adults, whereby information is shared and where the child's perspective is given due weight by adult decision makers commensurate with the age and maturity of the child. Participation in decision making does not mean that the child gets his or her own way all the time since outcome ultimately depends upon adults evaluating a number of factors, including the age and maturity of the child and whether the opinion articulated is reasonable. For example, a parent refusing to allow a three-year-old to play with a ball in a busy road is not violating the child's participation rights since the parent is protecting the best interests of the child by preventing the serious harm likely to result from following the child's wishes.

This chapter assesses the extent to which law and public policy in Canada currently recognizes child participation rights as specified in the UNCRC.

The laissez-faire, paternalistic, and children's rights stages will be used as the theoretical framework through which Canada's record will be categorized and evaluated. The social laissez-faire stage is characterized by the absence of any coherent legislation and policy concerning the participation of children in decision-making processes. In the laissez-faire stage, decisions regarding the lives of children are made exclusively by adults on whatever basis those adults deem most appropriate. In contrast, the paternalistic stage acknowledges the best interests of the child as a central principle guiding decision making, but designated adult decision makers in the government, school, family, or care facility are always assumed to know, and speak for, the best interests of the child. Only in the children's rights stage does legislation exist to empower the child with rights to communicate his or her own interpretations of the child's best interests to adult decision makers. And only in the children's rights stage are decision-making adults required to pay attention to the child's views in line with the age and maturity of the child.

This chapter finds that overall, Canada is stuck in the paternalistic stage. This finding will be explained by first introducing the reader to the substantive child participation rights codified in the UNCRC and the vital importance of those rights. Second, the chapter will provide an overview of the progress, and lack of progress, that Canada has made in recognizing participation rights on the federal, provincial, and territory levels. Third, the chapter focuses on three specific areas in identifying fundamental inconsistencies in how participation rights are recognized in Canada. Children's participation rights in the family will be introduced as an example of where policy remains in the laissez-faire stage. Civic participation will be examined to illustrate how policy reflects the paternalistic stage. Health care treatment will be examined as an example of an area where child participation rights have been recognized, at least in part, on the level of public policy. These three areas were selected on the grounds of their importance to the lives of children as well as characterizing different stages that Canada has reached in recognizing child participation rights. Educational institutions also play a key role in facilitating or neglecting child participation and the reader can be directed to the contribution from Katherine Covell in this edition for a discussion of this important topic.

LEGAL SOURCES OF THE RIGHT OF THE CHILD TO PARTICIPATE

Child participation rights are stipulated in a number of articles comprising the UNCRC. Article 12(1) ensures that any child capable of forming a view has the right to freely express that view in matters that affect him or her. Further, that view is to be given due weight commensurate to the age and maturity of the child, meaning that older and more mature children should have more autonomy than younger children. Article 12(2) assures the child the right to be heard in any judicial or administrative proceeding affecting him or her.

Article 9 of the UNCRC allows "all interested parties" to participate in proceedings involving the separation of parents. Article 13 guarantees the right of the child to freedom of expression; Article 14 to freedom of thought, conscience, and religion; Article 15 to freedom of association and peaceful assembly; Article 16 to privacy; Article 17 to access to information; Article 23 guarantees disabled children the right to active participation; Article 30 guarantees Indigenous children the right to practise their culture, religion, and language; and Article 31 guarantees children the right to participate fully in cultural and artistic life. The UNCRC requires in Articles 5 and 14 that children receive guidance from the parent or legal guardian so that the child can act upon his or her rights to participate in an appropriate and meaningful manner. When seen in combination, the above listed articles empower children to articulate their views in matters that affect them in family, cultural, artistic, social, and community life and ensure that these opinions are given due weight by adults in accordance with the age and maturity of the child. The state may limit these rights, but only through law and only for explicit purposes such as national security or public order (Campbell & Rose-Krasnor, 2007; Flekkoy & Kaufman, 1997).

WHY CHILD PARTICIPATION RIGHTS MATTER

Child participation rights tend to be more controversial than protection or provision rights since respecting participation rights often requires balancing competing rights, objectives, and concerns. It is subsequently problematic for law to codify participation rights through universally applicable mechanisms (Flekkoy & Kaufman, 1997; King, Wattam, & Blackstock, 2016). Social barriers also exist that further complicate the acceptance of child participation rights, including the prevalence of viewing children as inferior to adults and disregarding the potential of the child simply because of his or her age (Richards-Schuster & Checkoway, 2009).

Yet participation rights remain absolutely vital for four reasons. First, the assumption that adults always know best is not always accurate. The lived experiences of children are often distinct from those of adults in a myriad of ways that adults do not necessarily understand. Where the child develops in an environment that does not provide a supportive context for the child to articulate his or her emotional experiences, the child is less likely to talk to a teacher or legal guardian about important issues such as bullying. Adults operating under the paternalistic paradigm could subsequently make decisions on the basis of deficient information that places the child in potentially harmful situations.

Second, a growing body of research now demonstrates the importance of participation rights as attested by children themselves. Youth routinely rank the right to express themselves and to be listened to as one of their top 10 rights (Campbell & Rose-Krasnor, 2007; Ontario Provincial Advocate for Children and Youth, 2015). Birnbaum and Bala (2010) demonstrated that children involved in family law cases invariably want to be asked whether or not they wish to contribute their views. In an informative study, Covell (2007, p. 29) found that Canadian youth "overwhelmingly" articulated a sense of rejection and isolation, both at home and in broader society, due to the lack of opportunities to participate.

Third, giving due respect to participation rights is a requirement for ensuring healthy child development. Facilitating participation rights equips the child with the cognitive and communication skills, abilities, responsibilities, and experiences necessary to make considered decisions, and to participate in society in a constructive manner (Campbell & Rose-Krasnor, 2007; Mitra, Serriere, & Kirshner, 2014; Shen, 2006; Pearson, 2015). Encouraging child participation is an effective method of boosting self-esteem and building the resilience and character of the child (Flekkoy & Kaufman, 1997).

Fourth, and in light of the above three points, child participation should be interpreted not only as a guiding principle and as an important category of children's rights but also as an essential component of respecting the best interests of the child (Covell & Howe, 2001). Respecting the best interests of the child is required by Article 3 of the UNCRC to be a primary consideration when considering all actions concerning the child.

While participation rights may at times conflict with child protection rights, it should be noted that tensions between distinct categories of rights are not unusual. Tensions between participation and protection rights are dealt with in the UNCRC by requiring adults to always provide children with suitable guidance and to provide opportunities for the child to participate only as allowed by the age and maturity of the child (Article 5). Adults are required to consider the best interests of the child on a case-by-case basis when balancing participation and protection rights.

There is no lower age limit for the child to share in decision making, and innovative initiatives have successfully extended limited participation rights to even very young children who have demonstrated a capacity to form their own views. For example, since 2007 the Dolli Einstein nursery for under sixes in Pinneberg, Germany, has been giving children a say in decisions that have affected them. The nursery lists seven participation rights: to sleep; what and how much to eat; what to play with; where to sit; to voice opinions; which educator to cuddle; and which educator changes diapers. The decision on whether or not a diaper requires changing remains exclusively with the educators. The nursery is run by the Workers Welfare Institution, which reports such success with the model that there are now plans for the initiative to be extended to the other 57 nurseries also run by the charitable organization in Schleswig-Holstein (Ottermann, 2017).

PROGRESS ON PARTICIPATION RIGHTS IN CANADA

At the federal level, Canadian officials have recently voiced rhetorical support for the participation rights of the child (Campbell & Rose-Krasnor, 2007; Mitra et al., 2014). The Department of Justice can be commended for integrating child participation rights into legislation and initiatives. Indeed, the Canadian Foundation for Children, Youth and the Law has identified Canada as a model for how states can comply with Article 12 of the UNCRC because of how child participation has been facilitated in the area of the youth criminal justice system. For example, the 2002 *Youth Criminal Justice Act* guarantees legal representation to accused youth and allows the counsel of the youth to access information. A child aged 12 to 17 has the right to be heard in legal proceedings (Canadian Bar Association, 2016). In proceedings involving extrajudicial sanctions such as restorative justice, youth have the legal right to give or withhold their consent to their involvement and have rights to legal counsel before making decisions.

The Public Health Agency of Canada has taken some measures, albeit less systematically than the Department of Justice, to encourage child participation. For example, the agency funds the Centre of Excellence for Youth Engagement whose mandate is to engage youth in meaningful participation. However, child participation rights continue to be neglected by other notable federal departments. For example, Canadian Heritage, Citizenship and Immigration Canada, and Environment Canada have yet to integrate child participation rights into programs and services in any meaningful manner.

Considerable differences exist at the regional level in the extent to which participation rights are recognized since Canada's Constitution gives significant jurisdiction over matters of family law to provinces and territories. This arrangement has resulted in both positive and negative outcomes for ensuring child participation rights. The most positive feature has been the establishment of 11 provincial and territorial Child and Youth Advocates (CYA) tasked with giving a voice to children and advocating for the child (Hunter, 2017). CYAs in British Columbia and Alberta allow for input and dialogue with youth via youth advisory groups. In 2014 the Manitoba Office of the Child Advocate collaborated with a local TV station to give participating youth a platform to articulate stories about issues that mattered to them through the Digital Storytelling Project. CYAs in British Columbia and Ontario operate social media platforms to disseminate the voices, views, and concerns of young people directly to the broader public.

The Office of the Provincial Advocate for Youth and Children in Ontario has undertaken numerous youth-led initiatives, including the I Have Something to Say and Our Voice Our Turn initiatives, which allowed children in and from care to suggest how government might better meet their needs. The Our Voice Our Turn initiative involved the hiring of four young people in care to organize a two-day public hearing in the Ontario legislature to give voice to the experiences of children from the child welfare system. The initiative resulted in the publication of two reports and an action plan for improving the child welfare system in Ontario (Ontario Provincial Advocate for Children and Youth, 2016). The Our Voice Our Turn initiative also facilitated a meeting in 2016 between youth in care and the deputy minister of Children and Youth Services (Ontario Child Advocate, 2018). Ontario is also the first Canadian province to establish a permanent Premier's Council on Youth Opportunities. This council is comprised of 25 young people from a variety of backgrounds and advises government on how services for youth might be improved (Hunter, 2017).

Input from the CYA proved effective during the overhaul of laws relating to children's rights in Ontario. In the spring of 2018, Ontario's *Supporting Child, Youth and Family Services Act* came into force. This Act provides a comprehensive range of participation rights to a child receiving government services provided under the terms of the Act. Section 3 provides children with the right to express their views about matters that affect them; to engage in a dialogue regarding how decisions affecting them were made; to be consulted and to participate in deciding the nature of services provided to them; and to be advised of the decisions made with regard to those services; to raise concerns regarding the services provided; and to be informed of their rights to participate under the Act, and of the existence and role of the Provincial Advocate for Children and Youth. Section 8 goes on to guarantee the rights of a child in care to participate in decisions regarding their treatment, education, training or work programs. Sections 3 and 8 both guarantee that views expressed by the child must be given due weight by adults in accordance with the age and maturity of the child (*Supporting Child, Youth and Family Services Act*, 2017). The most significant shortcomings of the Act are that the provisions of sections 3 and 8 apply only to children receiving services or children in care.

As demonstrated above, the CYA in Ontario can be commended for raising public and political awareness of the experiences of children in the child welfare system as well as performing a lead role as an independent watchdog reviewing governmental policy toward children. Respect for children's rights at the political level in Ontario can therefore be seen to have suffered a major setback in November 2018, when the provincial government announced the elimination of the office of the Provincial Advocate for Children and Youth as a cost-saving measure.

The allocation of matters of family law to the provincial and territory level has led to a patchwork in the extent that participation rights are now recognized in Canada (Bala & Houston, 2015). In the case of custody proceedings, for example, considerable differences exist in the extent and age that children are allowed to participate. Section 37(2)(b) of the *Family Law Act* in British Columbia can be commended for requiring the court to consider the child's views in determining the best interests of a child for the purposes of drafting a parenting or contract order. Section 8(1) of the 1988 *Custody and Enforcement Act* in Prince Edward Island likewise requires courts to take the views and preferences of the child into consideration when addressing any application under the statute. A 2010 ruling by the Yukon Supreme Court decided that all children in that territory have the right to be heard in custody cases (Committee on the Rights of the Child, 2012). This ruling relied upon UNCRC Article 12 to establish the right of the child to be heard in disputes between separated parents (Bala & Houston, 2015).

With regard to child protection proceedings, children over age 12 have legal participatory rights in all jurisdictions except for Saskatchewan, which provides no right to participate, and Nova Scotia, which stipulates 16 as the minimum age to participate (Canadian Foundation for Children, Youth and the Law, 2013). In ignoring the requirement of Article 12 in the UNCRC to incorporate mechanisms into legal proceedings to also assess the maturity of the child, the government is neglecting the best interests of the child. Setting age as the sole factor in determining whether a child has legal rights to participate evidences the paternalistic stage since it prioritizes bureaucratic ease and convenience.

In Manitoba, the means through which the child may be heard in child protection proceedings can vary between the use of court-ordered assessments, children's lawyers, or the written statements of children. The relevant legislation reflects the paternalistic stage since procedures grant significant discretion to the courts rather than insisting on child participation rights. For example, legislation states that courts can or may (rather than shall) appoint lawyers, order assessments, or grant judicial interviews to facilitate child participation (Covell, Howe, & Blokhuis, 2018). While Ontario funds children's lawyers, other provinces do not with the consequence that while children retain formal rights to a lawyer, they invariably lack the resources and legal aid to act on this right in practice. Once again, we see weaknesses in the extent to which child participation rights are protected reflective of the paternalistic stage.

Only in Quebec are courts required to give the child the opportunity to be heard in all cases concerning the child, conditional upon the age and maturity of the child. Other provinces and territories remain stuck in the paternalistic stage since the question of deciding whether or not a child can participate is left to the discretion of the judge. Entrusting child participation to judicial discretion contravenes the UNCRC, which states that "all interested parties shall be given an opportunity to participate in the proceedings" (Article 9).

Therefore, as briefly detailed above in the context of custody and child protection proceedings, the participation rights currently afforded to the child in Canada vary considerably between provinces and territories both in substantive content and in the amount of resources allocated to enable children to realize those rights. Even in jurisdictions where the law prescribes clear rules on child participation, children have reported finding the system both confusing and inadequate (Canadian Foundation for Children, Youth and the Law, 2013).

A children's rights approach would see proper coordination among distinct jurisdictions so as to develop comprehensive and consistent child participation rights and to ensure legal representation to children involved in administrative proceedings. The Canadian Bar Association proposed a five-step best practice process that Canadian courts could adopt to ensure child participation rights. First, the child should be informed of his or her right to participate in a judicial process and of his or her option to communicate either directly or through a representative. Second, the child's views should be heard in a supportive context. Third, the cognitive capacity of the child to formulate and express his or her own views should be assessed. Fourth, the decision maker informs the child of the outcome of the process and explains how the views of the child, or of the child's representative, were considered. Finally, the process is to be made accountable to the child in terms of addressing any complaints and providing for redress (Canadian Bar Association, 2016).

HOW CANADA IS STILL FAILING THE PARTICIPATION RIGHTS OF THE CHILD

The UN Committee on the Rights of the Child (2012) contrasted the federal government's broad statements of support for participation rights to the absence of specific, coordinated, and properly resourced policies that could effectively deliver those rights in practice. Considerable evidence exists to support this assessment. For example, there are few guarantees that the child's views will be heard in immigration-related decisions made at the federal level since, in contradiction to Articles 3 and 12 of the UNCRC, children are not afforded standing, and therefore have no rights, to address the court under the *Immigration and Refugee Protection Act* (Canadian Foundation for Children, Youth and the Law, 2013). While the Public Health Agency of Canada (2017) has promoted November 20 as the official National Child Day by "celebrating children as active participants in their own lives," it appears as though such a celebration may be premature. Child participation rights remain absent from many programs and services offered through the agency. To pick just one example, while the Public Health Agency of Canada celebrates the Community Action Program for Children on its official website, this program focuses on parenting skills, nutritional support, physical activity programs, and outreach initiatives, none of which focus on child participation rights (Public Health Agency of Canada, 2017).

The first step to guaranteeing participation rights requires educating Canadian society so as to promote awareness of those rights. Yet federal programs aimed at educating parents on child participation rights remain patchy, superficial, and largely unevaluated. The federal government provides few opportunities for parents to become engaged in developing education programs on child participation rights, and few resources are placed into implementing or evaluating those programs that do exist (Matusicky & Russell, 2009). The Committee on the Rights of the Child subsequently expressed concern that awareness of key provisions of the UNCRC "remains limited" among Canadian children and the general public (2012, p. 5).

Moreover, the federal government has resisted calls to implement policies that could promote child participation rights in Canada. For example, the government has neglected to introduce a federal or national child advocate. Subsequently there is an ongoing lack of any federal coordination of the work of provincial and territorial CYAs and a lack of an official advocate for children at the federal level (Hunter, 2017). Canada's *Divorce Act* does not explicitly assure a child the right to have his or her views heard in court. Instead, the Act requires courts to take the "best interests" of the child into account only when making custody or access awards (Bala & Houston, 2015). While individual judges often take the child's views into consideration, leaving this crucial matter to the discretion of the judge reflects the paternalistic paradigm since it fails to provide the child with the right to participate. Such failings further justify criticisms from the Committee on the Rights of the Child that Canada employs "inadequate mechanisms for facilitating meaningful and empowered child participation in legal, policy, environmental issues, and administrative procedures that impact children" (Committee on the Rights of the Child, 2012, p. 8).

First Nations Children

Failings by the federal government to design an overall strategy for advancing child participation rights are exemplified in the case of First Nations children. In this instance, the government has gone so far as to take measures to block the efforts of children, and of their representatives, wanting to participate in political matters (Blackstock, 2011).

First Nations children face a combination of severe risks unparalleled to any other group of children in Canada. These include the legacy of colonialism; the ongoing prevalence of racism; legacy issues of trauma, abuse, or addictions caused by caregivers being forced to attend residential schools; and being displaced from traditional lands (Bennett & Auger, 2014; Ontario Provincial Advocate for Children and Youth, 2015). These risks manifest themselves in a multitude of grim statistics, perhaps the most shocking being that suicide was responsible for 38 percent of all deaths of First Nations children aged 10 to 19 in 2006 (Pearson, 2015). Meaningful efforts at promoting the participation rights of First Nations children would begin by recognizing the extraordinary challenges facing this demographic. A political strategy would then be formulated, adequately funded, and properly assessed to enable First Nations children to realize their participation rights. Further, the federal government could reasonably be expected to expedite the delivery of this political strategy because of its additional obligations to ensure participation rights to First Nations children under the terms of the Declaration on the Rights of Indigenous Peoples (King et al., 2016).

In fact, flagship programs directed toward First Nations children by the Public Health Agency of Canada, including Maternal Child Health, Prenatal Nutrition, Aboriginal Head Start, and the Fetal Alcohol Disorder Program, lack any coherent strategy for advancing child participation rights (Public Health Agency of Canada, 2012). It has therefore been left to First Nations children themselves to take proactive measures to assert their participation rights. For example, First Nations children played a role in the historic 2016 ruling from the Canadian Human Rights Tribunal (CHRT). This ruling found the federal government racially discriminated against Aboriginal children by providing between 22 and 34 percent less for services given on reservations compared to provincial funding for similar services provided elsewhere (Blackstock, 2011; King et al., 2016; Pearson, 2015). The complaint to the CHRT was first filed in 2007 by the First Nations Child and Family Caring Society of Canada and the Assembly of First Nations. Rather than addressing the merits of the case in a constructive manner, the federal government spent millions of dollars and nine years on eight unsuccessful attempts to have the case thrown out on legal technicalities. The federal government also objected to children participating in hearings. For example, the attorney general objected to a request from the Aboriginal Peoples Television Network (APTN) for permission to broadcast Tribunal proceedings. In 2012 the Federal Court ruled in favour of allowing the APTN to broadcast the hearings on grounds that receiving knowledge of events is a requisite for children to form their own opinions and to participate meaningfully in those proceedings. In another instance of attempting to prevent participation by children, Canada objected to allowing the Caring Society to include a video made by children in its opening statement. The government argued that inclusion of the video would be inappropriate, but provided no supporting evidence in defence of this claim (King et al., 2016).

First Nations children responded to government attempts to silence them by organizing the I am a Witness campaign, which offered an online forum for children to post their experiences and views on the hearings (First Nations Child and Family Caring Society of Canada, 2017). Refuting the misconception that children lack any interest in politics, children attended the hearing in such numbers that proceedings had to relocate to the Supreme Court of Canada courthouse.

Individual children have also demonstrated leadership in promoting their rights. At the age of 12, Shannen Koostachin from the Attawapiskat Cree Nation began a campaign to have a safe and comfortable school built in her community on the James Bay coast. This campaign was launched following a 2007 decision from the federal government to reverse a previous commitment to provide a new school on the reserve. A tragic car accident took the life of Shannen Koostachin in June 2010, but her campaign continued under the leadership of students determined to keep her dream of a new school alive. A letter-writing campaign by thousands of children across Canada demanding equitable funding for education on reserves resulted in a new school being opened in 2012.

Autumn Peltier from the Wikwemikong Unceded Indian Reserve began a campaign for access to clean drinking water rights as a universal right. At age 12, Autumn represented Canada at the 2015 Children's Climate Conference in Sweden and met with Justin Trudeau the following year. This meeting resulted in the Canadian prime minister publicly committing to better protections for water quality and access to clean water in Canada (Canadian 10th Annual Water Summit, 2019).

First Nations children led the Have a Heart Campaign on February 14, 2012, when 500 children, teachers, and parents went to the steps of

Parliament Hill to read letters that the children had written in support of equity for First Nations children. Demonstrating the centrality of the voice of the child in this campaign, only children were permitted to speak at the event (King et al., 2016). In utilizing UNCRC participation rights as political instruments, First Nations children can therefore be seen to be effective advocates for their own interests in the face of government paternalism and continuing refusal to respect those rights.

CHILDREN'S PARTICIPATION RIGHTS IN THE FAMILY

The child first learns rules of social interactions from relationships with family members. The role and status ascribed to the voice of the child in family decision making is consequently critical in familiarizing the child with fundamental democratic practices. Campbell and Rose-Krasnor (2007) point out that a child who is denied the opportunity to participate at home will likely not expect such opportunities in other contexts and is unlikely to know how to participate appropriately when such opportunities are provided.

Baumrind (1967) differentiated the way in which parents controlled children's actions into three categories. Children were found to have very different outcomes depending upon the parenting style under which they were raised. Under the permissive model, parents would typically exercise little control over their child's behaviour, demand little achievement, and accept anti-social behaviour. Under the authoritarian model, the parent exercised strict control over the child's behaviour, denying child participation. The permissive and the authoritarian parenting styles were found to lead to less beneficial outcomes for the development of the child when compared to the third style, the authoritative (or democratic) style. Authoritative parents would set and consistently enforce clear rules in a supportive environment receptive to the child's comments, questions, and input. The authoritative parent expected high levels of achievement and would devote considerable time and effort to helping the child to succeed. Recent research has demonstrated that children exposed to other than the authoritative parenting style are nine times as likely to be diagnosed with behavioural problems, while children of authoritative parents show higher levels of resilience, self-esteem, self-reliance, self-control, social maturity, and academic competence when compared to children raised under authoritarian or permissive parenting styles (Covell, Howe, & Blokhuis, 2018).

Child participation rights in the family are facilitated under the authoritative parenting style since only the authoritative parent encourages the child to reflect on different options and to express his or her views. The authoritative parent considers the child's view commensurate to the age and maturity of the child and provides explanations when the child's opinion is not decisive. In contrast, permissive parents typically set few limits and offer little input into decision making since children are allowed to follow their impulses. Authoritarian parents allow little input from the child since parents characteristically impose their own will on their children through, for example, closing down discussions by simply telling the child to do as he or she is told. Participation rights can guide the appropriate input from the child into the decision-making process based on the principle that the child and the parent should work together to make decisions. The evidence therefore commends the authoritative model as the most appropriate parenting style for realizing the best interests of most children. Government has two possible mechanisms for promoting authoritative parenting at the level of public policy.

First, government could use legislation to require parents to involve children in decision making in line with the age and maturity of the child. For example, child welfare legislation could be amended to incorporate the denial of child participation in family decision making as a component of emotional abuse. An alternative approach would see the enactment of specific legislation guaranteeing participation rights. A number of European countries, including Norway and Sweden, now have specific child participation rights legislation that places a legal obligation on parents to consult with, and hear the views of, the child before making decisions on personal matters that affect the child (Covell, Howe, & Blokhuis, 2018). In keeping with Article 12 of the UNCRC, Norway's *Children's Act* requires parents to allow children more autonomy to make their own decisions as they grow older. The purpose and effect of legislation in these countries is not to seek out and punish adults using permissive or controlling parenting styles. Rather, the purpose of the legislation is to stress the importance of participation rights and to help entrench those rights in society.

Second, government could invest in public education initiatives to inform the public of the benefits of authoritative parenting and of the importance of respecting child participation rights in terms of providing for the best interests of the child. Indeed, Article 18 of the UNCRC confers an obligation on states to assist parents in their performance of child-rearing responsibilities. Appropriately designed parenting education programs could help government to fulfill this obligation (Campbell & Rose-Krasnor, 2007).

Ideally, governments would employ a combination of legislation and public education programs to maximize acceptance and compliance with child participation rights in society. Yet, in contrast, Canada has done remarkably little to guarantee the participation rights of the child in the family. The Charter of Rights and Freedoms fails to assure child participation rights since the Charter does not apply to private associations, including the family. No Canadian government has yet introduced legislation specifically requiring parents to consult with their child when making family decisions.

In a report responding to the May 2002 special session on children, the Government of Canada (2004) formally declared its commitment to provide parents with the skills and knowledge necessary to become positive and effective parents. The Public Health Agency of Canada subsequently funded a number of parental education programs. For example, the Nobody's Perfect program is designed to meet the needs of parents of children aged under five years who are young, single, socially or geographically isolated, or have low income or limited formal education (Government of Canada, 2017). Yet this program targets marginalized families of very young children or families already facing difficulties. There continues to be a lack of education or programs directed at the broader population and specifically at parents of adolescent children. Most importantly, education surrounding participation rights continues to be excluded as a central component of those programs that do exist, as further discussed by Howe in Chapter 3 of this book. The dominant attitude of Canadian politicians concerning child participation rights in the family therefore remains largely stuck in the laissez-faire stage. Rather than advocating for the authoritative parenting style and providing broad-spectrum public education on participation rights in the family, government policy instead adopts a deferential position. The legal boundaries on parenting in Canada are set only by criminal and child protection laws. As Covell and Howe conclude, "[w]e seem to believe that if we are taught how to breathe during delivery, instinct will take over.... The current situation stands in complete contrast to children's participation rights and to their developmental needs" (2001, p. 108).

CIVIC PARTICIPATION

Canada can be placed in the paternalistic stage in terms of the extent to which children are allowed to participate in civic affairs. While initiatives facilitating child participation in civic affairs exist, power is invariably retained by adults in formal political structures.

It is perhaps instructive to view opportunities for child civic participation in Canada in light of initiatives undertaken in comparable states such as New Zealand, the United States, and Sweden. New Zealand was a leader in introducing youth forums to allow children to communicate their views and concerns to decision makers. Established in 1984, the Auckland City Youth Council, for example, advocates in City Hall on behalf of the youth living in the city of Auckland. Members are selected by a panel comprising a youth, a council officer, and a youth organization representative (Finlay, 2010). New Zealand also boasts a youth advisory forum that directly advises the prime minister and cabinet on youth matters (Bala & Houston, 2015).

While the United States lacks legal child participation rights at the federal level, the Detroit suburbs of Farmington and Farmington Hills have introduced innovative youth councils that allow participating teenagers to articulate their views to elected officials. Tangible outcomes resulting from the initiative include the development of a skateboard park and a community teen centre to provide more activities for young people (Richards-Schuster & Checkoway, 2009). Similarly, influence forums allowing children to articulate their views on local matters to councillors have been established in a number of Swedish municipalities (Bala & Houston, 2015).

Many Canadian municipalities have likewise adopted youth advisory forums, committees, or councils to represent the priorities of local youth to councils or mayors. For example, the Toronto Youth Cabinet was established in 1998 with the aim of giving youth a voice (Shen, 2006). Also in Ontario, the Ottawa Police Service established a Youth Advisory Committee with the aim of helping the Ottawa Police gain a broader understanding of youth aged 13–24 by collaborating on initiatives (Ottawa Police Service, 2017).

These examples succeed in terms of providing opportunities for individual youths to articulate concerns to decision makers. Yet this falls considerably short of guaranteeing rights for all children to participate in civic affairs in line with the age and maturity of the child. First, these opportunities are open only to some children, depending on whether or not the child is selected for a position on a youth committee and whether or not the child lives in a municipality that has a youth committee. Second, there are no mechanisms specifying how, or even whether, decision makers will pay regard to youth input. Third, the creation of a youth council is not, by itself, sufficient to engage children in civic affairs. For example, many children feel intimidated by speaking through a microphone in a formal council setting, making formal resolutions, or having to speak through a chairperson (Dibley & Gordon, 2006; Finlay, 2010). Mitra et al. (2014) explored the risks to children when they perceive youth participation initiatives as mere tokenism. In particular, the promise of a voice without actually having a say was found to increase, rather than reduce, participating children's feelings of alienation and disconnection from community decision-making processes (Callingham, 2013). For all three reasons, the simple existence of youth advisory committees fails to provide substantive civic child participation rights.

In an attempt to facilitate more meaningful youth participation in policy-making, the municipal council of Essex, Ontario, voted in April 2014 to allow two youth representatives to sit as members of the municipal council. While this initiative can be commended for moving beyond a mere advisory role for youth, the bylaw amendment establishing the positions nonetheless prevented youth members from having a formal vote or from participating in closed council sessions (Federation of Canadian Municipalities, 2015). Allowing youth representatives to sit as full voting members on council is currently prohibited by rules of order and procedure since youth representatives are unaccountable to the public.

Canada has yet to see the success of any campaign aimed at lowering the voting age to extend the vote to youth with a demonstrated capacity for making informed political decisions. Those projects that do exist are vulnerable to charges of tokenism since the votes of children are isolated from any impact on electoral results. Elections Canada has, for example, partnered with the civic education organization CIVIX to provide a student vote program to schools for recent elections, including the 2017 provincial elections in British Columbia and Nova Scotia and the 2015 federal election (CIVIX, 2017). Yet the student votes have no impact on the actual election outcome.

Extending the vote to children is typically rejected on the grounds that teenagers may be easily influenced when casting a vote and that they lack a detailed knowledge of politics. Yet maturity develops over time and the arbitrary age distinction separating the hypothesized politically naive child from a savvy adult is an artificial construct designed for bureaucratic ease and convenience. Children's citizenship is commonly conceived in terms of one of three representations in the political theory literature. Under the first two theories, children are either endowed with full citizenry or else are seen as citizens in waiting (Lister, 2007). As citizens in waiting, children are viewed as underdeveloped, unfinished, or apprentice human beings until they reach a certain age (Jenks, 2005). The full citizenry model fails since it neglects the aspects of children that make them exceptional and vulnerable. The citizens-in-waiting model fails as it assumes powerlessness and incapability, effectively precluding youth participation by constructing a notion of childhood as a deficit version of adulthood (Wyn, 2007).

In contrast to the above two positions, children's rights scholars typically stress the importance of apportioning rights in light of the child's evolving capacities. Instead of having full rights of citizenship, children are seen to have special vulnerabilities and dependencies that are best protected by grounding specific children's rights in a broader account of social obligations (Arthur, 2015). Electoral reform to facilitate child civic participation rights could consequently extend the vote to those under age 18 who are able to demonstrate a certain level of social responsibility and knowledge of politics. One possible model in keeping with Article 12 of the UNCRC would allow children of any age who wanted to cast vote to do so only after demonstrating a basic awareness of politics by successfully completing a rudimentary knowledge test. Another model could see participating children voting for one or more child representatives to sit alongside adult representatives in a council or Parliament. No such models currently exist in any national legislatures. States such as Argentina, Austria, and Brazil, which have extended the vote to children, have done so by lowering the voting age to 16. Although somewhat progressive, this measure is only partially successful at complying with Article 12 of the UNCRC since it relies solely on an arbitrary age cut-off to decide which children can or cannot vote.

No initiatives to extend the vote to children are currently under consideration in a Canadian jurisdiction. However, in 2001, two high school students initiated a legal challenge seeking to allow youth to vote in a civic election in Edmonton (Editorial, 2005). Eryn Fitzgerald and Christine Jairamsingh argued that voting age limits violated their democratic and equality rights guaranteed under the Charter of Rights and Freedoms. Court of Queen's Bench Justice Erik Lefsrud agreed with those arguments, but went on to rule against the plaintiffs on the grounds that those violations were justified in order to maintain the integrity of the electoral system. The justice remarked that "some restriction is necessary, since newborns and young children clearly do not have sufficient maturity to cast a rational and informed vote" (Editorial, 2005). The Alberta Court of Appeal subsequently upheld Judge Lefsrud's decision. This ruling exemplified paternalism for three reasons. First, the best interests of the child were not given the level of consideration that could be expected from a court prioritizing children's rights. Second, the court adopted the paternalistic position that allowing children to vote could jeopardize the integrity of the voting system. A children's rights perspective would, in contrast, see voting by engaged and informed children as a way to strengthen the integrity of the electoral system by addressing age-based discrimination. Third, Justice Lefsrud justified the age discrimination that continues to arbitrarily deny the vote to all children, including two highly articulate, engaged, and intelligent teenagers, by reference to the characteristics and incapacities of newborn babies. Such simplistic and paternalistic reasoning disregards Article 12 of the UNCRC, which requires that the child should be allowed to participate incrementally in accordance with his or her age and maturity.

Many children are asserting their participation rights in the face of indifference at the political level. School Strike for Climate is an international movement of school students "striking" from school in demanding their governments take immediate action against climate change as per their obligations under the December 2015 Paris Agreement. This movement was started in Sweden on August 20, 2018, by ninth grade student Greta Thunberg, who would demonstrate every subsequent Friday. In the Friday strikes that followed, Greta was joined by students first from within Sweden and then from around the world. On March 15, 2019, an estimated 1.4 million children took part in strikes held in 2,000 cities across the world, including Toronto, Vancouver, St. John's, Charlottetown, Regina, and Montreal in Canada (Stevenson, 2019). Fourteen-year-old Tara Schwiesow from the Max-Brauer School in Hamburg, Germany, articulated her reasons for taking part in the March 15, 2019, strike: "we have knowledge and interest in climate change. Every week children and teenagers from all over the world demonstrate to change things. Climate change affects us and our future. We have the right to stand up for our future" (email received March 18, 2019).

Empirical research by Zeglovits and Zandonella (2013) found that, rather than teenagers intrinsically lacking any interest in politics, it is the denial of the right to vote that causes a lack of interest among this demographic. Zeglovits and Zandonella examined the differences in political interest of 16- and 17-year-olds before and after Austria lowered the voting age for federal elections, presidential elections, and elections for the European Parliament to 16 in 2007. Measured both in terms of subjective political interest and in terms of the frequency of following news stories, these researchers found a "positive and highly significant" increase in the political interest of 16- and 17-year-olds in 2008 compared to 2004 (Zeglovits & Zandonella, 2013). Loreto (2015) likewise points out that many young people may appear disinterested in politics not because of apathy and indifference but rather because they have been disengaged by a political system that neglects their interests, leaves many to live in poverty, and continues to deny the relevance of their voice. As Wyn perceptively identifies, the amount of social and political participation by youth in civic affairs is itself a measure of the degree of adequacy of existent frameworks through which adults view youth and have created political institutions that either allow or prevent child participation (Wyn, 2007). In light of the above, Canada can be placed in the paternalistic stage since none of the limited opportunities that exist for children to participate in civic affairs guarantee actual rights for children to influence political decision making.

HEALTH CARE TREATMENT

Health care providers must decide whether children are passive objects receiving health care or subjects with rights in deciding the treatment they receive in line with their age and maturity (Clarke, 2015). This section documents how Canada has made significant moves toward the children's rights stage in deciding the health treatment of children, albeit in a manner with inconsistent applications among provinces and territories and with an overreliance on common law rights. Provincial legislation in Newfoundland and Labrador and New Brunswick specifies the age of 16 years at which children are presumed to have the capacity to provide their own consent to health treatment. The *Medical Consent of Minors Act* in New Brunswick allows for children under 16 to consent to treatment where a medical practitioner assesses that the child is capable of understanding the nature and consequences of treatment, and where the child's decision is assessed by the practitioner to be in the best interests of the child. The *Infants Act* in British Columbia applies a similar formula, except it does not set a minimum age for a child to give presumed consent (Bala & Houston, 2015).

Relevant legislation in neither Saskatchewan nor Alberta provides for decision making by children under the ages specified in the statute, which is 16 in the case of Saskatchewan and 18 in Alberta. In cases like this where statutory law fails to give decision-making rights to children under the stated age, the common law principle of mature minor applies. Under this principle, children who are deemed sufficiently mature are allowed to make their own treatment decisions (Bala & Houston, 2015). This principle is very much in line with the UNCRC since it allows capable children to have a say in the medical treatment they can receive, provided they are evaluated as sufficiently mature to make important decisions concerning their own health care as assessed by a health care practitioner. The notable caveat here is that, when tested in the courts, common law rights carry a very weak status when they conflict with statutory laws. Consequently, the mature minor principle has been overruled on numerous occasions. For example, the decision by a 16-year-old in Alberta to decline a blood transfusion on religious grounds was overridden in 2003, when the courts relied on child welfare legislation to empower the state to force the child to accept the procedure. This ruling came in spite of the fact that medical practitioners had deemed that child to be capable of considering complex issues as well as the implications of her decision. Since statutory law enjoys a higher status compared to common law, child protection legislation was deemed to overrule the child's common law rights derived from the mature minor principle. While the child was allowed to challenge the decision in this case, she was not allowed to present arguments based on her constitutional freedom to practise religion (Canadian Foundation for Children, Youth and the Law, 2013).

Ontario, Prince Edward Island, and the Yukon provide the most comprehensive rights for children to participate in matters of their own health treatment since all children are presumed capable of consenting to treatment unless they lack the understanding of the information pertinent to making a decision (Bala & Houston, 2015). Moreover, Ontario empowers a child with legal mechanisms to realize his or her participation rights. For example, when a child disagrees with a health practitioner's determination that he or she is not competent, the child can request a hearing before the Consent and Capacity Board to challenge the decision (Canadian Foundation for Children, Youth and the Law, 2013).

In contrast to Ontario, other provinces allow decisions made by a competent child to be overridden by a health practitioner in circumstances where that decision is deemed by the practitioner to contradict the child's best interests. Since this places decision-making power in the hands of health care professionals, this approach characterizes the paternalistic, rather than children's rights, framework.

Legislation relying solely on the age of a child in determining the ability of a child to participate in health care treatment is inherently problematic from the children's rights perspective since it prioritizes administrative convenience over considering the competency of the child, as required under UNCRC Article 12. Courts in Manitoba and British Columbia should be commended for upholding the principle that the degree to which children may participate in the health care that they receive is a function not simply of age but also maturity. In these two jurisdictions, maturity is evaluated on a case-by-case basis and depends upon the capability of the child to formulate and articulate his or her own views (Canadian Bar Association, 2016).

CONCLUSIONS: RESPECTING PARTICIPATION RIGHTS IN CANADA

This chapter has evaluated the progress that Canada has made in terms of recognizing and implementing child participation rights. It has noted the existence of a myriad of laws, policies, and practices that relate to child participation in Canada. The extent of these developments suggests that Canada has moved beyond the laissez-faire stage in offering children participation opportunities in many areas of their lives. Yet, all too often, these initiatives have failed to guarantee actual participation rights to children. Ongoing and serious omissions have been identified in Canada's record of implementing the participation rights contained in the UNCRC. The achievement of the children's rights stage remains elusive. Canada also falls short of implementing child participation rights when measured against developments in other states (KidsRights Foundation, 2017). Using indicators that measure quantitative data provided by UNICEF and qualitative data published by the UN Committee on the Rights of the Child, the KidsRights index assesses the extent to which states adhere to and are equipped to improve children's rights. While the research found that none of the 167 countries included in their analysis scored "good" in terms of guaranteeing participation rights,

Canada received a grade of "poor," scoring an overall mark of only 25 out of 100, placing Canada at 126 out of the 165 states examined.

This chapter has also illustrated notable differences in how participation rights are respected in laws governing three distinctive areas in the lives of children in Canada. Policies governing child participation rights in the family were found to be stuck in the social laissez-faire stage. Regulations governing child civic participation in Canada were found to be characteristic of the paternalistic stage. Health care treatment was then identified as an arena where child participation is recognized, at least in part, as a right in Canada. However, this conclusion came with the significant caveat that the situation varies considerably depending upon the age of the child and upon the province or territory in which that child resides. As previously referenced in this work, participation in the youth criminal justice system could provide another example of where child participation rights have been recognized in Canada. Yet the fact that progress on participation rights is so mixed between different areas of a child's life in Canada is itself indicative of ongoing political failure. As the relevant signatory to the UNCRC, the federal government has neglected its obligations to provide the leadership and direction necessary for ensuring ongoing improvements in child participation rights.

This chapter has suggested several measures for how policy and legislation might be more effectively mobilized to better align the policy and legislative framework in Canada with the child participation rights stated in the UNCRC. First, laws could advocate that the voice of the child be heard in a supportive and protective environment whenever decisions affecting the life of the child are made in a family setting. Second, legislation could require that the views of the child be given due weight by decision makers in accordance with the maturity, as well as the age, of the child in all areas of life concerning the child. Third, policy changes could ensure that children receive information from a range of perspectives to allow them to better understand their rights and formulate their own views. Currently there are widespread deficiencies in the extent to which Canadian children understand their rights. For example, in 2015 the Ontario Provincial Advocate for Children and Youth (2015) undertook a listening tour of over 400 youth and found that a majority of young people did not know their rights or how to exercise them properly. While the federal government distributes free copies of the UNCRC, Campbell and Rose-Krasnor (2007) reasonably question the extent to which children access and understand this information absent broader support structures. There is an urgent need to educate both children and adults since lack of awareness of children's participation rights currently stands as a major barrier to creating norms of adherence to those rights in Canadian society. Above all, public policy could move away from making child participation conditional upon simplistic and arbitrary age-based criteria. Efforts could instead be placed on developing mechanisms that allow and aid the child to increasingly participate in the context of his or her developing maturity. The continuing reticence from different levels of government to acknowledge the child's capacities to participate meaningfully in decision making in accordance with his or her age and maturity is perhaps itself the most conclusive evidence of the continuing dominance of the paternalistic paradigm in both Canadian political culture and legislation.

QUESTIONS FOR DISCUSSION

1. Identify why child participation rights matter and suggest two policy commitments that could be adopted by the federal government to enhance the profile of child participation rights in Canada.
2. Provincial legislation concerning child participation rights varies significantly. Which province or territory do you think has the most progressive legislation on child participation rights and what examples can you identify to defend your answer?
3. To what extent do you think parents in Canada currently provide for child participation in the family? Is legislation or parenting education more effective in ensuring that parents facilitate child participation?

ABBREVIATIONS

APTN	Aboriginal Peoples Television Network
CHRT	Canadian Human Rights Tribunal
CYA	Child and Youth Advocates
UNCRC	United Nations Convention on the Rights of the Child
US	United States

REFERENCES

Arthur, R. (2015). Recognising children's citizenship in the youth justice system. *Journal of Social Work and Family Law, 37*(1), 21–37.

Bala, N., & Houston, C. (2015). *Article 12 of the Convention on the Rights of the Child and Children's Participatory Rights in Canada*. Retrieved from http://www.justice.gc.ca/eng/rp-pr/other-autre.article12/Article12-eng.pdf

Baumrind, D. (1967). Child care practices anteceding three patterns of preschool behaviour. *Genetic Psychology Monographs, 75*(1), 43–88.

Bennett, M., & Auger, A. (2014). *The rights of First Nations children in Canada*. Retrieved from http://www.nccah-ccnsa.ca/Publications/Lists/Publications/Attachments/124/Rights_First_Nations_Children_EN_web.pdf

Birnbaum, R., & Bala, N. (2010). Judicial interviews with children in custody and access cases: Comparing experiences in Ontario and Ohio. *International Journal of Law, Policy and the Family, 24*(3), 300–337.

Blackstock, C. (2011). *Jordan and Shannen: First Nations children demand that the Canadian government stop racially discriminating against them*. Retrieved from https://fncaringsociety.com/sites/default/files/docs/UNCRC_report_Canada_2011_final.pdf

Callingham, M. (2013). Democratic youth participation: A strength-based approach to youth investigating educational engagement. *Youth Studies Australia, 32*(4), 48–56.

Campbell, K., & Rose-Krasnor, L. (2007). The participation rights of the child. In K. Covell & R. B. Howe (Eds.), *A question of commitment: Children's rights in Canada* (pp. 209–240). Waterloo: Wilfrid Laurier University Press.

Canadian Bar Association. (2016). *Convention on the Rights of the Child General comment no. 12*. Retrieved from http://www.cba.org/Publications-Resources/Practice-Tools/Child-Rights-Toolkit/theChild/Child-Participation

Canadian Foundation for Children, Youth and the Law. (2013). *Children's right to be heard in Canadian judicial and administrative proceedings*. Retrieved from https://jfcy.org/wp-content/uploads/2013/10/UNDiscussionPaper.pdf

Canadian 10th Annual Water Summit. (2019). *Autumn Peltier*. Retrieved from https://watersummit.ca/speaker/autumn-peltier/#

CIVIX. (2017). *Student vote*. Retrieved from http://studentvote.ca

Clarke, S. (2015). A child's rights perspective: The right of children and young people to participate in health care research. *Issues in Contemporary Pediatric Nursing, 38*(3), 161–180.

Committee on the Rights of the Child. (2012). *Concluding observations on the combined third and fourth periodic report of Canada*. Retrieved from http://docstore.ohchr.org/SelfServices/FilesHandler.ashx?enc=6QkG1d%2FPPRiCAqhKb7yhsh8%2FU426pHwccUxzN5kmnhLtdnrWm1hJzGwfirOtSF7im%2Btj4%2BJ5n5CPlpIDWXA35DpHXskxTdDvCoa0RW9yOJTACORyOJ17Auf%2Bpplgz6CB

Convention on the Rights of the Child. (1989). Retrieved from http://www.ohchr.org/EN/ProfessionalInterest/Pages/CRC.aspx

Covell, K. (2007). *Seen, heard and believed: What youth say about violence*. Retrieved from http://www.unicef.ca/childprotection/violencestudy

Covell, K., & Howe, R. B. (2001). *The challenge of children's rights for Canada*. Waterloo, ON: Wilfrid Laurier University Press.

Covell, K., Howe, R. B., & Blokhuis, J. (2018). *The challenge of children's rights for Canada* (2nd ed.). Waterloo, ON: Wilfrid Laurier University Press.

Dibley, G., & Gordon, M. (2006). *Talking participation, taking action: A local government guide to youth participation*. Retrieved from http://www.lgat.tas.gov.au/contentFile.aspx?filename=FINAL_Guide_to_youth_participation.pdf

Editorial. (2005, January 6). Supreme Court rejects challenge on voting age. *Globe and Mail*. Retrieved from https://beta.theglobeandmail.com/news/national/supreme-court-rejects-challenge-on-voting-age/article1112704/

Federation of Canadian Municipalities. (2015). *The municipal youth engagement handbook.* Retrieved from https://www.fcm.ca/Documents/tools/FCM/Municipal_Youth_Engagement_Handbook_EN.pdf

Finlay, S. (2010). Carving out meaningful spaces for youth participation and engagement in decision-making. *Youth Studies Australia, 29*(4), 53–58.

First Nations Child and Family Caring Society of Canada. (2017). *I am a witness.* Retrieved from https://fncaringsociety.com/i-am-witness

Flekkoy, M., & Kaufman, N. (1997). *The participation rights of the child: Rights and responsibilities in family and society.* London: Jessica Kingsley Publishers.

Government of Canada. (2004). *A Canada fit for children.* Retrieved from http://publications.gc.ca/collections/ollections/SD13-4-2004E.pdf

Government of Canada. (2017). *Nobody's perfect.* Retrieved from https://www.canada.ca/en/public-health/services/health-promotion/childhood-adolescence/parent/nobody-perfect.html

Hodgkin, R., & Newell, P. (2007). *Implementation handbook for the Convention on the Rights of the Child* (3rd ed.). Geneva: UNICEF.

Hunter, M. T. (2017). *Canadian child and youth advocates: A comparative analysis* (Unpublished doctoral dissertation). University of Victoria, Victoria, BC. Retrieved from https://dspace.library.uvic.ca/bitstream/handle/1828/8045/Hunter_Mary_Theresa_PhD_2017.pdf?sequence=1&isAllowed=y

Jenks, C. (2005). *Childhood.* Abingdon: Routledge.

KidsRights Foundation. (2017). *KidsRights index.* Retrieved from http://www.kidsrightsindex.org/

King, J., Wattam, J., & Blackstock, C. (2016). Reconciliation: The kids are here! Child participation and the Canadian Human Rights Tribunal on First Nations child welfare. *Canadian Journal of Children's Rights, 3*(1), 32–45.

Lister, R. (2007). Why citizenship: Where, when and how children? *Theoretical Inquiries in Law, 8*(2), 693–718.

Loreto, N. (2015, September-October). Canada's youth: From passivism to activism. *Canadian Centre for Policy Alternatives Monitor, 22*(3), 41–45.

Matusicky, C., & Russell, C. (2009). Best practices for parents: What is happening in Canada? *Paediatrics and Child Health, 14*(10), 664–665.

Mitra, D., Serriere, S., & Kirshner, B. (2014). Youth participation in US contexts: Student voice without a national mandate. *Children and Society, 28*(4), 292–304.

Ontario Child Advocate. (2018). *Our voice our turn.* Retrieved from https://www.provincialadvocate.on.ca/initiatives/our-voice-our-turn

Ontario Provincial Advocate for Children and Youth. (2015). *Children's rights matter to us: Over 400 children and youth speak out.* Retrieved from https://provincialadvocate.on.ca/documents/en/ChildrensRightsMatter_En.pdf

Ontario Provincial Advocate for Children and Youth. (2016). *Searching for home: Reimagining residential care.* Retrieved from https://www.provincialadvocate.on.ca/reports/advocacy-reports/english-reports/ResidentialCareReport_En.pdf

Ottawa Police Service. (2017). *Youth advisory committee.* Retrieved from https://www.ottawapolice.ca/en/news-and-community/Youth-Advisory-Committee-YAC.asp?_mid_=15405

Ottermann, P. (2017, August 11). Put to the vote: German nursery where children make the decisions. *Guardian.* Retrieved from https://www.theguardian.com/world/2017/aug/11/german-nursery-children-make-decisions-vote-dolli-einstein-haus

Pearson, L. (2015). *A Canada fit for children: Identity, rights and belonging*. Retrieved from http:www.landonpearson.ca/uploads/6/0/1/4/6014680/acffc_2015.pdf

Public Health Agency of Canada. (2012). *Evaluation of the Aboriginal Head Start in urban and northern communities program*. Retrieved from https://www.canada.ca/en/public-health/corporate/mandate/about-agency/office-evaluation-reports/evaluation-aboriginal-head-start-urban-northern-communities-program.html

Public Health Agency of Canada. (2017). *National child day*. Retrieved from http://www.phac-aspc.gc.ca/ncd-jne/index-eng.php

Richards-Schuster, K., & Checkoway, B. (2009). Youth participation in public policy at the local level. *National Civic Review, 98*(4), 26–30.

Shen, V. (2006). *Involve youth 2: A guide to meaningful youth engagement*. Retrieved from https://youthcore.ca/download.php?id=114

Stevenson, V. (2019, March 15). Tens of thousands rally in Montreal as part of international school strike against climate change. *CBC News*. Retrieved from https://www.cbc.ca/news/canada/montreal/climate-march-montreal-1.5058083

Supporting Child, Youth and Family Services Act. Bill 89, 2017. Retrieved from http://www.ontla.on.ca/web/bills/bills_detail.do?locale=en&BillID=4479

Wyn, J. (2007). Generation and class: Young people's new, diverse patterns of life and their implications for recognising participation in civic society. *International Journal of Children's Rights, 15*(1), 165–179.

Zeglovits, E., & Zandonella, M. (2013). Political interest of adolescents before and after lowering the voting age: The case of Austria. *Journal of Youth Studies, 16*(8), 1084–1104.

Chapter 13
Canadian Child and Youth Advocates' Roles in Supporting Children's Rights
M. Theresa Hunter

When Canada ratified the United Nations Convention on the Rights of the Child (UNCRC) (1989) in 1991, it made a significant commitment to implement the treaty and to be held accountable to the international community through regular reports to the UN Committee on the Rights of the Child (UNCRC Committee). Over the years, the Government of Canada has taken sporadic measures to acknowledge children and youth as intrinsic rights holders. Nine provinces and two territories have established independent child and youth advocates (CYAs) to play various roles in protecting and promoting the rights of young people in their jurisdictions. However, not all young Canadians have access to the sub-national CYAs. In addition, Canada does not have a national children's commissioner, despite many calls for this institution. Numerous pervasive, systemic barriers to children's rights, such as high rates of child poverty and inequitable access to public services, cannot be resolved without the significant involvement and co-operation of all levels of government. Establishing a national children's commissioner is an essential step toward achieving stage 3 of the child rights evolutionary framework: "Canada is one of the few countries in the industrialized world that lacks an independent mechanism to monitor the rights and well-being of its children and promote their best interests in law and policy" (UNICEF Canada, 2010, p. 3).

INTERNATIONAL CONTEXT

In 2002, world leaders held in a Special Session on Children and endorsed a unified plan of action called *A World Fit for Children* (UN General Assembly Special Session on Children, 2002). Following this session, the UNCRC Committee endorsed the establishment of national, independent, human rights institutions for children (HRICs) to support implementation of the UNCRC.

National HRICs are considered "one necessary indicator of political will to promote and protect children's rights ..." (UNICEF, 2001, p. 1). The UNCRC Committee (2002) outlined essential structural and functional features of HRICs to bolster their effectiveness. These guidelines are consistent with the UN General Assembly's *Principles Relating to the Status of National Institutions (Paris Principles)* (UN Centre for Human Rights, 1993). The *Paris Principles* set minimum standards for national human rights institutions (NHRIs), including their "legal foundation, membership, mandate, funding and so on ..." (International Council on Human Rights Policy, 2005, p. 9). At a minimum, NHRIs must operate independent of governments and be entrenched in the national constitution or legislation (UN Centre for Human Rights, 1995). So far, more than 70 countries have created national or subnational HRICs (UNICEF, 2013). Their roles are generally to monitor, support, and defend children's rights, and to play catalytic roles for changes to policies, laws, and social views, in keeping with the UNCRC (UNICEF, 2001).

CANADIAN CONTEXT

Since ratifying the UNCRC in 1991, the Government of Canada (1995, 2001, 2009) has taken some steps toward strengthening its commitment to children. There were temporary appointments of a national Secretary of State for Children (1997–2003) and a Minister of State for Children and Youth (2003–2004). The federal government and all provinces and territories participated in developing a National Children's Agenda, which was launched in 1997 (listed as 2000), followed by a national action plan called *A Canada Fit for Children* (2004). In February 1999, first ministers (except Quebec) signed the *Social Union Framework Agreement* to reform Canada's social services system and guarantee secure, pan-Canadian social programs (Canadian Centre for Management Development, 2000). Since then, there have been significant increases in federal transfer payments to the provinces and territories for programs and services for children, youth, and families. In 2007, a temporary Interdepartmental Working Group on Children's Rights was established, co-chaired by the Public Health Agency of Canada, to coordinate cross-government implementation of the UNCRC, and the Department of Justice, to oversee federal legislative implementation of the UNCRC (Government of Canada, 2009).

Despite these efforts, Canada has been criticized for failing to provide stable, national leadership on children's issues and coherent mechanisms to monitor and coordinate implementation of the UNCRC across all levels of government. Collins and Pearson (UNICEF and UNICEF Canada, 2009) observe that: "In reality, children are not always a priority for governments,

Canadian Child and Youth Advocates' Roles in Supporting Children's Rights   269

especially if the electorate wants other issues addressed. Without the vote, it is difficult for children to make themselves heard. As a result, children are not considered a priority in policy development and analysis; any assessment of how government policy might impact on children happens more by chance than by design. For these and other reasons, the absence of an independent institution for children's rights at the national level remains a serious obstacle to implementation of the Convention on the Rights of the Child in Canada" (p. 45).

ORIGINS AND EVOLUTION OF PROVINCIAL AND TERRITORIAL CHILD AND YOUTH ADVOCATES

Public advocacy for children and youth has a moderately long history in the Canadian provinces and territories (UNICEF, 2005). Following World War Two, as international human rights treaties emerged, children began to be viewed as the bearers of intrinsic rights. Changing notions about children and international agreements regarding their rights have influenced the evolution of provincial policies and child-serving systems (Canadian Children's Rights Council, 1997; Covell & Howe, 2001).

Provincial CYAs began to emerge even before Canada ratified the UNCRC. In 1979, Canada participated in celebrating the International Year of the Child, on the 20th anniversary of the United Nations Declaration of the Rights of the Child (1959), a precursor to the UNCRC (1989). Around this time, informal CYAs appeared within ministries and ombudsman offices in the provinces of Ontario, Alberta, and British Columbia. These early advocates emerged out of concerns for vulnerable children and youth who were involved with child welfare, youth justice, and other government programs. Ontario's first children's advocate describes the advent of this position as follows: "The Advocacy Office in Ontario developed out of a movement to combat hopelessness. We called hopeless children 'Hard to Serve.' We found them in jails, in hospitals, in treatment centres, and schools. The one thing they had in common was that nobody would or could help them.... There was a strong conviction that Ontario owed every child and young person the right to develop to his or her full potential and that no one was a throw-away" (Les Horne, in Geigen-Miller, 2003, p. i).

Following Canada's ratification of the UNCRC in 1991, sub-national CYAs continued to evolve and now exist in nine provinces and two territories. Table 13.1 presents a timeline of the CYAs' development from informal to formal institutions, and to independent statutory officers.

Ontario was a leader both nationally and internationally when in 1978, it created an informal child advocate (no legislation) within the Ministry of

Table 13.1 Origins and Evolution of Provincial and Territorial Child and Youth Advocates

PROVINCE/ TERRITORY	DATE FIRST ESTABLISHED	DATE BECAME FORMAL INSTITUTION	DATE BECAME INDEPENDENT
ON	1978	1984	2007
AB	1986	1989	2012
BC	1987	1996 2002[a] 2006	1996 2006
MB	1992	1999	1999
SK	1994	1994	1994
QC	1995	1995	1995
NS	1999	1999	1999
NL	2002	2002	2002
NB	2004	2006	2006
YT	2010	2010	2010
NU	2013	2013	2013
PEI	2019	2019	

a British Columbia has a history of discontinuity in establishing independent child and youth advocates.

Community, Family and Children's Services. In 1984, the Ontario Office of the Child and Family Service Advocacy was formally established within the Ministry of Community and Social Services and given a mandate under the *Child and Family Services Act* (1984). Many years later, an independent review of this office recommended that it be made independent from government (Whitehead, Bala, Leschied, & Chiodo, 2004). Following the Ontario Liberal Party's election in 2003, the *Provincial Advocate for Children and Youth Act* (October 2007) was passed and the Office of the Provincial Advocate for Children and Youth (OPACY) was established as an independent legislative officer in July 2008. The OPACY's mandate is to serve young people and families who receive or seek services under the *Child and Family Services Act* (1984), those attending provincial residential and demonstration schools, and youth in court holding cells. Following the general election in June 2018, the

Progressive Conservative Party formed a majority government. In November 2018, the government announced that the *Provincial Advocate for Children and Youth Act* (2007) would be repealed and the Ontario Child Advocate's Office would be closed. The Office of the Ombudsman Ontario will assume responsibility for children and youth (*Toronto Star*, 2018).

Alberta created the Children's Guardian in 1986, under the *Child Welfare Act* (1984), in response to a review of child welfare and community health services (Thomlison, 1984). The Children's Guardian operated within the Department of Family and Social Services to support children with guardianship orders (Knitel, 2003). In 1989, the Alberta Office of the Children's Advocate was established within the Ministry of Family and Social Services to provide advocacy for young people receiving services under the *Child Welfare Act* and to advise the minister regarding these services (Provincial Archives of Alberta, 2006). The Alberta Child and Youth Advocate (CYA) continued to operate within government for many years and began providing legal representation for children and youth receiving ministry services in 2006. Two review panels made recommendations to improve the delivery of child intervention services and supported the independence of the Alberta CYA (Alberta Child and Youth Advocacy Review Committee, 2009; Alberta Child Intervention Review Panel, 2010). In keeping with the Alberta NDP's election promise to create an independent CYA, the *Child and Youth Advocate Act* was passed in November 2011, and the Office of the Child and Youth Advocate (OCYA) was established in 2012 (Government of Alberta, 2011). The OCYA serves children and youth who receive "designated" child welfare services and continues to appoint legal representation for youth in relation to these types of services.

The British Columbia Ombudsman Office created an informal Deputy Ombudsman for Children and Youth in 1987 to monitor services for children and youth who were in the care or custody of the state (Reif, 2004). In 1996, British Columbia's NDP government established a formal, independent Child, Youth and Family Advocate (CYFA) in response to an in-depth inquiry into the tragic death of a young boy (Gove, 1995). British Columbia also created a Children's Commission in 1997, reporting to the attorney general, to review and investigate the deaths and critical injuries of all children and youth in the province. Following their election in 2001, the BC Liberals undertook a Core Services Review, including a review of the CYFA and Children's Commission (Morley, 2001) that led to their dissolution. A non-independent Office for Children and Youth was created in 2002, and the BC Coroners Service took over reviewing child deaths. Two subsequent heartrending deaths of young children and the discovery that many child death files had not been investigated led to an independent review of BC's child welfare system. In his review,

Hughes (2006) made a number of recommendations, including the creation of an independent representative for children and youth (RCY). Legislation was passed in May 2006 and British Columbia's RCY continues to serve children, youth, and their families who receive "designated" or "reviewable" services, including child welfare and youth criminal justice. More recently, the BC RCY extended its mandate to include young adults who receive services under the *Community Living Authority Act* (October 2004).

Manitoba established the Office of the Children's Advocate (OCA) in 1992, within the Ministry of Family Services and a mandate under *The Child and Family Services Act* (1985) (The Office of the Children's Advocate, ca. 2001). In 1999, the Manitoba OCA became an independent legislative officer under *The Child and Family Services Amendment and Consequential Amendments Act* (Manitoba Legislative Assembly, 1998); however, it was not given separate legislation. Several reviews were undertaken in relation to the death of a young girl in 2005 (e.g., Koster & Schibler, 2006), including a commissioned inquiry that recommended the creation of an independent Manitoba representative for children and youth with its own legislation (Hughes, 2013). Two bills pertaining to a new children's advocate were put forward under the Manitoba NDP government; however, they did not pass prior to the election of the Manitoba Progressive Conservatives in April 2016, and the Manitoba Office of the Children's Advocate continued to operate with a limited mandate under *The Child and Family Services Act* (1985). In March 2018, *The Advocate for Children and Youth Act* was passed with unanimous support from all parties. This new separate legislation phased in significant expansion of the CYA's roles.

Saskatchewan was the first province to create an independent children's advocate, in 1994, as one component of an *Action Plan for Children* (Legislative Assembly of Saskatchewan, 1994). The Action Plan was precipitated by numerous events, including the ombudsman's report (1992) on the deaths of several children due to neglect or abuse (Combes & Evans, 1998) and identification of fragmented government services (Bernstein & Schury, 2009). The Saskatchewan government responded by strengthening the child protection system and setting up a Task Force on Child and Youth Advocacy (Canadian Children's Rights Council, 1997). The Saskatchewan Advocate for Children and Youth (ACY) was created through *The Ombudsman and Children's Advocate Act* (1994) (Geigen-Miller, 2003). In 2010, the Child Welfare Review Panel (Pringle, Cameron, Durocher, & Skelton, 2010) called for fundamental changes to the delivery of child welfare services. In response, a Cabinet Committee for Children and Youth was established and the Saskatchewan Children and Youth Agenda was released in 2011. In September 2012, *The*

Advocate for Children and Youth Act was passed to give the independent ACY separate legislation to continue serving all children and youth in the province.

The Quebec Commission des droits de la personne et des droits de la jeunesse (CDPDJ) was established in 1995, through a merger of the Commission des droits de la personne and the Commission de protection des droits de la jeunesse (Geigen-Miller, 2003). The CDPDJ is a human rights institution with a broad mandate to serve all citizens in Quebec. It also provides special protection regarding the safety and development of young people under several pieces of legislation and the Convention on the Rights of the Child, which Quebec ratified in December 1991 (Quebec Commission des droits de la personne et des droits de la jeunesse, n.d.).

The Nova Scotia Office of the Ombudsman extended its mandate to include the Office of Youth Services (OYS) in 1999. This occurred in response to investigations into allegations of abuse in provincial youth facilities that occurred in the mid-1990s (Nova Scotia Office of the Ombudsman, ca. 2015). There is no legislation governing the OYS in the Nova Scotia *Ombudsman Act* (1989); however, services for young people are outlined on the Nova Scotia Office of the Ombudsman (n.d.) website and in the ombudsman's *Statement of Mandate* (2015). The Nova Scotia Office of the Ombudsman serves all citizens in the province. The province's Office of Youth Services primarily provides outreach and advocacy for children and youth, parents, guardians, and staff in provincial and municipal youth correctional and secure-care and residential care facilities.

In the early 1990s, Newfoundland and Labrador commissioned several inquiries into provincial laws and policies affecting children and youth. The Select Committee on Children's Interests (Newfoundland House of Assembly, Select Committee on Children's Interests, 1996; Newfoundland and Labrador House of Assembly, Select Committee on Children's Interests, 1996) recommended broad "fundamental changes" to the child welfare system and endorsed the creation of an independent child and youth advocate. The *Child and Youth Advocate Act* was passed in December 2001, and the Office of the Advocate for Children and Youth was created in 2002, to serve all young people in Newfoundland and Labrador (Office of the Child and Youth Advocate, Province of Newfoundland and Labrador, 2005).

New Brunswick enacted the *Child and Youth Advocate Act* in 2004. This was prompted by several events, including reports of the Child Death Review Committee (Koster, Hillier, New Brunswick Department of Health and Community Services, Canadian Intergovernmental Conference Secretariat, & Provincial-Territorial Meeting of Ministers Responsible for Social Services, 1996; Creaghan, 1998). The child and youth advocate position was not filled until the ombudsman took on the role in 2006. Following his retirement in 2011, the New Brunswick CYA became an independent, stand-alone office, serving all children and youth in the province (New Brunswick Child and Youth Advocate, 2011). In 2016, the *Child and Youth Advocate Act* (2007) was repealed and replaced with the *Child, Youth and Senior Advocate Act* (2016). The CYA assumed responsibility for both seniors and young people and now operates two advocacy offices.

The Yukon Territory *Child and Youth Advocate Act* was enacted in 2009. The government had undertaken a review of the *Children's Act* (2002) (Carvill, 2008) that included broad public consultation that indicated support for an independent child and youth advocate (Health and Social Service, Government of Yukon, February, 2009). The Yukon CYA office was established in April 2010, and has a comprehensive mandate to serve all children and youth in the region.

Shortly after the Territory of Nunavut was created in 1999, suggestions were made that a child advocate would be an important asset to protect the rights and interests of its young population (Nunavut Representative for Children and Youth, Territory of Nunavut, n.d.). Following recommendations made in a review of the Nunavut child welfare system in 2008–2009 (Phaneuf, Dudding, & Arreak, 2011), the Nunavut government made a commitment to create an independent child and youth advocate (Government of Nunavut, ca. 2009). The Nunavut *Representative for Children and Youth Act* passed in September 2013, and the position was filled in June 2014. Staff devoted 15 months to developing the office before opening for business in September 2015 to provide advocacy services for all young people in the territory (Representative for Children and Youth, Territory of Nunavut, 2015).

Prince Edward Island considered establishing a CYA since 2015 (*CBC News*, 2015) and adopted a children's lawyer program in 2016 (Campbell, 2016). On the basis of an Order in Council (January 30, 2019) Prince Edward Island appointed a children's commissioner and advocate and is expected to open an Office for Children and Youth by April 2019. The new child and youth advocate is not a stand-alone institution with separate legislation like the other CYAs.

Community feedback in the Northwest Territories has also acknowledged the need and desire for an independent CYA (MacLaurin, 2010); however, a CYA has not been created so far. Instead, the Northwest Territories' Office of the Children's Lawyer was established in the Department of Justice in 2011 to provide services for young people (Government of the Northwest Territories, 2011).

Only one province is known to have a dedicated advocate for Indigenous children and families. The Assembly of Manitoba Chiefs created the First

Nations Family Advocate in June 2015 to serve the large number of Indigenous children and families involved with Manitoba Child and Family Services (CFS): "The assembly created the position of family advocate to respond to mounting concerns about children in the care of CFS in Manitoba. More than 10,000 children are in care and roughly 90 per cent of them are aboriginal" (NationTalk, 2015).

Each provincial/territorial child and youth advocate is a distinctive institution with unique origins and legislation. The CYAs evolved over time and in response to local needs and conditions. Several were created or strengthened in response to local tragedies involving children and youth who were in the care or custody of the state (UNICEF, 2013). The CYAs' development was also influenced by norms and principles outlined in the UNCRC (1989), local politics and processes of acculturation (Pegram, 2010), where lessons were drawn from international models of human rights institutions for children, and in recent years, from other existing CYAs. Consequently, the CYAs are a diverse collection of agencies with variations in their institutional designs, mandates, target populations, and approaches to upholding children's rights.

INDEPENDENCE

In keeping with recommendations of the UN Committee on the Rights of the Child to Canada (2003, 2012), all of the provincial/territorial CYAs (except in Prince Edward Island) are now independent statutory officers that operate at arm's-length from government and report directly to their legislatures. There is a long-standing tradition of these types of officers in Canada at both the federal and provincial/territorial levels. Statutory officers assist their legislatures in monitoring the executive and protecting the rights of individual citizens and are a valuable source of information and advice (Thomas, 2003). Statutory officers play various roles, including audit, regulatory, ethical, judicial, and/or ombudsman (Gay & Winetrobe, 2003). While they have no authority to make changes to laws and public policies (Thomas, 2003), these officers may be very persuasive. They tend to be viewed by the public as trusted experts and often use the media to convey their authoritative messages and exert pressure on decision-makers (Good, 2007).

UNICEF (2013) views the independence and influence of human rights institutions for children as defining features of their effectiveness: "their combination of independence and 'soft power': the capacity to report, to convene, to mediate and to influence lawmakers, government bodies, public institutions and public opinion. Indeed, it is the ability to influence those with direct responsibility for policy and practice that distinguishes an effective institution" (p. 5).

INSTITUTIONAL MODELS

The child and youth advocates perform a number of different roles in keeping with their institutional designs and legislation. Two CYAs operate within broader provincial institutions that serve all members of the population. The Nova Scotia Office of the Ombudsman provides advocacy for young people through its Office of Youth Services (OYS). Ombudsmen have three traditional functions: to educate the public about their rights, to investigate citizens' complaints regarding administrative unfairness, and to make recommendations regarding administrative changes (Hyson, 2006). Quebec is unique in delivering youth advocacy through the Commission des droits de la personne et des droits de la jeunesse (CDPDJ). Human rights commissions traditionally focus on safeguarding citizens' civil and economic rights and protection from discrimination. All of the other CYAs operate as independent, stand-alone agencies and are considered to be "hybrid equalities institutions." Hybrid institutions are flexible models that carry out a blend of traditional functions and may be tailored to suit local needs (Rees, 2010).

LEGISLATED MANDATES

The CYAs' mandates, powers, and functions are defined in their enabling legislation. The Nova Scotia *Ombudsman Act* (1989) does not specifically address youth advocacy delivered by the Office of Youth Services. However, these services are outlined on the OYS website and in the ombudsman's *Statement of Mandate* (February 27, 2015). All but one of the other CYAs have separate, specific legislation.

Populations Served

The provinces of Ontario, Alberta, British Columbia, and Manitoba were the earliest to establish formal child and youth advocates. They emerged in direct response to concerns for young people involved with child welfare and youth justice systems, and other intensive government services and continue to provide advocacy services for children and youth (and their families) who receive or may be eligible for "designated services." The other CYAs arose later and serve all young people in their jurisdictions who may access any type of government services.

Functions

The child and youth advocates perform a range of functions pertaining to both the protection of young people and the promotion of their participation rights. These roles are outlined in their enabling legislation and implemented in various ways. The CYAs' formal roles are briefly summarized in Table 13.2 and explained in more detail below.

Individual Advocacy. All of the child and youth advocates provide individual advocacy for the populations they serve. Young people and concerned adults may contact the CYAs to file complaints and to seek help with resolving grievances related to government or publicly contracted services.

Systemic Advocacy. The CYAs also undertake systemic advocacy focused on broader issues related to government services, policies, practices, and laws that affect many young people. Through systemic advocacy, the CYAs seek to prevent harm to young people, enhance their well-being, and uphold their rights, including the right to be heard.

Systemic change is often a long-term goal of advocacy agencies because it may take years for public policy and social changes to occur and may be the result of many factors. The CYAs may use a number of approaches to advocate for changes to the child- and youth-serving systems, including raising awareness, facilitating discussions, developing networks, building consensus, reframing policy issues, and strengthening political will to lay the groundwork for change.

Table 13.2   CYAs' Legislated Advocacy Functions

ROLES/FUNCTIONS	BC	AB	SK	MB	ON	QC	NB	NS*	NL	YT	NU
Individual advocacy	✓	✓	✓	✓	✓	✓	✓		✓	✓	✓
Systemic reviews/investigations	✓	✓	✓	✓	✓	✓	✓		✓	✓	✓
Review/investigate child death and critical injuries	✓	✓		✓						✓	✓
Educate/raise public awareness	✓	✓	✓		✓	✓	✓		✓	✓	✓
Conduct research	✓	✓	✓		✓				✓		✓
Provide information/advice to government	✓	✓	✓	✓	✓	✓	✓		✓	✓	✓
Monitor implementation of recommendations	✓		✓		✓		✓		✓	✓	✓

The CYAs may undertake reviews and investigations of broad, recurring, or emergent issues that have implications for groups of young people. They may draw on research and the direct experiences of children and youth to develop recommendations to governments and publicly funded agencies regarding changes to improve programs, policies, practices, legislation, or other factors related to the overall child- and youth-serving system.

Most CYAs may undertake reviews and investigations into the deaths and critical injuries of children and youth in the populations they serve. By examining the circumstances surrounding these tragedies, the CYAs seek to identify underlying gaps and deficiencies in policies, programs, and service delivery that put young people at risk. Their recommendations to government address necessary changes to prevent future injuries and deaths.

Raising Awareness. Almost all of the CYAs have directives to raise awareness, provide information, and educate children, youth, families, and/or the public about children's rights and the services provided by the CYAs. Some CYAs also emphasize self-advocacy and provide instruction in their education and outreach activities. All of the CYAs provide information for young people and the general public about children's rights and the UNCRC through their websites, social media, and direct outreach and education.

Providing Information and Advice. All of the CYAs provide information and advice to their legislatures and governments and, in some cases, publicly funded service providers, such as Children's Aid Societies (Ontario) and delegated First Nations authorities. The CYAs may make recommendations regarding needed changes to public policies, laws, and services to improve conditions for children and youth. They deliver their advice through both formal channels, such as public reports, and in informal meetings or conversations with government representatives. While the CYAs can make recommendations to government, they have no authority to make changes. On the other hand, the CYAs may use the media to raise public awareness, put pressure on the government, and try to influence decision makers. The majority of CYAs also monitor implementation of their advice.

Forming Alliances. The CYAs' systemic advocacy efforts often overlap with the work of other institutions and they are only one source of influence on complex, open systems (International Council on Human Rights Policy, 2004). Systemic change depends on the support and cooperation of various individuals and public and civil agencies (International Council on Human Rights Policy, 2005; Reif, 2000; UNICEF, 2005). The UNCRC Committee (United Nations Committee on the Rights of the Child, 2002) recommends that human rights institutions for children work closely with non-governmental organizations (NGOs) that play complementary roles in the promotion of children's rights. The Annie E. Casey Foundation (2007) identifies building alliances as a key component of effective advocacy: "structural changes in community and institutional relationships and alliances have become essential forces in presenting common messages, pursuing common goals, enforcing policy changes and insuring the protection of policy 'wins' in the event that they are threatened" (p. 17).

Providing Legal Support. The Alberta Office of the Child and Youth Advocate has a unique role in appointing legal representation for young people who receive "designated services." The Saskatchewan Advocate for Children and Youth has a formal agreement with the Council for Children that provides independent legal representation for young people. None of the CYAs are permitted to provide legal counsel to young people.

Involvement of Young People. The UNCRC Committee (United Nations Committee on the Rights of the Child, 2002) recommends that human rights institutions for children should include children and youth in meaningful ways in their operations, such as through youth advisory councils. A few CYAs have established youth advisory groups. The Alberta Office of the Child and Youth Advocate's Youth Advisory Panel was created in 2013, and is made up of several young people who meet quarterly, provide input, guidance, and information to the Office of the Child and Youth Advocate (OCYA) and other agencies. In 2018, the OCYA created a handbook for the Youth Advisory Panel. The OCYA also invites young people to act as "Friends of the Advocate" so they can get involved and contribute through various events and other opportunities: "Young people are often best placed to speak about the impacts of government policies and services, and their voices can be powerful in delivering messages to key decision-makers" (Alberta Office of the Child and Youth Advocate, 2015, p. 13).

The Ontario Office of the Provincial Advocate for Children and Youth (OPACY) had the strongest legislated directive to engage with young people and ensure their participation. The *Provincial Advocate for Children and Youth Act* (2007) addressed two "Principles to be Applied," including those contained in the UNCRC, and to be an "exemplar" for youth participation. The OPACY put young people at the core of their work: "When the Advocate's Office engages in systemic advocacy, we draw on the expertise of young people who have direct experience with the issue. We work with them to recommend changes at the level of policy, funding, program delivery, and in how service providers, decision makers and the public view and treat young people who need government services" (Ontario Office of the Provincial Advocate for Children and Youth, 2015, p. 12).

The Ontario Office of the Provincial Advocate for Children and Youth did not have a youth advisory committee; however, it used other strategies to involve young people. The OPACY employed up to 15 "Youth Amplifiers" who performed various roles, including working with youth on specific issues (Ontario Office of the Provincial Advocate for Children and Youth, 2015). The OPACY facilitated a number of youth-led initiatives involving hundreds of young people, such as:

- *My REAL Life Book:* to present the views of youth who have experience being in care;
- *I Have Something to Say:* to elevate the voices of children and youth who have special needs regarding how government can better meet their needs; and
- *Feathers of Hope:* a First Nations Youth Action Plan.

The Ontario Office of the Provincial Advocate for Children and Youth demonstrated that facilitating young people to present their first-hand experiences with public services is very effective. The Ontario provincial government had made a commitment to involve young people in all decision-making processes that affect them. Ontario was the first province to establish a permanent Premier's Council on Youth Opportunities, made up of 25 young people who give advice on ways to improve government services and support young people (Province of Ontario, Office of the Premier, 2013). Of course, Ontario's past progressive advances in terms of youth engagement and participation now hang in the balance with the closure of the Ontario Child Advocate's Office.

All of the CYAs collaborate with young people on initiatives that elevate their voices. For example, the Manitoba Office of the Children's Advocate worked with a community agency and local television station to video-record young people's stories about issues that matter to them through the *Digital Storytelling Project* (Office of the Children's Advocate, Manitoba, 2015). The British Columbia Representative for Children and Youth collaborated with the province's Public Guardian and Trustee and the Federation of BC Youth in Care Networks to deliver 20 Plan Your Path workshops for youth and service providers focused on youth transitioning out of care (British Columbia Representative for Children and Youth, 2015). The Alberta Office of the Child and Youth Advocate submits written input from youth and co-presents with them to government on proposed changes to laws and services. The Nunavut Representative for Children and Youth Office conducted a survey of young people in 2017–2018 as part of its review of mental health services for children and youth, and incorporated input from 225 youth surveys into its final report (Nunavut Representative for Children and Youth Office, n.d.). Over most of 2017, Saskatchewan's Advocate for Children and Youth staff sought to gain a deeper understanding of the high incidence of youth suicide in northern Saskatchewan by undertaking extensive consultations with Indigenous youth in the north to gather "their perceptions, realities, and lived experiences related to youth suicide" (Saskatchewan Advocate for Children and Youth, 2017).

The CYAs participate in numerous events focused on young people, such as National Child Day. The CYAs also target educational materials and portions of their websites to young people. Some host workshops and conferences for youth and youth-serving agencies, such as periodic youth summits by the British Columbia's Representative for Children and Youth (2016), and Feathers of Hope youth forums by the Ontario Office of the Provincial Advocate for Children and Youth (2015).

CHILD AND YOUTH ADVOCATES AND THE UNCRC

All of the CYAs make extensive use of the UNCRC to guide their work and support their arguments for changes to policies, programs, and procedures. The CYAs also promote the UNCRC in their educational materials, workshops, and through their websites and social media. However, the UNCRC is embedded in the legislation of only three CYAs, including Ontario's *Provincial Advocate for Children and Youth Act* (2007), the Yukon's *Child and Youth Advocate Act* (2010), and Nunavut's *Representative for Children and Youth Act* (2013). The Quebec Commission des droits de la personne et des droits de la jeunesse (n.d.) explains on its website that it protects young people's rights under the UNCRC, although this is not explicit in their legislation. The norms and principles expressed in the UNCRC (1989) are reflected in most of the CYAs' enabling legislation, such as promoting/protecting children's rights, best interests, and well-being, and ensuring that young people's viewpoints are sought and respected. Only BC's *Representative for Children and Youth Act* (2006) does not refer to these types of norms. Instead, it focuses on the protection of vulnerable children and youth who are in the care and custody of the state and improving "designated" and "reviewable" services. The BC Representative for Children and Youth was established in response to an in-depth, independent review of the child welfare system (Hughes, 2006) and its legislation reflects efforts to mitigate failings identified in this system.

CANADIAN COUNCIL OF CHILD AND YOUTH ADVOCATES

In 1996, the provincial CYAs formed an alliance through the Canadian Council of Provincial Child and Youth Advocates (CCPCYA). Through this informal network, the CYAs could "identify issues of mutual concern and strive to promote improvements nation-wide" (Canadian Council of Child and Youth Advocates, 2010). As new CYAs were established, membership in the council grew from five affiliates in 2005 to 10 members in 2010. The name was changed to the Canadian Council of Child and Youth Advocates (CCCYA) to be inclusive of all the CYAs. In 2015, the CCCYA adopted National Advocacy Standards (Canadian Council of Child and Youth Advocates, 2015), grounded in the legal norms outlined in the UNCRC, to help ensure consistent quality of services provided by all of the CYAs.

The CCCYA has delivered several joint statements and reports on issues of national concern with regard to children and youth (Canadian Council of Child and Youth Advocates, 2010, 2011a), including a Special Report (2011b) to the UNCRC Committee regarding the need for a coordinated, comprehensive plan across all levels of government to better serve the needs and interests of Indigenous children and youth.

THE NEED FOR A NATIONAL CHILDREN'S ADVOCATE

Over the years, there have been many calls for Canada to establish a national children's advocate. The United Nations Committee on the Rights of the Child (1995, 2003, 2012) has consistently urged Canada to create an independent, national ombudsman for children and youth to provide broad oversight of the rights of all young people and ensure that they are aware of advocacy services available in the provinces and territories. The Standing Senate Committee on Human Rights (2005, 2007) endorsed the creation of a national, independent children's commissioner to uphold the rights of all young Canadians and to oversee implementation of the UNCRC. The Canadian Council of Child and Youth Advocates (2010, 2011a; November 20, 2015) has repeatedly called for a national children's commissioner, with an emphasis on ensuring the rights of Indigenous children and youth who are overrepresented in child welfare and youth custody systems across the country. UNICEF Canada (UNICEF & UNICEF Canada, August, 2009, 2010, testimony at Standing Senate Committee on Human Rights, 2013) and other agencies have also advocated for a national children's advocate to address systemic concerns, including high rates of child poverty (Family Service Toronto, 2015) and lower levels of child health and well-being compared to other wealthy nations (UNICEF Canada, 2016).

A national children's commissioner could also hold the Government of Canada to account for ensuring that public policies, laws and budgets undergo child rights impact assessments (CRIAs). In keeping with Article 3 of the UNCRC, UNICEF (United Nations Children's Fund, n.d.) emphasizes the importance of using CRIAs for all government decisions concerning young people: "A CRIA should be undertaken whenever there are new policies, proposed legislation, regulations or budgets being adopted, or other administrative decisions at national, provincial/territorial, and local levels that can have an impact on children" (United Nations Children's Fund, n.d.).

Two bills were put forward in 2009 and 2011 by a Liberal MLA, the Hon. M. Garneau (An Act to Establish a Children's Commissioner of Canada, Bill C-418, 2009; An Act to Establish the Office of the Commissioner for Children and Young Persons in Canada, 2011), to establish a national children's commissioner; however, these bills did not pass First Reading. Since the Liberal Party of Canada formed a majority government in 2015, there has been no indication that a national human rights institution for children will be created to support implementation of the UNCRC.

DISCUSSION

There are reasons for optimism about Canada's progress in formally recognizing children and youth as rights holders. The evolution of public child and youth advocates in almost every province and territory indicates a growing recognition of young people's rights, including their rights to protection and participation in decisions that are made about them. However, the subnational CYAs are not invulnerable to shifts in political climates. The Ontario Progressive Conservative government's decision to repeal the *Provincial Advocate for Children and Youth Act* (2007) and close the Office of the Provincial Advocate for Children and Youth is a significant step backward for young people in Ontario and a poor reflection on Canada's commitment to uphold the rights of its children and youth. Canada's failure to create a national children's commissioner is a significant barrier to achieving stage 3 of the child rights evolutionary framework.

The CYAs are a diverse collection of institutions that perform a range of important functions to advocate for the rights of young people in their jurisdictions. The CYAs also play broader roles in raising public awareness about children's rights and identifying and elevating issues of national concern. The CYAs are uniquely positioned to monitor a range of public policies, laws, and services. However, there are gaps in the provision of public advocacy for young people. CYAs do not exist in all jurisdictions and some serve only specific populations. On their own, the CYAs cannot resolve many significant systemic issues that compromise the rights of numerous young people across the country.

A national, independent children's commissioner is essential to ensure the rights of all young Canadians. National leadership and coordination, and the development of comprehensive strategies with firm commitments from all levels of government are needed to address wide-ranging, systemic concerns. In lieu of a national children's commissioner, the CYAs will continue to play vital roles in protecting young people's rights and holding Canada to account for implementing the UNCRC.[1]

QUESTIONS FOR DISCUSSION

1. In what ways are the child and youth advocates visible in your community?
2. How could the CYAs' roles be enhanced to strengthen young people's participation rights?
3. Why does Canada need a national children's commissioner?

NOTE

1 For more detailed analysis, please see my dissertation (Hunter, 2017).

REFERENCES

An Act to Establish a Children's Commissioner of Canada, Bill C-418 [M. Garneau]. (2009, June 11). House of Commons of Canada. Retrieved from: http://www2.parl.gc.ca/HousePublications/Publication.aspx?Docid=3979987&file=4

An Act to Establish the Office of the Commissioner for Children and Young Persons in Canada, Bill C-418 [M. Garneau]. (2011, June 2). House of Commons of Canada. Retrieved from http://www.parl.gc.ca/LEGISInfo/BillDetails.aspx?billId=5514117&Mode=1&View=3&Language=E

The Advocate for Children and Youth Act Chapter A-5.4. (2012, September 1). As amended by the Statutes of Saskatchewan, 2014, c. E-13.1; and 2015, c. 16.

Alberta Child and Youth Advocacy Review Committee. (2009, March). *Review of child and youth advocacy in Alberta*. Edmonton, AB: Government of Alberta.

Alberta Child Intervention Review Panel. (2010, June 30). *Closing the gap between vision and reality: Strengthening accountability, adaptability and continuous improvement in Alberta's child intervention system: Final report*. Edmonton, AB: Author.

Alberta Office of the Child and Youth Advocate. (2015). *Annual report 2014–15*. Edmonton AB: Author.

Annie E. Casey Foundation. (2007). *A guide to measuring advocacy and policy*. Baltimore, MD: Organizational Research Services.

Bernstein, M. M., & Schury, R. A. (2009). Passion, action, strength and innovative change: The experience of the Saskatchewan Children's Advocate's Office in establishing rights-based "Children and Youth First" principles. In S. McKay, D. Fuchs, & I. Brown (Eds.), *Passion for action in child and family services: Voices from the Prairies* (pp. 15–47). Regina, SK: Canadian Plains Research Center.

British Columbia Representative for Children and Youth. (2015, September 28). *2014/15 Annual Report and 2015/16–2016/17 Service Plan*. Victoria, BC: Author.

British Columbia Representative for Children and Youth. (2016, October 24). *2015/16 Annual Report and Service Plan 2016/17–2017/18*. Victoria, BC: Author.

Campbell, K. (2016, April 21). Children's Lawyer Program to offer protection in custody disputes. *CBC News*. Retrieved from http://www.cbc.ca/news/canada/prince-edward-island/custody-disputes-child-lawyer-advocates-1.3547635

Canadian Centre for Management Development. (2000). *Implementing the social union framework agreement: A learning and reference tool*. Retrieved from http://www.publications.gc.ca/collections/Collection/SC94-76-2000E.pdf

Canadian Children's Rights Council. (R. Volpe, S. Cox, L. Goddard, & K. Tilleczek). (1997). *Children's rights in Canada: A review of provincial policies*. Toronto: Dr. R. G. N. Laidlaw Research Centre. Institute of Child Study. OISE, University of Toronto.

Canadian Council of Child and Youth Advocates. (2010, June 23). *Position paper: Aboriginal children and youth in Canada: Canada must do better*. Retrieved from http://www.gnb.ca/0073/PDF/positionpaper-e.pdf

Canadian Council of Child and Youth Advocates. (2011a, March). *Submission to the House of Commons Standing Committee on Justice and Human Rights respecting an act to amend the Youth Criminal Justice Act*. Retrieved from http://www.cccya.ca/images/english/pdf/Memoire_CCDDEJ_C-4_En.pdf

Canadian Council of Child and Youth Advocates. (2011b, November). *Special report. Aboriginal children: Canada must do better: Today and tomorrow*. Submitted to UN Committee on the Rights of the Child. N.p.: Author. Retrieved from http://www.cccya.ca/images/english/pdf/aboriginal_children_youth_advocates_position_paper_2010.pdf

Canadian Council of Child and Youth Advocates. (2015, June). *National advocacy standards*. Retrieved from http://www.cccya.ca/images/english/pdf/NationalAdvocacyStandards_EnFr.pdf

Canadian Council of Child and Youth Advocates. (2015, November 25). *Letter to the Right Honourable Justin Trudeau*. Retrieved from https://rcybc.ca/sites/default/files/documents/pdf/reports_publications/151120_2_en_trudeau_justin_the_right_honourable_-_prime_minister_of_ca_.pdf

Carvill, A., Grand Chief of the Council of Yukon First Nations. (2008, April 19). Letter to the editor: Children's act: Let's get it right. *Yukon News*.

CBC News. (2015, June 16). *Premier promises action in light of murder-suicide of mother, 4-year-old son*. Retrieved from http://www.cbc.ca/news/canada/prince-edward-island/premier-promises-action-in-light-of-murder-suicide-of-mother-4-year-old-son-1.3116195

Child and Family Services Act SO Chapter 55. (1984). Toronto: Queen's Printer for Ontario.

The *Child and Family Services Act* C.C.S.M. c. C80. (1985, July 11). Winnipeg: Queen's Printer.

Child and Youth Advocate Act SNL2001 Chapter C-12.01. (2001, December 13). St. John's, NL: Queen's Printer.

Child and Youth Advocate Act Chapter C-2.5. (2004). Fredericton, NB: Queen's Printer for New Brunswick.

Child and Youth Advocate Act Chapter 1. (2009, May 14). Whitehorse, YT: Yukon Legislative Counsel Office.

Child and Youth Advocate Act SA Chapter C-11.5. (2011, November). Edmonton, AB: Alberta Queen's Printer.

Child Welfare Act S.A., cC-8.1. (1984). Edmonton, AB: Alberta Queen's Printer.

Child, Youth and Senior Advocate Act. (2016). Chapter C-2.7, c. 54, s. 1. Fredericton, NB: Queen's Printer for New Brunswick.

Children's Act RSY c. 31 (2002). Whitehorse, YT: Yukon Legislative Counsel Office.

Combes, J., & Evans J. (1998). Canada, Saskatchewan: United efforts to integrate from the top-down and bottom-up. In *Co-ordinating services for children and youth at risk: A world view*. Paris: OECD Publishing and Centre for Educational Research and Innovation. Retrieved from http://www.worldcat.org/title/co-ordinating-services-for-children-and-youth-at-risk-a-world-view/oclc/64595039

Community Living Authority Act SBC Chapter 60. (2004, October). Victoria, BC: Queen's Printer.

Covell, K., & Howe, R. B. (2001). *The challenge of children's rights for Canada*. Waterloo, ON: Wilfrid Laurier University Press.

Creaghan, W. L. M. (1998). *A report by the Child Death Review Committee on the death of Jacqueline Dawn Brewer*. Fredericton, NB: Department of Health and Community Services.

Family Service Toronto. (2015). *Let's do this: Let's end child poverty for good. 2015 report card on child and family poverty in Canada*. Toronto, ON: Author.

Gay, O., & Winetrobe, B. K. (2003). *Officers of Parliament: Transforming the role*. London: Constitution Unit.

Geigen-Miller, M. (2003). *It's time to break the silence: Creating meaningful access to rights and advocacy services for young people in care in Ontario*. Toronto: Defence for Children International Canada.

Good, D. (2007). *The politics of public money: Spenders, guardians, priority setters, and financial watchdogs inside the Canadian government*. Toronto: University of Toronto Press.

Gove, T. J. (1995, April). *Report of the Gove inquiry into child protection in British Columbia*. Vancouver: The Inquiry.

Government of Alberta. (2011, November 21). *News release: New legislation to create an independent child and youth advocate who reports to the Legislature*. Retrieved from https://www.alberta.ca/release.cfm?xID=31561C7AF5C4F-946F-08A9-95530E3837E26637

Government of Canada. (May. 1995). *UN Committee on the Rights of the Child: Canada's Reporting 1994. Canada's Reports to the UN Committee on the Rights of the Child Canada's 1st Report - 9th Session of the Committee*. Retrieved from http://www.canadiancrc.com/UN_CRC/UN_Committee_Rights_Child_Canada_1st_Reports-Overview_MAY_1995_9th_Session.aspx

Government of Canada. (2001). *Canada's second report on the Convention on the Rights of the Child*. Ottawa: Human Rights Program Department of Canadian

Heritage. Retrieved from http://www.collectionscanada.gc.ca/webarchives/20061216060240/http://www.pch.gc.ca/progs/pdp-hrp/docs/crc-2001/index_e.cfm

Government of Canada. (2009, November 20). *Convention on the Rights of the Child: Third and fourth reports of Canada covering the period January 1998–December 2007.* Ottawa: Human Rights Program Department of Canadian Heritage. Retrieved from http://www.pch.gc.ca/ddp-hrd/docs/pdf/canada3-4-crc-reports-nov2009-eng.pdf

Government of the Northwest Territories. (2011, December). Office of the Children's Lawyer. Retrieved from http://www.gov.nt.ca/newsroom/office-childrens-lawyer

Government of Nunavut. (ca. 2009). *Building our future together: The Government of Nunavut's action plan: CL^CC Tamapta 2009–2013.* Iqaluit, NU: Author.

Health and Social Service, Government of Yukon. (2009, February). *What we heard about a Child and Youth Advocate Act: Summary of comments on discussion paper.* Whitehorse, YT: Author.

Hughes, Hon. T. (2006, April). *BC children and youth review: An independent review of BC's child protection system.* Report Submitted to the Minister of Children and Family Development. Retrieved from http://cwrp.ca/sites/default/files/publications/en/BC-HuguesReviewReport.pdf

Hughes, Hon. T. (2013, December). *The legacy of Phoenix Sinclair: Achieving the best for all our children. Vol. 1.* Winnipeg, MB: Commission of Inquiry into the Circumstances Surrounding the Death of Phoenix Sinclair.

Hunter, M. T. (2017). *Canadian Child and Youth Advocates: A Comparative Analysis.* (Doctoral dissertation). Retrieved from https://dspace.library.uvic.ca//handle/1828/8045

International Council on Human Rights Policy. (2004). *Performance & legitimacy: National human rights institutions* (2nd ed.). Bellegarde/Valserine, France: Imprimerie SADAG.

International Council on Human Rights Policy. (2005). *Assessing the effectiveness of national human rights institutions.* Geneva, Switzerland: ATAR Roto Press SA.

Knitel, F. (2003). *Child protection: Trends and issues in Alberta.* (Master's thesis). University of Alberta, Calgary. Retrieved from https://www.uleth.ca/dspace/bitstream/handle/10133/1151/Knitel_Faye.pdf;sequence=1

Koster, A., Hillier, B., New Brunswick Department of Health and Community Services, Canadian Intergovernmental Conference Secretariat, & Provincial-Territorial Meeting of Ministers Responsible for Social Services. (1996). *A report.* Ottawa: Canadian Intergovernmental Conference Secretariat.

Koster, A. J., & Schibler, B. (2006, September). Commission of Inquiry into the circumstances surrounding the death of Phoenix Sinclair. *A special case review in regard to the death of Phoenix Sinclair.* Submitted to the Minister of Family Services and Housing, Province of Manitoba. Winnipeg, MB: Author.

Legislative Assembly of Saskatchewan. (1994, February). *Saskatchewan's action plan for children: Investing in Saskatchewan's future.* Regina, SK: Author. Retrieved from http://lin.ca/sites/default/files/attachments/skaction.htm

MacLaurin, B. (2010, July). *A report on the Northwest Territories Child and Family Services Act: Submitted to the Northwest Territories Standing Committee on Social Programs.* Calgary, AB: Faculty of Social Work, University of Calgary.

Manitoba Legislative Assembly. (1998). *The Child and Family Services Amendment and Consequential Amendments Act* (1998). Retrieved from https://web2.gov

.mb.ca/laws/statutes/1998/c00698e.php

Morley, J. (2001, December). *Report of the Core Services Review of the Children's Commission and overlapping services provided by the Child and Youth Advocate, the Ombudsman, Coroner and Ministry of Children and Family Development*. Victoria, BC: Author.

NationTalk. (2015, June 16). *First Nations family advocate discouraged after 1st week working with [Child and Family Services Manitoba] CFS–CBC*. Retrieved from http://nationtalk.ca/story/first-nations-family-advocate-discouraged-after-1st-week-working-with-cfs-cbc

New Brunswick Child and Youth Advocate. (2011, April). *News bulletin*. Fredericton, NB: Author. Retrieved from http://www.gnb.ca/0073/Child-YouthAdvocate/PDF/Newsletter/april2011%20.pdf)

Newfoundland and Labrador House of Assembly, Select Committee on Children's Interests. (1996, June). *LISTENing and ACTing: A plan for child, youth and community empowerment: The report of the Select Committee on Children's Interests*. St. John's, NL: Author.

Newfoundland House of Assembly, Select Committee on Children's Interests. (1996). *Strategic plan for government and society on children, youth and families*. St. John's, NL: Author. Retrieved from http://www.assembly.nl.ca/pubinfo/CHILD/plan.htm

Nova Scotia Office of the Ombudsman. (n.d.). *Office of Youth Services*. Retrieved from https://www.novascotia.ca/ombu/youth.htm

Nova Scotia Office of the Ombudsman. (2015, February 27). *Statement of mandate 2015–16*. Halifax, NS: Author.

Nova Scotia Office of the Ombudsman. (ca. 2015). *Annual report 2014–15*. Halifax, NS: Author.

Nunavut Representative for Children and Youth. (n.d.). *Business Plan 2019–2022*. Iqaluit, NU: Author.

Nunavut Representative for Children and Youth. (n.d.). "Our History." Retrieved from http://www.rcynu.ca/families-public/about-us/our-history

Nunavut Representative for Children and Youth. (2015, September 15). *Young people have rights, we support them. Representative for children and youth 2014–15 Annual Report*. Iqaluit, NU: Author.

Office of the Child and Youth Advocate, Province of Newfoundland and Labrador. (2005, December 2). *Annual Report 2004–2005*. St. John's NL: Author.

Office of the Children's Advocate, Manitoba. (ca. 2001). *Annual report of the Office of the Children's Advocate of Manitoba 2000–2001*. Winnipeg, MB: Author.

Office of the Children's Advocate, Manitoba. (2015). *The Office of the Children's Advocate annual report 2014–2015: Little voices, big echo*. Winnipeg, MB: Author.

Ombudsman Act Chapter 327 of the Revised Statutes. (1989). Halifax, NS: Queen's Printer. Retrieved from http://nslegislature.ca/legc/statutes/ombudsm.htm

The Ombudsman and Children's Advocate Act c. 7, s. 5. (1994). Regina, SK: Queen's Printer.

Ontario Office of the Provincial Advocate for Children and Youth. (2014). *2014 Report to the Legislature*. Toronto, ON: Author.

Ontario Office of the Provincial Advocate for Children and Youth. (2015). *2015 report to the Legislature*. Toronto ON: Author.

Pegram, T. (2010). Diffusion across political systems: The global spread of national human rights institutions. *Human Rights Quarterly, 32*(3), 729–760.

Phaneuf, G., Dudding, P., & Arreak, J. (2011, July). *Nunavut social services review: Final report*. Ottawa: Child Welfare League of Canada.

Prince Edward Island Executive Council. (2019, January 30). EC2019-34 Civil Service Act Executive Division Children's Commissioner and Advocate Designation and Appointment Michele M. Dorsey, Q.C. Charlottetown, PEI: Author.

Pringle, B., Cameron, H., Durocher, A., & Skelton, Hon. C. (2010, November). *For the good of our children and youth: A new vision, a new direction*. Saskatoon: Saskatchewan Child Welfare Review.

Province of Ontario, Office of the Premier. (2013, March). *News release: First-ever Premier's Council on Youth Opportunities*. Retrieved from https://news.ontario.ca/opo/en/2013/03/first-ever-premiers-council-on-youth-opportunities.html

Provincial Advocate for Children and Youth Act S.O. c. 9. (2007, October). Ottawa: Queen's Printer for Ontario.

Provincial Archives of Alberta. (2006). *Children's services 1999–present. An administrative history of the Government of Alberta, 1905–2005*. Edmonton, AB: Author,

Quebec Commission des droits de la personne et des droits de la jeunesse (CDPDJ). (n.d.). *Youth Rights: Your Rights*. Retrieved from http://www.cdpdj.qc.ca/en/droits-de-la-jeunesse/vos-droits/Pages/default.aspx

Rees, O. (2010). Dealing with individual cases: An essential role for national human rights Institutions for Children? *International Journal of Children's Rights, 18*(3), 417–436.

Reif, L. C. (2004). *The ombudsman, good governance and the international human rights system*. Leiden: Martinus Nijhoff Publishers.

Representative for Children and Youth Act. SBC. (2006). Chapter 29. [British Columbia].

Representative for Children and Youth Act c. 27. (2013, September). Iqaluit, NU: Territorial Printer for Nunavut.

Saskatchewan Advocate for Children and Youth. (2017, December 5). *Shhh ... listen!! We have something to say: Youth voices from the North. A special report on the youth suicide crisis in Northern Saskatchewan*. Saskatoon, SK: Author.

Standing Senate Committee on Human Rights (Hon. R. Andreychuk, & Hon. L. Pearson). (2005, November). *Who's in charge here? Effective implementation of Canada's international obligations with respect to the rights of children. Interim report of the Standing Senate Committee on Human Rights*. Ottawa: Senate of Canada.

Standing Senate Committee on Human Rights (Hon. R. Andreychuk, & Hon. J. Fraser). (2007, April). *Children: The silenced citizens: Effective implementation of Canada's international obligations with respect to the rights of children. Final report*. Ottawa: Senate of Canada.

Standing Senate Committee on Human Rights. (2013, March 25). *Evidence* (testimony of D. Morley, president and CEO, UNICEF Canada). Ottawa: Senate of Canada.

Thomas, P. G. (2003). The past, present and future of officers of Parliament. *Canadian Public Administration, 46*(3), 287–314.

Thomlison, R. J. (1984). *Case management review: Northwest region*. Edmonton, AB: Department of Social Services and Community Health, Province of Alberta.

Toronto Star. (2018, November 19). *Marv Bernstein & Birgitte Granofsky Opinion: Eliminating the Ontario Child Advocate's Office a mistake*. Retrieved from https://www.thestar.com/opinion/contributors/2018/11/19/eliminating-the-ontario-child-advocates-office-a-mistake.html

UNICEF. (2001). Independent human rights institutions protecting children's rights. *Innocenti Digest 8*. Florence: UNICEF Innocenti Research Centre.

UNICEF (Alston, P., & Tobin, J.). (2005). *Laying the foundations for children's rights: An independent study of some key legal and institutional aspects of the impact of the Convention on the Rights of the Child*. Florence: UNICEF Innocenti Research Centre.

UNICEF. (2013). *Championing children's rights: A global study of independent human rights institutions for children*. Florence: UNICEF.

UNICEF and UNICEF Canada (Pearson, L., & Collins, T). (2009, August). *Not there yet: Canada's implementation of the general measures of the Convention on the Rights of the Child*. Florence: UNICEF Innocenti Research Centre.

UNICEF Canada. (2010). *It's time for a national children's commissioner for Canada*. Toronto: Canadian UNICEF Committee.

UNICEF Canada. (2016). *UNICEF report card 13: Fairness for children; Canada's challenge*. Toronto ON: Author. Retrieved from https://www.unicef.ca/en/node/8951

United Nations Centre for Human Rights. (1993, December 20). *Resolution. 48/134 on National institutions for the promotion and protection of human rights: Annex, principles relating to the status of national institutions*. Geneva: Author.

United Nations Centre for Human Rights. (1995). *National human rights institutions: A handbook on the establishment and strengthening of national institutions for the promotion and protection of human rights*. Professional Training, Series no. 4. Geneva: UN Centre for Human Rights.

United Nations Children's Fund (UNICEF). (n.d.). *What is a child rights impact assessment?* Retrieved from https://www.unicef.ca/fr/discover-fr/article/what-is-a-child-rights-impact-assessment

United Nations Committee on the Rights of the Child. (1995, June 20). *Concluding observations of the Committee on the Rights of the Child: Canada*. Geneva: Author. Retrieved from http://www.unhchr.ch/tbs/doc.nsf/(Symbol)/a6daf2f3b9d386da4125623700565bcb?Opendocument

United Nations Committee on the Rights of the Child. (2002, November 15; 34th Session). *General comment no. 2: The role of independent national human rights institutions in the promotion and protection of the rights of the child*. Geneva: Author.

United Nations Committee on the Rights of the Child. (2003, October 3; 34th Session). *Consideration of reports submitted by states parties under Article 44 of the Convention: Concluding observations of the Committee on the Rights of the Child: Canada*. Geneva: Author.

United Nations Committee on the Rights of the Child. (2012, December 6). (61st Session; September 7, October 5, 2012). *Implementation of the Convention on the Rights of the Child: List of issues concerning additional and updated information related to the combined third and fourth periodic reports of Canada (CRC/C/CAN/3-4)*. Geneva: Author.

United Nations Development Programme and Office of the High Commissioner for Human Rights. (1989, November 20). *Convention on the Rights of the Child.* Printed in Canada by the Human Rights Directorate, Department of Multiculturalism and Citizenship. Ottawa: Minister of Supply and Services Canada.

United Nations General Assembly Special Session on Children. (2002, May). A/RES/S-27/2, Para. 31.

Whitehead, P. C., Bala, N., Leschied, A. W., & Chiodo, D. (2004). *A new model for child and youth advocacy in Ontario. Prepared for the Ministry of Children and Youth Services.* Toronto: Whitehead Research Consultants.

Chapter 14
Shaking the Movers
A Decade Later – Does Our Voice Stick?
Judy Finlay and Landon Pearson

The concept of "Shaking the Movers" (STM) emerged from our shared experience. Both of us have long been committed to finding a meaningful way for children and youth to have an impact on public policy; to exercise, in effect, their civil and political rights as guaranteed by the United Nations Convention on the Rights of the Child (UNCRC). STM was created to challenge our way of thinking and behaving about the perceived vulnerability and dependency of children and youth. By viewing children and youth as competent players in society who are able to participate in meaningful ways as full citizens in social, economic, cultural, civil, and political contexts, their voices guided the original intention, creation, and design of STM. Subsequently, the identification and development of annual themes, the organization, preparation and planning, and the implementation and evaluation of all STM events and initiatives are facilitated by youth leaders themselves. The purpose of STM from the onset was for youth to identify themes from their own lived experiences that would be discussed at each workshop. Their reporting of the discussion—including issues, problems, and recommended solutions—is collated into a report each year and distributed to the "Movers" (the Children's Rights Academic Network). These reports capture verbatim the words of the youth participants at STM, and their voices and opinions are intended to "shake the movers."

The Child Rights Academic Network (CRAN) has been evolving along with the STM workshops, which become richer every year. CRAN is made up of 64 academics in Canada and the United Kingdom who have a declared interest in children's rights. They listen to and are moved by what the STM participants have had to say and come together to respond. New insights they have gained from paying attention to the youth's ideas are then taken back to enrich both their classroom practice and their research.

Therefore, the challenge for the youth participants involved in STM workshops, and to those of us who are enabling them, is to shake up the adults to whom they are directing their voices so they will actually begin to see issues related to youth from a child-rights perspective and will reframe how they make decisions about them. In so doing, the existing imbalance of power between children and adults is disrupted.

BACKGROUND HISTORY

For Landon Pearson, this effort began in 1979 with the International Year of the Child, and was focused on recognizing children as true rights holders and the rest of us as duty bearers obligated to respond. For Judy Finlay, it began with her work as Ontario's official child and youth advocate from 1991 to 2007. From the time we first met in the early 1990s and began to inform each other's work with and on behalf of children, our shared commitment to enabling the authentic and experience-based ideas of children and young people to influence decision makers in the public sphere has only grown. In 2006, after her retirement from the Senate of Canada, Pearson founded the Landon Pearson Resource Centre for the Study of Childhood and Children's Rights (LPRC) at Carleton University in Ottawa, and in 2007 Judy took up an academic position in the Faculty of Community Services, School of Child and Youth Care at Ryerson University in Toronto. We continued to stay in close touch and together we jointly crafted the model of significant child and youth participation in matters that concern us, now known as "Shaking the Movers."

Landon Pearson's initial attempt to open up the political sphere to the voices of children occurred in 1979 when she was vice-chair of the Canadian Commission for the International Year of the Child (IYC) and editor of the Commission's Report to Parliament: "For Canada's Children: A National Agenda for Action, 1980" (For Canada's Children, 1980). Pearson insisted that the commission needed to hear from children and not just study their situation, and therefore she crisscrossed the country with some of her colleagues to meet with children of all ages and in all sorts of circumstances. Their message to the commissioners was consistent and twofold and it is as relevant today as it was then. What they said then is that every child needs someone in his or her life who is "crazy" about him or her and prepared to engage with the child in increasingly complex ways over the long haul. The young people also said that all children have to be given opportunities from a very early age to make choices that matter not only to them but also to those around them. This double message is firmly embedded in the IYC Commission's Report.

Pearson's next major experience of engaging children and youth under the age of 18 in political processes, this time on a global scale, came with the World Summit on Children at the United Nations in 1990, when as president of the Canadian Council on Children and Youth, she was able, with government support, to bring together a group of children and youth from across the country to draft and then personally deliver a strong message about their understanding of their rights to Prime Minister Brian Mulroney, who co-chaired the summit. As proof that he had heard them, he invited Pearson to organize a similar group to come on December 13, 1991, to the Great Hall of Parliament, ablaze with Christmas lights, to witness his signature on the official document affirming Canada's ratification of the UNCRC.

Once Pearson was called to the Senate in 1994, opportunities to engage young people in actual parliamentary processes opened up. Asked to represent that significant portion of the Canadian population who, being under the age of 18, are unable to vote, she ensured that they were invited to speak as witnesses at parliamentary committees studying, for example, the new *Youth Criminal Justice Act*, possible reforms to the *Divorce Act* related to child custody and access, and the constitutional change that was required to transform the multiple faith-based schools of Newfoundland and Labrador into a single public system.

In 1996 Pearson was formally named adviser on children's rights to the minister of foreign affairs, enabling her to be active on the international issues affecting children's rights, which had become increasingly visible as a result of attention raised by the UNCRC. As a senior delegate to meetings and conferences in Europe, Asia, Latin America, and throughout Canada related to child labour, child protection, children in armed conflict, child trafficking, and sexual exploitation, she brought the views of the children involved back to the federal government and helped to make sure that the policies, programs, and new legislation related to these issues would be more respectful of children's rights.

Perhaps the most influential of these conferences in terms of impact on government legislation, as well as on Pearson personally, was the First World Congress against the Commercial Sexual Exploitation of Children held in Stockholm in September 1996. The Canadian delegation included a young woman, Cherry Kingsley, who was the only experiential youth at the whole event, and whose words had a profound effect on the assembled delegates from 131 countries. A year and a half later, Pearson and Kingsley were able, with the support of both the federal government and UNICEF, to co-chair a "summit" of experiential youth from the Americas whose carefully considered and well-articulated words have changed the language about this issue forever. "Juvenile prostitutes" are now known as "sexually exploited youth" and having non-consensual sex with anyone under the age of 18 is now universally recognized as child abuse.

In June 1999, Prime Minister Jean Chrétien appointed Pearson as his personal representative to the processes leading up to and including the United Nations Special Session on Children. Scheduled to take place in New York in September 2001, the Special Session was postponed for a year by the events of 9/11. This provided more time for preparations and, having secured the prime minister's commitment to child and youth participation, there were increased opportunities to engage them. The presence of young people on the Canadian delegations to regional and preparatory sessions encouraged other countries to include children and youth on their delegations, and their collective voice in September 2002 had a very profound influence on the outcome document of the Special Session, entitled "A World Fit for Children" (A World Fit for Children, 2002). Subsequently Canada's own young delegates, augmented by others involved in Canada-wide consultations, had significant input into the National Plan of Action prepared under the guidance of Pearson in response to the Special Session. Pearson shepherded "A Canada Fit for Children" (A Canada Fit for Children, 2004) through cabinet in 2004, where it was adopted as government policy.

Pearson's final opportunity as a senator to engage children in parliamentary processes came the same year when she was vice-chair of the Senate Standing Committee on Human Rights studying Canada's implementation of the UNCRC. By this time her colleagues were fully prepared to embrace their obligation to call young witnesses. They heard a good deal of frustration from the young people who appeared before them, and the telling title of the committee's final report is "Children: The Silenced Citizens" (Children: The Silenced Citizens, 2007). Its first recommendation reads: "Pursuant to articles 12 to 15 of the Convention on the Rights of the Child, the Committee recommends that the federal government dedicate resources towards ensuring that children's input is given considerable weight when laws, policies and other decisions that have a significant impact on children's lives are discussed or implemented at the federal level."

Finlay came to the Office of Child and Family Service Advocacy (OCFSA) as the chief advocate (for Ontario) in 1991, having worked throughout the province of Ontario as a social worker and clinician for two decades. Early in her career, she worked in residential care, child welfare, and policing. Most of her professional life however, has been spent in the field of children's mental health. In 1977, Finlay co-founded the first non-government women's shelter built on a feminist framework in Ontario. In the early 1980s she co-founded the Social Welfare Action Group in Perth, Australia, where she was teaching in a School of Social Work at a local university. Advocacy initiatives included influencing legislative change regarding care of seniors in residential care; Indigenous rights related to land, language, and culture; and police practices in domestic violence. In the mid-1980s, Finlay opened the dialogue in communities in Ontario about the range of trauma experienced by children in the context of the family.

Finlay has been characterized as a change-maker, disrupting the traditional understanding of child and youth work practice and creating knowledge with, not for, youth who are marginalized or oppressed. Despite complex adversities facing these young people, elevating their voice and facilitating meaningful participation is a fundamental commitment.

In 1991, the legislated mandate of the Office of Child and Family Service Advocacy was embedded in the *Child and Family Services Act* and indeed the Office itself was engulfed in the operations of the Ministry of Community and Social Services. The Office at that time served not only children and youth (particularly those with complex needs), but also adult recipients of social welfare and developmentally challenged adults. It was at that time as well, that Canada was ratifying the UNCRC. Finlay negotiated with the provincial government, drawing on the language promoted by the UNCRC, to ensure that the Office was entirely dedicated to children and youth seeking or receiving services from the Ministry. The Office evolved quickly to embrace the rights of all children or youth in any form of out-of-home-care in which they didn't have a parent available as their primary advocate. This included youth in youth justice settings that were designated for adults. She reinforced that these settings were founded on the principles of rehabilitation, not correction, and that youth were separate and apart from adult inmates. Finlay publicly advocated that parents should not have to give up guardianship of their children in order that they receive the specialized services they deserved. She ensured that youth had a strong voice at inquests by offering them "standing" because they had an inimitable perspective, having walked the same path as the deceased youth. She spoke out with youth to restrict the use of intrusive measures as a means of behavioural intervention in all residential settings. Finlay partnered with Indigenous youth leaders in remote First Nations to heighten public awareness about the impact of not having access to any of their rights or entitlements.

As illustrated, child and youth advocacy at the OCFSA evolved beyond case advocacy to include program advocacy and policy advocacy. Case advocacy continued to reflect the amplification of youth voice, intervention in rights violations or harsh treatment, and the navigation of the service systems on behalf of families and rights education. Program advocacy was informed by case advocacy. The opinions and lived experience of the youth in residential settings were collated to represent a unified voice to influence programmatic change. Policy advocacy was also driven by youth participation. A policy or legislative change was targeted based on the accumulation of opinions by youth across programs and sectors. The principles that propelled the Office from 1991 to 2007 were voice, partnerships that were relational, and a rights-based approach, all of which were intended to influence systemic change.

In 1996, Finlay co-founded and provided leadership in the development of the Canadian Council of Provincial Child and Youth Advocates (CCPCYA). There appeared to be no political will at the national level to establish an office of a children's commissioner. Although not federally appointed and the mandates of each advocate differed through the council, they shared a common commitment to further the voice, rights and dignity of children. The CCPCYA offered the opportunity for provincial advocates across the country to present a unified voice on policy issues of national interest related to children and youth. The members identified issues of mutual concern and strived to develop ways to address the issues at the national level. CCPCYA made representations to legislative bodies, including the Senate, on the introduction of new legislation such as the *Youth Criminal Justice Act* and the *Divorce Act*. The council made numerous representations to standing committees related to children's rights, particularly as it concerned vulnerable populations of youth.

For seven years, Finlay promoted and advocated for the introduction of legislation for an independent office of the child and youth advocate. For several years she suffered the consequences of speaking out on behalf of children and youth in a political environment that didn't support the concept or principles of advocacy. This reinforced the importance of independence for the role of the advocate to ensure that the rights of children and youth were respected and valued in Ontario communities and in government practice, policy, and legislation. The *Provincial Advocate for Children and Youth Act* was proclaimed in October 2007.

Finlay has been a professor in the Faculty of Community Services at Ryerson for 10 years. This role offers greater autonomy to pursue advocacy initiatives than what she was afforded at OCFSA. She is presently championing two projects that she began as the advocate. First, Mamow Ki-ken-da-ma-win: Everyone Searching for Answers Together, is a partnership-based approach to identifying priorities and issues of importance in remote First Nations in Ontario. The collective goal of this partnership is to learn from one another in the context of northern First Nations lived realities. Youth leadership plays an essential role in the initiative. Second, the Cross-over Youth Project is designed to implement and evaluate a range of best-practice options that are aimed at improving outcomes of youth who are "dually involved" in the child welfare sector and youth justice system.

Finlay's belief as an academic is that outcomes of ethical and participatory gathering of knowledge must be reflected not just in words, but also in action, practice, innovation, and change. There is, therefore, a role and responsibility for academics to advocate, based on new learning. Each initiative undertaken by Finlay addresses the challenges faced by those who are seeking voice, but are thwarted by cumbersome institutional structures.

Due to their cumulative and parallel experiences, Pearson and Finlay were uniquely positioned to create and implement a vehicle for young people to have a voice and to participate in a significant manner to influence their rights under the UNCRC. When Pearson retired from the Senate and moved to Carleton University to open the Landon Pearson Resource Centre for the Study of Childhood and Children's Rights in 2006, she took all that she had learned about engaging children and youth in the public policy process with her and was determined to continue providing them with opportunities to speak up and speak out. In conversation with Judy Finlay and further discussions with Virginia Caputo,[1] who had become the academic director of the Landon Pearson Centre, the idea of Shaking the Movers evolved to make it possible for young people to continue to speak truth to power with respect to their rights with the promise that their voices would be heard. With funding from the Public Health Agency of Canada, about 40 young people from across Canada, most sponsored by youth-serving agencies, came to Ottawa in June 2007 to engage in two days of intense conversation. They stayed in the student residences at Carleton and visited Parliament. The theme of the first Shaking the Movers (STM) workshop was "The Civil and Political Rights of Children" (Shaking the Movers, 2007) and the keynote speaker was Lt. Gen. (Rtd.) Roméo Dallaire. He told the participants that in order to fully exercise their civil and political rights, "you must engage with the world around you and the *movers* of the world; the adult decision-makers must create the conditions in which your ideas can *shake them up*."

With the success of the first STM workshop, Pearson and Finlay sought funding from the Laidlaw Foundation for three years, funding that was augmented by a continuing commitment from the Public Health Agency and the Collaborating Centre for Aboriginal Public Health to support the presence of Indigenous youth. After the second STM workshop in June 2008, which focused on "Identity and Belonging" (Shaking the Movers II, 2008), Pearson and Finlay decided that it would be a good idea to create a Child Rights Academic Network (CRAN) to respond annually to what the children and youth had to say at each STM gathering. Funding was obtained from the Muttart

Foundation in Edmonton and the inaugural meeting was held at Carleton University later in 2008.

Two more STM gatherings took place at Carleton University. In June 2009, the theme was "Child Rights in Education" (Shaking the Movers III, 2009) and in late May 2010, the theme was "Child Rights in the Media" (Shaking the Movers IV, 2010). Finlay then recommended that the venue of the STM workshops be moved to Ryerson University, where the facilitation and reporting could be done by students in the School of Child and Youth Care and tied in with their own curriculum in Child Rights and Advocacy. Pearson and Finlay continued to guide the process and guarantee the physical and emotional safety of young people engaged in the difficult personal issues that would sometimes arise. Everyone else involved with STM gatherings was, at the time of the event, under the age of 25. This has assured that none of the young participants feel coerced to say something they think they ought to say rather than something they really think. The Public Health Agency of Canada was now prepared to fund the creation of a template so that the model could be used in other venues and so the first STM gathering in Toronto in November 2011—a time chosen because the Ryerson students were in class— was able to use and adapt this template to what were now slightly changed circumstances. The theme was "Youth Justice" (Shaking the Movers V, 2011). In 2012, it was "The Rights of Children with Mental Health Issues" (Shaking the Movers VI, 2012); in 2013 it was "The Right to Play and to Artistic Expression" (Shaking the Movers VII, 2013), and in 2014, "The Right to be Free from Exploitation" (Shaking the Movers VIII, 2014). By this time, partly as a result of the interest generated through CRAN, other parts of the country became interested in organizing STM gatherings. Simon Fraser University in Vancouver, in conjunction with Equitas, organized two connected STM gatherings on the theme of "The Sexual Exploitation of Children" (Shaking the Movers IX, 2015), and in 2016 when "Children's Rights in the Context of Climate Change" (Shaking the Movers X, 2016) was the theme, STM workshops were held in Fredericton, New Brunswick (bilingual), Montreal (French), Toronto (at Ryerson), and Vancouver.

All of the reports from these gatherings feature what the young people actually had to say, including their recommendations to "movers," and are available on Pearson's website (landonpearson.ca). The cumulative impact of all of these young voices is very powerful.

GATHERING OF VOICES

The Shaking the Movers workshops that have taken place over the past decade in Ontario have resulted in annual reports, which describe the structure and expectations for youth participation and, more specifically, capture the words of the youth participants. These reports were written by the youth facilitators of the workshop following a standardized format for the ease of the youthful writers. In the early STM workshops, youth narratives were captured in writing by the facilitators and posted on flip charts for discussion during the event and for use in the preparation of the reports. In the last number of years, Ryerson child and youth care students were assigned purposefully to record, in writing and verbatim, the words of the youth participants during those smaller group discussions, which are not open to adults. Youth were also encouraged to comment at the end of each conference by means of a written evaluation. These words were also captured in the written reports. The youth facilitators responsible for writing the annual reports selected what they believed to be the most relevant quotes to include in that year's report. Youth participants remain anonymous throughout all the annual reports.

This method of gathering, collating, analyzing, and reporting the words and conversations of youth participants at the 10 STM Ontario-based workshops for the annual reports is therefore not rigorous. Indeed, emphasis at the workshops is explicitly placed on the ability of the youth participants to have a voice and to be heard in a safe space that is youth-centred. The gathering of their voices is secondary to ensuring the ability for youth participants to have a voice in a manner that is ethical and meaningful to them. Youth facilitators, through experience over time at the workshops, create and model the values, principles, and practices for meaningful, safe, and active engagement of the youth participants. This has become the framework for each event.

A content analysis of the 10 annual Ontario-based reports was undertaken by Sabrin Hassan.[2] Themes were generated from the reports by means of a structured qualitative methodology. The data were in the form of direct quotes from the youth participants across all reports. All quotes were extracted from the reports and placed in one document. Categories were then derived inductively from the words of the participants by the student. These were cross-checked with one of the writers herein. All quotes were then organized according to category. These categories were then reviewed, and the 10 most salient themes emerged from across the categories. These 10 themes had up to 15 quotes each and were named using the words of the youth participants. The content analysis process was consistently youth-centred and honoured the meaning attached to their words. The themes are described here, again relying on the words and interpretation of those words by the youth participants or facilitators.

The student/youth facilitator who conducted the content review decided that it wasn't necessary to prioritize the themes as she thought all were equally relevant. Although some themes were mentioned more frequently by the youth participants, the salience of the quote as perceived by the youth facilitators and the student writer gave weight to its use. However, we organized the themes into three areas for the purposes of this chapter. In summary, it is important to note, that all the gathering, collating, analysis, and reporting of the voice of the youth participants who attended all 10 Shaking the Movers workshops was undertaken by young people themselves.

Initial Themes

A series of themes identified by participants generally at the beginning of each of the 10 workshops were: the lack of knowledge and understanding of rights, particularly related to the UNCRC; the diminished value placed on their ideas and opinions because of their age; and when given the opportunity to engage, participants felt that their voice did not influence consequential change.

We Didn't Know We Had Rights. A common theme across all 10 conferences was that youth participants were under the impression that they had no rights and they viewed themselves merely as an extension of their parents/guardians with no independent agency to have or access their rights:

- "If parents take on the responsibility of having a child, they also have to respect the child, as a separate entity with their own rights."
- "You have to wait until you're a certain age to learn about rights, and by that point a lot of kids don't care about them anymore."

Some participants indicated that they thought that rights were a privilege that youth had to earn. For example, having high marks in school made you eligible for participation in rights education: "Many youth don't know that they can participate, or that it's not just for the top students—the right to participate needs to be widely communicated."

Youth participants clearly stated that "If you don't know what your rights are, how do you know what you're not getting?"

They realized their vulnerability when they didn't know or understand their rights and/or how to access them: "If something happens at school and we get in trouble for it, we can't defend ourselves properly because we don't know our rights."

A shared response by most participants was the need to be informed about their rights in a way that leads to comprehension and awareness so that they "know how to use them" effectively or how to speak out when their rights are not being respected. They were frank about the need to take responsibility for knowing their rights:

- "We've never really been told about our rights; we need to know what our rights are."
- "It's important to understand the rights—you can read them, but if you don't understand them, it's pointless."
- "It's one thing to know your rights; it's another to know how to use them."
- "We need to educate each other and have more knowledge of what our rights are, this was the first time I heard about my rights."
- "There needs to be a way for young people to know their rights, to know what to do, and to know what process is in place to help if your rights are not being met."
- "Give us life examples to show how we can use our rights to defend ourselves. How can we defend our rights if we don't know them?"

Because We Are Young. The theme "because we are young" appeared to be prevalent among the youth participants in all 10 conferences. They believed that their thoughts, feelings, and perceptions are often overlooked and disregarded because they are young and don't have the requisite lived experience to offer an opinion. Even in settings in which youth are the "biggest stakeholder" and therefore should have the ability to influence decision making, they were frequently confounded when they were not taken seriously. They expressed the importance of having their voice honoured regardless of their age and inexperience in order to feel equally valued as a person with equity and agency:

- "The youth voice is questioned because it comes from youth who know less and have experienced less."
- "Sometimes our ideas get through but other times our opinions and ideas are just put aside because we are young."
- "People don't see children as people."
- "Adults tell us that we don't know anything, we haven't had enough experience. They don't take us seriously because we our [sic] young."

- "It seems backwards that school administrators are not taking youth seriously when they have a problem."
- "Students are the biggest stakeholders of all."
- "It's really important that everyone knows everyone is a person."
- "Childhood is a big step in a person's life. If they don't feel important, that's what they will carry."

Does Our Voice Stick? Youth participants uniformly acknowledged that they often did feel heard by adults; however, they did not see concrete changes that flowed from their engagement and participation. They wondered if their intentions and opinions were of equal value and meaning as those of adults:

- "As a youth, there is always a question—does our voice stick? The youth voice is questioned because it comes from youth who know less and have experienced less."
- "Listening isn't enough; adults must act on our concerns."
- "Participation means having a say in anything that has anything to do with you, like simple things, like having to move."

The outcome of this common experience as expressed in these three themes was a sense of disempowerment, which nurtured complacency and eventual resistance. This hindered youth's willingness to pursue opportunities to voice their opinions about their life experience or civic or political concerns. Distrust of the authenticity or worthiness of engagement processes ensued. In conjunction with these central themes, additional themes emerged from the discussion among participants that were directly related to the content of the conferences.

Additional Themes

No-normal. The concept of "no-normal" was discussed in many workshops and it explored the different issues that the youth participants faced daily that were identified and labelled by society as abnormal. Topics included how society views mental health, youth justice, education, and the media. The participants reappropriated the term "abnormal" and changed it to "no-normal," illustrating that nothing in society is actually normal:

- "Mental health has different aspects; people label the kids at school as having a certain mental illness, but I don't really know what it means."

- "The knowledge we receive is always limited. This allows the media to control our perception of the world and govern society by the information they choose to give us."

Education and opportunities to explore life beyond the classroom were recognized as ways of giving a more informed and less judgmental context to societal issues:

- "Information about accessing good information is not well known and must be. Education is the key!!!"
- "Whenever you come across information, you have to be critical of it; you can't trust any of it."
- "We focus on academics but not on basic principles of being out in the world."

Stigma. Asserting the concept of "no-normal" gave rise to rich dialogue about stigma. Participants in each workshop highlighted the social impact of stigma from their own personal experiences and explained how it affected their identity and their daily life. They were very aware of how society stigmatized minority groups. They felt that stigma was attached directly to being a young person, which led to their belittlement or other unjustified consequences:

- "When we voice our opinions, we get in trouble for being out of line."
- "Youth are often portrayed as a group that needs to be served, not one that contributes."
- "They think that we're clueless, and because we're not adults, it won't really matter much to us."
- "People are quick to judge young people and assume that they are up to no good."
- "Labelling is unfair because they only look at what people have done and not what they will do or who they are—people can change."

The youth participants demonstrated over and over again their attunement to the impact of stigmatization and its intent to marginalize those groups not considered "mainstream." They appreciated the value of education and advocacy in these disturbing circumstances:

- "Canadians are not accustomed to different religions and therefore form an unfair bias towards the people who practise them."

- "If everyone keeps thinking of someone negatively, they start to believe the same thing about themselves."
- "Your parents put stuff in your head ... racism starts with parents; they put it in our heads ... parents want their kids to hang around people of their own race ... it's hard to disobey your parents."
- "Judgment needs to stop. People living with mental illness can be judged and have been judged; this needs to stop."
- "Advocate means to speak up and represent others."
- "You need to remove the stigma, not the people."
- "Get students to come together about something that relates to all groups, no matter where they come from."
- "Inclusivity is about recognizing that each individual is a person, no less, no more than anyone."

Our Experiences as Aboriginal Children. Youth participants who identified as First Nations, Inuit, and/or Métis were present at eight of the 10 workshops. Their perspectives about the experiences of Indigenous children and youth in Canada were compelling and had a powerful impact on all participants and leaders:

- "Canada has a facade of how good things are but there are a lot of things under the surface."
- "When you are young, having people love you is very important. A lot of neglect happens in Inuit communities because of isolation of communities, lack of access to services, traditions that are against girls, no parenting skills, fetal alcohol syndrome, etc."
- "We lost a lot of students because they couldn't handle the change from reserve to city. The transition is sometimes too much for students to take and it affects their education."

Participants acknowledged their lack of knowledge and understanding of Canada's First Peoples and the role that the education system played in perpetuating that ignorance:

- "I have never learned anything about Aboriginal health in school."
- "There is such ignorance about the issues that Aboriginal youth face."
- "Within the Ontario education system, there is a lack of Indigenous teachings (history), rather it is a much more Eurocentric focus."

This Is Native Land. Despite the lack of school curriculum dedicated to Canada's history related to Indigenous peoples, youth participants had strong opinions about the destructive role that colonialism played in devastating the land, language, and culture, which are determinants of identity and well-being for Indigenous communities. Participants expressed their support to people who identify as First Nations, Inuit, and/or Métis and openly recognized the inequalities and racism that they continue to face. One of the most compelling quotes was: "We need to remember that this is Native Land." Other quotes follow:

- "Overall evaluation of Canada ... Grade B–."
- "Health should be 'community-specific, not pan-Aboriginal but status-blind'—so no one has to present a status card."
- "Many Aboriginal people feel they aren't Canadian because their language isn't recognized as official."
- "Language can act to marginalize people."
- "Language has overt and covert ways of displacing people."
- "Why are Canada's official languages French and English? What happened to the Indigenous languages? Is it based on a certain perception of Canadian history? This gives everyone a false sense of Canadian history."
- "Canadians try to keep the Americans out, the French in, and hide the Aboriginals."

Notably, participants were acutely aware of culturally safe and appropriate approaches to take in any interaction with Indigenous peoples: "It is important that people advocate in support of Aboriginal youth, not on their behalf, because this takes away power."

The final set of themes that arose usually at the end of the STM workshops illustrated the youth participants' vision to drive change. They had developed new friendships and had a greater sense of self-efficacy when it came to understanding and advocating for their rights and the rights of other young people. They articulated very clearly what needed to change in order to boost their individual capacity to voice their opinion. They also offered their ideas, tactics, and strategies that could influence systemic change related to their rights generally and, more specifically, to their rights linked to the various conference topics.

Our Rights Should Be Considered. After two days of learning and collaborating with other youth and the youth facilitators, the participants had a greater knowledge of their rights and were able to clearly convey the difficulty in accessing them. They became comfortable offering examples of the dilemmas that they faced and were self-reflective about how to approach them. They saw the need for equity and collaboration between adults and youth:

- "When you're looking at your rights, ask yourself whose story am I telling, whose standards am I holding myself to?"
- "Adults speak past and youth speak future."
- "There can be lots of programmes set out to educate young people about rights, but if adults don't learn too, then it is difficult."
- "We have the right to stand up and say, 'this is what's wrong'—adults should give us that chance."
- "We want respect to be mutual so that everyone is on an even playing field."
- "Walking away sometimes doesn't help, sometimes you have to fight."

We Need to Change the Way Things Are. By the end of the workshop, the participants felt energized and inspired by one another to consider tactics and strategies to change the status quo and influence the policy agenda. They tackled real-life issues that they faced related to the authorities in their lives such as parents, teachers, and the police. They frankly confronted issues related to broader societal structures such as religion, economics, governments, politics, and social systems. The words below capture some of these themes:

- "Adults will tailor their questions so that you say what they want ... we need systems that are more youth-friendly."
- "We need someone we can talk to in the community who's there to listen to youth because that's their job."
- "Professionals and people in authority are sometimes the very ones who are violating our rights."
- "The way a child is treated by a society, is an indication of what that society is all about."
- "Child and youth involvement is a strategic investment in human capital instead of hoping a good leader will come along; we need to build a good leader."
- "Youth should be involved in promoting, implementing, and maintaining the physical, mental, and spiritual health of their unique community."

- "If the 'day of the child' becomes the 'month of the child,' the momentum is carried."
- "Canada cannot have credibility on an international scale because we have racism and inequalities here."
- "Once I sent in the same résumé under two different names, a white girl's name and a black girl's name. The résumé that seemed like it came from a white girl got a call from the company, the other one didn't."
- "There should be legal consequences for government if they don't fulfill their obligations."

Education Should Be to Empower Us. Remarkably, education was cited invariably at each workshop by the majority of youth participants as the most powerful strategy for change when considering the rights of young people. However, they simultaneously conveyed that the current education system promotes "Eurocentric views, language, and learning" and is devoid of a curriculum about youth rights. Participants suggested that the education system should be the agent to promote rights, learning through experience, and civic responsibility:

- "In our world, post-secondary education is more important than anything."
- "Education causes prevention."
- "Everything starts with education ... proper allocation of funding, to be able to break stereotypes."
- "The main reason behind education should be to empower children."
- "An important part of education is to learn to make decisions and to deal with issues properly. We need to be allowed to learn from our mistakes."
- "Educate youth on issues that are relevant to them; this empowers them to be passionate."
- "Every Teachers' College student should take an oath to uphold the Convention on the Rights of the Child."
- "Place students and teachers in situations where they have to exercise their rights together."
- "Respect should be taught in schools."

On looking at the analysis of the major themes that emerged from every one of the Shaking the Movers gatherings that have taken place over the last 10 years, no matter the actual topic under discussion, we have come away with two strong impressions. First of all, most of the participants, regardless of their background, came to the workshops unaware that they actually have rights and were disappointed that no one had ever told them about these rights. Once they learned about them, they were excited and highly motivated to exercise them. However, they were only too aware that the balance of power is always tilted toward the adults in all the institutions and systems that surround them as they grow up. The participants were clearly not convinced that rights are actually relational and that adults have a duty to respond. The second message is that these young people would like us to understand that there is no such thing as a "normal" adolescent, so they are very wary of any stereotypes that are used to classify them. Non-discrimination is an important issue. Over a decade of gatherings, the message remained the same. The young people revealed a strong sense of social justice as well as recognition that adolescence is a time for trying on identities, not for being trapped inside them.

CONCLUSION: THE STRENGTHS AND BENEFITS OF STM

In conjunction with Gerison Lansdown,[3] a widely respected child rights consultant and an expert on child and youth participation, and on the basis of our own experience, we propose the following analysis of the strengths and benefits of STM as a model for the promotion of the civil and political rights of children:

1. STM has demonstrated positive outcomes for participating young people; greater knowledge of their rights, enhanced self-esteem, a sense of self-efficacy, building new friendships, growing awareness of the potential for collaboration between adults and children and the opportunities to influence the policy agenda.

2. STM provides a good practice model of meaningful consultative participation embodying the four key dimensions necessary for compliance with Article 12 of the United Nations Convention on the Rights of the Child: space, voice, audience, and influence. In addition, it fully complies with the nine basic requirements of quality participation:

    - **Transparent and informative:** Young people understood exactly what STM can and cannot achieve, what it is for and their role within it.

- **Relevant to children's lives:** The young people chose the topic.
- **Voluntary:** No young person was under any compulsion or pressure to participate.
- **Respectful:** Methods of working were designed to promote self-esteem and confidence.
- **Child-friendly:** Environment and activities were all appropriate for young people, and designed explicitly with them in mind.
- **Inclusive:** Young people from different environments and context were included and treated equitably within the meetings.
- **Supported by trained adults:** Young adults were trained and supported to lead the sessions.
- **Safe and sensitive to risk:** All adults were fully aware of child-protection issues and safeguards were in place to minimize risks.
- **Accountable:** The findings from the young people were shared with the participants at the Children's Rights Academic Network (CRAN), and their discussions and reflections were fed back to the young people through a youth-friendly report.

As such, STM provides an exemplar to others of how to construct participatory spaces for children. Furthermore, as it evolves, it is building toward becoming a more collaborative space, affording young people opportunities to follow up with their concerns and to maintain ongoing contact both with the other participating children and the CRAN members.

3. STM workshops have become an invaluable source of information, providing stimulus for the creation of knowledge to inform research agendas, policy priorities, and advocacy efforts. It provides orientation as to the perspectives of young people, their priorities for change, and the strength of their concerns. But the workshops are more than just youth engagement exercises.

When they are followed up by the Child Rights Academic Network meetings, they not only create a space for researchers in different disciplines to share their thinking, explore their different fields of current research, and identify points of potential shared interest and future collaboration, but also inspire all concerned to become activists on behalf of the young people. The annual nature of the event builds a close-knit community that increasingly utilizes the opportunities for identifying gaps and orienting future research.

QUESTIONS FOR DISCUSSION

1. Has there been adequate attention to children's rights and participation in Canada since the ratification of the UNCRC? What evidence is there to support this conclusion?
2. How do we as practitioners and educators ensure that youth "voices stick"?
3. There were elements of the STM model that resonated with the youth participants. How do educators and practitioners facilitate the introduction of these elements in institutional settings?
4. How do educators and practitioners encourage and ensure active youth engagement in civil and political processes?

NOTES

1 Virginia Caputo is currently an associate professor in the Department of Sociology and Anthropology and the director of the Landon Pearson Resource Centre for the Study of Childhood and Children's Rights at Carleton University. From 2005 to 2009 she directed the Pauline Jewett Institute of Women's and Gender Studies, helping to design and launch a graduate program on the themes of transnational feminisms and globalization. Her particular contribution is her expertise on girlhoods, gendered childhoods, and the changing contours of young people's lives in the context of globalization.
2 Sabrin Hassan is a youth facilitator/student at Ryerson University.
3 Gerison Lansdown, was founder director of the Children's Rights Alliance for England, and is now an international children's rights consultant and advocate who has published and lectured widely on the subject of children's rights. She was actively involved in the drafting of the Convention on the Rights of Persons with Disabilities, is an honorary fellow of UNICEF–UK, an associate of the International Institute for Child Rights and Development in Victoria, Canada, and co-director of Child Rights Education for Professionals, an international initiative to develop child rights educational programs for professionals working with children.

REFERENCES

A Canada Fit for Children. (2004, April). *Canada's follow-up to the United Nations General Assembly Special Session on Children*. Government of Canada. Retrieved from https://canadiancrc.com/PDFs/Canadas_Plan_Action_April2004-EN.pdf

Children: The Silenced Citizens. (2007). *Effective implementation of Canada's international obligations with respect to the rights of Children*. Final report of Standing Senate Committee on Human Rights.

For Canada's Children: A National Agenda for Action. (1980). Report of the Canadian Commission for the International Year of the Child issued under the signature of Judge Doris Ogilvie.

Shaking the Movers: Speaking Truth to Power: Civil and political rights of children. (2007). Landon Pearson Resource Centre for the Study of Childhood and Children's Rights. Final Report. Carleton University, Ottawa.

Shaking the Movers II: Identity and Belonging. (2008). Landon Pearson Resource Centre for the Study of Childhood and Children's Rights. Carleton University, Ottawa. Final Report.

Shaking the Movers III: Children's Rights in Education. (2009). Landon Pearson Resource Centre for the Study of Childhood and Children's Rights. Carleton University, Ottawa. Final Report.

Shaking the Movers IV: Child Rights and the Media. (2010). Landon Pearson Resource Centre for the Study of Childhood and Children's Rights. Carleton University, Ottawa. Final Report.

Shaking the Movers V: Divided We're Silent: United We Speak: Standing up for Youth Justice. (2011). Faculty of Community Services, Ryerson University and Landon Pearson Resource Centre for the Study of Childhood and Children's Rights. Toronto. Final Report.

Shaking the Movers VI: Standing up for Children's Mental Health. (2012). Faculty of Community Services, Ryerson University and Landon Pearson Resource Centre for the Study of Childhood and Children's Rights. Toronto. Final Report.

Shaking the Movers VII: Standing up for Children's Right to Play. (2013). Faculty of Community Services, Ryerson University and Landon Pearson Resource Centre for the Study of Childhood and Children's Rights. Toronto. Final Report.

Shaking the Movers VIII: Child Exploitation. (2014). Faculty of Community Services, Ryerson University and Landon Pearson Resource Centre for the Study of Childhood and Children's Rights. Toronto. Final Report.

Shaking the Movers BC IX: Standing Out against Sexual Exploitation. (2015). Landon Pearson Resource Centre for the Study of Childhood and Children's Rights. Vancouver. Final Report.

Shaking the Movers X: Youth Rights and the Environment. (2016). Faculty of Community Services, Ryerson University and Landon Pearson Resource Centre for the Study of Childhood and Children's Rights. Toronto. Final Report.

A World Fit for Children. (2002). *Millennium Development Goals Special Session on Children documents the Convention on the Rights of the Child.* UNICEF. Retrieved from https://www.unicef.org/bangladesh/wffc-en_main.pdf

Chapter 15
Conclusion: A Children's Rights Pathway to Status and Recognition
Thomas Waldock

INTRODUCTION

At the outset, before the journey through areas of public policy, practice, and the law, the book's preoccupation with the following question was highlighted: To what extent has Canada fulfilled its obligations under the United Nations Convention on the Rights of the Child (UNCRC) to treat children as rights-bearing citizens, respecting their dignity as fully human persons in their own right? The Howe and Covell framework was also identified and this provided authors and readers with a context for the analysis and discussion of Canada's record in various areas of policy, practice, and law. Three general stages are outlined in the framework, corresponding to the evolution of the human rights story of children. While this story shares to some degree the general trajectory from property to persons that characterizes other human rights stories, it is also unique in terms of its specific application to children. The three overlapping, evolutionary stages of development—as children transition from being regarded as objects/property to subjects/citizens in their own right—are as follows: social laissez-faire, paternalistic protection, and children's rights. Of course, for the purpose of analysis and discussion, these stages are also the possibilities. General evidence of the transition aside, authors have provided more specific analysis and discussion of their respective areas of policy, practice, and the law, allowing for an overall assessment of Canada's general level of progress in terms of the evolving status of children and the extent to which children have been afforded the type of recognition associated with the children's rights evolutionary stage.

Prior to offering such an overall assessment and some conclusions about Canada's level of progress with regard to the children's rights stage, it is appropriate, in the spirit of critical thinking, to note the following: readers and in particular students are free to draw their own conclusions about Canada's progress or lack thereof, either in relation to particular areas of policy, practice, and law—where hopefully the "Questions for Discussion" have been helpful—or in terms of a general, overall assessment. In what follows, a general assessment and some conclusions are provided that represent the views of the editor. At the very least, perhaps these observations can serve as a basis for further discussion.

In Canada, overall progress toward the children's rights stage and recognizing children as rights bearers has been slow; in addition, development has been uneven, with some areas of policy, practice, and the law demonstrating signs of progress, while other areas continue to be mired in the past, notably as this relates to paternalistic conceptions of children. Before summoning the evidence in this regard—provided by authors in relation to their specific areas of analysis—suffice to say that there are only limited and sporadic signs that Canada is treating its children and youth as rights-bearing citizens. That is not to say that real progress is not discernible in some areas of policy and law. As will be noted, at times there are signs of progress, and real reasons for optimism in particular areas. But too often, positive signs are confined to particular, limited aspects of the area in question, and there is not enough evidence to support the conclusion that stage 3 has been fully achieved, and that a view of children as rights bearers and citizens has been sufficiently incorporated. More often than not, paternalistic conceptions of children dominate, with only limited indications and sporadic signs of moving beyond what is defined as stage 2 (paternalistic protection) in the framework. Even when there are indications in law—for example, the incorporation of children's rights into legislation in the area—and perhaps some elements of the UNCRC incorporated into practice, often practices on the ground fail to exemplify the children's rights evolutionary stage, and sometimes in important respects. Again, progress is uneven and some areas are further ahead than others in this regard, but it is sobering to note that the above conclusion holds across all the areas focused on by authors in this book. In short, Canada has work to do if it is to live up to its obligations under the UNCRC.

LIMITED PROGRESS AND ONGOING CHALLENGES

The Status of the UNCRC in Canadian Law

Part of the context for limited progress in treating children as rights bearers and achieving stage 3 in the framework relates to the status of the UNCRC in Canadian law. Canada ratified the Convention in 1991, committing the country under international law to its provisions. As noted in Chapter 1's

"Introduction," there is a mechanism of accountability around this commitment—reports, responses, peer pressure on the international stage—but in order for the Convention to be enforceable in Canadian courts, this requires implementing legislation. Recall that countries are obligated under Article 4 to "take all appropriate legislative, administrative, and other measures for the implementation of the rights recognized in the present Convention," and they are to do so "to the maximum extent of their available resources...." Some countries have been at the forefront in this regard: in Belgium—under the doctrine of monism—the UNCRC is self-executing, meaning that its provisions were automatically and directly incorporated into domestic law; in Norway—under the doctrine of dualism (like Canada), whereby countries must incorporate treaties through legislation into domestic law—the UNCRC has been incorporated into key pieces of legislation, notably their human rights act (Howe & Covell, 2007). In these countries, the UNCRC has the force of hard law in their domestic courts.

Substantial commitments and efforts related to the incorporation of the UNCRC would be required in order to conclude that a country was serious about treating children as rights-bearing citizens—associated with stage 3 in the Howe and Covell framework. To date it remains generally true that Canada has not directly incorporated the UNCRC into domestic legislation and policies. Two observations are relevant in this regard, the second of which relates to a legitimate, ongoing challenge. First, authorities have tended to assume—certainly incorrectly to a significant extent, based on the general thrust of the chapters herein—that laws and policies already are sufficiently in conformity with the Convention's dictates (Howe & Covell, 2007). Secondly, as noted by J. C. Blokhuis (Chapter 8), the federal system presents challenges and the federal government's concerns around the separation of powers may in part account for the lack of progress on incorporation, since many areas related to the Convention (for example, education) fall within provincial jurisdiction. Each province and territory would have to incorporate the Convention into its own legislation for children's rights to be realized in their areas of jurisdiction. And as J. C. Blokhuis points out, Canada has a "long way to go" in this regard. Of course, the challenge posed by federalism is no excuse for Canada's record, since in itself this in turn simply becomes an argument for federal leadership and responsibility, and the institution of coordinating and monitoring systems. Has the federal government done enough in this regard (the subject matter of the next subsection)? Moreover, the provinces are signatories to the UNCRC as well, so their record becomes part of Canada's by default when the country is being assessed. In the final analysis, the most that can be said regarding incorporation of the UNCRC is that Canada has proceeded in a piecemeal fashion, falling short of anything that could be construed as a substantial commitment to children's rights.

The good news is that there are some positive signs. While the UNCRC has been incorporated into only a few areas, there are signs of progress. At present, the Convention has been incorporated into the *Youth Criminal Justice Act* (Preamble) (see Moore's Chapter 5), and in child welfare legislation in Yukon (Preamble), Northwest Territories (Principles), Nunavut (Principles), and more recently Ontario (Preamble) (see Waldock's Chapter 6); and the *Immigration and Refugee Protection Act* is to be construed and applied consistent with international human rights instruments (Birdsell & Chan, 2017). In particular, the recent incorporation of the Convention into Ontario child welfare legislation was an important step forward (Waldock's Chapter 6) and signifies progress in the right direction. It should also be noted that the UNCRC is embedded in provincial advocate for children and youth legislation in Yukon, Nunavut, and Ontario (Hunter's Chapter 13).

In addition, while no substitute for actual incorporation, the Supreme Court of Canada has recognized the UNCRC in important decisions chronicled by J. C. Blokhuis in Chapter 8. While these decisions have not always been supportive in terms of viewing children as rights bearers (more on this below), the court has recognized that the values reflected in international human rights law can inform a contextual approach to statutory interpretation and judicial review. The UNCRC is also recognized as a significant interpretive tool when it comes to key legal concepts like the "best interests of the child" (Birdsell & Chan, 2017) and the *parens patriae* doctrine. Moreover, the Supreme Court uses international agreements like the Convention to interpret the Charter. It also bears keeping the following observation in mind: for the most part, in the majority of cases where the court's decisions or even the judgments of individual judges have been counterproductive from a children's rights perspective, the failure to incorporate the UNCRC into domestic law in the area has been an important factor. J. C. Blokhuis's conclusion (Chapter 8) about the role of the Supreme Court in the absence of implementing legislation is worth emphasizing: "The halting and piecemeal recognition of the Convention by the Supreme Court has achieved in part what implementing legislation and widespread children's rights education would surely achieve more fully. Much remains to be done if children are actually to enjoy the substance of their rights under the Convention in Canada."

The point is this: in terms of the status of the UNCRC in Canadian law, any positive signs of progress—whether this relates to developments regarding incorporation (child welfare legislation in Ontario), or supportive

Supreme Court decisions (*Baker v. Canada*: see Chapter 8)—are something on which to build, but they do not belie the general conclusion that Canada has a long way to go. With regard to the incorporation of the UNCRC, there is no uniformity across policy and practice areas, and progress itself has been uneven. In addition, it should be noted in this context that while incorporation itself is significant, it is not sufficient; evidence provided in the relevant chapters alluded to above suggests that even where Canada has incorporated the UNCRC, it continues to fall short of stage 3 by not fully realizing the Convention's dictates in policy and practice (on the ground). Moreover, with regard to the Supreme Court, at times there have been counterproductive decisions and significant setbacks in terms of realizing stage 3 (children's rights stage) and recognizing children as right bearers.

The upholding of section 43 (2004 decision) of the Criminal Code, allowing for the corporal punishment of children, is a prime and notorious example in this regard. As articulated so well by Joan Durrant in Chapter 9, Canada's legal justification of corporal punishment is more than a symbol. Sweden was the first country to prohibit all corporal punishment of children (1979), and as Durrant argues, "Sweden's law is the embodiment of stage 3 law" because it recognizes children as independent rights bearers. Where does that leave Canada, aside from being increasingly isolated because over 50 countries have followed Sweden's lead and banned corporal punishment? Identifying section 43 as stage 1 law because it conceives of children as the objects of adult authority, Durrant suggests that the 2004 decision "might push the legal status of corporal punishment into stage 2—paternalistic protection," by increasing the protections for children, but even then, the court's "concept of protection was not based on universal human rights standards" and "did not recognize in any way the inherent rights of children." The judgments of the dissenting judges (6–3 decision) also were noteworthy, with phrases and terms like "second-class citizens" (Justice Binnie) and "property" (Justice Deschamps) being employed to describe the status of children in relation to the section 43 provision.

Concerns about children's status in Canadian law also arise in Sonja Grover's piece (Chapter 10) on the Canadian courts' approach to so-called "wrongful life" and "wrongful birth" cases, and in these cases, it is the status of children with disabilities that is in question. At issue in the *Bovingdon et al. v. Hergott* case was whether a doctor's negligence could result in legal damages being awarded separately to parents and their disabled children. In assessing the eventual outcome of the case at the Court of Appeal for Ontario—the Supreme Court declined to hear the appeal of that court's decision, leaving the decision to stand—Grover concludes that the "denial by the high courts in Canada of the born-alive disabled child's right to a civil remedy in erroneously labelled 'wrongful life' cases grossly undermines the child's status as a rights holder." In her view, the decision "undermines the live-born disabled child's status as legal person by effectively denying access to the courts for a tort remedy for the disabilities suffered by the born-alive child due to another's negligence"; in such a scenario, the "live-born child ... is effectively considered no more than parental property that was negligently damaged...."

While the incorporation of the UNCRC into domestic law would add clarity to the question of status by solidifying the concept of children as rights holders, it also would likely facilitate a better framework for judicial decision making generally, which would be particularly important in difficult and contentious cases. In Chapter 11, J. C. Blokhuis and Amy Smoke outline the "extraordinary cases of J. J. and Makayla Sault," the two Indigenous girls who opted for alternative treatment against the recommendation of the hospital to continue chemotherapy. The resulting lawsuit (concerning J. J.) pitted the hospital on one side against the local Children's Aid Society—the latter had refused to consider J. J. a child in need of protection under provincial child welfare legislation—and the Indigenous community of Six Nations on the other side. Readers of this chapter cannot but be struck by the complexity of the case, which required a weighing of constitutional claims (subsection 35 (1) of the *Constitution Act*) recognizing Aboriginal and treaty rights, the *parens patriae* responsibility of the government, the best interests of the child principle, and the participation rights of the child. While there is no guarantee that the formal incorporation of the UNCRC would have made the decision any easier, it seems logical to suggest that since the Convention incorporates many of the principles involved, it would provide additional context and allow for decisions to be informed by years of philosophical discussion and legal decisions related to the relationship between these principles.

Coordination and Monitoring

The realities of a federal system, along with the absence of implementing legislation, make the need for coordination and monitoring systems that much more pronounced, and this in turn demands federal leadership and responsibility. This begs the question: Has the federal government done enough in this regard? Unfortunately, the answer to this question is no. As pointed out by M. Theresa Hunter in Chapter 13, there are "numerous pervasive, systemic barriers to children's rights, such as high rates of child poverty and inequitable access to public services," and the significant involvement and cooperation of all levels of government is required if these are to be addressed.

In terms of coordination, a national children's commissioner could oversee a more consistent and even implementation of Convention principles and articles across the provinces and territories. Yet despite repeated calls for a national-level human rights advocate and institution, Canada still does not have a national children's commissioner.

Canada does have provincial/territorial child advocates; nine provinces and two territories have established independent child and youth advocates (CYAs), and as Hunter notes, these offices play important roles and fulfill various roles in protecting and promoting the rights of young people in their jurisdictions. As will be pointed out in more detail in discussing participation rights, Canadian child and youth advocates have a significant role to play in supporting children's rights and achieving stage 3 (children's rights stage) in the Howe and Covell framework, and there are some real success stories in this regard, where such advocates have enhanced the voice of children to real effect on policies and practices. But as Hunter argues, on their own, the CYAs cannot resolve the many significant systemic issues that compromise the rights of numerous young people across the country: "A national, independent children's commissioner is essential to ensure the rights of all young Canadians. National leadership and coordination, and the development of comprehensive strategies with firm commitments from all levels of government are needed to address wide-ranging, systemic concerns."

It is not as though the federal government is unaware of the need for coordination and monitoring, and at times national initiatives have been undertaken to provide this to some degree. In this regard, Hunter references the efforts of the temporary Interdepartmental Working Group on Children's Rights—established in 2007 and co-chaired by the Public Health Agency of Canada—to coordinate cross-government implementation of the UNCRC and the Department of Justice to oversee federal legislative implementation of the UNCRC. But such temporary, sporadic initiatives are insufficient, and are no substitute for "stable national leadership on children's issues and coherent mechanisms to monitor and coordinate implementation of the UNCRC across all levels of government" (Hunter's Chapter 13).

In the absence of significant national leadership—and to their credit—the provincial CYAs formed an alliance (1996) that ultimately resulted in the formation of the Canadian Council of Child and Youth Advocates (CCCYA). In order to achieve some level of consistency across the country, this group adopted national advocacy standards grounded in UNCRC norms. The CCCYA also puts out joint statements and reports when seeking to address common issues and concerns. As we have seen, within areas of policy and practice, similar efforts exist to ensure coordination. Recall that one example of this was in child welfare (Waldock's Chapter 6), where occasional meetings occur between provincial and territorial directors of service.

While such measures are important in terms of facilitating progress in realizing the rights of children, there is always the sense that such efforts are seeking to make up for more formal, ongoing coordination and monitoring at the national level. Recognizing this, the CCCYA itself has called for a national advocate, joining the chorus of such requests emanating from a variety of sources. Yet despite repeated calls for a national advocate and consistent criticism from the Committee on the Rights of the Child, the federal government has shown little willingness to institute such an office. This remains a real challenge moving forward, but one that has to be confronted in order to achieve more substantial progress. Hunter's conclusion in this regard is direct: "Establishing a national children's commissioner is an essential step toward achieving stage 3 of the child rights evolutionary framework."

Policy and Practice Areas

While authors outlined in detail the challenges specific to their policy and practice areas, a common theme has emerged, and some general observations are possible. The main theme is the following: no author suggests the full realization of stage 3, whereby children's rights have been fully entrenched in the area in question, and children are being respected as independent, rights bearers consistent with the UNCRC. Given that the analyses are critical in nature, perhaps the normative and legal ideal associated with stage 3 is a somewhat unrealistic standard and difficult to live up to. Unfortunately, the general scenario outlined by authors is that Canada is not even close to achieving this standard in the areas assessed.

Generally—and this will be elaborated in the observations to follow—there are three possibilities or classifications within which the analyses fall. First—and at best—the analysis suggests that progress has been made in so far as there is some limited evidence of children's agency and participation rights being incorporated into the area in question. In other words, there is some indication of movement beyond the paternalistic approaches characteristic of stage 2. It should be noted that the approach taken here is generous in this regard because the indications of a transition generally are somewhat superficial, and for the most part are offset by other problematic aspects of the area in question. Nevertheless, it will be included within this first classification as a result of providing some recognition of agency and participation rights. Second—and this is the case more often than not—the analysis suggests that the area in question is deeply entrenched in stage 2 (paternalistic protection). Children continue to be perceived as "not-yets" (future citizens) and objects of paternalistic concern; there may be some evidence of consistency with the UNCRC within the confines of stage 2, but overall, the policies and practices in the area don't allow for meaningful participation or agency because children are assumed to be incapable in this regard. And finally—at worst—the author suggests that even stage 2 is in question, and that the area falls somewhere between stage 1 and stage 2, with evidence that children are to some extent still being conceptualized and treated as property.

Before considering authors' conclusions about their respective policy and practice areas, it bears keeping in mind that such categorizations can be simplistic. There are no hard and fast lines between the possibilities alluded to here, and reality often is more grey than black and white. Nevertheless, the categorizations are useful when trying to come to terms with Canada's progress or lack thereof with regard to children's human rights. In addition, it should be pointed out that the assessments below are those of the editor—not the authors themselves—based on a careful reading of the chapters herein. At times, authors state their conclusions about the possible stages and children's status very directly, so categorizing the analysis into one of the possibilities above is fairly straightforward; at other times, authors are not as direct, in which case more responsibility for the classification falls on the editor. In what follows, authors' conclusions about their respective policy and practice area are situated within the three possibilities or classifications alluded to above.

Education. The assessment of policy and practice areas began with education. The reason for this is that no area is more important than education if progress toward the children's rights stage (stage 3) is to be achieved. Rights-respecting education has the power to engage and animate children's agency and participation, and is inextricably interconnected with the fundamental principle of participation (Article 12) in the Convention, a principle that marks the transition to the children's rights stage. Given the importance of education, Katherine Covell's conclusions in Chapter 2 should be real cause for concern. Covell highlights Article 29, which focuses on the aims of education, and the development of the whole child as articulated in the UNCRC. In a thorough and in-depth analysis of curricula, pedagogical methods, and the school environment, Covell's conclusions are sobering: "At this time, curricula are not infused with rights, pedagogy is non-democratic with little (if any) allowance for participation, and school cultures do not embrace and reflect the rights of the child. Current practices across jurisdictions do not recognize the child as a contemporaneous citizen" (Covell's Chapter 2).

Far from reaching the stage where children are understood to be and treated as independent bearers of rights, Covell identifies policies and practices in education where the state continues to act like an "authoritarian parent," exemplifying "lingering concepts of children as parental property." At the same time, she argues that the "disregard for student participation, together with the orientation toward preparing children for future (adult) citizenship, may also be seen as indicators of beliefs in children as not-yets." Ultimately, Covell concludes that "current education is best described as transitioning from understanding children as parental property to not-yets." The analysis of education, then, falls into the lowest classification of the range of scenarios identified previously—the author suggests that the area falls somewhere between stage 1 and stage 2, with evidence that children are to some extent still being conceptualized and treated as property. It is particularly revealing, ironic, and indeed somewhat disturbing that education falls into the same classification that would apply to Joan Durrant's analysis of corporal punishment (Chapter 9) when discussing the status of children in law.

The education of adults is important as well in terms of developing a children's rights consciousness, and fulfilling the Article 42 requirement to make the Convention's principles and articles known to children and adults alike. Parenting education programs have a central role to play in this regard. Unfortunately, as noted by R. Brian Howe in Chapter 3, current programs in Canada have failed to spread awareness about the rights of the child. While such programs have grown in number, and have real potential to advance the rights and best interests of children, they largely disregard the Convention and ignore the rights of the child. In particular, participation rights—so associated with stage 3—are rarely incorporated into such programs. Aside from one exception identified by Howe—the Positive Discipline in Everyday Parenting program, where parents learn that "children are persons with rights in the here and now, not possessions or objects to be moulded"—most programs do not explain the benefits of child participation, or the parenting approaches consistent with it.

Howe situates the historical development of parenting programs, and the current situation, within the context of the evolving the status children. His conclusions in this regard are clear. Parenting education programs, like other government-sponsored protective and support programs for children and families, did not emerge during stage 1 (social laissez-faire) because children were seen as the property and responsibility of their parents. Only during stage 2 (paternalistic protection), when children came to be seen as vulnerable and in need of protection, did governments begin to provide such supports. With the advent of stage 3 (children's rights) and another elevation in the status of children as rights bearers, parenting education programs would be expected to evolve as well. This has not happened. Howe concludes:

"Although children have the official status of persons with rights, this goes unrecognized in programs of parenting education. Governments and those responsible for designing and administering programs continue to see children as objects of welfare, to be given a helping hand when there is a need and when resources permit. They fail to appreciate that children are entitled to the best possible conditions for their development not out of compassion or charity but out of their status as persons with rights" (Howe's Chapter 3).

For our purposes here—in terms of the classification of authors' conclusions—it is safe to say that parenting education in Canada is firmly embedded within stage 2 (paternalistic protectionism) of the framework.

Health Care. With regard to health care policy and practice, Cheryl van Daalen-Smith, Brenda LeFrançois, and Devon MacPherson-Mayor provide a wide-ranging assessment of the field that includes the interrogation of policies, associations, law (consent), and practices (that relate, for example, to nurses and pediatricians). Given the importance of participation rights (Article 12)—and children's ability to exercise those rights in practice—to the achievement of stage 3 (children's rights stage) in the framework, it is particularly helpful that the authors pay significant attention to the role that children play in decision making related to their health care, and the degree to which children are involved in treatment decisions. Aware of the exacting standard of participation embedded in the UNCRC, the authors address whether or not health care in Canada moves beyond "a mere protectionist status, where outdated and adultist lenses, coupled with paternalistic approaches, deny young persons their capacity and voice."

Their analysis is complex in the sense that the authors chronicle a good deal of evidence that suggests promising policies in line with UNCRC dictates, but they probe deeper to find ambiguous practices, particularly as these relate to children's real experiences on the ground. For example, as the authors note, "the provision, protection, and especially ... the *participation* rights afforded to Canadian children in the UNCRC *fit* with the various codes of ethics of all the health professionals who work with children in Canada's health care systems." There are references to the need to respect rights and dignity and at times, on the issue of consent, there are no distinctions regarding age (Code of Ethics for Canada's Psychologists). But in practice, as the authors point out, there "remains widespread confusion surrounding young people's right to consent," and often this leads to ambiguity in practice. Other factors impeding children's full participation come into play as well, including adultist assumptions about children being "inherently incompetent or incapable of making an informed, rational decision"; and at times a paternalistic approach in practice overrides children's participation on the ground, especially with regard to high-stakes decisions. Of the additional factors that authors discuss—for example, a lack of awareness of rights, and a lack of consistency in policies across the country—one is emphasized: "Who the Young Person Is Matters." Marginalized children can experience the health care system in a way that undermines their ability to participate:

> Although white abled-bodied middle-class children may find it difficult to be taken seriously and have their rights to informed consent to treatment realized in practice, this situation is much more tenuous for children who are further marginalized by their status as racialized, Indigenous, queer-identified, poor, in care, or being seen as physically, intellectually, or psychiatrically disabled. In short, who the young person is matters when it comes to the closing down of possibilities for participatory practice in health care situations. And who the young person is matters in terms of who practitioners tend to regard as worthy of being accorded their rights.

The authors conclude that to date, Canada's efforts have been a "piecemeal approach of good intentions" that are insufficient. It continues to be the case that when "young people interact with Canadian health care, a status of protectionist paternalism remains the default." In terms of classifying authors' conclusions, then, health care falls into stage 2 of the framework (paternalistic protection), perhaps with the caveat that policies and principles often project beyond the reality on the ground.

Youth Justice. As noted previously, the UNCRC has been incorporated into legislation governing the field of youth justice, through the preamble of the *Youth Criminal Justice Act* (YCJA). Earlier legislation was viewed as too punitive, and in this context, there was hope that the UNCRC's guiding principles and relevant articles would transform the nature of youth justice in Canada. Moore makes the case that a "rights-based restorative justice" approach to youth justice would be consistent with international law, but that despite the promise of such an approach and Canada's reputation as a leader in this regard, it "remains a challenge to move principles of child rights into practice in adultist systems" that "often abandon an appreciation of the citizenship, the innate dignity, and the increased vulnerability to risk of young offenders in favour of legitimizing power relations in paternalistic, hierarchical systems."

UNCRC Articles 37 and 40 serve as the backdrop for Moore's analysis by highlighting the standards that should guide juvenile justice policy-makers and practitioners. Article 37 highlights the conditions under which young people can be deprived of liberty, and Article 40 focuses on the need to avoid deprivation of liberty and emphasizes that young people are to be treated in a manner consistent with dignity and worth. While the Ashley Smith case represents an egregious failure to abide by these provisions, Moore's larger point is that retributive approaches to youth justice are not consistent with children's rights. As she notes, the retributive justice system was inherited from Europeans during colonization in the 17th and 18th centuries, and while Indigenous justice systems continued to exist informally in Indigenous communities, Canada's dominant approach to justice was based on retribution and punishment. Defining characteristics of this system include children being "isolated from community and context as they are taken into custody, an act that places in jeopardy the full range of needs and rights of young people at the very moment they are the most vulnerable ... with respect to power relations within adultist institutions." Importantly, Moore adds that conceptualizations of young people condition responses in policy and practice, and in this regard, the "social construction of youthful offending is frequently described as deviance," often leading to retributive responses focused on social control. Combined with the legacy of colonialism, the dislocation of communities, associated discrimination (for example, racism), and the "institutionalization of inequity that has perpetuated the silencing of minority voices," the result is the marginalization of particular youth—for example, Indigenous and black youth are seriously overrepresented in the youth justice system.

In contrast, rights-based restorative justice practices "encourage the voices of victims, offenders, and young people to be heard in socially just sorts of ways through non-discriminatory, safe, authentic, and complete participation." The aim is to move away from a focus on isolated behaviours and deviance toward "understanding risk as the critical edge of potential," in order to facilitate the creation of "safety nets to support young people in conflict with the law to stay accountable and engaged in community." In this regard, Moore observes, "Such a construction of youthful offending behaviours would reflect an understanding of young people as rights bearers and full citizens responding to their unique social worlds, which may include experiences of structural and social injustice manifest in multiple nodes of inequities and violence. In this context, a rights-based approach to youth justice may aim to teach community (hooks, 2003); creating the opportunity for young people to have their dignity respected and, in turn, young people may gain tools to be increasingly accountable for the human rights of others" (Moore's Chapter 5).

The positive news in terms of evaluating Canada's record is that the basic principles of restorative justice are found within youth justice legislation

(YCJA), and there has been "an expansion of restorative justice community-based programming." In this regard, the legal mandate and potential is there to "support the integration of the UNCRC and ... principles of restorative justice into systems impacting young people." But according to Moore, this potential "remains largely unrealized." Canada is "mired in policy and practice at the edge of abeyant action."

In terms of classifying authors' conclusions, then, youth justice also falls into stage 2 of the framework (paternalistic protection). The conclusion in this regard is similar to that arrived at in relation to health care, although one might argue that there is a clearer inclination toward stage 3 (children's rights), given the incorporation of the UNCRC into legislation governing the area, and the expansion of restorative justice programming. But Moore's conclusions about the nature of the dominant "adultism" and paternalism governing the area call into question the "conditions" experienced by youth in the system, with regard to rights consistency (UNCRC) even within the confines of a stage 2 assessment; moreover, these "conditions" also affect children's agency and undermine the ability to participate. Ultimately, Moore's conclusions ("abeyant" action and "unrealized" potential) speak to a lack of sufficient progress in the area, particularly as this relates to Indigenous and other marginalized youth, and notably with regard to a lack of "participation." For this reason, a stage 2 categorization is warranted until there is a more substantial realization of the apparent "promise" associated with legislation and restorative justice programming.

Child Welfare. Thomas Waldock employs a UNCRC framework to assess Canada's record in the area of child welfare (Chapter 6), with a particular focus on whether or not the dignity and integrity of marginalized children requiring the care and support of child welfare have been respected. After discussing a central challenge for child welfare in Canada related to discrimination (Article 2) and marginalized children—with a focus on Indigenous children—Waldock turns to three relevant subject matters: (1) the existing paradigm of social work practice in the field (Anglo-American); (2) child welfare systems of care and the quality of caregiving in the field; and (3) the extent to which child welfare has incorporated participation rights. The third, of course, is particularly important in assessing the status of children, since the ability to participate is indicative of status and recognition as rights-bearing citizens (stage 3 in Howe and Covell's template of analysis).

Historically, child welfare has always interacted with marginalized children and families. Issues related to poverty, housing conditions, food insecurity, to name a few, have plagued such children and families throughout Canada's history. Waldock notes that Canada has a long way to go in terms of instituting proactive, preventative family policies, a requirement under the UNCRC. But the situation with regard to particular groups of marginalized children stands out. With regard to Indigenous children and families, child welfare has been part of the problem. Paternalistic approaches associated with the dominant paradigm of practice, and discriminatory, racist practices, have led to the serious overrepresentation of Indigenous children in care. This is an ongoing challenge for child welfare.

Waldock argues that the existing paradigm of child welfare practice (Anglo-American), which "flows out" of a "child-saving" past, does not accord with the UNCRC framework that he identifies. Among other characteristics, the existing model is punitive, reactive, and paternalistic. He identifies a family service model with a children's rights focus as most in line with the Convention; at present, Canada is not close to having such a model in any jurisdiction. With regard to systems of care, Waldock's criticisms are direct: these systems have been in crisis for decades; there have been only minimal efforts to reform them, nothing close to what is required; and Canada is not meeting its requirements to provide quality care that would promote the recovery and reintegration of children in care. Lastly, Waldock points out that some tangible progress is evident in the area of participation rights for children in care. While the UNCRC itself is incorporated in only a few jurisdictions, some form of participation rights is included in most jurisdictions across the country. And child advocates, who often operate on UNCRC principles, have provided productive support to children in terms of enhancing their voice. At the same time, real challenges continue to exist in terms of providing what Waldock calls "embedded advocacy"—support to marginalized children in their day-to-day lives.

Overall, in terms of classifying authors' conclusions, then, child welfare is an area that is in need of serious reform. At present, it falls into stage 2 of the framework (paternalistic protection), and with regard to its role in the further marginalization of particular groups of children, its counterproductive paradigm of practice, and seriously inadequate systems of care, any signs of stage 3 progress seem virtually non-existent. Indeed, in the case of systems of care, once again the conditions of paternalistic protection should be called into question as not rights-consistent (UNCRC), and these also affect agency and undermine the ability to participate. Incorporation of the UNCRC in a few jurisdictions, and some progress in the area of participation rights, signifies some movement in the direction of children being regarded as right bearers and is helpful in terms of addressing the marginalization of children requiring the care and support of child welfare, but in the final analysis, Waldock calls such progress a "glimmer of light on the horizon in the Canadian context."

Marginalized Groups of Children

When considering limited progress and ongoing challenges, we would be remiss not to include and single out particularly marginalized children. These children experience the world as "lesser-thans." This bears keeping in mind when we consider the general evolution of conceptualizations of children from being viewed as objects or property, as sacred trusts and "not-yets" under the authority of adults and the state, and increasingly as subjects and bearers of rights. In relation to all of these classifications and at every stage, particularly marginalized children's status has been lived and experienced as "lesser than" the general population. For example, historically it was one thing to be viewed as property, and quite another to be seen as property to be used or abused (Waldock, 2012). These are related but distinguishable conceptualizations of children, and in the real world, some children experience the difference.

While authors have focused on or referenced some of these groups—for example, children with disabilities (Grover's Chapter 10), minority children (cultural, ethnic, or racial), and LGBTQ+ community members—two groups are singled out in the book. The first group is Indigenous children, and beyond Chapter 11 by Blokhuis and Smoke, they figure prominently throughout the book in many of the chapters. In part this is sad commentary due to the history of colonialism and the related, contemporary situation of many Indigenous children and families; for example, areas like child welfare and youth justice simply couldn't be discussed without recognizing the experience of Indigenous youth. But at the same time, identifying this experience, and attempting to account for it, is a necessary step to a better future. In the aftermath of the Truth and Reconciliation Commission (2015), it is particularly appropriate to highlight the experience of Indigenous children when considering the status of children in Canada today.

The second group to be singled out is refugee children, given the global refugee crisis and the growing concerns today about the situation of these marginalized children in Canada and around the world. Against the backdrop of UNCRC requirements regarding refugee children, Myriam Denov and Maya Fennig provide an in-depth overview of the realities of war-affected refugee children in Canada (Denov and Fennig's Chapter 7). While the Syrian refugees have received the most attention in the media and elsewhere, these authors point out that armed conflict is affecting the lives of children and families around the world; in a sobering observation, they note that the "increase in armed conflict in countries like Syria, Democratic Republic of the Congo, Iraq, South Sudan, and Afghanistan represents the highest level of human suffering since World War Two." Since the effects of exposure to armed conflict on children and families have been well documented—it "ruptures healthy child development, causes injury, illness, severs familial and social networks, and breaks down the structures that provide preventive, curative, and ameliorative care"—and the process of resettlement comes with additional psychosocial challenges and post-migration stressors related to mental health and well-being, the question of whether or not Canada is fulfilling its obligations to these children and families is important. As the authors note, the numbers are significant; each year, Canada receives between 25,000 and 35,000 refugees, and between 2015 and 2016, due to the resettlement of Syrian refugees throughout 2016, there was a 133 percent increase (62,000 refugees).

In terms of Canada's obligations, Denov and Fennig focus on Article 38(4) and Article 39 of the United Nations Convention on the Rights of the Child (UNCRC). Article 38(4) includes the requirement that states "take all feasible measures to ensure protection and care of children who are affected by an armed conflict." In relation to the postwar and resettlement context, Article 39 requires states to "take all appropriate measures to promote physical and psychological recovery and social reintegration" of children victimized in armed conflicts, in environments that foster "the health, self-respect and dignity of the child." The authors examine Canada's response to war-affected refugee children with a focus on unaccompanied refugee minors, children in detention, family reunification responses, and refugee children's access to education and health services, and they ultimately conclude that Canada's commitment to refugee children falls short of international obligations.

Denov and Fennig's analysis is comprehensive in detailing the challenges that need to be addressed, among them the lack of a cohesive *federal* policy concerning the protection of refugees, the fact that there are considerable inconsistencies in terms of the services available to unaccompanied children across the country, family reunification policies not in accordance with children's rights to family (Article 9)—and the prevention of separation and preservation of family unity—and difficulties accessing services, like health care and education. But the detention of migrants stands out as a particularly egregious violation of Canada's obligations. As the authors note, every year thousands of migrants are placed in detention (7,300 in 2013), and a "third of these individuals were put in provincial jails, alongside inmates facing criminal charges or serving sentences." This practice is not in the best interest of children—research shows that it can cause psychological harm—and it violates international law. Moreover, the United Nations Committee on the Rights of the Child "has repeatedly admonished and chastised Canada for its practice of child detention."

Important in terms of identifying the classification of these authors' observations and conclusions within the framework of assessment (status), and also in understanding the particular nature of the marginalization experienced, there is an emphasis on honouring and promoting children's voices and perspectives. Denov and Fennig are conscious of "dominant attitudes and assumptions concerning children's agency and competence," and the extent to which adults and other authority figures minimize children's capacities to understand and express themselves; according to the authors, this is especially pronounced in the case of children affected by armed conflict because they are "presumed to be too vulnerable, traumatized, naive, unknowledgeable, and irrational to contribute to decision-making processes." Denov and Fennig conclude that "much work lies ahead to ensure the treatment and status of this population as rights bearers and full citizens." "An analysis of Canada's responses ... shows that Canada falls short. Not only are there instances of a failure to protect, and a neglect of the best interest of the child (as seen in relation to detention), but also there are few instances and spaces where refugee children have the ability to participate in key decision making, and where refugee children's agency, competence, and voice can be clearly articulated."

In terms of classifying authors' conclusions, then, commitments in this area fall predominantly into stage 2 of the framework (paternalistic protection), with some evidence of stage 1—for example, treating children as the objects of control through the practice of detention. Moreover, the authors cite "a failure to protect" (for example, detention), calling into question the level of adherence to children's protection rights. And it is clear that some policies and practices in the area contribute to the further marginalization of these children. At any rate, recognition of agency and participation rights is notably absent, with no real evidence that these children are being regarded as rights-bearing citizens, characteristic of stage 3 progress.

A PATHWAY TO STATUS AND RECOGNITION

The previous overview of limited progress and ongoing challenges related to four areas: (1) the status of the UNCRC in Canadian law; (2) coordination and monitoring; (3) policies and practices; and (4) marginalized groups of children. The overview confirms that Canada has a good deal of work to do in terms of meeting UNCRC requirements and treating children as rights-bearing citizens. There is simply not enough evidence to suggest that Canada is close to achieving stage 3 (children's rights stage) of the Howe and Covell framework. Certainly, positive signs in this regard are apparent—related to the four areas above—but limited and sporadic signs are not enough to support a conclusion that substantial progress associated with stage 3 is evident. As we have seen, despite some variation that suggests a classification of either somewhere between stage 1 and 2, or stage 2 with some minimal indications of stage 3, stage 2 (paternalistic protection) is the default position to date and paternalistic conceptions of children continue to dominate in the Canadian context.

Given this conclusion, a question arises: What are the prospects for the future? In one sense, when we consider that in not much more than a century—on a global scale—children have gone from being viewed as objects or property to "not-yets" in need of paternalistic protection, to now being considered as subjects and bearers of rights, there seems every reason to be optimistic about the future. Perhaps patience is a virtue in this regard, and the direction of historical currents regarding children's human rights is clear (Waldock's Chapter 1)—that it is just a matter of (more) time. Of course, nothing should be taken for granted, particularly today, when the current geopolitical context is to some extent relegating human rights to the sidelines (Goldberg, 2017). The aforementioned question, then, demands a more concrete answer. One approach might be to consider whether or not there is a discernible and tangible pathway to status and recognition for children as rights bearers and full citizens. The nature of the road or pathway ahead might be clear enough in the sense that the challenges outlined by the authors in this book need to be addressed, and Canada needs to fulfill its children's rights obligations. But is there an impetus for change, a kind of driving force capable of nudging us forward on the pathway?

Today, is it possible that there are clearer indications that children's participation itself—children's voices aided and supported by advocates seeking to amplify their volume and effect—is pushing the envelope of paternalism and giving more hope that stage 3 is on the horizon, even if the prospects in Canada look better over the long haul? After all, historically the UNCRC itself was an important achievement in the evolution of views of children and childhood precisely because it incorporated children's agency and their rights to participation. Could it be that the impetus for change, the driving force for progress on the path ahead, might come through children's participation itself? The image suggested here is one of gradual, incremental advancement, built on a progress-reinforcing dynamic between increasing opportunities to participate and a developing appreciation and capacity for participation among children themselves.

The last section of the book focuses on participation rights for a reason. As conveyed by Jan Hancock in Chapter 12, "Participation Rights of the Child: At the Crossroads of Citizenship," children themselves value participation rights, and the right to express themselves and be listened to is ranked very highly when children consider their rights. With the facilitation of participation rights and the opportunity to participate, children develop "the cognitive and communication skills, abilities, responsibilities, and experiences necessary to make considered decisions, and to participate in society in a constructive manner." Other effects of participation are evident as well, among them the boosting of self-esteem and the building of resilience and character. Given opportunities to participate, and the encouragement of advocacy support, children become engaged and want to make a difference.

The experience of Landon Pearson and Judy Finlay with the Shaking the Movers (STM) workshops (Chapter 14) bears out the positive effects and potential of participation facilitated by advocacy support; throughout their careers, a fundamental commitment of both authors has been to elevate children's voice and facilitate meaningful participation. As Pearson and Finlay point out, "STM provides a good practice model of meaningful consultative participation embodying the four key dimensions necessary for compliance with Article 12 of the United Nations Convention on the Rights of the Child: space, voice, audience, and influence." They add that it "fully complies with the nine basic requirements of quality participation": Transparent and informative; Relevant to children's lives; Voluntary; Respectful; Child-friendly; Inclusive; Supported by trained adults; Safe and sensitive to risk; and Accountable. As such, STM "provides an exemplar to others of how to construct participatory spaces for children," and it allows for the voices of children to be heard directly.

There is no question that translating this into practice on a larger scale comes with challenges, particularly in a context where paternalistic protection (stage 2) is the default position. These challenges have been chronicled throughout the chapters in the book. As Hancock concludes (Chapter 12), directly in relation to participation rights and the Canadian landscape, the paternalistic paradigm continues to dominate, and the "achievement of the children's rights stage remains elusive." At this point, that dominance must be conceded. But in terms of the argument being made here, incremental advancement requires only some progress and some signs of increasing opportunities for participation. In this regard, Hancock's observations mirror those found in many of the other chapters in the book, where some progress at times is acknowledged with respect to stage 3 and participation rights.

But perhaps the most revealing evidence relates to outcomes and success stories when children's participation is facilitated and opportunities to participate are increased; the energy, passion, and strength that can be brought to bear by children and youth themselves through the process of participation is powerful, and they can be difference makers in terms of affecting decision makers. Consider the example of child and youth advocates (CYAs) and their efforts to engage and collaborate with youth. Such advocates have facilitated numerous youth-led initiatives that have had a demonstrable impact on legislators (Hancock's Chapter 12; Hunter's Chapter 13).

Examples of marginalized children exercising their participation rights are particularly inspirational. As pointed out by Hancock (Chapter 12), Indigenous children "played a role in the historic 2016 ruling from the Canadian Human Rights Tribunal," which dealt with the federal government racially discriminating against Indigenous children by underfunding services on reserves compared to funding for similar services elsewhere (Hancock's Chapter 12; Waldock's Chapter 6). In this case, the federal government opposed children's participation in the hearings and even attempted to prevent the broadcast of proceedings. As explained by Hancock (chapter 12), the Federal Court allowed the broadcasts on the grounds that "receiving knowledge of events is a requisite for children to form their own opinions and to participate meaningfully in those proceedings." Children then organized the I Am a Witness online campaign, which offered a forum for children to express their views regarding the hearings. Hancock aptly observes, "Refuting the misconception that children lack any interest in politics, children attended the hearing in such numbers that proceedings had to relocate to the Supreme Court of Canada courthouse."

Hancock provides other examples as well, including the case of Shannen Koostachin from the Attawapiskat Cree Nation, who led thousands of children in successfully advocating for a new school in the community.

These and other examples provide reason for optimism. Increased opportunities for and facilitation of participation, combined with a developing appreciation and capacity for participation among children themselves, might provide the impetus for a gradual, incremental advancement toward the children's rights stage and the full realization of children's status as rights-bearing citizens. But this will take time; it is a long journey on the pathway to stage 3 from where we are today, still largely mired in a paternalistic protection paradigm. Yet what the above examples provide is an answer to the question asked earlier; children's participation itself—children's voices aided and supported by advocates seeking to amplify their volume and effect—is indeed pushing the envelope of paternalism and giving more hope that stage 3 is on the horizon. Children's activism—the exercise of their participation rights—puts children's agency on full display, and provides examples for children and adults alike that are hard to reconcile with conceptions of children as objects or incomplete beings.

Ultimately, however, sufficient momentum on the pathway to stage 3 will require overcoming some of the challenges identified by authors throughout this book, and two areas stand out if Canada is to move forward. The area of education needs to be prioritized. Education has the potential to develop a children's rights consciousness, and a cultural shift in conceptions of children is much more likely with progress in this area. To date, efforts here have been inadequate. In addition, Canada must abolish corporal punishment. This practice, and the law supporting it—still mired to a large degree in stage 1 of the framework—sets up children for vulnerability by highlighting and projecting a counterproductive image of children as property; as long as this practice continues, it is hard to imagine much progress on the road to conceptualizing children as full citizens and independent bearers of rights.

At the same time, there are also reasons for optimism. Views of children have evolved in the past, and images of children as objects or property are no longer dominant. Today, there are some signs that the transition from the dominant conception of children as incomplete adults ("not-yets") to a view of children as rights-bearing citizens already is under way in Canada, and evidence in this regard also can be found in some of the chapters herein. As discussed in Chapter 1, on a global scale children's rights have a rich history, situated within the history of human rights generally. A greater level of commitment will be required if Canada is going to help children take their rightful place in the human rights story that is still being written.

REFERENCES

Birdsell, M., & Chan, E. (2017). *Application of the UNCRC in Canadian law—children's participation in justice processes: Finding the best way forward*. Retrieved from http://findingthebestwaysforward.com/Materials/4B%20PPt%20 CRC%20and%20Charter%20-%20Birdsell%20Chan.pdf

Goldberg, M. L. (2017, December 20). The well respected UN High Commissioner for Human Rights is leaving because his job has become impossible. *UN dispatch: United Nations news and commentary (global news—forum)*. Retrieved from https://www.undispatch.com/well-respected-un-high-commissioner -human-rights-resigning-job-become-impossible/

Howe, R. B., & Covell, K. (Eds.). (2007). *Children's rights in Canada: A question of commitment*. Waterloo, ON: Wilfrid Laurier University Press.

Truth and Reconciliation Commission of Canada (TRCC). (2015). *Honouring the truth, reconciling for the future: Summary of the final report of the Truth and Reconciliation Commission of Canada*. Retrieved from http://www.trc.ca/web sites/trcinstitution/File/2015/Findings/Exec_Summary_2015_05_31_web_o.pdf

Waldock, T. (2012). Apologize ... for goodness sake: Canada's "home children" and our history of discrimination against marginalized children. *Relational Child and Youth Care Practice, 25*(2), 69–75.

About the Contributors

J.C. BLOKHUIS (Renison University College, University of Waterloo—Social Development Studies) holds a Ph.D. from the University of Rochester and a J.D. from the University of Ottawa. He is an Associate Professor in Social Development Studies at Renison University College, University of Waterloo, and a former Kluge Fellow at the Library of Congress. He is lead author of *Education Law*, 6th ed. (Routledge, 2020), and co-author, with Katherine Covell and R. Brian Howe, of *The Challenge of Children's Rights for Canada*, 2nd ed. (Wilfrid Laurier University Press, 2018).

KATHERINE COVELL (Cape Breton University—Psychology) is a Professor Emerita and a former Executive Director of the Children's Rights Centre, Cape Breton University. She has developed teaching resources and has published widely, including six books, on children's rights. As an advocate she has worked with the Canadian Coalition for the Rights of Children, UNICEF, Save the Children, and the Canadian Government. Covell was the lead researcher for North America for the UN Global Study on Violence Against Children in 2005. From 2007 to 2014 she represented North America on the International NGO Council on Violence against Children.

MYRIAM DENOV (McGill University—Social Work) is a Full Professor at McGill University and holds the Canada Research Chair in Youth, Gender and Armed Conflict. Her research focuses on children and families affected by war and migration. She is the author of *Child Soldiers* (Cambridge University Press) and co-editor of *Children Affected by Armed Conflict: Theory, Method & Practice* (Columbia University Press). Denov is a Trudeau Fellow and member of the College of the Royal Society of Canada. She holds a Ph.D. from the University of Cambridge, where she was a Commonwealth Scholar.

JOAN DURRANT (University of Manitoba—Community Health Sciences) is a Child-Clinical Psychologist and Full Professor of Community Health Sciences at the University of Manitoba. Her research focuses on physical punishment of children in Canada and worldwide. She co-authored the Canadian *Joint Statement on Physical Punishment of Children and Youth* and was a member of the Research Advisory Group to the *United Nations Secretary-General's Study on Violence against Children*. She is the creator of the program *Positive Discipline in Everyday Parenting*, which is being delivered in many countries around the world.

MAYA FENNIG (McGill University, Ph.D. candidate—Social Work) locates her research interests at the intersections of social work, psychiatry, and ethnography. Her dissertation research explores how culture and context shape the way Eritrean refugees living in Israel express, experience, and make sense of psychological distress. She is a recipient of the Vanier Canada Graduate Scholarship.

JUDY FINLAY (Ryerson University—Child and Youth Care) is an Associate Professor and the Graduate Program Director in the School of Child and Youth Care at Ryerson University. Her areas of research include the Cross-over Youth Project and the Mamow ki ken da ma win: Searching Together Project. As Ontario's Chief Advocate (1991–2007), Judy was the longest-standing Child Advocate in Canada. Judy has worked for more than three decades in the development of children's rights agendas, youth capacity building, and leadership across Canada and internationally in Turkey, Mexico, Japan, Jamaica, Guatemala, and Sierra Leone.

SONJA C. GROVER (Lakehead University—Faculty of Education) is a Full Professor in the Faculty of Education, Lakehead University, and an Associate Editor of the *International Journal of Human Rights*. Her research area is international law generally with a focus on children's fundamental human rights. She has published extensively in her field. She is a co-investigator on the SSHRC project The International and Canadian Child Rights Partnership and is the editor of *Peremptory International Legal Norms and the Democratic Rule of Law* (Routledge).

JAN HANCOCK (Cape Breton University—Political Science) is an Assistant Professor in Public Administration in the Department of L'nu, Political and Social Studies at Cape Breton University. Prior to joining the department he held lectureships at Birkbeck College, London, and Manchester University in the UK. He was awarded a Hallsworth Research Fellowship to study human rights at Manchester University, 2004–2007. His research focus is in rights. He has published several books, including *Environmental Human Rights* (Ashgate) and *Human Rights and US Foreign Policy* (Routledge).

About the Contributors

R. BRIAN HOWE (Cape Breton University—Political Science) is a Professor Emeritus at Cape Breton University and author of numerous books and articles on children's rights. His books include *Empowering Children* and *The Challenge of Children's Rights for Canada*. The latter was selected for two national awards and *Empowering Children* received an award by the Canadian Education Association for work in citizenship education. He was also the co-recipient of a children's rights award by the Canadian Coalition for the Rights of Children. His current research is on populism as a threat to children's rights.

M. THERESA HUNTER (University of Victoria, Ph.D.—Public Administration) is a consultant in Victoria, British Columbia. She has worked with young children and families in child welfare and child daycare settings in Canada and the United States, has undertaken research and teaching at the University of Victoria, has conducted evaluation, training, and policy analysis for public sector and community organizations, has coordinated academic and health care research ethics boards, and has provided administrative coordination and research services for the Canadian Consortium of Universities for Evaluation Education.

BRENDA LEFRANÇOIS (Memorial University of Newfoundland—Social Work) is a Full Professor at Memorial University of Newfoundland. Her doctoral research was on the topic of children's rights and power relations within child and adolescent mental health services. Her current teaching, scholarship, and activism focus on children's psychiatrization, sanism, and anti-sanist praxis from the perspectives of mad studies, the sociology of childhood, and critical children's rights. She has edited and authored many books, special volumes, and journal articles on these issues. Her most notable contributions appear in the anthology *Mad Matters* and in the edited volumes *Children & Society* and *Intersectionalities*.

DEVON MACPHERSON-MAYOR (York University—Critical Disability Studies) has a master of arts degree in Critical Disability Studies from York University and currently works as a non-profit copywriter.

SHANNON A. MOORE (Brock University—Child and Youth Studies) is an Associate Professor in the Department of Child & Youth Studies and holds a Ph.D. in Counselling Psychology. Her approach to scholarship, teaching, and professional practice is shaped by transdisciplinarity and critical pedagogy. Moore's research focuses on the intersection of transdisciplinary, restorative justice, human rights, and mental health in practice with children, young people, and communities. Registered since 2000 with the Canadian Counselling and Psychotherapy Association, she has practised within educational, social service, mental health, and correctional service contexts in Canada and the UK.

LANDON PEARSON OC (Carleton University—Landon Pearson Resource Centre for the Study of Childhood and Children's Rights) is a long-time advocate for the rights and well-being of children. Throughout her career, whether working with or on behalf of children at home and abroad, serving on various councils and commissions or in her role as a Canadian senator responsible for children, Pearson has been an outspoken champion for children. Upon her retirement from the Senate in 2005 she was invited by Carleton University to establish a centre to ensure that her years of work and her passion for children's rights would continue to inspire others to carry her vision forward.

AMY SMOKE (Wilfrid Laurier University, M.S.W.) is Mohawk Nation, Turtle Clan, from the Six Nations of the Grand River. They are two-spirit, a single parent, a public speaker, a singer, and a community member. They have recently graduated from Wilfrid Laurier University with a Master of Social Work—Indigenous Field of Study. They share their story of overcoming intergenerational trauma, drug addiction, homelessness, and domestic violence. They advocate for urban First Nations, Métis, and Inuit folks, and work continually to decolonize spaces.

CHERYL VAN DAALEN-SMITH (York University—Nursing) is a critical feminist nurse who is an Associate Professor in the School of Nursing at York University in Toronto, with cross appointments to the Children's Studies Program in the Department of Humanities and to The School of Gender, Sexuality and Women's Studies. Her areas of specialization include children's rights to health and quality of life, women's health, girls' and women's anger, and women's lived experiences of psychiatric hospitalization and electroshock. She recently completed a film documenting women's experiences of psychiatric hospitalization in Canada (www.yorku.ca/indiff).

THOMAS WALDOCK (Nipissing University—Child and Family Studies) is a Full Professor of Child and Family Studies at Nipissing University. His recent research relates the UN Convention on the Rights of the Child to the child welfare field, with a focus on child welfare paradigms that characterize different child welfare systems. His numerous publications in social work and child- and youth-care journals have examined the connection between caregiver competency and the provision of quality care to marginalized children. Waldock also has authored legal case reports on the status of caregiving and governmental liability for marginalized children in care.

Index

Abella, Rosalie, 173–74, 174–75
Aboriginal Head Start, 43, 44, 45, 47, 250
Aboriginal Peoples Television Network (APTN), 251
abortion: *Cherry* case, 214; unborn as property, 213–14
absenteeism, 23; monitoring of attendance, 27
abuse and neglect: Canadian Incidence Study of Reported Child Abuse and Neglect, 197–98; child welfare system, 122; correlation to denial of rights, 107–8; vs discipline, 189; emotional abuse, 253; home visitation programs, 46; intergenerational aspects of, 120; protection from, 5, 9; reasonable force, 193–94
A. B. v. Bragg Communications, 174–75
A Canada Fit for Children, 268
access to information, 20, 243
A. C. v. Manitoba, 173–74, 229
addiction services, as parental support, 36
adolescent children, 254
adultism, 57; developmentalist assumptions, 73
adults: children's rights awareness, 307–9, 324–25; communication processes with children, 241; rights to protection, 194–95
advocacy. *See* child and youth advocates (CYA)
ageist bias, capacity/incapacity in best interest models, 75
agency: and activism, 335; awareness of rights, 302–3; of marginalized groups, 76–77; recognition of, 322, 332, 333; right of, 205
age of consent, 58–59; age-based consent practices, 56, 79; capacity as relational process, 67, 71–73; Consent and Capacity Review Board (CCRB), 228, 259–60; evolving capacity, 4, 56–57, 75; law, and decision-making capacity, 59–60; mature minor principle, 59, 229, 259; maturity vs chronological age, 5, 58–59, 173–75, 242–43; presumed capacity to consent, 59; presumed competence, 79, 80; traditional medicine vs Western medical treatment, 223–24. *See also* consent to care
age of majority, 58, 72; diminished moral culpability, 173
Alberta: *Child and Youth Advocate Act*, 271; child and youth advocates (CYA), 269; Children's Guardian, 271; *Child Welfare Act*, 271; corporal punishment, 200n13; health care decision making, 67; law, and decision-making capacity, 59; Office of the Child and Youth Advocate, 271, 280; Office of the Child and Youth Advocate's Youth Advisory Panel, 279; Office of the Children's Advocate, 271; youth advisory groups, 245, 246
Anglo-American child welfare model, 117, 118–19, 329
Annie E. Casey Foundation, 279
Arbour, Louise, 170–71, 192, 196
Arneson, Richard, 226
Article 1 (UNCRC): rights of children under 18, 215
Article 2 (UNCRC): non-discrimination, 5, 21, 109–10, 328–29; without discrimination, 89
Article 3 (UNCRC): best interests of the child, 5, 37, 89, 170, 188; child welfare, 109, 111, 117
Article 4 (UNCRC): incorporation of UNCRC into domestic law, 5–8, 317–19

Article 5 (UNCRC): parents obligation, 36, 243
Article 6 (UNCRC): right to life, 227–28; survival and development, 5, 89, 111–12
Article 7 (UNCRC): parental care, 111
Article 9 (UNCRC): separation from parents, 111, 140, 243, 331
Article 12 (UNCRC), 325–26; age, and maturity, 257, 258; participation rights, 5, 79, 89, 109, 112–13, 253, 334; right of expression, 19–20, 40, 56, 78, 111; right to be heard, 243, 247
Article 13 (UNCRC): and education rights, 26; freedom of expression, 40, 243; right to access and impart information, 20
Article 14 (UNCRC): and education rights, 26, 243; freedom of thought, conscience, and religion, 20, 40, 162, 243
Article 15 (UNCRC): freedom of association and assembly, 20, 243
Article 16 (UNCRC): right to privacy, 243
Article 17 (UNCRC): access to information, 243
Article 18 (UNCRC): best interests of the child as parental concern, 36, 188; child care, 36; government investment in parenting education, 40, 42–43, 253
Article 19 (UNCRC): protection from harm, 40, 112, 117–18, 170, 188
Article 20 (UNCRC): quality alternative placements, 118
Article 23 (UNCRC): children with disabilities, 21, 36, 243; rights of the disabled "eligible child," 217–18
Article 24 (UNCRC): health care decision making, 56; health care education for parents, 36; health education, right to, 21; prenatal/postnatal health care, 36, 41, 206, 214–15; provision of basic needs, 40; right to health care, 142, 228
Article 27 (UNCRC): provision of basic needs, 40; standard of living, 37, 111–12
Article 28 (UNCRC): access to education, 20, 21; guidance counselling, 27; school discipline, 170, 188
Article 29 (UNCRC): aims of education, 28–29, 323–24; development of child's potential, 20–21; education rights compliance, 26; pre-service/in-service training, 23, 30; rights-consistent pedagogy, 21–22
Article 30 (UNCRC): linguistic and cultural rights, 21, 111, 230, 243
Article 31 (UNCRC): cultural and artistic participation, 243
Article 33 (UNCRC): protection from harm, 40
Article 34 (UNCRC): protection from harm, 40
Article 37 (UNCRC): degrading treatment, 170; justice provisions, 89–90, 91, 326–27
Article 38 (UNCRC): war-affected refugees, 133, 134–35, 331
Article 39 (UNCRC): foster care, and alternative placements, 112, 118; postwar resettlement, 133, 135–36, 331
Article 40 (UNCRC): justice provisions, 89, 90, 91, 326–27
Article 42 (UNCRC): awareness of children's rights, 49, 110, 162, 324–25; children's rights education, 20; right to a name, 28
Article 43 (UNCRC): reports on implementation of UNCRC, 162
Assembly of First Nations (AFN), 114; Canadian Human Rights Tribunal 2016 ruling, 250–51
association, freedom of, 20, 243
Attawapiskat Cree Nation, 251, 335
Auckland City Youth Council, 254–55
authoritarian parenting, 253
authoritative parenting, 48, 252–53; government mechanisms for promotion of, 253

Baker v. Canada, 167–68
Bala, Nicholas, 163
basic needs, provision of, 40
Beijing Rules (UN, 1985), 100
Belgium, 317; child welfare legislation, 110; incorporation of UNCRC into domestic law, 5–6
Bellotti v. Baird, 229
Bennett, Carolyn, 115
best interests of the child, 5, 99; and Canadian use of detention, 138–40; and child welfare, 109, 111; consent to care,

233–34, 320; custody disputes, 164–66; described, 37; education rights, 21; health provisions, 56–57; *parens patriae*, 163, 165, 170, 173; parental supports, 36; participation rights, 244; paternalism in health care decision making, 75; and Supreme Court of Canada, 161, 176n1; unaccompanied refugee minors, 175
Bill C-126, 186
Bill C-148, 283
Bill S-206, 187
Binnie, Justice, 191–92, 319
Blackstock, Dr. Cindy, 58, 77, 115
Blackstone, William, *Commentaries on the Laws of England*, 182, 183
black youth, overrepresentation of in juvenile justice system, 94–95, 327
Blais, Pierre, 186
Blokhuis, J. C., 12, 161–78, 317–18, 320; and Amy Smoke, 223–35
born-alive disabled children: legal rights of, 205–6, 215–18; medical negligence claims, 206–8; recognition as legal persons, 218; recovery of legal damages, 219–20; rights of the disabled "eligible child," 217–18; tort paradigm, 208, 215–16; wrongful life lawsuits, 206–8, 209–13
Bovingdon et al. v. Hergott, 319–20; medical negligence claim, 208; wrongful life lawsuit, 209–13
de Bracton, Henry, 182
Bragg Communications, 174–75
Breakey, Dr. Vicky, 224
British Columbia: *Child, Family, and Community Services Act*, 124; Child, Youth and Family Advocate (CYFA), 271–72; child and youth advocates (CYA), 269; Children's Commission, 271; *Community Living Authority Act*, 272; Coroners Service, and child deaths, 271; Deputy Ombudsman for Children and Youth, 271–72; *Family Law Act*, 247; Federation of BC Youth in Care Networks, 280; home-schooling, 19; Indigenous children in care, 114; *Infant's Act*, 57, 67, 259; law, and decision-making capacity, 59; Office for Children and Youth, 271; Plan Your Path workshops, 280; representative for children and youth, 272; *Representative for Children and Youth Act*, 281; restorative justice system, 102; *R. v. Sharpe*, 169; school discipline, 27; social media platforms, 246; *Young v. Young*, 164–65; youth advisory groups, 245, 246
Bulgaria, 180
bullying, 23, 24, 25

Camitta, Bruce, 223
Campbell, Kim, 186
Canada: absence of participation rights policies, 248–50; *A Canada Fit for Children*, 268; child detention, 138–40; child participation mechanisms, 56; child welfare legislation, 117; child welfare system, 109–10, 118–19, 125–26; civic participation, 254–58; commitment to children's rights, 268–69; corporal punishment, legal justification of, 12, 169, 170–71, 181, 182–84; Criminal Code, 75; *Divorce Act*, 249; dualism of, 6, 317; education rights compliance, 23, 24–31; evolutionary stages of development, 8–9; family reunification, 140–42; federal/provincial/territorial jurisdictions, 163; human rights challenges, 181; *Immigration and Refugee Protection Act* (IRPA), 140, 141, 318; Indigenous cultural genocide policy, 91–92; Indigenous incarceration rates, 92–93; integration of restorative justice, 98–102; Interim Federal Health Program (IFHP), 143; international ranking on family supports spending, 45; justice system historical overview, 91–93; juvenile justice, federal/provincial/territorial jurisdictions, 91; juvenile justice system, 87–89; law, and decision-making capacity, 59–60; legislative process, 185–86, 199n4, 200nn5–6; as liberal welfare state, 115–16; National Children's Agenda, 268; national children's commissioner, call for, 267; Office of the Federal Commissioner for Children and Youth, 81; parenting education implementation, 43–49; participation rights, 245–48, 260–62; paternalistic protection stage of, 78, 242, 254, 316, 332, 333;

346 Index

presumed capacity to consent, 59; provincial/territorial jurisdiction on education, 18–19; ratification of UNCRC, 5, 36, 88–89, 273; refugee resettlement, 132–33, 136–42; *Social Union Framework Agreement*, 268; *Young Offenders Act*, 87–88; youth advisory forums, 255–56; *Youth Criminal Justice Act* (YCJA), 87–88, 91, 94–95, 98, 100, 245, 318, 326. *See also* Charter of Rights and Freedoms
Canada Border Services Agency: immigration detention, 137, 138–40, 331
Canada Prenatal Nutrition program, 44
Canada's Pediatric Nurses, 62–63
Canada–US Safe Third Country Agreement, 142
Canadian Association of Occupational Therapists, 73
Canadian Association of Paediatric Nurses, 72
Canadian Association of Pediatric Health Centres (CAPHC): youth health care engagement, 57–58, 79–80
Canadian Association of Social Workers, 72
Canadian Bar Association: five-step best practice process, 248
Canadian Coalition for the Rights of Children (CCRC), 25; *Right in Principle, Right in Practice*, 71–72
Canadian Coalition for the Rights of the Child, 74
Canadian Council of Child and Youth Advocates (CCCYA), 282, 321–22
Canadian Council of Provincial Child and Youth Advocates (CCPCYA), 282, 298
Canadian Council on Children and Youth, 295
Canadian Foundation for Children, Youth, and the Law: child participation in youth criminal justice system, 245; constitutional challenge to section 43, 188–90; spanking, as corporal punishment, 169–71
Canadian Heritage, 245
Canadian Human Rights Tribunal: 2016 ruling on First Nations funding, 250–51; on Indigenous children, 77; underfunding on reserves, 114–15
Canadian Incidence Study of Reported Child Abuse and Neglect, 197–98
Canadian Institute for Child Health, 75; *The Rights of the Child in the Health Care System*, 60–61
Canadian Medical Protective Association (CMPA): consent, and communication issues, 58–59
Canadian Nurses Association: ethical nursing practice, 62
Canadian Paediatric Nursing Standards, 62–63
Canadian Paediatric Society (CPS): age of consent, 72; health care decision making, 63–64
Canadian Physiotherapy Association, 72
Canadian Teachers' Federation, 25
Cancellor, Reginald, 183
Caputo, Virginia, 299
Caring Society, 251
Carnevale, Dr. Franco, 75, 78
Carstairs, Sharon, 186
case advocacy, 297
Centre for Medicine, Ethics and Law, 232
Centre for Professional and Applied Ethics, 232
Centre of Excellence for Youth Engagement, 245
Charron, Louise, 172–73
Charter of Rights and Freedoms, 225; best interests of the child principle, 164–66; and children's rights, 25; education rights, 145; equality rights test cases, 188; health care violations, 143; inclusion of participation rights, lack of, 253–54; spanking, as corporal punishment, 169–71, 172, 188–90; Supreme Court of Canada interpretation, 164, 318; violation of rights, 166–67
Cherry case, 214
Chicago Child–Parent Center program, 42
Child, Family, and Community Services Act (BC), 124
Child, Youth, and Family Services Act (ON), 111, 124
Child Advocacy International, 78
child and youth advocates (CYA), 12, 124–25, 334–35; advocacy initiatives, 297–98; alliances, 277, 278–79; Canadian

Council of Child and Youth Advocates (CCCYA), 282; child welfare system, 122–23, 124; and the UNCRC, 281; enabling legislation, 281, 318; establishment of, 267; functions of, 276–77; gaps in provision of, 283–84; health care decision making, 64–66, 69; as hybrid equalities institutions, 276; as independent statutory officers, 275; individual advocacy, 277; information and advice, provision of, 277, 278; institutional models, 276; involvement of young people, 277, 279–81; legal support, provision of, 277, 279; legislated advocacy functions, 277; legislated mandates, 276–81; national children's advocate, need for, 282–83, 284; origin and evolution of, 269–75; participation rights, 245–47; populations served, 276; rights awareness education, 277, 278; role of in child custody evaluations, 321–22; systemic advocacy, 277–78

child benefits, 45

child care, as parental support, 36

child-centred care, 62–63; vs family-centred care, 74–75, 81

Child-Friendly Health Care Initiative: standards, 78

Child Health UK, 78

childhood: conceptualizations of, 7–8; revision of ideas about, 3

child maltreatment: parenting education, 41–42; protection from, 40

child pornography, 169

children: as agents of decision making, 241; awareness of rights, 302–3, 310; as "blank slates," 2; as citizens in waiting, 256; denial of rights, correlation to abuse, 107–8; evolution of status, 49–50, 336; as incomplete adults, 2; as not-yets, 17, 30, 117, 322–23, 324; as objects of welfare, 50, 107–9; as property, 117, 175, 324; as rights-bearing citizens, 11, 17, 29, 122, 322; vulnerability of, 88, 101–2, 175

Children's Act (Norway), 253

Children's Aid Society (CAS): age of consent, 223, 224; *B. (R.) v. Children's Aid Society of Metropolitan Toronto*, 225; *In Re L. D. K.*, 226

Children's Climate Conference (2015, Sweden), 251

children's rights: awareness of, 49; barriers to, 267, 320–21; Canadian context, 268–69; denial of, 73–77; education on, 20, 261–62; as entitlements, 7–8; evolution of, 1–4; international context, 267–68; international recognition of, 180–81, 199n1; judicial recognition, 175–76; and obligations of parents, 75; *Right in Principle, Right in Practice* (CCRC), 71–72; stages of, 315–16; stages of legal evolution, 8–9; status of in Canadian law, 332–36

Children's Rights in Juvenile Justice (UN, 2007), 100

children's rights stage, 205, 315; Canadian achievement of, 332–36; children as bearers of rights, 179–80; evolution to, 195–97; legal participatory rights, 248; and participation rights, 8, 9, 11, 242

"Children: The Silenced Citizens," 296

children with disabilities, 330; born-alive disabled children, legal rights of, 205–6, 319–20; education rights, 21; government support of parents, 36; parenting education programs, 41; participation rights, 243; personhood and agency of, 205–6

Child Rights Academic Network (CRAN), 293, 311; creation and funding of, 299–300

child rights impact assessments (CRIAs), 283

child welfare models, 115–19

child welfare system, 12, 328–29; access to health care, 123; advocacy support, provision of, 122–23; Anglo-American model, 117, 118–19, 329; *Child, Youth, and Family Services Act* (ON), 111; child-centred approach, 118–19; continuity of care, 120; and UNCRC standards, 109–13; culturally appropriate placements, 120; development of, 9; family service model, 117–18, 121; foster care, and alternative placements, 112, 119–20; inappropriate language in objectification of children, 110–11; Indigenous children, 113–15, 120; kinship care, 119–20; legislation governing,

110, 124; and marginalized children, 107; organizational culture, 114; participation rights, 122–25; paternalistic approach to child interaction, 110–11; paternalistic protection stage of, 329; as provincial/territorial responsibility, 109–10; reform priorities, 119–22, 125–26; shortages of caregivers/homes, 120–21; Sixties Scoop, 113, 117, 118; state approaches to, 109; stigmatization of, 110; systems of care, 119–22; welfare state classifications, 115–16
child welfare: parenting education program evaluations, 46
Chrétien, Jean, 200n7, 296
Citizenship and Immigration Canada, 245
civic participation, 242, 254–58, 335; climate activism, 257–58; electoral reform, 256–57; paternalistic protection stage, 261
CIVIX, student vote school program, 256
Clement, Brian, 224
Collaborating Centre for Aboriginal Public Health, 299
College of Nurses of Ontario, informed consent, 62
Committee on the Rights of the Child (UN), 162, 321–22; absence of participation rights policies, 248–50; awareness of children's rights, 249; best interests of the child, 37; Canadian child participation mechanisms, 56; Canadian reports to, 267; on child and youth advocates, 275; children's rights education, 20; child's right to be heard, 56; "Concluding Observations," 6–7; on corporal punishment, 170, 198; criticism of child detention, 139, 331; education rights compliance, 23, 24–31; on evolving capacity, 75; family reunification, 140; human rights institutions for children (HRICs), 267–68; KidsRights index, 260–61; national children's advocate, need for, 282, 284, 322; national legislation in implementation of child rights, 149; parenting education program evaluations, 45–46
common law: defence of necessity, 194–95, 196; de minimis defence, 196; necessities of life, provision of, 2

Community Justice Initiatives, 96–97, 98
Consent and Capacity Review Board (CCRB), 228, 259–60
consent to care, 79, 258–60; *A. C. v. Manitoba*, 173–74; coercion, 65; competency requirements, 62–63; and denial of rights, 73–77; evolving capacity, 4, 56, 58–59, 64, 71–73; *I Do Care Project* (OPACY), 65; informed consent, 59, 60–64; law, and decision-making capacity, 59–60; marginalized groups, 76–77; of mature minor, 229, 259; maturity vs chronological age, 5, 58–59; mental health treatment, 68; nursing, 62–63; as process, 65–66; recommendations, 78–81; *The Rights of the Child in the Health Care System*, 60–61; right to refuse, 67; traditional medicine vs Western medical treatment, 223–24, 320; voluntariness, 67; youth experiences, 68–70. *See also* age of consent
conservative welfare states, 116
Convention on the Rights of Persons with Disabilities (UN), 25
Convention on the Rights of the Child (UN): as advocacy tool, 7–8; approval, and ratification, 1, 4; Canadian ratification, 36; child welfare, 108, 109–13; complaint procedure, 205; coordination and monitoring, 320–22; core principles, 89; cross-government implementation, 321; education rights, 19–23, 145; enforcement mechanisms, 161–62; government obligations, 36–37; as holistic treaty, 94; implementation of legislation, 10–11, 317–19; incorporation into domestic law, 5–8; integration into juvenile justice system, 87–88; as moral commitment, 161; Optional Protocol to the Convention on the Sale of Children, Child Prostitution and Child Pornography, 169; participation rights, 5; policy and practice areas implementation, 322–29; principles of, 5, 21; protection rights, 5; provision rights, 5; Quebec ratification, 273; reporting system, 6–7; status of in Canadian law, 316–20; and Supreme Court of Canada, 161, 176n1; Supreme Court of Canada decisions, 12. *See also* Articles by number

Convention Relating to the Status of Refugees (UN), 142, 145
corporal punishment: abolishment of, 336; vs abuse, 179; ancient roots of, 182; as assault, 195, 200n10; discipline as "non-abusive physical punishment," 189–90; federal/provincial/territorial jurisdictions, 197, 200nn12–14; global progress, 181–82; history of, 182–84; Joint Statement on Physical Punishment of Children and Youth, 198; legal justification of in Canada, 12, 181; national charging protocol, 195–96, 200n11; non-violent discipline, education on, 39; in penitentiaries, 184, 199n3; prohibition of, 196–97; reasonable force, 182–83, 187–88, 190–91, 193–94, 200n9; reasonable vs unreasonable punishment, 183, 187–88; school discipline, 20, 22, 27, 30, 170; section 43 defence, 169, 170–71, 188–92, 319; spanking, 169–71, 172, 188; Swedish prohibition of, 179, 180
Correctional Services Canada: Ashley Smith case, 90–91
correctional system: corporal punishment, 184, 199n3
Cory, Peter, 167, 225
Council of Ministers of Education (CMEC): human rights in education, view of, 25–26; *Learn Canada 2020*, 26; rights-consistent education, 25–26
Council of Ministers of Education, Canada (CMEC), 18
Covell, Katherine, 11, 17–31, 323–24; implementation of legislation, 10–11; stages of legal evolution, 8–9, 179–80
Criminal Code: constitutional challenge to section 43, 188–92; criminalization of corporal punishment, 195–96, 200nn10–11; de minimis defence, 196; section 43, efforts to repeal, 184–88; section 43 as stage 1 law, 184; section 43 defence of corporal punishment, 12, 169, 170–71, 181, 182–83, 319
Cross-over Youth Project, 298–99
cultural rights, 21, 111, 243; in health care practice, 61
cyberbullying, 174–75

Dallaire, Roméo, 299
David Asper Centre for Constitutional Rights, 233
Davies, Libby, 186
Declaration of Geneva, 3
Declaration on Human Rights (UN), 145
Declaration on the Rights of Indigenous Peoples (UN), 28, 250
Declaration on the Rights of the Child (UN), 3–4, 215, 269
defence of necessity, 194–95
de minimis defence, 196
democratic parenting, 48, 252–53; government mechanisms for promotion of, 253
Denmark: as social democratic welfare state, 116
Denov, Myriam, 11, 131–50, 331–32
Department of Justice (Canada): legislative implementation of the UNCRC, 268; participation rights, 245
Deschamps, Marie, 171, 175, 192, 319
Dewdney, Edgar, 231
Dickson, Brian, 164
Digital Storytelling Project, 246, 280
DiManno, Rosie, 230–31
diminished moral culpability, 173
disability medical negligence cases, 12, 208, 209–13
disabled children. *See* born-alive disabled children; children with disabilities
discrimination: child welfare system, 123; and non-discrimination, 5, 21, 89; war-affected refugees, 146
Dolli Einstein nursery, participation rights, 244–45
Douglas, William O., 227
drug abuse, 40
dualism, 6, 317
Durrant, Joan, 12, 47, 179–99, 319, 324

early childhood education, 25, 42, 45
Early Head Start, 42
early school leaving, 23, 24, 25
education: cut-off age of public secondary education, 148; empowerment through, 19, 309–10; Indigenous teachings, lack of, 306–7; language proficiency issues, 146; LEAD program, 147; as means of social inclusion, 145–46;

post-resettlement education, barriers to, 146–47; programs on child participation rights, need for, 249; school funding for war-affected refugees, 147–48
educational cultural brokers, 147
education rights, 11; access to education, 20; compulsory schooling, age of, 18; consistency with the Convention, 26–27; curricula content, 21–22, 28; development of child's potential, 20–21; empowerment of children, 19, 309–10; equitable funding on reserves, 251; experiential learning, 22; faith-based private schools, 19; federal/provincial/territorial jurisdictions, 18–19; federal role in, 25–26; First Nations reserves, 18; guidance counselling, 20, 27; home-schooling, 19; inconsistency with the Convention, 27–30; pedagogical methods, 22; physical punishment, 22; private schools, 18–19; rights-consistent curricula, 24; rights-consistent pedagogy, 21–22; rights-respecting education, 323–25; school discipline, 20, 22, 27, 30; school environment, 23, 29; school management strategies, 22; student participation in school/classroom functioning, 22, 27–28; teachers, authority of in *loco parentis*, 17, 184; technology, impact on student outcomes, 24; war-affected refugees, 145–48
Edward, Gethin, 224, 228–29, 232, 233–34
electoral reform: voting age, 256–57, 258
Elman, Irwin, 124; health care decision making, barriers to, 65–66; *Reality Check*, 81
embedded advocacy, 122–23
emotional abuse, 253
England, as liberal welfare state, 115–16
Environment Canada, 245
Equality, and shared rights, 3
equality, and equal treatment, 99
Esping-Anderson, E., 115, 116
evidence-based programs, 38; evaluation of, 41–43
evolving capacity, 4, 56, 58–59, 64
experiential learning, 22
expression, right of, 19–20, 40, 111, 243; health care decision making, 56, 223–24, 226, 228–29; and voice, 99, 150, 244, 303–4

family: participation rights within, 252–54
family breakdown: *Divorce Act*, 249; parenting education programs, 41, 46
family-centred care, 62–63; ambiguity in, 74–75, 78; vs child-centred care, 74–75, 81
family law: child protection proceedings, 247; custody and access disputes, 247, 249; legal participatory rights, 247; provincial/territorial jurisdiction, 247–48
family reunification, 140–42, 331
family services, 45
Feathers of Hope, 280, 281
Feinberg, Joel, 227
Fennig, Maya, 11, 131–50, 331–32
Finland: as social democratic welfare state, 116
Finlay, Judy, 12, 293–312, 334; background history, 294, 296–99; Canadian Council of Provincial Child and Youth Advocates (CCPCYA), 298; Cross-over Youth Project, 298–99; Mamow Ki-ken-da-ma-win, 298; Office of Child and Family Service Advocacy (OCFSA), 296
First Nations: federal jurisdiction of reserves, 197, 200n12. *See also* Indigenous children; Indigenous peoples
First Nations Caring Society, 77
First Nations Child and Family Caring Society of Canada, 114; Canadian Human Rights Tribunal 2016 ruling, 250–51
First World Congress against the Commercial Sexual Exploitation of Children, 295–96
Fitzgerald, Dr. Peter, 230
Fitzgerald, Eryn, 257
Focus on the Family, 170
foster care: advocacy by caregivers, 125; and alternative placements, 112, 118, 121–22; caregivers, significance on, 121; competency of caregivers, 119–20; continuity of care, 120; kinship care, 119–20; *Looking After Children in Ontario*, 76; negligence, 122; parent involvement, 121; shortages of caregivers/homes, 120–21
foster parents, 38

France: as conservative welfare state, 116
freedom of expression, 4, 40. *See also* expression, right of
freedom of the press, 174–75
freedom of thought, conscience, and religion, 20
Freeman, Michael, 7, 10, 37

Galston, William, 225
Garneau, Marc, 283
Gartner, Hana, 76
Germany: as conservative welfare state, 116
Gilbert, N., 115, 116
Glavin, Terry, 230–31, 232
globalization, and criminology, 98
Gordon v. Goertz, 166
Grover, Sonja C., 12, 205–20, 319–20
Guichon, Juliet, 234
Guide to Health Care Rights for Children and Youth, 59–60

Hamilton Health Sciences v. D. H., 230–31
Hammarberg, T.: categories of rights, 109
Hancock, Jan, 123, 241–65, 333–34, 335
hard law, 317; vs soft law, 6
Harper, Stephen, 200n7
Harrison, Dr. Christine, 63
Hart, H.L.A., 162
Hassan, Sabrin, 301
Have a Heart Campaign, 251–52
head start programs, parenting education, 41–42
health care, 11, 12, 325–26; advocates, 64–66; ambiguity in family-centred care, 74–75, 78; awareness of children's rights, 67–68, 74, 79; barriers to accessing services, 144–45; best interest models, 75; child participation in, 242; and child welfare system, 123; denial of medical care, 143–44; denial of rights, 73–77; duty to protect, 73–74; factors affecting decision making, 55–57; *Guide to Health Care Rights for Children and Youth*, 59–60; *Health Care Consent Act* (ON), 59, 60, 66; *I Do Care Project* (OPACY), 65; and immigration status, 144–45; *Infant's Act* (BC), 57, 67; informed consent, 60–64; Jordan's Principle, 58; law, and decision-making capacity, 59–60; lenses of young persons' status, 56–57; listening, 81; marginalized groups, 76–77; *Medical Consent of Minors Act* (NB), 59; mental health treatment, 60, 68; nursing, 62–63; as parental support, 36; and parenting education, 44; participation rights, 258–60, 261; participation rights in practice, 60–64; pediatricians, 63–64; policy inconsistencies, 74; prenatal/postnatal health care, 206–8; protectionist paternalism of, 326; recommendations, 78–81; *Right in Principle, Right in Practice* (CCRC), 71–72; rights awareness of service providers, 64–66; right to refuse, 67; role of geography, 68; war-affected refugees, access to, 142–45; youth experiences, 68–70. *See also* consent to care
Health Care Compliance Association (HCCA): age of consent, 59
Health Care Consent Act (ON): age of consent, 228; traditional medicine vs Western medical treatment, 232
health centres: policies on health care decisions, 57–59
health education, right to, 21
health institutions: culture of care, 65–66
Hervieux-Payette, Céline, 186
High Commissioner for Refugees (UN), 132
Hill, Ava, 230
Hill, Dr. Karen, 232
Hippocrates Health Institute, 224
"Home children," 113
Home School Legal Defense Association, 170
home visitation, 42, 46
hopeless children, 269
Hopley, Thomas, 183
Howe, Edward, 24
Howe, R. Brian, 35–50, 324–25; implementation of legislation, 10–11; parental education, 11; stages of legal evolution, 8–9, 179–80
Hughes, Bethany, 67
human rights: classroom education on, 28; evolution of children's rights, 1–4
human rights institutions for children (HRICs), 267–68
humility: adult attitude of, 95
Hunter, M. Theresa, 12, 124, 267–84, 320–21

Iacobucci, Frank, 167
I am a Witness campaign, 251, 335
Ianno, Tony, 186
Iceland: corporal punishment as assault, 195, 200n10
I Do Care Project (OPACY), 65
I Have Something to Say program, 246, 280
immigration: *Baker v. Canada*, 167–68; Canada–US Safe Third Country Agreement, 142; dependent child, definition of, 141; detention, 137, 138–40; family reunification, 140–42; Government-Assisted Refugee (GAR) program, 136–37; *Immigration and Refugee Protection Act* (IRPA), 140, 141, 168, 249, 318; *Immigration and Refugee Protection Regulations* (IRPR), 141; and legal status, 132; processing times, 141, 144–45; Refugee and Humanitarian Resettlement Stream, 133; refugee determination process, 136; sponsored refugees, 133
incarcerated children: treatment of, 76
income support, 36, 45
Incredible Years, 41, 42
Indigenous children, 328–29, 330; Aboriginal Head Start, 43, 44, 45, 47; access to health care, 77; Canadian Human Rights Tribunal 2016 ruling, 250–51, 335; clean water, access to, 181, 251; colonialism legacy, 250, 307; culturally appropriate placements, 120; Declaration on the Rights of Indigenous Peoples, 250; experiences of, 306–7; Feathers of Hope, 280, 281; First Nations Caring Society, 77; First Nations Family Advocate, 274–75; Have a Heart Campaign, 251–52; health care decision making, 58, 61, 230–31; I am a Witness campaign, 251, 335; incarceration rates, 101; Jordan's Principle, 58, 77; Mamow Ki-ken-da-ma-win, 298; marginalization, and child welfare, 12, 113–15, 181; "Millennium Scoop," 114; overrepresentation of in care, 113–15; overrepresentation of in juvenile justice system, 94–95; parenting education, 38; and post-colonial trauma, 95; racism, 250; residential schools experience, 187, 231–32, 250; Sixties Scoop, 113, 117, 118; suicide rates, 250, 281; treatment of in child welfare system, 115; underfunding on reserves, 114–15; vulnerability of, 101–2. *See also* Indigenous peoples
Indigenous peoples: cultural genocide of, 91–92; justice system, pre-colonization, 91–92; multi-generational effects of colonization, 101; residential schools experience, 92, 187, 231–32; restorative justice approach of, 96, 327; traditional medicines, and Indigenous identity, 233–34; traditional medicine vs Western medical treatment, 230–31. *See also* Indigenous children
infanticide, 2
Infant's Act (BC), 57, 67, 259
In Parham v. J. R., 229
In Re L. D. K., 226
In R. v. B. W. P., 172–73
Institute for Patient and Family-Centred Care, 63
Inter-American Commission on Human Rights: prohibition of corporal punishment, 181–82
Interdepartmental Working Group on Children's Rights, 268, 321
Interim Federal Health Program (IFHP): policy changes, 143
International Bureau for Children's Rights, 145
International Covenant on Civil and Political Rights, 170
International Covenant on Economic, Social and Cultural Rights, 142
international human rights law: accountability, 6–7; UNCRC as legal obligation, 5; evolution of children's rights, 1–4
International Human Rights program: children in detention centres, 138
International Year of the Child (1979), 4, 269, 294
Italy: as conservative welfare state, 116

Jairamsingh, Christine, 257
Jebb, Eglantyne, 3
J.J., 12; age of consent, 224, 226; as child in need of protection, 228–29, 230–31, 320
Jordan's Principle, 58

Justice for Children and Youth (JCY): awareness of children's rights, 74; *Guide to Health Care Rights for Children and Youth*, 59–60
juvenile justice system, 11, 12, 326–28; development of, 9; deviance, and youthful offending, 95–96; gender differences, 94; general deterrence, 172–73; integration of UNCRC, 87–88; international instruments on, 100; no-normal, concept of, 304–5; overrepresentation of marginalized groups, 77, 94–95; participation rights, 245, 261; pro-social approaches, 93–94; and restorative justice, 95–102, 245, 326–28; rights-based approach to, 88, 89–90; rights-based justice, barriers and opportunities to, 93–95; secure custody, 91; *Young Offenders Act*, 87–88; *Youth Criminal Justice Act* (YCJA), 87–88, 91, 98, 100, 172, 245, 326

Kanthasamy, Jeyakannan, 175
Kanthasamy v. Canada, 175
KidsRights index, 260–61
King, Thomas, 231
Kingsley, Cherry, 295
kinship care, 119–20
Koffka, Jurt, 28
Koostachin, Shannen, 251, 335
Korczak, Janusz, 4
Koster, Andrew, 223, 230, 232

La Forest, Gérard, 225, 226
LaForme, Bryan, 232
Laidlaw Foundation, 299
laissez-faire stage. *See* social laissez-faire stage
Lamer, Antonio, 226
Landon Pearson Resource Centre for the Study of Childhood and Children's Rights (LPRC), 294, 299
language, 295–96; education, and proficiency issues, 146; in health care practice, 61; linguistic rights, 21, 111, 230, 243; marginalization through, 307; *Official Languages Act*, 200n7
Lansdown, Gerison, 310
Latvia, 180

law: and decision-making capacity, 59–60; as social policy tool, 163
League of Nations: Declaration of Geneva, 3
Learn Canada 2020 (CMEC), 26
LeFrançois, Brenda, 11, 55–81, 325
Lefsrud, Erik, 257
legal rights: vs moral rights, 161–62
legislation: evolution of, 195–97; federal/provincial/territorial jurisdictions, 163, 317–18
LGBTQ+ community, 330
L'Heureux-Dubé, Claire, 164–65, 166–67, 167–68, 168–69
liberal welfare states, 115–16
linguistic rights, 21, 111, 230, 243
Locke, John: children as "blank slates," 2
Looking After Children in Ontario, 76

MacPherson-Mayor, Devon, 11, 55–81, 325
Macrae, J. A., 231
Main, D. R., 226
Mamow Ki-ken-da-ma-win, 298
Manitoba: *A. C. v. Manitoba*, 173–74; *Advocate for Children and Youth Act*, 272; Child and Family Services, 275; *Child and Family Services Act*, 173–74, 272; corporal punishment, 200n13; Digital Storytelling Project, 246, 280; First Nations Family Advocate, 274–75; Indigenous children in care, 114; law, and decision-making capacity, 59; *Manitoba Child and Family Services Act*, 168–69; Office of the Child Advocate, 245–46; Office of the Children's Advocate, 272; parenting education, 45; right to be heard, 247; *In R. v. B. W. P.*, 172–73; *R. v. L. (D.O.)*, 166–67; Safe and Caring Schools policy, 29; Triple P (Positive Parenting Program), 43; youth involvement, 280
marginalized groups, 326, 328–29; foster care, 76–77; incarcerated children, 76; Indigenous children, 12, 113–15; as "lesser-thans," 330; overrepresentation of in incarceration statistics, 94–95; overrepresentation of in juvenile justice system, 92–93, 237; power imbalances, 76–77; psychiatrized children, 76; war-affected refugees, 11

Martin, Douglas L., 232
mature minor principle, 59, 229, 259
McCombs, Justice, 189
McLachlin, Beverly, 166, 170, 171
McMaster Children's Hospital: consent to care, and age of consent, 223–24, 230
media coverage: no-normal, concept of, 304–5; of youth crime, 93
Medical Consent of Minors Act (NB), 59, 259
medical negligence claims: *Bovingdon et al. v. Hergott*, 208, 209–13
Mennonite Central Committee, 96
mental health concerns, 64; family-centred solutions, 149–50; no-normal, concept of, 304–5; of refugees, 132, 140, 146, 149–50
mental health services: overrepresentation of marginalized groups, 93
mental health treatment: consent to care, 68; psychiatrized children, 70–71
Mexico: international ranking on family supports spending, 45
Meyer v. Nebraska, 225
"Millennium Scoop," 114
Milne, Cheryl, 233
Minister of State for Children and Youth (Canada), 268
Mongolia, 180
monism, 6, 317
Moore, Shannon A., 11, 87–102, 326–27
Mulroney, Brian, 186, 200n7, 295
Muttart Foundation, 299–300
mutuality, 99
My REAL Life Book, 280

National Child Day, 281
national children's advocate, need for, 282–83, 284
national children's commissioner: call for, 267, 321, 322
National Inquiry into Missing and Murdered Indigenous Women and Girls, 101
National Network for Youth in Care, 77
neglect: in child welfare legislation, 118
New Brunswick: *Child, Youth and Senior Advocate Act*, 274; *Child and Youth Advocate Act*, 273–74; Child Death Review Committee, 273; corporal punishment, 200n14; *Medical Consent of Minors Act*, 59, 259; school discipline, 27; student participation in school/classroom functioning, 27
Newfoundland and Labrador: *Child and Youth Advocate Act*, 273; Office of the Advocate for Children and Youth, 273; Select Committee on Children's Interests, 273
New Zealand: Auckland City Youth Council, 254–55
Nobody's Perfect, 43, 44, 45, 48; evaluations, 46–47
non-discrimination, 5, 21, 89, 99, 310; and child welfare, 109
no-normal, concept of, 304–5
North America: children's lack of legal protection, 181
Northwest Territories: child welfare legislation, 110; Office of the Children's Lawyer, 274
Norway, 6; *Children's Act*, 253; child welfare legislation, 110, 117, 253; incorporation of UNCRC into domestic law, 6; as social democratic welfare state, 116
Nova Scotia: *Education Act*, 27; legal participatory rights, 247; Office of the Ombudsman, 276; Office of Youth Services (OYS), 273, 276; *Ombudsman Act*, 273, 276; ombudsman *Statement of Mandate*, 273, 276; *R. v. R.C.*, 171–72; school discipline, 27; student participation in school/classroom functioning, 27
Nunavut: child welfare legislation, 110, 124; *Representative for Children and Youth Act*, 274, 281; Representative for Children and Youth Office, 280–81
Nurse Family Partnership program, 42
nursing, 62–63; awareness of children's rights, 67–68

Office of Child and Family Service Advocacy (OCFSA), 296; *Consent and Confidentiality in Health Services*, 79; principles to guide health care consent with young persons, 79–80
Office of the Child and Youth Advocate (AB), 271, 280

Office of the Federal Commissioner for Children and Youth: establishment of, 81
Ontario: *Canadian Foundation for Children, Youth and the Law v. Canada*, 169–71, 172; *Child, Youth, and Family Services Act*, 111, 124; *Child and Family Services Act*, 66, 228–29, 270, 297; child welfare legislation, 110, 124; Consent and Capacity Review Board (CCRB), 228, 259–60; constitutional challenge to section 43, 188–90, 200n8; *Health Care Consent Act*, 59, 60, 66, 228, 232; Indigenous children in care, 113–14; law, and decision-making capacity, 59; legal participatory rights, 247–48; Ministry of Community, Family and Children's Services, 269–70; office of the child advocate, removal of, 82, 124; Premier's Council on Youth Opportunities, 246, 280; *Provincial Advocate for Children and Youth Act*, 270–71, 279, 281, 283, 298; *R. v. D. B.*, 173; social media platforms, 246; Student Voice project, 27; *Supporting Child, Youth and Family Services Act*, 246; youth advisory forums, 255–56. *See also* Ontario Office of the Provincial Advocate for Children and Youth (OPACY)
Ontario Human Rights Commission Report: overrepresentation of marginalized groups in care, 114
Ontario Office of the Provincial Advocate for Children and Youth (OPACY): closing of, 82, 271, 283; creation of, 269–71; Feathers of Hope, 280, 281; health care rights, 65–66; I Have Something to Say, 246, 280; listening tour, 261; My REAL Life Book, 280; and Office of the Ombudsman Ontario, 271; Our Voice Our Turn program, 246; social media platforms, 246–47; Youth Amplifiers, 280; youth participation, 279–80, 281
Openheimer, Todd, 24
Optional Protocol to the Convention on the Rights of the Child on a Communications Procedure, 205
Optional Protocol to the Convention on the Sale of Children, Child Prostitution and Child Pornography, 169

Organization of American States: prohibition of corporal punishment, 181–82
original sin, 2
Ottawa Police Service: Youth Advisory Committee, 255
Our Voice Our Turn program, 246

Paraguay, 180–81
parens patriae, 163, 165, 170, 173, 225–27, 229, 231–32, 318
parental authority: in agricultural societies, 2; *patria potestas*, 2, 182
parental leave, 36, 45
parental power, and state control, 226–27
parental supports: government obligations, 36–37
Parenthood and Guardianship Code, 196–97
parenting education, 11; and children's rights, 47–48, 324–25; conflicting views of, 39; described, 35–36; early childhood education, 42; evidence-based programs, 38, 41–43; foster parents, 38; funding, 44–45; government investment in, 40, 42–43, 49–50; head start programs, 41–42; home visitation, 42; implementation in Canada, 43–49; importance of, 37–40; Indigenous parents, 38; non-violent discipline, 39; Nurse Family Partnership program, 42; participation rights, 48–49; Positive Discipline in Everyday Parenting, 47–48, 324; prenatal/postnatal health care, 36, 41; *Seen, Heard and Believed*, 49; shortcomings in implementation, 44–49; single parents, 38; social need for, 38–40; support services, 35–36; Systemic Training for Effective Parenting, 43; teen parents, 38; therapeutic interventions, 41–42
parenting education programs: Aboriginal Head Start, 43, 44, 45, 47, 250; Chicago Child–Parent Center program, 42; Early Head Start, 42; Head Start programs, 43; Incredible Years, 41, 42; Nobody's Perfect, 43, 44, 45, 46–47, 48, 254; Nurse Family Partnership program, 42; Positive Discipline in Everyday Parenting, 47–48; Save the Children, 47–48;

Triple P (Positive Parenting Program), 41, 42, 46
parenting norms, pressure to conform to, 75
Parent Management Training (Oregon Model), 41
parents: abusive parenting, risk factors, 41; authoritarian parenting, 252, 253; authoritative parenting, 48, 252–53; corporal punishment, 191; custodial authority of, 225; democratic parenting, 48, 252–53; health care decision making, 57, 61; permissive parenting, 252, 253; pressures to conform to parenting norms, 75; role of, in relationship to children's rights, 4, 48, 70–71, 111; role of in children's education, 148; separation from, 111, 140, 243
Parliament: Court Challenges program, 188–90, 200n7; legislative process, 185–86, 199n4, 200n6; private members' bills, 185–86, 199n4, 200n5
participation rights, 99, 322, 325–26; age, and capacity, 4; age, and maturity, 5, 241, 242–43; Article 12 (UNCRC), 5; awareness of, 261–62; of children as citizens, 4, 12, 333–34; in children's rights stage, 8, 9, 11; and child welfare, 109; child welfare system, 122–25; civic participation, 254–58; climate activism, 257–58, 335; education rights, 21; within the family, 242, 252–54; freedom of expression, 40; health care, 258–60; health care decision making, 55–57, 58, 64–70; within health care practice, 60–64; Indigenous children, 250–52; law, and decision-making capacity, 59–60; legal sources of, 242–43; omissions in implementation, 260; in parenting education programs, 48–49; as political instruments, 251–52; reasons for, 243–44; regional differences, 245–47; right of expression, 19–20; right to be heard, 56; *Seen, Heard and Believed*, 49; social barriers to, 243; student participation in school/classroom functioning, 22, 27–28; suggested measures, 261–62; voice, and agency, 112–13, 123. *See also* age of consent; consent to care

paternalism, 57; in health care decision making, 75
paternalistic protection stage, 8, 205, 315, 322, 333; and adult decision makers, 242; civic participation, 254–58, 261; legal participatory rights, 247–48; section 43, 192–95; state paternalism, 9, 179
patria potestas (paternal power), 2, 182
Paxton v. Ramji, 216–17
peaceful assembly, 20
Pearson, Landon, 12, 81, 293–312, 334; "A Canada Fit for Children," 296; background history, 294–96; "For Canada's Children," 294
pediatricians: health care decision making, 63–64; pediatric ethicists at tertiary care centres, 66–68
Peltier, Autumn, 251
permissive parenting, 252, 253
Philpott, Jane, 114
physician duty of care: *Bovingdon et al. v. Hergott*, 208, 209–13; *Cherry* case, 214; to future children, 216, 218; and medical negligence, 208; *Paxton v. Ramji*, 216–17; prenatal/postnatal health care, 214–15
Pierce v. Society of Sisters, 225, 227
Planned Parenthood v. Danforth, 229
Plan Your Path workshops (BC), 280
policy advocacy, 297, 298
Positive Discipline in Everyday Parenting, 47–48, 324
post-traumatic stress disorder (PTSD): war-affected refugees, 146, 147
poverty: and equal opportunity of education, 20
Premier's Council on Youth Opportunities (ON), 246, 280
Prince Edward Island: children's lawyer program, 274; *Custody and Enforcement Act*, 247; Office for Children and Youth, 274; school discipline, 27
Prince v. Massachusetts, 227
privacy, right to, 243
program advocacy, 297
protection from harm, 40, 112, 168–69, 170; provincial/territorial jurisdiction, 197, 200nn13–14; Supreme Court of Canada interpretation, 192–94, 200n9

Index 357

protection rights: and child welfare, 109; and participation rights, 244
Provincial Advocate for Youth and Children (ON), 246–47
provincial/territorial jurisdiction: on education, 18–19, 25–26; separation of power, 317–18
provision rights: and child welfare, 109
psychiatric treatment: consent to care, 60; psychiatrized children, 70–71, 76
Public Health Agency of Canada: Aboriginal Head Start, 47, 250; Community Action Program for Children, 249; Fetal Alcohol Disorder Program, 250; Interdepartmental Working Group on Children's Rights, 268, 321; Maternal Child Health, 250; National Child Day, 249; Nobody's Perfect, 254; parenting education, 43; participation rights, 245; Prenatal Nutrition, 250; Shaking the Movers (STM) workshops, 299, 300
public policy: Canadian context, 8–11; education, 11; evolutionary stages of development, 8–9; gap with reality, 81; in implementation of children's rights, 5; implementation of legislation, 10–11; incorporation of rights in immigration/refugee legislation, 148–49; law as social policy tool, 163; low priority of children in, 268–69; and participation rights, 242; participation rights, and social laissez-faire stage, 261; refugee services, training for, 149
P. (D) v. S. (C), 165–66

Quebec: age of consent, 58, 59; Commission des droits de la personne et des droits de la jeunesse, 273, 276, 281; curricula content, 28; parenting education newsletters, 45; *P. (D) v. S. (C)*, 165–66; right to be heard, 248

racism: and child removal, 114; systemic, and Indigenous children, 77, 95, 101, 250; war-affected refugees, 146
Reality Check (Elman), 81
reasonable force, 182–83, 187; criteria for, 190–91, 193–94; *R. v. Earl*, 193, 200n9; *R. v. Kaur*, 193; *R. v. Morrow*, 193

reasonable vs unreasonable punishment, 183
religion, freedom of, 20, 26, 164–65, 243; and medical treatment, 225–26
Re Public Service Employee Relations Act, 164
residential schools: impact on Indigenous parents, 38; legacy of, 113, 187, 231–32, 250
restoration, 99
restorative justice, 95–102; Community Justice Initiatives, 96–97, 98; contemporary sense of, 96–97; global history of, 102; participation rights, 245; principles of, 97; vs retributive justice, 97; rights-based approach to, 88, 94, 99–100, 326–28; social construct of youthful offending, 95–96; spiritual roots of, 96–97; in truth and reconciliation process, 101
Right in Principle, Right in Practice (CCRC), 71–72
Rights, Respect and Responsibility Initiative (RRR), 31
rights-consistent education, 25–26
right to access and impart information, 20, 26
right to a name, 28
right to be heard, 56, 245, 303–4
Riyadh Guidelines (UN, 1990), 100
Robinson, Svend, 185
Roman law: Law of Chastisement, 183–84; *patria potestas* (corporal punishment), 2, 182
Rousseau, Jean-Jacques, 3
Royal College of Nursing, 78
Royal College of Paediatrics, 78
R. v. B. V. N., 172–73
R. v. Earl, 193, 200n9
R. v. Kaur, 193
R. v. Morrow, 193
R. v. R.C., 171–72
R. v. Van der Peet, 233
Ryerson University School of Child and Youth Care, 300

Safe and Caring Schools policy, 29
Saskatchewan: *Action Plan for Children*, 272; Advocate for Children and Youth,

272, 281; *Advocate for Children and Youth Act*, 273; Children and Youth Agenda, 272; Child Welfare Review Panel, 272; consultations on Indigenous youth suicide, 281; *Education Act*, 30; law, and decision-making capacity, 59; legal participatory rights, 247; *Ombudsman and Children's Advocate Act*, 272; Task Force on Child and Youth Advocacy, 272
Sault, Makayla, 12; competency to consent, 226, 320; media criticisms, 232–33; traditional medicine vs Western medical treatment, 223–24
Save the Children: founding of, 3; parenting education, 47–48
Scalia, Justice, 229
Schafer, Arthur, 232, 233
School Strike for Climate, 257–58
Schwiesow, Tara, 258
Secretary of State for Children (Canada), 268
Seen, Heard and Believed, 49
self-advocacy, 278
sexual exploitation, 40
Shaking the Movers (STM) workshops, 12, 334; background history, 294–300; Child Rights Academic Network (CRAN), 293; funding, 299, 300; methodology/content analysis of annual reports, 301–2; purpose of, 293–94; right to be heard, 303–4; strengths and benefits, 310–11; themes, 299–300, 302–10; voice and agency, 301; youth participation, 301
Shapiro, Ian, 226
Shue, Henry, 176
Simpson, Sandra, 167
Sinclair, Murray, 187
single parents, 38
Sixties Scoop, 113, 117, 118
Smith, Ashley, 76, 90–91, 327
Smoke, Amy, 12, 223–35, 320; First Nations identity issues, 234–35
social democratic welfare states, 116, 117
social justice: pro-social approaches, 93–94
social laissez-faire stage, 205, 315; absence of child's participation in decision making, 242, 254; children as objects of parental authority, 8–9, 179

social media, 24
social services: overrepresentation of marginalized groups, 93
Social Union Framework Agreement (Canada), 268
soft law: vs hard law, 6
solitary confinement, 90–91
Somerville, Margaret, 232
South Sudan, 181
spanking, 169–71, 172, 188; Canadian Incidence Study of Reported Child Abuse and Neglect, 197–98; public attitudes, 198
Special Session on Children (UN): *A World Fit for Children*, 267–68, 296
standard of living, 37
Standing Senate Committee on Human Rights: "Children: The Silenced Citizens," 296; national children's advocate, need for, 282
state parties: access to education, obligation of, 20
state paternalism, 9
stigmatization, 305–6
Student Voice project (Ontario), 27
Supporting Child, Youth and Family Services Act (ON), 246
Supreme Court (US): *Bellotti v. Baird*, 229; *Meyer v. Nebraska*, 225; *In Parham v. J. R.*, 229; *Pierce v. Society of Sisters*, 225, 227; *Planned Parenthood v. Danforth*, 229; rights of self-determination, 229–30; *Vernonia School District 47 v. Acton*, 229–30; *Wisconsin v. Yoder*, 225, 227
Supreme Court of Canada: *A. B. v. Bragg Communications*, 174–75; *A. C. v. Manitoba*, 173–74, 229; *Baker v. Canada*, 167–68; *B. (R.) v. Children's Aid Society of Metropolitan Toronto*, 225; *Canadian Foundation for Children, Youth and the Law v. Canada*, 169–71, 172; concept of protection, 192–94; court decisions, 12; and UNCRC, 318; *Gordon v. Goertz*, 166; judicial recognition of UNCRC, 161, 176n1; *Kanthasamy v. Canada*, 175; *parens patriae*, and state intervention, 225–27, 318; *P. (D) v. S. (C)*, 165–66; *Re Public Service Employee Relations Act*, 164; *R. v. B. V. N.*, 172–73; *In R. v. B. W. P.*, 172–73; *R. v. D. B.*, 173; *R. v. L.*

(D.O.), 166–67; *R. v. R.C.*, 171–72; *R. v. Sharpe*, 169; *R. v. Van der Peet*, 233; section 43 defence, 12, 169, 170–71, 181, 182–83, 184–88, 319; *Winnipeg Child and Family Services v. K. L. W.*, 168–69; *Young v. Young*, 164–65

survival and development, 5, 21, 89, 99; participation rights, 244; right to life, 227–28; role of the state in, 111–12

Sustainable Development Goals (UN), 145

Sweden: child welfare legislation, 253; civic participation, 254, 255; prohibition of corporal punishment, 179, 180, 195, 196, 319; as social democratic welfare state, 116

Syrian refugees, 331–32; Canadian resettlement of, 132–33; health care needs, 144

systemic advocacy, 277–78

Systemic Training for Effective Parenting, 43

teachers: assessment strategies, 22; classroom management strategies, 24; in *loco parentis* authority, 17, 184, 189–90; pedagogical methods, 22; pre-service/in-service training, 23, 30; reasonable force, 191; rights-consistent pedagogy, 21–22; training on rights-consistent education, 25–26, 28, 30; and war-affected refugees, 147

technology: impact on student outcomes, 24

teen parents, 38

The New Mentality, 68

Thunberg, Greta, 257–58

Toronto Youth Cabinet, 255

traditional medicine vs Western medical treatment, 232; consent to care, 223–24, 230–31; *Hamilton Health Sciences v. D. H.*, 230–31

Triple P (Positive Parenting Program), 41, 42; evaluations, 46

Trudeau, Justin, 200n7, 251

Trudeau, Pierre: Court Challenges program, 188–90, 200n7

Truth and Reconciliation Commission, 12, 92, 187, 198

Turpel-Lafonde, Mary Ellen, 120

unaccompanied refugee minors, 131–32, 136–42, 150; categories of, 136–37; defined, 136; deportation of, 137; detention of, 137, 138–40, 331; gender differences, 136; *Kanthasamy v. Canada*, 175

UNICEF, 78; on child and youth advocates, 275; national children's advocate, need for, 282–83; participation rights, 260–61

United Nations: Convention on the Rights of Persons with Disabilities, 25; Declaration on the Rights of Indigenous People, 28, 250; Declaration on the Rights of the Child, 3–4, 215, 269; High Commissioner for Human Rights, 25; juvenile justice instruments, 100; Kids-Rights index, 260–61; Optional Protocol on the Involvement of Children in Armed Conflict, 134; *Principles Relating to the Status of National Institutions (Paris Principles)*, 268; Special Session on Children, 267–68. *See also* Convention on the Rights of the Child (UN)

United Nations Educational, Scientific and Cultural Organization (UNESCO): rights-consistent education, 25

United States, 163–64; child welfare legislation, 117; civic participation, 254, 255; international ranking on family supports spending, 45; as liberal welfare state, 115–16; *parens patriae*, 227

Universal Declaration of Human Rights, 142

van Daalen-Smith, Cheryl, 11, 55–81, 325

victimization of children during armed conflict, 134–35

Vienna Guidelines (UN, 1997), 100

voice: and agency, 112–13, 123, 150, 244, 301; right of expression, 99, 303–4

voluntariness: and consent to care, 67

volunteerism, 99

vulnerability: and deprivation of rights, 7

Waldock, Thomas, 1–14, 11, 107–26, 315–36

war: child recruitment, 134; impact on family system, 149–50; internally displaced persons, 131–33
war-affected refugees, 11, 331–32; access and quality of services, 142–48, 150; categories of, 136–37; child refugees, 133; detention of, 137, 138–40; education, access to, 145–48; family reunification, 140–42; family separation within detention centres, 138–39; fear and insecurity of, 134–35, 139–40; gender differences, 136; health care, access to, 142–45; impact on psychological functioning, 131–32; mental health concerns, 139, 140; post-resettlement education, barriers to, 146–47; protection of children during war, 134–35; resettlement, and post-migration stressors, 132–33, 135–36, 142; school enrolment, 146; unaccompanied minors, 131–32, 136–42
Watkinson, Dr. Ailsa, 188
Weinrib, Lorraine, 233
welfare system: "cross-over" into justice system, 101
well-being, 99
White, Byron, 227
Wikwemikong Unceded Indian Reserve, 251
Winnipeg Child and Family Services v. K. L. W., 168–69
Wisconsin v. Yoder, 225, 227
Workers Welfare Institution, 245
World Health Organization (WHO), 78
World Summit for Children (UN, 1990), 89, 295
Worth, Dave, 96

wrongful birth: *Bovingdon et al. v. Hergott*, 209–13, 319–20; as legally viable lawsuit, 207, 213–14
wrongful life lawsuits, 12, 319–20; and born-alive disabled children, 206–8; "non-existence dilemma," 219–20; as non-viable, 207, 213–14; recovery of legal damages, 219–20

Yantzi, Mark, 96, 98
young offenders: within child rights discourses, 93; diversion of, 195–96, 200n11; and ideology of childhood, 93; vulnerability of, 88
Young Offenders Act, 87–88
young persons: health care decision-making experiences, 68–70
Young v. Young, 164–65
youth advisory councils, 279
youth advisory forums, 245–46; civic participation, 255–56
youth advocates. *See* child and youth advocates (CYA)
Youth Criminal Justice Act (YCJA), 87–88, 91, 318, 326; diversion of young offenders, 195–96, 200n11; impact on youth incarceration rates, 94–95; introduction of, 172; participation rights, 245; and restorative justice, 98, 100
youth justice system. *See* juvenile justice system
Yukon: *Child and Youth Advocate Act*, 274, 281; child welfare legislation, 110, 124; custody cases, right to be heard, 247; non-attendance of school, sanctions for, 27; school discipline, 27

Books in the Studies in Childhood and Family in Canada Series Published by Wilfrid Laurier University Press

Making Do: Women, Family, and Home in Montreal during the Great Depression by Denyse Baillargeon, translated by Yvonne Klein • 1999 / xii + 232 pp. / ISBN 0-88920-326-1 / ISBN-13: 978-0-88920-326-6

Children in English-Canadian Society: Framing the Twentieth-Century Consensus by Neil Sutherland with a new foreword by Cynthia Comacchio • 2000 / xxiv + 336 pp. / illus. / ISBN 0-88920-351-2 / ISBN-13: 978-0-88920-351-8

Love Strong as Death: Lucy Peel's Canadian Journal, 1833–1836 edited by J.I. Little • 2001 / x + 229 pp. / illus. / ISBN 0-88920-389-x / ISBN-13: 978-0-88920-389-230-x

The Challenge of Children's Rights for Canada by Katherine Covell and R. Brian Howe • 2001 / viii + 244 pp. / ISBN 0-88920-380-6 / ISBN-13: 978-0-88920-380-8

NFB Kids: Portrayals of Children by the National Film Board of Canada, 1939–1989 by Brian J. Low • 2002 / vi + 288 pp. / illus. / ISBN 0-88920-386-5 / ISBN-13: 978-0-88920-386-0

Something to Cry About: An Argument against Corporal Punishment of Children in Canada by Susan M. Turner • 2002 / xx + 317 pp. / ISBN 0-88920-382-2 / ISBN-13: 978-0-88920-382-2

Freedom to Play: We Made Our Own Fun edited by Norah L. Lewis • 2002 / xiv + 210 pp. / ISBN 0-88920-406-3 / ISBN-13: 978-0-88920-406-5

The Dominion of Youth: Adolescence and the Making of Modern Canada, 1920–1950 by Cynthia Comacchio • 2006 / x + 302 pp. / illus. / ISBN 0-88920-488-8 / ISBN-13: 978-0-88920-488-1

Evangelical Balance Sheet: Character, Family, and Business in Mid-Victorian Nova Scotia by B. Anne Wood • 2006 / xxx + 198 pp. / illus. / ISBN 0-88920-500-0 / ISBN-13: 978-0-88920-500-0

The Social Origins of the Welfare State by Dominique Marshall, translated by Nicola Doone Danby • 2006 • xx + 278 pp. / ISBN 978-0-88920-452-2

A Question of Commitment: Children's Rights in Canada edited by R. Brian Howe and Katherine Covell • 2007 / xiv + 442 pp. / ISBN 978-1-55458-003-3

Taking Responsibility for Children edited by Samantha Brennan and Robert Noggle • 2007 / xxii + 188 pp. / ISBN 978-1-55458-015-6

Home Words: Discourses of Children's Literature in Canada edited by Mavis Reimer • 2008 / xx + 280 pp. / illus. / ISBN 978-1-55458-016-3

Depicting Canada's Children edited by Loren Lerner • 2009 / xxvi + 442 pp. / illus. / ISBN 978-1-55458-050-7

Babies for the Nation: The Medicalization of Motherhood in Quebec, 1910–1970 by Denyse Baillargeon, translated by W. Donald Wilson • 2009 / xiv + 328 pp. / illus. / ISBN 978-1-5548-058-3

The One Best Way? Breastfeeding History, Politics, and Policy in Canada by Tasnim Nathoo and Aleck Ostry • 2009 / xvi + 262 pp. / illus. / ISBN 978-1-55458-147-4

Fostering Nation? Canada Confronts Its History of Childhood Disadvantage by Veronica Strong-Boag • 2011 / x + 302 pp. / ISBN 978-1-55458-337-9

Cold War Comforts: Maternalism, Child Safety, and Global Insecurity, 1945–1975 by Tarah Brookfield • 2012 / xiv + 292 pp. / illus. / ISBN 978-1-55458-623-3

Ontario Boys: Masculinity and the Idea of Boyhood in Postwar Ontario, 1945–1960 by Christopher Greig • 2014 / xxviii + 184 pp. / ISBN 978-1-55458-900-5

A Brief History of Women in Quebec by Denyse Baillargeon, translated by W. Donald Wilson • 2014 / xii + 272 pp. / ISBN 978-1-55458-950-0

With Children and Youth: Emerging Theories and Practices in Child and Youth Care Work edited by Kiaras Gharabaghi, Hans A. Skott-Myhre, and Mark Krueger • 2014 / xiv + 222 pp. / ISBN 978-1-55458-966-1

Abuse or Punishment? Violence Towards Children in Quebec Families, 1850–1969, translated by W. Donald Wilson • 2014 / xii + 396 pp. / ISBN 978-1-77712-063-0

Girls, Texts, Cultures edited by Clare Bradford and Mavis Reimer • 2015 • x + 334 pp. • ISBN 978-1-77112-020-3

Engendering Transnational Voices: Studies in Families, Work and Identities edited by Guida Man and Rina Cohen • 2015 / xii + 344 pp. / ISBN 978-1-77112-112-5 (hc)

Growing Up in Armyville by Deborah Harrison and Patrizia Albanese • 2016 • xii + 250 pp. • ISBN 978-1-77112-234-4

The Challenge of Children's Rights for Canada, Second Edition by Katherine Covell, R. Brian Howe, and J.C. Blokhuis • 2018 • x + 248 pp. • ISBN 978-1-77112-355-6

A Question of Commitment: The Status of Children in Canada, Second Edition, edited by Thomas Waldock • 2020 • xiv + 363 pp. • ISBN 978-1-177112-405-8